THE BEST
MOVIE
QUIZ BOOK
Ever!

THIS IS A CARLTON BOOK

Copyright © 2000 Carlton Books Limited

Published by Carlton Books Limited 2000
20 Mortimer Street
London
W1N 7RD

A CIP catalogue for this book is available from the British Library.

ISBN 1 85868 948 1

Questions set by The Puzzle House
Design: Adam Wright
Production: Garry Lewis

THE BEST
MOVIE
QUIZ BOOK
Ever!

CARLTON
BOOKS

CONTENTS

Welcome to *The Best Movie Quiz Book Ever!*. As the wife of the only movie actor to become US president said, 'Where would we be without the movies?'

Whether your first experience of the cinema was the first talkie or *Toy Story*, there's lots to enjoy among these pages. So much has happened since the early days of the movies that there's plenty to quiz you on. Many different subjects and interests are catered for. Are action movies your speciality? Is your knowledge of classic movie moments second to none? Or are you an all-round mine of information? If you answered yes to at least one of these questions, then this book is for you. In *The Best Movie Quiz Book Ever!* you'll find 7,750 questions all about the first hundred years of movie history. All the family can join in, so start quizzing!

You will see that the book is divided into three main sections – easy, medium and hard questions. For those of a nervous disposition, begin with the easy questions and work your way on to the hard ones when you've got the hang of things. Who knows, you may get hooked and be the movie quiz champion before you know it. In addition to the themed sections you will find Pot Luck questions. Use these if specialist subjects are not what you want, and you just need questions on general movie knowledge.

We know that you, the reader of this book, would never ever dream of taking a sly peek at an answer if you weren't sure what the correct answer was. Well, not everyone is as honest as you are. That is why the answers to the questions are on a different page from the questions themselves. We tell you where to find the answers underneath the quiz number and topic heading. You won't have far to look. The correct answers will be just a few pages before or after the questions.

Running a quiz which just involves family and friends is usually a simple affair. All you really need is a copy of *The Best Movie Quiz Book Ever!*

If you are going to run a quiz and invite the public to attend, preparation is the key. When you organize the questions, have them all ready in the order you want to ask them. The whole event will disintegrate into chaos if you're fumbling around for the questions, and – even worse – hesitating over the answers. At a public quiz people don't want to be made to look stupid. It's a night out, remember. They've probably had a hard day at the office and the last thing they need is an evening of supposed relaxation where they're made to look as though they know nothing at all. They want to have fun, so start with easy questions to get everyone in the mood. Only when you've lulled them into a false sense of security should you step up the pressure by adding the medium and finally the hard questions.

ESSENTIAL EQUIPMENT :
A copy of *The Best Movie Quiz Book Ever!*
Sheets of paper for people to write their answers on
Pens or pencils in case people don't bring their own

YOU'VE SEEN THE MOVIE.

YOU'VE GOT THE BOOK.

NOW ENJOY THE QUIZ!

There are those who say that any question is easy if you know the answer. Well maybe. In this section most people will be able to come up with most of the answers without too much difficulty. The questions are about well-known films and famous names. There are no trick questions. The questions are short and snappy. The answers are brief and simple.

Use these questions in an organized quiz in the early rounds so that everyone will get something right. There is nothing worse than announcing the score in the first round and finding Team 1 got zero. They'll all want to go home and will never come back again. Give them plenty of easy questions to get them in the mood. The pressure comes later!

An easy question certainly won't ask you the name of the third extra on the left on the deck of the Titanic. However, if you didn't even know that there was a movie called *Titanic*, then there will certainly be some questions in this section that you simply won't be able to answer. Broadly speaking, we assume most people would consider these questions to be straightforward!

Finally a word of warning. Don't always say the first thing that comes into your head, however easy the question may seem. If you can't answer one of the difficult questions in the final section of this book most of your fellow contestants will be not at all surprised, and probably relieved. If you get a really easy question wrong because you were too impulsive, the embarrassment factor goes off the scale!

Answers – see page 11

1   Which film centre is also known as Tinseltown?
2   Which writer was 'in Love' in the 1998 movie?
3   In which movie based on a Jane Austen novel did Gwyneth Paltrow play Emma Woodhouse?
4   What follows the names of Harry Connick and Robert Downey?
5   Who played the lead role in *The African Queen* after David Niven turned it down?
6   Who sang the title song of *Who's That Girl*?
7   In which decade was *Star Wars* first released?
8   Who played the villain in the 90s movie *Silence of the Lambs*?
9   Who won the Best Actor Oscar for *One Flew over the Cuckoo's Nest*?
10 In which decade was *Goldfinger* released?
11 How is Demetria Guynes better known?
12 Who won the Best Director Oscar for *Annie Hall*?
13 From which country did Mikhail Barishnikov defect to the USA?
14 In which country was Britt Ekland born?
15 In which eastern bloc country was the movie *Reds* set?
16 In which decade was *Mission: Impossible* released?
17 Who was Paul Newman's wife whom he directed in *Rachel, Rachel*?
18 What did T stand for in *E.T.*?
19 How is former Bond girl, Mrs Ringo Starr, Barbara Goldbach better known?
20 Which Apollo mission was the subject of a movie starring Tom Hanks?
21 Which comedian Bob has hosted the Oscars ceremony over 20 times?
22 Rupert Everett starred in 'The Madness of' which king?
23 Burt Bacharach was a former accompanist for which actress Marlene?
24 Which movie did the song 'Fame' come from?
25 Which Phoebe of TV mini-series *Lace* married actor Kevin Kline?

Answers Pot Luck 2 (see Quiz 3)
1 India. 2 Thompson. 3 3 hours. 4 Mike Newell. 5 *The Boxer*. 6 Marlon Brando. 7 1930s. 8 Cage. 9 Boxing. 10 Julia Roberts. 11 *The Godfather*. 12 Oldman. 13 Quentin. 14 Brad Pitt. 15 Sister. 16 Curtis. 17 Mitty. 18 *Jaws*. 19 Winona. 20 Reynolds. 21 Stone. 22 1980s. 23 Harlow. 24 *Green*. 25 Elton John.

Answers – see page 12

1   *Anna Christie* was the first talkie for which Swedish star?
2   *The Blue Angel* with Marlene Dietrich was shot in English and which other language?
3   Which 'modern' film was Chaplin's last silent movie?
4   In *Stagecoach* which actor John played the Ringo Kid?
5   Which 1939 movie featured a Yellow Brick Road?
6   Which dancers appeared in *The Story of Vernon and Irene Castle*?
7   *Mr Smith Goes to* where in the title of the 1939 movie?
8   Which Laurence played Heathcliff to Merle Oberon's Cathy in *Wuthering Heights*?
9   What were Katharine Hepburn and Cary Grant *Bringing Up* in the 1938 comedy?
10   Which King was a successful ape?
11   Which Clark Gable film, the name of a city, was about a Californian earthquake at the beginning of the 20th century?
12   *The Adventures of* which English hero was the title of a 1938 movie with Errol Flynn?
13   What type of character did James Cagney play in *Angels with Dirty Faces*?
14   *Thoroughbreds Don't Cry* teamed Judy Garland with which Mickey?
15   Which Busby did the choreography for *Footlight Parade*?
16   Which *Hotel* was the title of a Garbo movie?
17   Which zany brothers made *Animal Crackers* in 1930?
18   In which city is *The Hunchback of Notre Dame* set?
19   Bela Lugosi starred as the first sound version of which character?
20   Where was it *All Quiet* in the movies in 1930?
21   The movie *Scarface* was based on the life of which gangster?
22   Which 1939 movie was about a schoolmaster called Mr Chipperfield?
23   What was the heroine of *Gone with the Wind* called?
24   Boris Karloff starred in one of the first horror movies about which Mary Shelley character?
25   What completes the title of the Mae West movie, *She Done Him ___*?

Answers Animation (see Quiz 4)
1 Gibson. **2** Gromit. **3** Disney. **4** *The Lion King.* **5** Williams. **6** The Beast.
7 Rowan Atkinson. **8** Jane. **9** Bugs Bunny. **10** 1940s. **11** Phil Collins.
12 Dalmatians. **13** *Jungle Book.* **14** 1960s. **15** Cat. **16** *Antz.* **17** The Aristocats.
18 *101 Dalmatians.* **19** Donald. **20** 1930s. **21** Bugs Bunny. **22** 1990s.
23 *Jungle Book.* **24** Irons. **25** *Toy Story.*

Answers – see page 9

1   Which Asian country is home to 'Bollywood'?

2   Which Emma starred in *Sense and Sensibility*?

3   To the nearest hour, how long does *Titanic* last?

4   Who directed *Four Weddings and a Funeral*?

5   In which 1997 movie did Daniel Day Lewis play a boxer?

6   Who won the Best Actor Oscar for *On the Waterfront*?

7   In which decade of the 20th century was Joan Collins born?

8   Which Nicolas starred in *Face/Off*?

9   Is *Raging Bull* about American football, boxing or bull-fighting?

10   *My Best Friend's Wedding* and *Sleeping with the Enemy* featured which actress?

11   The character Sonny Corleone was in which sequence of movies?

12   *Air Force One* starred which Gary?

13   What is the first name of the *Pulp Fiction* director?

14   Which actor links *Se7en, Sleepers* and *Thelma and Louise*?

15   What relation is Shirley MacLaine to Warren Beatty?

16   Which Tony starred in *Some Like It Hot*?

17   'The Secret Life of' which Walter formed a movie title?

18   Which early Spielberg blockbuster featured a shark?

19   Which Ms Ryder had her big break in *Beetlejuice*?

20   Which 70s actor Burt was *Cosmopolitan*'s first male nude centrefold?

21   Which Oliver won the Best Director Oscar for *Born on the Fourth of July*?

22   In which decade was *Batman* with Michael Keaton released?

23   Which famous Jean tested for the role of Scarlett O'Hara?

24   Which colour completes the film title, *How ____ Was My Valley*?

25   Which pop singer wrote the music for Disney's *The Lion King*?

Answers Pot Luck 1 (see Quiz 1)

1 Hollywood. **2** Shakespeare. **3** *Emma*. **4** Junior. **5** Humphrey Bogart.
6 Madonna. **7** 1970s. **8** Anthony Hopkins. **9** Jack Nicholson. **10** 1960s.
11 Demi Moore. **12** Woody Allen. **13** USSR – Latvia. **14** Sweden. **15** USSR.
16 1990s. **17** Joanne Woodward. **18** Terrestrial. **19** Barbara Bach. **20** 13.
21 Hope. **22** George. **23** Dietrich. **24** *Fame*. **25** Cates.

Answers – see page 10

1   Which Mel was the voice of Captain Smith in *Pocahontas*?
2   Who did Nick Park create as Wallace's faithful hound?
3   Who worked with Pixar to make *Toy Story*?
4   Which movie has the cub Simba and his evil uncle Scar?
5   Which Robin was the voice of the genie in *Aladdin*?
6   Who appeared with Beauty in the 1991 Disney movie?
7   Which alter ego of Mr Bean was the voice of Zazu in *The Lion King*?
8   Which Tarzan mate did Minnie Driver provide the voice for in *Tarzan*?
9   Who featured in *Knighty Knight Bugs* in 1958?
10   In which decade was *Fantasia* released?
11   Who provided the music for the Disney *Tarzan* film?
12   Pongo and Perdita were which types of black-and-white dog in the 1961 Disney movie?
13   Which 'Book' movie featured a jazz-loving bear, Baloo?
14   In which decade was *Jungle Book* released?
15   What type of creature was Felix, an early animation character?
16   Anne Bancroft provided a voice in which 1998 movie about insects?
17   Which felines were the stars of a 1970 Disney classic?
18   In which canine caper was there a 'Twilight Bark'?
19   Which cartoon duck was usually dressed in blue and white?
20   In which decade was *Snow White and the Seven Dwarfs* released?
21   Which Bunny did Mel Blanc provide the voice for?
22   In which decade was *The Lion King* released?
23   Which film featured the song 'The Bare Necessities'?
24   Which English actor Jeremy was the voice of Scar in *The Lion King*?
25   Which movie featured Buzz Lightyear and Mr Potato Head?

Answers – see page 15

1   Which Hugh Grant/Julia Roberts movie set in London featured 'She'?
2   Who first sang 'Somewhere over the Rainbow'?
3   Gene Autry was usually billed as a singing what?
4   Which Newman/Redford movie featured, 'Raindrops Keep Falling on My Head'?
5   John Barry is linked with the music for films about which celebrated secret agent?
6   'Colours of the Wind' was from which movie about a native North American heroine?
7   'When You Wish upon a Star' was from which film about a puppet?
8   Which Mrs was a character and the theme song in *The Graduate*?
9   'Can You Feel the Love Tonight' came from which Disney movie?
10 'Whole New World' was heard in which Disney hit about a genie?
11 'Bright Eyes' from *Watership Down* was about which animals?
12 Which 'Top' 80s movie had the hit song 'Take My Breath Away'?
13 'Up Where We Belong' was used in which movie with Richard Gere and Debra Winger?
14 Which French–Canadian sang the theme from *Titanic*?
15 Who sang 'You Must Love Me' from *Evita*?
16 Which 'Cowboy' movie provided the hit 'Everybody's Talkin'' for Nilsson?
17 Which Oscar-winner featured 'My Heart Will Go On'?
18 Who wrote the music for *Evita*?
19 'The Streets of Philadelphia' from which movie won Best Song Oscar?
20 Which Shirley sang the title song for the 007 movie *Goldfinger*?
21 What type of 'River' was the theme from *Breakfast at Tiffany's*?
22 Scott Joplin's music for *The Sting* is played on which musical instrument?
23 Which 'Melody', a hit for The Righteous Brothers, featured in *Ghost*?
24 How is composer and Oscar-winner Hoagland Howard Carmichael better known?
25 Which Welshman Tom sang the theme song for 007's *Thunderball*?

Answers Arnold Schwarzenegger (see Quiz 7)
1 Austria. **2** Iron. **3** Conan. **4** *The Terminator*. **5** Red. **6** DeVito. **7** Total.
8 George Bush. **9** Los Angeles. **10** Her husband. **11** *Conan the Barbarian*.
12 Preston. **13** Maria. **14** Cameron. **15** Pregnant. **16** Austrian Oak.
17 *Terminator 2*. **18** *True Lies*. **19** 'The Last'. **20** 1940s. **21** Kindergarten.
22 Computers. **23** J.F. Kennedy. **24** Planet Hollywood. **25** Jeff Bridges.

QUIZ 6 POT LUCK 3

Answers – see page 16

1   *Top Gun* and *City of Angels* featured which actress?
2   The character Vincent Vega appeared in which movie?
3   Which Susan starred in *The Witches of Eastwick*?
4   In 1998 who separated from her husband Bruce Willis?
5   In which decade was the remake of *Godzilla* released after the 1955 movie?
6   Who played Jack in *Titanic*?
7   In which decade does *The Talented Mr Ripley* take place?
8   Who played the title role in *Citizen Kane*?
9   Which Matt starred in *Wild Things*?
10   Which word links a 'Hawk' and a 'Wolf' to give two film titles?
11   Who played Rosemary in *Rosemary's Baby*?
12   Was *Beverley Hills Cop* first released in the 1960s, 70s or 80s?
13   *Ghostbusters* and *Alien* featured which actress?
14   Who played the police captain in *Casablanca*?
15   Which actress links *The Silence of the Lambs* and *Taxi Driver*?
16   Which superhero gets involved with Cat Woman?
17   Who starred in the *Lethal Weapon* series of films?
18   What is the name of Jamie Lee Curtis's actor father?
19   Which fruit would complete this title, *The ____ of Wrath*?
20   Which Jamie starred in *Halloween*?
21   Does *Mary Poppins* last for 140, 200 or 240 minutes?
22   Who won the Best Director Oscar for *Titanic*?
23   In which decade was *Rain Man* released?
24   Which group had a giant hit with the movie-linked song 'Take My Breath Away'?
25   In which decade of the 20th century was Sean Connery born?

Answers Horror (see Quiz 8)
1 Kenneth Branagh. **2** The Devil. **3** *Bram Stoker's Dracula.* **4** *Scream 2.*
5 William Peter Blatty. **6** Bela. **7** Invisible. **8** King. **9** Dracula. **10** Cruise.
11 Spiders. **12** Kubrick. **13** The creature. **14** *Halloween.* **15** Spacek. **16** Elm
Street. **17** 1970s. **18** Mia Farrow. **19** Victor. **20** In London. **21** *The Birds.*
22 Anthony Perkins. **23** Anthony Hopkins. **24** Pfeiffer. **25** Hammer.

Answers – see page 13

1   In which European country was he born?
2   What was he 'Pumping' in the 1977 documentary film about himself?
3   What was the name of 'the Barbarian' he played in 1982?
4   Which smash hit movie gave him the line 'I'll be back'?
5   What colour went before 'Sonja' in his 1985 movie?
6   Which Danny was his co-star in *Twins*?
7   What type of 'Recall' was his 1990 movie?
8   In 1990 which Republican President made him chairman of the Council on Physical Fitness?
9   In which Californian city was *The Terminator* set?
10   Which muscleman relative of Jayne Mansfield did he play in the TV biopic?
11   What was *Conan the Destroyer* the sequel to?
12   Which Kelly co-starred in *Twins*?
13   Which journalist Ms Shriver did he marry?
14   Which James, later famous for *Titanic*, directed *The Terminator*?
15   What very unmasculine condition was he in *Junior*?
16   In weightlifting circles he was billed as what type of Austrian tree?
17   Which *Terminator* film was subtitled 'Judgment Day'?
18   What sort of 'Lies' did he make for James Cameron in 1994?
19   What sort of 'Action Hero' was he in 1993?
20   In which decade was he born?
21   What sort of 'Cop' was he in 1990?
22   In *True Lies* Schwarzenegger is a salesman of what?
23   He married the niece of which late US President?
24   Which 'Planet' restaurant chain did he back?
25   Who was Schwarzenegger's male co-star in *Stay Hungry*?

Answers Music on Film (see Quiz 5)
1 *Notting Hill.* **2** Judy Garland. **3** Cowboy. **4** *Butch Cassidy and the Sundance Kid.* **5** Bond films. **6** *Pocahontas.* **7** *Pinocchio.* **8** Robinson. **9** *The Lion King.* **10** *Aladdin.* **11** Rabbits. **12** *Top Gun.* **13** *An Officer and a Gentleman.* **14** Celine Dion. **15** Madonna. **16** *Midnight Cowboy.* **17** *Titanic.* **18** Andrew Lloyd Webber. **19** *Philadelphia.* **20** Bassey. **21** 'Moon River'. **22** Piano. **23** 'Unchained Melody.' **24** Hoagy Carmichael. **25** Jones.

Answers – see page 14

1   Who directed Kenneth Branagh in *Mary Shelley's Frankenstein*?

2   Who, according to the movie, fathered *Rosemary's Baby*?

3   In which Dracula movie did Anthony Hopkins play Professor van Helsing?

4   What was the sequel to *Scream* called?

5   Who wrote the screenplay of William Peter Blatty's *The Exorcist*?

6   What was the first name of Dracula actor Lugosi?

7   What sort of 'Man' was Claude Rains in 1933?

8   Which Stephen's first novel *Carrie* was a successful 70s movie?

9   Who was Transylvania's most famous vampire?

10   Which Tom played a vampire with Brad Pitt in *Interview with the Vampire: The Vampire Chronicles*?

11   Which creepy-crawlies are the subject of *Arachnophobia*?

12   Which Stanley made *The Shining* with Jack Nicholson?

13   What part did Boris Karloff play in the pre-World War II *Frankenstein*?

14   Which 1978 movie shares its name with the spooky 31st October?

15   Which Sissy played the title role in *Carrie*?

16   On which street was the 'Nightmare' in the 80s movie series?

17   In which decade was *The Exorcist* first released?

18   Who was the female star of *Rosemary's Baby*?

19   What was Frankenstein's first name in the Kenneth Branagh version?

20   Where was the 'American Werewolf' in the 1981 movie with David Naughton?

21   Which Hitchcock movie featured feathered attackers?

22   Who directed and starred in *Psycho 3* in 1986?

23   Which British actor won an Oscar for *The Silence of the Lambs*?

24   Which Michelle co-starred with Jack Nicholson in *Wolf*?

25   Which British studios were famous for their horror movies?

Answers Pot Luck 3 (see Quiz 6)
1 Meg Ryan. **2** *Pulp Fiction*. **3** Sarandon. **4** Demi Moore. **5** 1990s. **6** Leonardo DiCaprio. **7** 1950s. **8** Orson Welles. **9** Dillon. **10** Sea. **11** Mia Farrow. **12** 80s. **13** Sigourney Weaver. **14** Claude Rains. **15** Jodie Foster. **16** Batman. **17** Mel Gibson. **18** Tony Curtis. **19** *Grapes*. **20** Lee Curtis. **21** 140 minutes. **22** James Cameron. **23** 1980s. **24** Berlin. **25** 1930s.

Answers – see page 19

1   Which detective has been portrayed on screen over 200 times?
2   Which 1988 film did rock star Phil Collins star in?
3   Which Ewan starred in *Emma*?
4   *Batman Forever* and *To Die For* featured which actress?
5   Which *Home Alone* star was the 20th century's highest paid child in the movies?
6   Who played the young Obi Wan Kenobi in *Star Wars Episode I: The Phantom Menace*?
7   Which Anthony played *Zorba the Greek*?
8   Who sang 'I Will Always Love You' in her film, *The Bodyguard*?
9   Which film legend Mack inspired the musical *Mack and Mabel*?
10   Which Buzz appeared in *Toy Story*?
11   Which veteran actor Richard was Dr Hammond in *Jurassic Park*?
12   Which James starred in the original *Harvey*?
13   Which singer Diana starred in *Lady Sings the Blues*?
14   Which French sex symbol became an animal rights campaigner?
15   Which children's toys are linked with 'Guys' in the title of a film based on a musical?
16   In which TV soap did Larry Hagman find fame after appearing on the big screen?
17   In which decade was *Return of the Jedi* released?
18   Which actor links *The Magnificent Seven* and *The King and I*?
19   Val Kilmer played Jim Morrison in the movie about which rock band?
20   Which Robin starred in *Mrs Doubtfire*?
21   Which actor links *Mission: Impossible, A Few Good Men* and *Days of Thunder*?
22   What was the name of the movie based on TV's *The X-Files*?
23   Which Glenda won the Best Actress Oscar for *Women in Love*?
24   In which decade of the 20th century was Jamie Lee Curtis born?
25   What was the Bond theme for *A View to a Kill* called?

Answers Late Greats (see Quiz 11)
1 Car. **2** Gish. **3** Marvin. **4** Rex Harrison. **5** Gable. **6** Niven. **7** England.
8 Pub. **9** Clark Gable. **10** Vivien Leigh. **11** Richard Burton. **12** Charlie Chaplin &
Paulette Goddard. **13** Rock Hudson. **14** Laurence Olivier. **15** Gardner. **16** Davis.
17 Davis. **18** W.C. Fields. **19** Cary Grant. **20** Nose. **21** Jackie Gleason.
22 Stewart. **23** *Citizen Kane* **24** Dean. **25** Betty Grable.

Answers – see page 20

1   Which pop superstar did Sean Penn marry in 1985?

2   Which ex Mrs Sonny Bono played Loretta Castorini in *Moonstruck*?

3   When Billy Crystal was Harry, who was Meg Ryan?

4   Which 24-year-old Michael played teenager Marty in *Back to the Future*?

5   Which husband of Demi Moore played John McLane in *Die Hard*?

6   Which Kirstie appeared in *Star Trek II*?

7   Which tough guy actor has the nickname Sly?

8   Which Melanie was a 'Working Girl' for Harrison Ford?

9   Who played Tom Cruise's autistic brother in *Rain Man*?

10   Which Patrick practised 'Dirty Dancing' with Jennifer Grey?

11   Which Glenn's 'Attraction' looked 'Fatal' to Michael Douglas in 1987?

12   Which successful US talk show hostess appeared in *The Color Purple*?

13   Who changed her name from Susan Weaver before appearing in movies such as *Ghostbusters*?

14   In *Born on the Fourth of July*, Tom Cruise played a veteran from which war?

15   Which Canadian Leslie found big-screen fame as Lieutenant Frank Drebin?

16   Which Richard was the *American Gigolo*?

17   Which Mel played the title role in *Mad Max II*?

18   Which Kevin played opposite Meryl Streep in *Sophie's Choice*?

19   Which animal was a star with Clint Eastwood in *Any Which Way You Can*?

20   What did Elliott call his pet alien in the 80s Spielberg movie?

21   What sort of busters were Dan Aykroyd and Bill Murray?

22   Which Michael was in *Romancing the Stone* in 1984?

23   What was the name of the cartoon rabbit in the title of the movie with Bob Hoskins?

24   Michael Keaton starred as which caped crusader in 1989?

25   Which 007 joined Harrison Ford in *Indiana Jones and the Last Crusade*?

Answers Pot Luck 5 (see Quiz 12)
1 Danny Boyle. **2** 1950s. **3** *Kitty*. **4** 85 minutes. **5** Ingrid Bergman. **6** Winona Ryder. **7** Diamonds. **8** Madness. **9** *A Return to Oz*. **10** Tina Turner. **11** *Gone with the Wind*. **12** Oldman. **13** Nazis. **14** *The Full Monty*. **15** Dolly Parton. **16** Audrey Hepburn. **17** Michelle Pfeiffer. **18** *Sophie's Choice*. **19** Stockholm. **20** Michael Jackson. **21** Diane Keaton. **22** Whoopi Goldberg. **23** 1960s. **24** Peter Sellers. **25** 1930s.

Answers – see page 17

1	In what type of crash did James Dean meet his death?
2	Which Lillian was dubbed The First Lady of the Silent Screen?
3	Which Lee turned down George C. Scott's role in *Patton*?
4	Who won the Best Actor Oscar for *My Fair Lady*?
5	Which Clark's last movie was *The Misfits*?
6	Which David's autobiography was called *The Moon's a Balloon*?
7	Where was Jessica Tandy born?
8	In what type of building did Oliver Reed die?
9	Who died 12 days after finishing *The Misfits*?
10	Who won the Best Actress Oscar for *Gone with the Wind*?
11	Which Welsh actor directed and starred in *Dr Faustus* in 1968?
12	Which husband and wife starred in *The Great Dictator* in 1940?
13	Who was Bogart talking to when he said, 'You look very soft for a rock'?
14	Which British actor won an Oscar for *Hamlet* in 1948?
15	Which Ava was Oscar-nominated for *Mogambo*?
16	Which Bette tested for the role of Scarlett O'Hara?
17	Which Sammy starred in *Sweet Charity*?
18	How was William Claude Fields known to cinema goers?
19	Jennifer Grant is the only daughter of which great from the heyday of Hollywood?
20	Which part of him did Jimmy Durante insure for $100,000?
21	How was John Gleason known in movies?
22	Which James died in 1997 aged 89?
23	What was Orson Welles's first film, in 1941?
24	Which doomed James starred in *Rebel Without a Cause*?
25	How was Elizabeth Ruth Grable better known?

Answers Pot Luck 4 (see Quiz 9)
1 Sherlock Holmes. **2** *Buster*. **3** McGregor. **4** Nicole Kidman. **5** Macaulay Culkin.
6 Ewan McGregor. **7** Quinn. **8** Whitney Houston. **9** Mack Sennett. **10** Lightyear.
11 Attenborough. **12** Stewart. **13** Ross. **14** Brigitte Bardot. **15** Dolls. **16** *Dallas*.
17 1980s. **18** Yul Brynner. **19** The Doors. **20** Williams. **21** Tom Cruise. **22** *The X-Files*. **23** Jackson. **24** 1950s. **25** 'A View to a Kill'.

Answers – see page 18

1   Which Danny directed *Trainspotting*?
2   In which decade of the 20th century was Kevin Costner born?
3   Which girl's first name completes the film title, ____ *Foyle*?
4   Did *Ace Ventura, Pet Detective* run for 65, 85 or 155 minutes?
5   Who got the lead in *Casablanca* after Hedy Lamarr turned it down?
6   Which actress links *Bram Stoker's Dracula* and *Beetlejuice*?
7   What, according to Monroe's song, are 'a girl's best friend'?
8   Which ailment is mentioned in the title of a movie about King George III?
9   What was the sequel to *The Wizard of Oz* called?
10 Which female pop star featured in *Mad Max Beyond Thunderdome*?
11 Scarlett O'Hara was heroine of which epic film?
12 Which Gary starred in *The Fifth Element*?
13 Which political group is central to the plot of *The Sound of Music*?
14 Which 90s movie told of a group of stripping Sheffield steelworkers?
15 Which blonde country star had a cameo role in *The Beverly Hillbillies*?
16 Which Audrey starred in *My Fair Lady*?
17 Who played the female lead in *Grease 2*?
18 In which movie did Meryl Streep play a Polish holocaust survivor?
19 Greta Garbo was born in which European capital city?
20 Martin Scorsese directed the video *Bad* for which pop superstar?
21 Which Diane was in *The First Wives' Club*?
22 *The Color Purple* and *Sister Act 2* featured which actress?
23 In which decade was *The Graduate* released?
24 Which Peter played *Inspector Clouseau*?
25 Did Shirley Temple first win an Oscar in the 1930s, 50s or 70s?

Answers 1980s Stars (see Quiz 10)
1 Madonna. **2** Cher. **3** Sally. **4** J. Fox. **5** Bruce Willis. **6** Alley. **7** Sylvester Stallone. **8** Griffith. **9** Dustin Hoffman. **10** Swayze. **11** Close. **12** Oprah Winfrey. **13** Sigourney Weaver. **14** Vietnam. **15** Nielsen. **16** Gere. **17** Gibson. **18** Kline. **19** Orang Utan. **20** E.T. **21** Ghostbusters. **22** Douglas. **23** Roger. **24** Batman. **25** Sean Connery.

Answers – see page 23

1   Which musical set in New York won 10 awards in 1961?
2   'Dances with' what was the first winner of the 1990s?
3   The chauffeur was 'Driving Miss' whom in 1989?
4   Who was 'in Love' in 1998 to take Best Film honours?
5   *Chariots of Fire* was about events at which 1924 sporting event?
6   What was 'Confidential' in the movie with Kim Basinger?
7   Which musical Mary had 13 nominations and five awards in 1964?
8   Judi Dench played which queen in *Shakespeare in Love*?
9   Which 'List' won in 1993?
10 *The English Patient* tells of a desert explorer during which war?
11 Which continent was in the title of an 80s winner with Meryl Streep?
12 Which pacifist leader of India was the subject of a 1982 biopic?
13 What was the name of the sequel to *The Godfather* which won two years after the original?
14 Which 'Hunter' was the 1979 winner?
15 What was the name of the musical based on a Dickens novel about the boy who asked for more?
16 In which country was *Gigi* set?
17 Who was the 1984 winner *Amadeus* about?
18 Which 80s film is about The Dragon Throne?
19 Which 'Connection' was Best Picture of 1971?
20 *Platoon* was set during which Asian conflict?
21 *The Greatest Show on Earth* was about what type of entertainment?
22 *The Sting* won Best Picture during which decade?
23 The most successful winner of the 90s had the shortest name: what?
24 Who was 'versus Kramer' in 1979?
25 In which European country was *Cabaret* set during the 1930s?

Answers 1940s (see Quiz 15)
1 Hitchcock. 2 *Pinocchio*. 3 *The Outlaw*. 4 St Louis. 5 Old Lace. 6 Horses.
7 Christmas. 8 Hayworth. 9 Easter. 10 The Ambersons. 11 Elephant. 12 *The Philadelphia Story*. 13 *Green*. 14 Maltese. 15 Kane. 16 34th Street. 17 Red.
18 *Casablanca*. 19 Vienna. 20 Sailors. 21 Philip. 22 Hitler. 23 *Bambi*.
24 Walt Disney. 25 Coronets.

Answers – see page 24

1   Which Geena starred in *A League of their Own*?
2   In which country was Leslie Nielsen born?
3   Which Helen was the only American nominated for Best Actress Oscar in 1998?
4   Which actor links *Batman, A Few Good Men* and *Wolf*?
5   Steven Spielberg made 'Close Encounters of' which kind?
6   Which much-quoted actress wrote an autobiography called *Goodness Had Nothing to Do with It*?
7   Which whale was played by Keiko in a 90s movie?
8   *Top Gun* was about which of the armed services?
9   Was *Bambi* first released in the 1920s, 40s or 60s?
10   Which Frank starred in the 50s movie *From Here to Eternity*?
11   What is Nicolas Cage's real surname?
12   Real-life character Lee Harvey Oswald appears in which Oliver Stone movie?
13   Which word completes the film title, *I Am a ____ from a Chain Gang*?
14   Which character was voiced by Robin Williams in *Aladdin*?
15   Which James Bond has an actor son called Jason?
16   *Total Recall* and *Casino* both featured which actress?
17   Who played opposite Ginger Rogers 10 times?
18   Which pop star Tina did Angela Bassett play in the 1993 biopic?
19   In which decade was *Batman Forever* released?
20   Who won the Best Actor Oscar for *The Godfather*?
21   Which actress Natalie did Robert Wagner marry twice?
22   In which decade of the 20th century was Michelle Pfeiffer born?
23   Which mode of transport completes the film title, *Night ____ To Munich*?
24   Which Kevin played Bottom in the 1990s *A Midsummer Night's Dream*?
25   Which Mark starred in *The Empire Strikes Back*?

Answers – see page 21

1   *Rebecca* was the first Hollywood movie for which director Alfred?

2   Which Disney movie featured a wooden puppet?

3   Which 1943 movie was outlawed for six years because of Jane Russell's attributes?

4   The 1944 Judy Garland movie says 'Meet Me in' which town?

5   What went with 'Arsenic' in the comedy with Cary Grant?

6   *National Velvet* centred on what type of animals?

7   *It's a Wonderful Life* is set at which festive time of year?

8   Which Rita played the title role in *Gilda*?

9   At what time of year was the 'Parade' which starred Fred Astaire and Judy Garland?

10   Which 'Magnificent' family was the subject of a 40s movie directed by Orson Welles?

11   What sort of animal was Dumbo?

12   Which 'Story' with Cary Grant and Katharine Hepburn had the name of a US state in its title?

13   Which colour completes the title of 1941 Oscar winner, *How ____ Was My Valley*?

14   What was the nationality of the 'Falcon' in the 1941 movie with Humphrey Bogart and Peter Lorre?

15   Which 'Citizen' was a debut for Orson Welles?

16   On which street was there a 'Miracle' in a 1947 film?

17   What colour were the dancing shoes in the movie with Moira Shearer?

18   Which movie has the line, 'Here's lookin' at you kid'?

19   In which Austrian city is *The Third Man* set?

20   What type of servicemen were on leave in *On the Town*?

21   Which private detective Marlowe is the subject of *The Big Sleep*?

22   Which dictator did Chaplin play and mock in *The Great Dictator*?

23   Which Disney movie was the tale of a young fawn?

24   Who was the most famous director of *Fantasia*?

25   What went with 'Kind Hearts' in the movie with Alec Guinness?

Answers Oscars – Best Films (see Quiz 13)

1 *West Side Story*. **2** Wolves. **3** Daisy. **4** Shakespeare. **5** Olympic Games. **6** LA. **7** *Mary Poppins*. **8** Elizabeth I. **9** *Schindler's List*. **10** World War II. **11** (Out of) Africa. **12** Gandhi. **13** *The Godfather Part II*. **14** *The Deer Hunter*. **15** *Oliver!* **16** France. **17** Mozart. **18** *The Last Emperor*. **19** *The French Connection*. **20** The Vietnam War. **21** Circus. **22** 1970s. **23** *Titanic*. **24** Kramer. **25** Germany.

Answers – see page 22

1   What colour are Paul Newman's eyes?
2   Which Elizabeth was his co-star in *Cat on a Hot Tin Roof*?
3   In which decade was he Oscar-nominated for *The Hustler*?
4   Which Martin directed him in *The Color of Money*?
5   Who was his co-star in *Butch Cassidy and the Sundance Kid*?
6   In which 70s disaster movie did he play the architect of a skyscraper?
7   In which city is *The Sting* set?
8   In which decade was *Butch Cassidy* first released?
9   Which actor Sidney is co-partner in his production company First Artists?
10 He founded the Scott Newman Foundation in memory of his son who died from what?
11 Which actress Joanne did Paul Newman marry in 1958?
12 What 'Menagerie' did he direct in 1987?
13 Which singer Julie was his co-star in *Torn Curtain* in 1966?
14 Which speed sport is he involved in, which he used in 1969 in *Winning*?
15 Which western hero Billy did he play in *The Left-Handed Gun*?
16 In 1978 which Democratic US President appointed him a US delegate to the UN Conference on Nuclear Disarmament?
17 In *Butch Cassidy and the Sundance Kid*, which part did he play?
18 Which 'Long Hot' season was the title of a 1958 movie?
19 In which movie did he play conman Henry Gondorff?
20 How was his character Eddie Felson described?
21 Which 'Cool Hand' character did he play in 1967?
22 What type of salad product did he market for charity?
23 He and his wife played 'Mr and Mrs' who in 1990?
24 Which Oscar did he win for *The Color of Money*?
25 In which decade did he team up again with Redford for *The Sting*?

Answers Pot Luck 6 (see Quiz 14)
1 Davis. **2** Canada. **3** Hunt. **4** Jack Nicholson. **5** The Third Kind. **6** Mae West.
7 Willy. **8** The Air Force. **9** 1940s. **10** Sinatra. **11** Coppola. **12** *JFK*. **13**
Fugitive. **14** The Genie. **15** Sean Connery. **16** Sharon Stone. **17** Fred Astaire.
18 Tina Turner. **19** 1990s. **20** Marlon Brando. **21** Wood. **22** 1950s. **23** *Train*.
24 Kline. **25** Hamill.

Answers – see page 27

1   *Mrs Doubtfire* and *Jumanji* both featured which actor?
2   Which Danny starred in *LA Confidential*?
3   *Gregory's Two Girls* was the sequel to which film?
4   Which Michael played Marty in *Back to the Future*?
5   Which musical set in gangland New York won 11 Oscars in the 60s?
6   Which Henry wrote the score for *The Pink Panther*?
7   Peter Lawford was the brother-in-law of which late US president?
8   In the film's title, which word describes Clint Eastwood's character Harry?
9   Who wrote the musical score for *Star Wars*?
10   Who was billed in his first movie as Arnold Strong?
11   Forties movie *The Outlaw* featured which Jane?
12   Which actress links *Ghost* and *The Juror*?
13   Which musical about Danny and Sandy was re-released in the 90s?
14   Which Nicolas starred in *Leaving Las Vegas*?
15   Who was Vincente Minnelli's famous daughter?
16   Which word completes the film title, *A Room with a ___*?
17   *Land Girls* starred which Anna?
18   Which Meg starred in *When Harry Met Sally*?
19   Madonna bought a burial plot next to where which blonde icon is buried?
20   In which decade of the 20th century was Al Pacino born?
21   Which Ralph starred in the film version of *The Avengers*?
22   According to the film title, what should you do to your wagon?
23   Which Annette was Warren Beatty's first wife?
24   In which decade was *Some Like It Hot* released?
25   Did *Babe* run for 52, 92 or 182 minutes?

Answers Pot Luck 8 (see Quiz 19)
1 Redford. **2** Dustin Hoffman. **3** The Spice Girls. **4** Wayne's. **5** Piano. **6** Tom Hanks. **7** Black. **8** Tarzan. **9** Mulder & Scully. **10** *10*. **11** Patrick Swayze. **12** Sutherland. **13** Jacques Tati. **14** *Robin Hood: Prince of Thieves*. **15** 1930s. **16** Red. **17** Sergeant Bilko. **18** Glenn Close. **19** Ryan O'Neal. **20** Dinosaurs. **21** Bette Midler. **22** American. **23** 1970s. **24** 'The Living Daylights'. **25** Demi Moore.

Answers – see page 28

1	Which 'Park' was a blockbuster of the 1990s?
2	Who played Jack in *Titanic*?
3	What was the nationality of Oskar Schindler in Spielberg's movie?
4	Which shark-infested movie was the first to take $100 million at the box office?
5	In which movie was someone told to "phone home"?
6	What sort of 'Menace' was Episode I in the *Star Wars* movies?
7	What mythical sea creature did Daryl Hannah play in *Splash!*?
8	Who played Schindler in *Schindler's List*?
9	Which song was used for the hugely successful *The Full Monty*?
10	What was the most expensive film made in the 20th century?
11	What was the last Bond movie of the 20th century?
12	Who played Dan Gallagher in *Fatal Attraction*?
13	Which musical was made about Eva Peron?
14	How was the 'Mission' described in the 1996 release with Tom Cruise?
15	For which role was Faye Dunaway Oscar-nominated in *Bonnie and Clyde*?
16	Mel Gibson's movie *Gallipoli* was set during which war?
17	Which 'King' grossed the fourth highest sum in the US in the 1990s?
18	What did E stand for in *E.T.*?
19	Which singer played Rachel Marron in *The Bodyguard*?
20	Who won the Best Director Oscar for *Schindler's List*?
21	Which 'Day' was released just before the 4th of July in the US?
22	'Tomorrow is another day' is the last line of which movie?
23	In which movie did Warren Beatty say, 'We rob banks'?
24	*The Empire Strikes Back* was the sequel to which blockbusting film?
25	Which David won the Best Director Oscar for *The Bridge over the River Kwai*?

Answers – see page 25

1   Which Robert starred in *The Horse Whisperer*?
2   Who won the Best Actor Oscar for *Rain Man*?
3   Which pop group starred in *Spiceworld*?
4   Whose 'World' was a 1992 film with Mike Myers and Dana Carvey?
5   *Shine* is about a musician playing which instrument?
6   Which actor links *Forrest Gump*, *You've Got Mail* and *A League of their Own*?
7   Which colour goes before 'Narcissus' and 'mail' to form film titles?
8   Johnny Weissmuller portrayed which jungle hero?
9   Who are the two main characters in *The X-Files*?
10 Which Bo Derek film had a number as the title?
11 Who starred opposite Jennifer Gray in *Dirty Dancing*?
12 Which Donald played Hawkeye in the film *M*A*S*H*?
13 Who starred in and directed *Monsieur Hulot's Holiday*?
14 Which movie used the song 'Everything I Do (I Do it for You)'?
15 In which decade of the 20th century was Jack Nicholson born?
16 Which colour links 'Shoes' and 'Dust' in film titles?
17 Which sergeant created by Phil Silvers featured in a 90s movie?
18 Which actress links *Fatal Attraction* and *101 Dalmatians*?
19 What is the name of Tatum O'Neal's actor father?
20 Which creatures dominated *Jurassic Park*?
21 *The First Wives' Club*, *Ruthless People* and *Hocus Pocus* all feature which actress?
22 A werewolf in London and a man in Paris were both of what nationality?
23 In which decade was *The Godfather* released?
24 What was the Bond theme for *The Living Daylights* called?
25 Who played opposite Patrick Swayze in *Ghost*?

Answers Pot Luck 7 (see Quiz 17)
1 Robin Williams. **2** Danny DeVito. **3** *Gregory's Girl*. **4** Michael J. Fox. **5** *West Side Story*. **6** Mancini. **7** John F. Kennedy. **8** Dirty. **9** John Williams. **10** Arnold Schwarzenegger. **11** Russell. **12** Demi Moore. **13** *Grease*. **14** Cage. **15** Liza Minnelli. **16** *View*. **17** Friel. **18** Ryan. **19** Marilyn Monroe. **20** 1940s. **21** Fiennes. **22** *Paint Your Wagon*. **23** Bening. **24** 1950s. **25** 92 minutes.

Answers – see page 26

1   What was the first talkie?
2   In the first *Toy Story*, which child owns the toys?
3   Which film company opened the first ever theme park?
4   Where in Italy did the first film festival take place?
5   Which monster lizard, first seen in 1955, was in a 1997 blockbuster?
6   What was the first movie in which Eastwood was Harry Callahan?
7   Which Fay was the first scream queen, in *King Kong*?
8   What was Disney's first feature film – with eight people in the title?
9   Which oriental detective Charlie first appeared on screen in 1926?
10 Where were India's first studios, giving rise to the name 'Bollywood'?
11 What was the first two-colour system used in movie making?
12 *The Robe* was the first movie with what type of screen?
13 *The Scent of Mystery* was the first movie with sight, sound and what?
14 Which 1995 'Story' was the first computer-animated film?
15 What was the first major movie about the Vietnam War?
16 Which 1946 Oscar-winning Dickens film gave Alec Guinness his major movie debut?
17 Which movie with an all-child cast was Alan Parker's directorial debut?
18 Which Ralph played Steed in the first Avengers movie to hit the big screen?
19 In which decade were the Oscars first presented?
20 Which Christmas classic was first heard in *Holiday Inn*?
21 Who was Oscar-nominated for his directorial debut in *Ordinary People*?
22 Which Brothers made the first talkie?
23 In which movie did Al Jolson say, 'You ain't heard nothin' yet'?
24 Which Katharine won the first BAFTA Best Actress award?
25 In which French city was the first movie in Europe shown?

Answers – see page 31

1   What sort of films did the Keystone Company make?
2   Samuel Goldfish changed his name to what after founding a film company?
3   In which state did William Fox found his film production company in 1912?
4   Which 'Little Lord' was played by Mary Pickford, who also played his mother?
5   Which movie about the little boy who asked for more starred Jackie Coogan?
6   In which decade did Chaplin make *The Kid*?
7   How many 'Horsemen of the Apocalypse' were there in the Valentino movie?
8   In which decade of the 20th century was Keystone founded?
9   Which Gloria found fame in *The Danger Girl* in 1916?
10   'The Taming of' what was the only movie to star Douglas Fairbanks and Mary Pickford together?
11   Ford Sterling led which Kops?
12   What was the first name of Langdon of *Tramp Tramp Tramp* fame?
13   Which regal first name did director/producer/writer Vidor have?
14   Which Fred's tours to the US brought Chaplin from England?
15   Pathe Weekly showed what on their reels?
16   Which Brothers released their first major feature in 1915?
17   Which Rudolph shot to stardom in *The Sheik*?
18   Who was forced out of Goldwyn Pictures in 1922?
19   Cecil B. de Mille's *King of Kings* was about whom?
20   *Birth of a Nation* was the first movie screened at which presidential home?
21   Which Cecil made the spectacular *Ten Commandments*?
22   Who made *The Gold Rush*?
23   Lon Chaney starred as which Phantom in 1925?
24   Which D.W. made *Birth of a Nation*?
25   Which 'Singer' marked the end of the silent era?

Answers Elizabeth Taylor (see Quiz 23)
1 England. 2 Grand National. 3 Cleopatra. 4 Fisher. 5 *The Taming of the Shrew*.
6 Agatha Christie. 7 8. 8 Richard Burton. 9 Flintstone. 10 AIDS. 11 Jackson.
12 American. 13 Virginia Woolf. 14 Perfume. 15 Violet. 16 *The Simpsons*.
17 Carrie Fisher. 18 Rooney. 19 *Cat on a Hot Tin Roof*. 20 Richard Burton.
21 *Little Women*. 22 1940s. 23 *Jane Eyre*. 24 Tracy. 25 Clowns.

Answers – see page 32

1	Which Woody starred in *Natural Born Killers*?
2	Which 007 starred in *The Lawnmower Man*?
3	What is the first name of FBI agent Starling in *The Silence of the Lambs*?
4	In which country was Jean-Claude Van Damme born?
5	In which TV soap did Joan Collins and John Forsythe find fame after appearing on the big screen?
6	Did *Aladdin* run for 60, 90 or 130 minutes?
7	Which Diane played Steve Martin's wife in *Father of the Bride*?
8	Which *Grease* star danced with Princess Diana at the White House?
9	Which Julie links *Darling* in the 1960s and *Afterglow* in the 90s?
10	In which decade of the 20th century did James Stewart die?
11	Which actor was tennis star John McEnroe's first father in law?
12	The character Harry Lime appears in which spy thriller?
13	What was Crocodile Dundee's homeland?
14	*The Sunshine Boys* starred which Walter?
15	Which western star John first acted as 'Duke Morrison'?
16	In which decade was *Psycho* released?
17	In a movie title, which word goes before 'of the Lost Ark'?
18	Which actress links *Se7en* and *Sliding Doors*?
19	Which Kim likened Hollywood to the Mafia?
20	*Three Kings*, with George Clooney, takes place during which war?
21	In which decade of the 20th century was Liam Neeson born?
22	In which 1976 movie did Sylvester Stallone play a boxer?
23	What type of snack completes the film title *Animal ___*?
24	Which famous Loretta tested for the role of Scarlett O'Hara?
25	Who sang 'Fame' in *Fame*?

Answers Unforgettables (see Quiz 24)
1 Davis. **2** *High Society*. **3** *Paint Your Wagon*. **4** Swanson. **5** Oliver Reed.
6 Richard Burton. **7** Humphrey Bogart & Lauren Bacall. **8** Mae West. **9** Henry
Fonda. **10** Dietrich. **11** Elvis Presley. **12** Jeanette Macdonald. **13** Charlie Chaplin.
14 Durante. **15** John Wayne. **16** Transylvania. **17** Legs. **18** 1970s. **19** Rex
Harrison. **20** Joan Crawford. **21** Spencer Tracy. **22** Car. **23** Laurence Olivier.
24 First. **25** Kelly.

Answers – see page 29

1 In which country was Elizabeth Taylor born?

2 Which horse race was her movie *National Velvet* about?

3 Which Egyptian queen did she play in the 1960s?

4 Which singer Eddie did she marry after her third husband was killed?

5 Which Shakespeare play, with Taylor as the volatile Katherine, did Taylor and Burton bring to the big screen?

6 Who wrote the whodunnit on which her 1980 movie *The Mirror Crack'd* was based?

7 Which number followed 'Butterfield' in her first Oscar-winning movie?

8 Which husband did she fall in love with on the set of *Cleopatra*?

9 Which Fred's mother-in-law was she when she played Pearl Slaghoople in 1994?

10 In 1993 she received an award at the Oscars ceremony for her work with sufferers from what?

11 On which pop star Michael's estate did she marry for the eighth time?

12 What was the nationality of her parents?

13 'Who's Afraid of' whom was the title of her second Oscar-winner?

14 What type of beauty product did she launch towards the end of the 20th century?

15 What colour are her famous eyes?

16 She was the voice of Baby Maggie in which cartoon series?

17 Which star of *Star Wars* was her one-time step-daughter?

18 Which Mickey was her co-star in *National Velvet*?

19 In which movie based on a Tennessee Williams play was she the 'cat' Maggie?

20 Which actor did Elizabeth Taylor marry twice?

21 Which 'Little' film was based on the classic by Louisa May Alcott?

22 In which decade did she make her very first movie?

23 In which movie about Charlotte Bronte's most famous heroine did she appear in 1944?

24 Which Spencer played the title role in *Father of the Bride*?

25 In *A Little Night Music* she sang 'Send in the' what?

Answers The Silent Years (see Quiz 21)
1 Comedy. 2 Goldwyn. 3 California. 4 Fauntleroy. 5 *Oliver Twist.* 6 1920s.
7 Four. 8 Second decade (1912). 9 Swanson. 10 The Shrew. 11 Keystone.
12 Harry. 13 King. 14 Karno. 15 News. 16 Warner Brothers. 17 Valentino.
18 Sam Goldwyn. 19 Jesus Christ. 20 The White House. 21 B. de Mille. 22 Charlie Chaplin. 23 Phantom of the Opera. 24 Griffith. 25 *The Jazz Singer.*

Answers – see page 30

1 Which Bette said, 'Until you're known in my profession as a monster, you're not a star'?
2 What was Grace Kelly's last film, with Frank Sinatra and Bing Crosby?
3 In which 1961 movie did Lee Marvin have a singing role?
4 Which Gloria played Norma Desmond in *Sunset Boulevard*?
5 Which famous hell-raising actor wrote an autobiography called *Reed All About It*?
6 Which Welshman's real name was Richard Jenkins?
7 Which husband and wife starred in *Key Largo* in 1948?
8 Which film star wrote the novel *Constant Sinner*?
9 Who played the father of real-life daughter Jane in *On Golden Pond* in 1981?
10 Which Marlene found fame with *The Blue Angel*?
11 Who played two parts in *Kissin' Cousins* in 1964?
12 Who played opposite Nelson Eddy eight times?
13 Robert Downey Jr was Oscar-nominated for playing which unforgettable star of the silent screen?
14 Which Jimmy's nickname was Schnozzle?
15 Who played The Ringo Kid in the classic western *Stagecoach*?
16 Where was Bela Lugosi born?
17 Which part of her did Cyd Charisse insure for $5 million?
18 In which decade of the 20th century was River Phoenix born?
19 Which British actor won an Oscar for *My Fair Lady*?
20 Whose autobiography was called *A Portrait of Joan*?
21 Who died 15 days after finishing *Guess Who's Coming to Dinner*?
22 In what type of crash did Jayne Mansfield meet her death?
23 Who directed and starred in *Hamlet* in 1948?
24 In which World War did Humphrey Bogart receive a facial injury which gave him his trademark sneer?
25 Which Gene discovered Leslie Caron?

Answers – see page 35

1   Who, in the movie title, is the 'International Man of Mystery'?
2   Who directed *Forrest Gump*?
3   Which song won Best Song Oscar for *Breakfast at Tiffany's*?
4   What word links a 'Book' and 'Asphalt' to form two film titles?
5   Which Jane starred in *Barbarella*?
6   Which British movie is about the 1924 Olympics?
7   What's the name of the chief villain of *The Lion King*?
8   Which Emma wrote the screenplay for *Sense and Sensibility*?
9   Which boxer appeared in *The Greatest*?
10   *Love Me Tender* was the first film for which rock 'n' roll star?
11   Which actor links *True Lies, Total Recall* and *Twins*?
12   The character Richard Hannay appears in a film about how many steps?
13   Who played Dolly in the 60s movie *Hello Dolly*?
14   Which creatures were 'in the Mist' in the title of the Sigourney Weaver movie?
15   Was *Ghostbusters* first released in the 1960s, 70s or 80s?
16   Which hard man English football player appeared in *Lock, Stock and Two Smoking Barrels*?
17   In which decade of the 20th century was Dennis Quaid born?
18   Which wife of Kenneth Branagh has also been Oscar nominated?
19   Who did Timothy Dalton play in *Licence to Kill*?
20   Which word completes the film title, ____ *Largo*?
21   Who played the Fay Wray role in the remake of King Kong?
22   Which Tom starred in *A Few Good Men*?
23   Who created the accident prone Mr Bean?
24   Which Tom won the Best Actor Oscar for *Philadelphia* in 1993?
25   In which decade was *You Only Live Twice* released?

Answers Superstars (see Quiz 27)
1 Sean Connery **2** Meryl Streep. **3** Henry Fonda. **4** Clooney. **5** Marilyn Monroe.
6 Madonna. **7** Sophia Loren. **8** John Wayne. **9** Leonardo DiCaprio. **10** Olivia
Newton-John. **11** Paul Newman. **12** Nicolas Cage. **13** Tom Cruise & Nicole
Kidman. **14** *Rocky* **15** Katharine Hepburn. **16** 1940s. **17** Julie Andrews.
18 *Carlito's Way*. **19** West Germany. **20** *G.I. Jane*. **21** Cher. **22** *Se7en*.
23 Picasso. **24** *The Color Purple*. **25** *Dick Tracy*.

Answers – see page 36

1. What is Harrison Ford's real name?
2. Which 007 played his father in *Indiana Jones and the Last Crusade*?
3. Which Steven directed Ford in *Raiders of the Lost Ark*?
4. Which Kate was his co-star in *Indiana Jones and the Temple of Doom*?
5. In which sci-fi movie did he first find fame?
6. Which Melanie was a co-star in *Working Girl*?
7. In which movie did he play Richard Kimble in a film version of the TV series?
8. What sort of 'Graffiti' was the title of a 1973 movie?
9. In which decade did he star in *Witness*?
10. In which decade was Ford born?
11. In which California city was *Blade Runner* set?
12. What is the occupation of Indiana Jones?
13. What was 'Presumed' in the title of the 1990 movie?
14. In which decade did he star in the first *Star Wars* movie?
15. Which 1997 film was the name of a special aircraft?
16. 'Clear and Present' what was the title of Ford's 1994 movie?
17. Which Annette co-starred with him in *Regarding Henry*?
18. Who directed him as Col Lucas in *Apocalypse Now*?
19. What relation to Harrison Ford is scriptwriter Melissa Mathison?
20. In *Air Force One* he plays the role of a man in which office?
21. In what sort of 'Games' did he play ex-CIA agent Jack Ryan in 1992?
22. How many 'Nights' go with the 'Six Days' in a movie title?
23. What was the first *Star Wars* sequel in which he starred?
24. Which Bonnie plays Ford's wife in *Presumed Innocent*?
25. Which 'Solo' part did he play in the *Star Wars* movies?

Answers Pot Luck 11 (see Quiz 28)
1 *Eyes Wide Shut.* 2 Hawke. 3 Grasshoppers. 4 Pierce Brosnan. 5 80 minutes.
6 Ireland. 7 Attenborough. 8 1950s. 9 Popeye. 10 Uma Thurman. 11 The
Vietnam War. 12 Willis. 13 Kramer (*Kramer versus Kramer*). 14 *Apollo 13.*
15 Dog. 16 Guinness. 17 Jerry Lewis. 18 Faye Dunaway. 19 Wayne.
20 Anna. 21 *Alien.* 22 Michelle Pfeiffer. 23 1960s. 24 Charlie Chaplin.
25 Gerry and the Pacemakers.

Answers – see page 33

1   Which 007 has a tattoo with 'Scotland Forever' on it?
2   Who links *Silkwood* and *The French Lieutenant's Woman*?
3   Who died shortly after finishing *On Golden Pond*?
4   Which George, a superstar of the small screen, had a big-screen flop with *The Peacemaker*?
5   Whose real first names were Norma Jean?
6   Which singer/actress's surname is Ciccone?
7   How is Sofia Scicolone better known?
8   Who was dying of cancer when he made *The Shootist* about a gunman dying of cancer?
9   Whose boat sank while making *The Beach* after becoming a star in *Titanic*?
10   Which blonde reached superstar status after playing Sandy in *Grease*?
11   Who played opposite Joanne Woodward 11 times?
12   Whose real name is Nicholas Coppola?
13   Which husband and wife starred in *Eyes Wide Shut* in 1999?
14   In which 1976 movie did Sylvester Stallone play a boxer?
15   Who first starred with Spencer Tracy in *Woman of the Year*?
16   In which decade of the 20th century was Michael Douglas born?
17   Who won the Best Actress Oscar for *Mary Poppins*?
18   In which movie did Al Pacino play Carlito Brigante?
19   Where in Europe was Bruce Willis born?
20   In which 'G.I.' movie did Demi Moore shave her head?
21   Who played Winona Ryder's eccentric mother in *Mermaids*?
22   Brad Pitt's affair with Gwyneth Paltrow began on the set of which movie?
23   Which painter did Anthony Hopkins play on screen in 1996?
24   What was Whoopi Goldberg's first film, in 1985?
25   Which cartoon character did Warren Beatty play in a 1990 movie?

Answers Pot Luck 10 (see Quiz 25)
1 Austin Powers. 2 Robert Zemeckis. 3 'Moon River'. 4 Jungle. 5 Fonda.
6 *Chariots of Fire.* 7 Scar. 8 Thompson. 9 Muhammad Ali. 10 Elvis Presley.
11 Arnold Schwarzenegger. 12 39 (*The Thirty-Nine Steps*). 13 Barbra Streisand.
14 Gorillas. 15 1980s. 16 Vinnie Jones. 17 1950s. 18 Emma Thompson.
19 James Bond. 20 *Key.* 21 Jessica Lange. 22 Cruise. 23 Rowan Atkinson.
24 Hanks. 25 1960s.

Answers – see page 34

1	What was the last movie made by Stanley Kubrick?
2	Which Ethan starred in the 1998 *Great Expectations*?
3	What type of insects were posing the greatest threat in *A Bug's Life*?
4	Who replaced Timothy Dalton as James Bond?
5	Did *Toy Story* last 45, 80 or 240 minutes?
6	Where was 1990s James Bond, Pierce Brosnan, born?
7	Which Richard won the Best Director Oscar for *Gandhi*?
8	In which decade of the 20th century was Kirstie Alley born?
9	Robin Williams played which cartoon sailor?
10	*The Avengers* and *Dangerous Liaisons* both featured which actress?
11	*The Deer Hunter* was about which war?
12	Which Bruce starred in *The Jackal*?
13	Who did Kramer take to court?
14	Ed Harris played the mission controller in which Tom Hanks film?
15	Is Gromit a person, a dog or a sheep?
16	Which Sir Alec starred in *Star Wars*?
17	Which zany comedian often co-starred with Dean Martin in the 50s?
18	Who played a lead role in *Bonnie and Clyde* after Jane Fonda turned it down?
19	Which John won the Best Actor Oscar for *True Grit*?
20	Which woman's name links the King of Siam and Karenina?
21	'In space no one can hear you scream' was the cinema poster line for which Sigourney Weaver movie?
22	Which actress links *Batman Returns*, *One Fine Day* and *Scarface*?
23	In which decade was *Butch Cassidy and the Sundance Kid* released?
24	Who played the Little Tramp in *The Kid*?
25	Which Liverpool band appeared in the movie *Ferry Cross the Mersey*?

Answers Harrison Ford (see Quiz 26)
1 Harrison Ford. **2** Sean Connery. **3** Spielberg. **4** Capshaw. **5** *Star Wars*.
6 Griffith. **7** *The Fugitive*. **8** American. **9** 1980s. **10** 1940s. **11** Los Angeles.
12 Archaeologist. **13** Innocent. **14** 1970s. **15** *Air Force One*. **16** Danger.
17 Bening. **18** Francis Ford Coppola. **19** Wife. **20** US President. **21** *Patriot Games*. **22** Seven. **23** *The Empire Strikes Back*. **24** Bedelia. **25** Hans Solo.

Answers – see page 39

1	Bette Davis starred in a film 'All About' whom?
2	What sort of 'Holiday' was had by Gregory Peck and Audrey Hepburn?
3	James Dean was 'East of' where in 1955?
4	In which principality, a favourite with millionaires, was *To Catch a Thief* with Grace Kelly set?
5	Which movie named after a US state includes 'Oh What a Beautiful Morning'?
6	How long did Phileas Fogg have to go round the world in?
7	'The African' what was a 1951 movie with Bogart and Hepburn?
8	Which 1959 Charlton Heston movie is famous for its chariot races?
9	Which massacre takes place at the start of *Some Like It Hot*?
10	Which tragic diary was filmed in 1959?
11	'The Bridge on' which Asian river was a big hit of the 50s?
12	In a 1951 film, where was 'An American in', as played by Gene Kelly?
13	Which 'Place' was a top 50s film which later became a top soap with Ryan O'Neal and Mia Farrow?
14	Whose dress is blown up by the air from a subway grating in *The Seven Year Itch*?
15	What was 'A Streetcar Named' in the Brando and Vivien Leigh movie?
16	What 'light' was Chaplin's last US movie, made in 1952?
17	Which James appeared in *Vertigo* and *Rear Window*?
18	Which story set in Never Never Land was made by Disney in 1953?
19	How many 'Leagues under the Sea' were in the title of the 1954 movie with Kirk Douglas?
20	What were the 'Stockings' made from in the title of the 1957 movie?
21	What type of animal is Harvey in the movie of the same name?
22	What was *Les Vacances de Monsieur Hulot* called in English?
23	What did you Dial for Murder in Hitchcock's classic?
24	How many brides were there 'for Seven Brothers' in 1954?
25	Where were 'Strangers' in the title of a 1951 Hitchcock movie?

Answers 1960s Stars (see Quiz 31)
1 Steve McQueen. **2** *Lawrence of Arabia.* **3** Sean Connery. **4** Shirley MacLaine.
5 Richard Burton. **6** Janet Leigh. **7** Mia Farrow. **8** Ann-Margret. **9** Audrey
Hepburn. **10** Barbra Streisand. **11** Nicholson. **12** *Midnight Cowboy.* **13** Michael
Crawford. **14** Kirk Douglas. **15** John Wayne. **16** Yul Brynner. **17** Lemmon &
Matthau. **18** James Bond. **19** Andress. **20** Julie Christie. **21** Mills. **22** Marilyn
Monroe. **23** The Beatles. **24** Lancaster. **25** Paul Newman.

Answers – see page 40

1 Where in America was Leonardo DiCaprio born?
2 Which Dan starred in *The Blues Brothers*?
3 A 90s movie title was 'The Bridges of' which county?
4 The song 'Circle of Life' features in which animated movie?
5 Who played the title role in *Gandhi*?
6 Who played herself in *Dear Brigitte* in 1965?
7 Which actor links *Face/Off* and *Grease*?
8 The Japanese attack on where is central to *From Here to Eternity*?
9 Who played Truman in *The Truman Show*?
10 *Postcards from the Edge* was based on the life of which Carrie?
11 Which Ms Smith played the Mother Superior in Whoopi Goldberg's *Sister Act*?
12 Which 1997 movie equalled *Ben Hur*'s record haul of Oscars?
13 Who played the Caped Crusader in *Batman Forever*?
14 Which Melanie married Antonio Banderas?
15 Robert De Niro sang about New York in which film?
16 Which Jane was one of the first movie stars to produce fitness videos?
17 Who was Kenneth Branagh's wife whom he directed in *Much Ado About Nothing* in 1993?
18 What was the Bond theme for *For Your Eyes Only* called?
19 What is Bruce Willis' profession in *The Sixth Sense*?
20 Which James was the knife thrower in *The Magnificent Seven*?
21 In which decade was *The Sting* released?
22 Which word completes the film title, *In ____ We Serve*?
23 In which decade of the 20th century was Julie Andrews born?
24 Who directed *Evita*?
25 Which Jeff starred in *Tron*?

Answers Weepies (see Quiz 32)
1 USA. **2** Blind. **3** Barbra Streisand. **4** Cancer. **5** *Romeo and Juliet*. **6** Turner. **7** Jack. **8** Brief. **9** Binoche. **10** Danes. **11** Antonio Banderas. **12** *The Horse Whisperer*. **13** Clint Eastwood. **14** Deeply. **15** Omar Sharif. **16** *Kramer versus Kramer*. **17** *William Shakespeare's Romeo and Juliet*. **18** Tyler Moore. **19** *Tess of the d'Urbervilles*. **20** Meryl Streep. **21** Geraldine. **22** 1990s. **23** Dustin Hoffman. **24** Cinderella. **25** *Love Story*.

Answers – see page 37

1   Whose movies included *The Great Escape* and *Bullitt*?
2   Peter O'Toole played the title role in which movie set in the sands of the Middle East?
3   Which 007 played opposite Tippi Hedren in *Marnie*?
4   Which sister of Warren Beatty starred with Jack Lemmon in *The Apartment*?
5   Who was Elizabeth Taylor's husband on and off screen in *Who's Afraid of Virginia Woolf*?
6   Which star of *Psycho* is the mother of Jamie Lee Curtis?
7   Which sometime partner of Woody Allen starred in *Rosemary's Baby*?
8   Whose real name is Ann-Margret Olsson?
9   Which star of *My Fair Lady* was born in Belgium?
10   Which singing superstar was the Funny Girl in the title of the movie?
11   Which Jack found fame in *Easy Rider*?
12   Which 'Cowboy' was played by Jon Voight in 1969?
13   Which future star of *Phantom of the Opera* appeared in *Hello Dolly*?
14   Which actor father of *Fatal Attraction*'s Michael starred in *Spartacus*?
15   Which star of westerns starred in, produced and directed *The Alamo*?
16   Which *The King and I* star was 'the old Cajun' in *The Magnificent Seven*?
17   Which Jack and Walter played *The Odd Couple*?
18   George Lazenby played whom in *On Her Majesty's Secret Service*?
19   Which Ursula's first major English language film was *Dr No*?
20   Which long-haired blonde starred in *Darling*, for which she won an Oscar?
21   Which Hayley played both twins in *The Parent Trap*?
22   Which blonde's last movie was *The Misfits*, written by Arthur Miller?
23   Which pop group starred in *A Hard Day's Night*?
24   Which Burt frolicked in the surf with Deborah Kerr in *From Here to Eternity*?
25   Who starred as Fast Eddie Felson in *The Hustler*, a role he was to reprise 25 years later in *The Color of Money*?

Answers 1950s (see Quiz 29)
1 Eve. **2** Roman. **3** Eden. **4** Monaco. **5** *Oklahoma!*. **6** 80 Days. **7** Queen.
8 *Ben Hur*. **9** St Valentine's Day Massacre. **10** *The Diary of Anne Frank*. **11** The
River Kwai. **12** Paris. **13** *Peyton Place*. **14** Marilyn Monroe's. **15** Desire.
16 *Limelight*. **17** Stewart. **18** *Peter Pan*. **19** Twenty Thousand. **20** Silk.
21 Rabbit. **22** *Monsieur Hulot's Holiday*. **23** M. **24** Seven Brides. **25** On a Train.

Answers – see page 38

1   In which country does the action of *The Horse Whisperer* take place?
2   What disability does Al Pacino have in *Scent of a Woman*?
3   Which singer starred in and directed *The Prince of Tides*?
4   In *Terms of Endearment* Debra Winger is dying from which disease?
5   Which doomed lovers were played by Leonard Whiting and Olivia Hussey in 1968?
6   Which Lana was the star of *Imitation of Life*?
7   What was the name of Leonardo DiCaprio's character in *Titanic*?
8   What type of 'Encounter' occurred between Celia Johnson and Trevor Howard in the movie classic?
9   Which Juliette nursed the 'English Patient'?
10   Which Claire starred in *Little Women* and *Romeo and Juliet*?
11   Which husband of Melanie Griffith starred opposite Tom Hanks in *Philadelphia*?
12   Which Nicholas Evans novel was *The Horse Whisperer* based on?
13   Who falls for Meryl Streep in *The Bridges of Madison County*?
14   What follows 'Truly, Madly' in the Anthony Minghella weepie?
15   Who played the title role in *Dr Zhivago*?
16   Which movie had the ad line, 'There are three sides to this love story'?
17   The 1996 version of *Romeo and Juliet* mentioned its writer's name in the title; what was it called?
18   Which Mary, famous for her TV roles, starred opposite Donald Sutherland in *Ordinary People*?
19   Which Thomas Hardy novel was *Tess* based on?
20   Who played Mrs Kramer in the 1979 weepie?
21   Which daughter of Charlie Chaplin starred in *Dr Zhivago*?
22   In which decade was *Ghost* released?
23   Who won the Best Actor Oscar for *Kramer versus Kramer*?
24   *Ever After* was a remake of which fairy story?
25   Ryan O'Neal's affair with Ali McGraw began on the set of which movie?

Answers Pot Luck 12 (see Quiz 30)
1 Hollywood. 2 Aykroyd. 3 Madison County. 4 *The Lion King*. 5 Ben Kingsley.
6 Brigitte Bardot. 7 John Travolta. 8 Pearl Harbor. 9 Jim Carrey. 10 Fisher.
11 Maggie Smith. 12 *Titanic*. 13 Val Kilmer. 14 Griffith. 15 *New York, New York*.
16 Fonda. 17 Emma Thompson. 18 'For Your Eyes Only'. 19 Child psychologist.
20 Coburn. 21 1970s. 22 *Which*. 23 1930s. 24 Alan Parker. 25 Bridges.

Answers – see page 43

1   *Maverick* and *Freaky Friday* both featured which actress?
2   Which character battles against The Joker?
3   Which star of *Sliding Doors* split with fiancé Brad Pitt in 1997?
4   Who wrote most of the songs for *Saturday Night Fever*?
5   *Philadelphia* became the first mainstream Hollywood movie to focus on which disease?
6   Which Shirley sang the Bond song 'Diamonds Are Forever'?
7   In a Disney film title, which animal did Pete own?
8   Which actress links *Batman and Robin* and *Pulp Fiction*?
9   Was *King Kong* first released in the 1930s, 50s or 70s?
10 Which Bruce is the voice of Mikey in *Look Who's Talking*?
11 Which blonde French actress's real name is Camille Javal?
12 Which Disney movie was based on the life of a native American?
13 Who met husband-to-be Richard Burton on the set of *Cleopatra*?
14 The cop Popeye Doyle first appeared in which classic thriller?
15 In which decade of the 20th century was Richard Attenborough born?
16 Which Ernest starred in *The Wild Bunch*?
17 To the nearest hour, how long does *Lady and the Tramp* last?
18 According to the film title, Lawrence was 'of' which country?
19 Who played the lead role in *Fatal Attraction* after Debra Winger turned it down?
20 In which decade was *E.T.* released?
21 Which actor was in *A River Runs Through It*, *Meet Joe Black* and *Legends of the Fall*?
22 What colour is Queen Victoria, according to the film title?
23 Who sang 'A Groovy Kind of Love' in *Buster*?
24 Which Robert won the Best Actor Oscar for *Raging Bull*?
25 Marlene Dietrich was born in which European capital?

Answers Pot Luck 14 (see Quiz 35)
1 Affleck. 2 Jack Nicholson. 3 Cher. 4 Emily Watson. 5 Johnson. 6 Scorsese.
7 Michael Caine. 8 Prince. 9 Straw. 10 Austria. 11 *Toy Story*. 12 Basinger.
13 *Sue*. 14 Richard Burton. 15 *Columbo*. 16 Fonda. 17 Little (*The Little Foxes*
and *The Little Mermaid*). 18 1950s. 19 Andress. 20 Venice. 21 Mel Gibson.
22 Cat (*The Cat and the Canary* and *Cat on a Hot Tin Roof*). 23 Duchovny.
24 *Stand By Me*. 25 1960s.

Answers – see page 44

1 Which Sam said, 'A producer shouldn't get ulcers, he should give them'?
2 In which country was Stanley Kubrick born?
3 Which English producer David was head of Columbia for two years in the 80s?
4 What was Bob Fosse's contribution to *Cabaret* and *All That Jazz*?
5 What was the first name of producer Thalberg who has given his name to a special movie award?
6 Which Winner appeared in *You Must Be Joking* as well as directing?
7 Which actor directed *Star Trek V: The Final Frontier*?
8 Which letter was used to show the superior film when there was a cinema double-feature?
9 Which soft-drinks company once owned Columbia Pictures?
10 What was the name of MGM's lion?
11 *The Peacemaker* was the first release from which Spielberg stable?
12 Which man and dog were the creation of Briton Nick Park?
13 Who did Martin Scorsese direct in *Raging Bull* and *Taxi Driver*?
14 Which actor Leonard stayed behind the camera for *Three Men and a Baby*?
15 Which Mrs Minnelli, Judy, did Vincente direct in *The Pirate*?
16 What name is given to the hinged board which shows the film's details during shooting?
17 Who was Oscar-nominated for his debut as director of *Dances with Wolves*?
18 What precedes 'Star' in the name of the studio which made *Men in Black*?
19 In which of his own movies did Cecil B. de Mille appear in 1950?
20 Which George links *Star Wars* and *Raiders of the Lost Ark*?
21 What is the first name of director Zemeckis of *Back to the Future*?
22 Which member of Dire Straits wrote the music for *Local Hero*?
23 Buena Vista was set up to distribute which studio's films?
24 What geographical symbol did Paramount use as its logo?
25 What is the name of Garry Marshall's sister who is also a film director?

Answers Child Stars (see Quiz 36)
1 Macaulay Culkin. 2 Donald. 3 *Mary Poppins*. 4 Natalie Wood. 5 The Artful Dodger. 6 1930s. 7 Drew Barrymore. 8 New York. 9 Durbin. 10 *The Piano*. 11 Elliott. 12 Judy Garland. 13 *Little Women*. 14 Pickford. 15 Jodie Foster. 16 Ryan O'Neal. 17 James. 18 Lassie. 19 1970s. 20 Coogan. 21 Seven. 22 *E.T.* 23 *Kramer versus Kramer*. 24 Rooney. 25 Hawke.

Answers – see page 41

1   Which Ben co-wrote *Good Will Hunting*?
2   Who won the Best Actor Oscar for *As Good as it Gets*?
3   How is Oscar-winning actress, former Mrs Sonny Bono, better known?
4   Which actress was BAFTA nominated for *Angela's Ashes*?
5   Which Celia starred in the tearjerker *Brief Encounter*?
6   Which director Martin did Isabella Rossellini marry?
7   Who was born Maurice Micklewhite?
8   Which pop star's first film was *Purple Rain*?
9   Dustin Hoffman was in a movie about what kind of 'Dogs'?
10   In which country was Arnold Schwarzenegger born?
11   Which 'Story' was the first ever completely computer-animated movie?
12   Which Kim did Alec Baldwin marry?
13   Which name completes the film title, *Peggy ____ Got Married*?
14   Elizabeth Taylor was twice married to which Welsh actor?
15   In which TV cop series did Peter Falk find fame after appearing on the big screen?
16   Which Henry won the Best Actor Oscar for *On Golden Pond*?
17   In film titles, what sizes are foxes and a mermaid?
18   In which decade of the 20th century was Sharon Stone born?
19   Which Ursula co-starred with Elvis in *Fun in Acapulco*?
20   *Don't Look Now* is set in which Italian city?
21   Which actor links *Mad Max* and *Braveheart*?
22   Which animal links a canary and a tin roof in film titles?
23   Which David starred in *The X-Files*?
24   Which movie did the song 'Stand By Me' come from?
25   In which decade was *West Side Story* released?

Answers Pot Luck 13 (see Quiz 33)
1 Jodie Foster. **2** Batman. **3** Gwyneth Paltrow. **4** The Bee Gees. **5** AIDS.
6 Bassey. **7** Dragon. **8** Uma Thurman. **9** 1930s. **10** Willis. **11** Brigitte Bardot.
12 *Pocahontas*. **13** Elizabeth Taylor. **14** *French Connection*. **15** 1920s.
16 Borgnine. **17** 1 hour. **18** Arabia. **19** Glenn Close. **20** 1980s. **21** Brad Pitt.
22 Brown (*Mrs Brown*). **23** Phil Collins. **24** De Niro. **25** Berlin.

Answers – see page 42

1   Who found fame when he was left *Home Alone*?
2   Which O'Connor was a child star before being a huge success in *Singin' in the Rain*?
3   In which musical movie did Karen Dotrice appear as a child with a superhuman nanny?
4   Which child star later played Maria in the musical *West Side Story*?
5   Jack Wild played which cheeky role in *Oliver!*?
6   In which decade did Shirley Temple win a Special Oscar for her outstanding contribution to movies?
7   Which star of *E.T.* wrote an autobiography called *Little Girl Lost*?
8   In *Home Alone 2* Macaulay Culkin is lost where?
9   Which Deanna was a contemporary of Judy Garland?
10 Anna Paquin won an Oscar with Holly Hunter for which movie?
11 What was the name of Henry Thomas's character in *E.T.*?
12 Who co-starred with Mickey Rooney 10 times on screen?
13 Which movie based on Louisa M. Alcott's novel starred a young Elizabeth Taylor?
14 Which Mary was the 'world's sweetheart' and made her first movie aged 16 in 1909?
15 Who played the gangster's moll in *Bugsy Malone* before later becoming a multiple Oscar winner?
16 Who played the father of Tatum in *Paper Moon*?
17 Which member of the Fox family, brother of Edward, was known as William when he was a child star?
18 Who was asked to 'Come Home' in Elizabeth Taylor's 1943 movie?
19 In which decade of the 20th century was Drew Barrymore born?
20 Which Jackie was immortalized in Chaplin's *The Kid*?
21 How many Von Trapp children were there in *The Sound of Music*?
22 In which movie did Drew Barrymore find fame as Gertie?
23 Justin Henry was Oscar-nominated for which movie where his parents Meryl Streep and Dustin Hoffman are to divorce?
24 Which Mickey married eight times?
25 Which Ethan starred in *Explorer* before his 20th birthday?

Answers Behind the Camera (see Quiz 34)
1 Goldwyn. **2** USA. **3** Puttnam. **4** Choreography. **5** Irving. **6** Michael. **7** William Shatner. **8** A. **9** Coca Cola. **10** Leo. **11** Dreamworks. **12** Wallace & Gromit. **13** Robert De Niro. **14** Nimoy. **15** Garland. **16** Clapperboard. **17** Kevin Costner. **18** Tri. **19** *Sunset Boulevard*. **20** Lucas. **21** Robert. **22** Mark Knopfler. **23** Disney. **24** Mountain. **25** Penny.

Answers – see page 47

1   Was *The Ten Commandments'* running time nearer to 60, 100 or 220 minutes?
2   *Shakespeare in Love* and *A Perfect Murder* both feature which actress?
3   According to a movie title, 'Only Angels Have' what?
4   Which word follows 'Never Say Never' in a Sean Connery movie title?
5   What is the name of Michael Douglas's actor father?
6   Which star actor was in *Apollo 13, Sleepless in Seattle* and *Big*?
7   Who sang the theme song for *Titanic*?
8   Which word follows 'Dirty Rotten' in a Steve Martin movie title?
9   War veteran Ron Kovic features in which movie?
10 Which Barbra starred with Nick Nolte in *The Prince of Tides*?
11 Who sang the title song of *Help!*?
12 Which famous Carole tested for the role of Scarlett O'Hara?
13 In which decade of the 20th century was Rowan Atkinson born?
14 Which Melanie starred in *Working Girl*?
15 According to the film title, how many 'Degrees of Separation' are there?
16 Which Elliott featured in *M*A*S*H*?
17 Which director had a long custody battle for his children with Mia Farrow?
18 *The Empire Strikes Back* was a sequel to which blockbuster?
19 Which actor Martin was assigned to assassinate Brando in *Apocalypse Now*?
20 Which actress links *Pretty Woman* and *Hook*?
21 Dancer Eugene Curran Kelly became known under which name?
22 In *Mary Poppins*, what job does Mary take?
23 Which Jonathan starred in *Evita*?
24 Which spread can complete the film title, *A Taste of ____*?
25 *Lady and the Tramp* were what type of animals?

Answers Westerns (see Quiz 39)
1 Kilmer. 2 Civil War. 3 Clint Eastwood. 4 Cat. 5 Cooper. 6 Marvin.
7 Mitchum. 8 Bob Dylan. 9 *Paint Your Wagon*. 10 1960s. 11 Horse operas.
12 Autry. 13 Van Cleef. 14 *True Grit*. 15 Clint Eastwood. 16 Stanwyck.
17 Freeman. 18 Newman. 19 1950s. 20 Costner. 21 *Shane*. 22 Hackman.
23 Wayne. 24 *The Magnificent Seven*. 25 Marvin.

Answers – see page 48

1   Which 'Raging' animal won for Robert De Niro in 1980?
2   In which movie did Anthony Hopkins play Hannibal Lecter?
3   Which street made Michael Douglas an 80s winner?
4   Who was the only actor to win two Best Actor Oscars in the 1990s?
5   Which body part is in the title of a Daniel Day-Lewis winning movie?
6   Which Gary is one of only a handful of actors to win Best Actor twice?
7   Which fields made a Best Supporting winner of Haing S. Ngor?
8   Which 007 was Best Supporting Actor in *The Untouchables*?
9   Which 70s Mafia movies both won three nominations for Best Supporting Actor?
10   Best Actor winners in 1990 and 1991 came from which kingdom?
11   Which man made Dustin Hoffman a 1988 winner?
12   Which Henry was the oldest Best Actor winner of the 20th century?
13   Which two Jacks were 70s winners in the Best Actor category?
14   What is the nationality of 1998 winner Roberto Benigni?
15   In 1992 Al Pacino won for 'Scent of a' what?
16   What is the middle initial of Best Actor Scott who won for *Patton*?
17   Which simple fellow with a heart of gold won Tom Hanks a second Oscar?
18   Which Paul won for *The Color of Money*?
19   Which James was nominated for *The Godfather*?
20   Which Robin won Best Supporting Actor for *Good Will Hunting*?
21   Geoffrey Rush won for *Shine*, a biopic about what type of musician?
22   Which Kevin was Best Supporting Actor in *A Fish Called Wanda*?
23   Nicolas Cage was 'Leaving' where in his 1995 winning role?
24   Who, with the name of the American capital in his name, won Best Supporting Actor for *Glory*?
25   Which Tom Hanks winning portrayal was a ping-pong star?

Answers Pot Luck 16 (see Quiz 40)
1 Gary Shandling. **2** China. **3** *Falcon Crest*. **4** Myers. **5** Christie. **6** Diaz.
7 Samuel L. Jackson. **8** They dress as women. **9** Kate Winslet. **10** Kline.
11 *Raging Bull*. **12** Accept it. **13** *Aladdin*. **14** Eye patch. **15** Costner. **16** *West*.
17 Never. **18** Park. **19** Wayne. **20** Indiana Jones. **21** Hackman. **22** *Daughter*.
23 Warren Beatty. **24** 1960s. **25** Reynolds.

Answers – see page 45

1   Which Val starred in *Tombstone*?
2   During which American war was *Dances with Wolves* set?
3   Which spaghetti western icon was 'The Good' in *The Good, The Bad and The Ugly*?
4   Which animal name precedes 'Ballou' in the Jane Fonda western spoof?
5   Which Gary won the Best Actor Oscar for *High Noon*?
6   Which Lee won the Best Actor Oscar playing opposite Jane Fonda?
7   Which Robert co-starred with John Wayne in *El Dorado*?
8   Which 60s folk singer had a minor role in *Pat Garrett and Billy the Kid*?
9   'I Was Born under a Wandrin' Star' comes from which western?
10   In which decade did spaghetti westerns first hit the screens?
11   Westerns were referred to as what type of operas?
12   Which Gene was dubbed the Singing Cowboy?
13   Which Lee found fame in spaghetti westerns?
14   In which 'True' western did John Wayne famously wear an eye patch?
15   Who won the Best Director Oscar for *Unforgiven*?
16   Which Barbara, star of *Forty Guns*, was one of the few female members of the National Cowboy Hall of Fame?
17   Which Morgan appeared with Clint Eastwood in *Unforgiven*?
18   Which blue-eyed Paul starred in *Hud*?
19   In which decade was *High Noon* released?
20   Which Kevin won the Best Director Oscar for *Dances with Wolves*?
21   'Come back, Shane' is the last line of which movie?
22   Which Gene won an Oscar as the sheriff in *Unforgiven*?
23   Which western legend John's final movie was *The Shootist*?
24   Which movie was a remake of *Seven Samurai*?
25   Which Lee starred in *The Man Who Shot Liberty Valance*?

Answers – see page 46

1   Which US comic star Gary featured in the 90s *Doctor Dolittle*?
2   Which country links 'town' and 'Syndrome' in movie titles?
3   In which TV soap did Jane Wyman find fame after appearing on the big screen?
4   Which Mike starred in *Wayne's World*?
5   Which 60s star Julie was Oscar-nominated in 1998?
6   *There's Something About Mary* featured which Cameron?
7   Which actor links *Jurassic Park* and *Coming to America*?
8   In *Some Like It Hot*, what disguise do Curtis and Lemmon adopt?
9   Which actress appeared on the cinema poster for *Titanic*?
10   Which Kevin featured in *A Fish Called Wanda*?
11   In which 1980 movie did Robert De Niro play a boxer?
12   What did George C. Scott refuse to do with his Oscar for *Patton*?
13   The song 'A Whole New World' comes from which animated movie?
14   What did John Wayne wear on his face in *True Grit*?
15   Which Kevin won a Best Director Oscar for *Dances with Wolves*?
16   Which direction completes the film title *Once Upon a Time in the ____*?
17   How many times did Greta Garbo marry?
18   Which Nick won an Oscar for *The Wrong Trousers*?
19   Which John starred in *Stagecoach*?
20   Which Mr Jones was a character in *Raiders of the Lost Ark*?
21   Which Gene won the Best Actor Oscar for *The French Connection*?
22   Which family member completes the film title, *Ryan's ____*?
23   Who directed *Dick Tracy*?
24   In which decade of the 20th century was Nicolas Cage born?
25   Which Debbie starred in *Singin' in the Rain*?

Answers Oscars – Best Actors (see Quiz 38)
1 Bull. **2** *The Silence of the Lambs.* **3** *Wall Street.* **4** Tom Hanks. **5** (My Left) Foot.
6 Cooper. **7** *The Killing Fields.* **8** Sean Connery. **9** *The Godfather* & *The Godfather Part II.* **10** United Kingdom. **11** *Rain Man.* **12** Fonda. **13** Lemmon & Nicholson.
14 Italian. **15** Woman. **16** C. **17** Forrest Gump. **18** Newman. **19** Caan.
20 Williams. **21** Pianist. **22** Kline. **23** Las Vegas. **24** Denzel Washington.
25 Forrest Gump.

Answers – see page 51

1   Which movie had the ad line, 'They're young, they're in love and they kill people'?
2   What sort of race was a main feature of *Ben Hur*?
3   Who won the Best Actor Oscar for *It Happened One Night*?
4   Which movie begins with the line, 'Yes, this is Sunset Boulevard, Los Angeles, California'?
5   In which decade was *The Sound of Music* released?
6   What was the profession of Mr Chips, in *Goodbye, Mr Chips*?
7   In which city was *Breakfast at Tiffany's* set?
8   'I Could Have Danced All Night' comes from which musical movie?
9   'Rosebud' was a significant word in which classic movie?
10   In *The Wizard of Oz* what sort of animal is Dorothy's pet, Toto?
11   In which decade was *Top Hat* with Astaire and Rogers released?
12   Which blonde was originally destined for *Move Over Darling* before Doris Day stepped in?
13   Which James won Best Actor Oscar for *The Philadelphia Story*?
14   Who sings the opening song in *The Sound of Music*?
15   What is the town in question in *On the Town*?
16   Which movie had the ad line, 'You are cordially invited to George and Martha's for dinner'?
17   'Louis, I think this is the beginning of a beautiful friendship' is the last line of which movie?
18   In which decade was *The Wizard of Oz* first released?
19   In which movie did Dustin Hoffman say, 'Mrs Robinson, you're trying to seduce me, aren't you?'?
20   Who won the Best Actor Oscar for *The King and I*?
21   Which Basil played Sherlock Holmes in *The Hound of the Baskervilles*?
22   Which British actor won an Oscar for *Gandhi*?
23   'Raindrops Keep Fallin' on My Head' won an Oscar when it was used in which movie in 1969?
24   Which movie is set in Rick's bar in North Africa?
25   In which decade was *Gone with the Wind* first released?

Answers 1960s (see Quiz 43)
1 *Romeo and Juliet.* **2** World War I. **3** Plants. **4** Jane. **5** Pink. **6** Italy. **7** Simon & Garfunkel. **8** *Bonnie and Clyde.* **9** 2001. **10** Katharine Hepburn. **11** Liberty Valance. **12** Cactus. **13** Seven. **14** Russia. **15** Rome. **16** *The Birds.* **17** San Francisco. **18** Shower. **19** *Cleopatra.* **20** Julie Andrews. **21** Tiffany's. **22** One Million. **23** *The Apartment.* **24** World War II. **25** Russia (*From Russia with Love*).

Answers – see page 52

1   Who was described as the 'Prince of Thieves' in the title of a 90s blockbuster?
2   Which Anthony starred in *Silence of the Lambs*?
3   Does *South Pacific* last nearly 1, 2 or 3 hours?
4   Which actress links *Sleepless in Seattle* and *You've Got Mail*?
5   Was *Alien* first released in the 1960s, 70s or 80s?
6   Which Jessica became the then-oldest Oscar winner for *Driving Miss Daisy*?
7   Which Burt starred in *Smokey and the Bandit*?
8   For which role is Bela Lugosi best remembered?
9   Which famous US family did Arnold Schwarzenegger marry into?
10 The song 'Who Will Buy' features in which musical movie?
11 In which decade was *Forrest Gump* released?
12 Which city was Macaulay Culkin lost in, in *Home Alone 2*?
13 Who co-wrote and starred in the *Rambo* films?
14 Which singer/actress won the Best Actress Oscar for *Cabaret*?
15 Which Redgrave was nominated for an Oscar in 1999?
16 At what Fahrenheit temperature do books burn in the film title?
17 In which decade of the 20th century was Alec Baldwin born?
18 Catherine Zeta Jones comes from which country?
19 Which Jack starred in *Some Like It Hot*?
20 Which wife of Richard Burton has also been Oscar-nominated?
21 Upon which day of the week does 'Night Fever' occur?
22 Which silent screen heartthrob starred in *The Sheik*?
23 What was the Bond theme for *Live and Let Die* called?
24 In which decade was *Twins* released?
25 Which soap did Hollywood actress Demi Moore star in?

Answers Pot Luck 18 (see Quiz 44)
1 Goldie Hawn. **2** Holland. **3** *Top Gun*. **4** Mel Gibson. **5** Cop. **6** Gary Oldman.
7 *Kojak*. **8** Shatner. **9** Before. **10** Foster. **11** Anthony Hopkins. **12** A Fish.
13 Superman. **14** Mia Farrow. **15** Twelve (*The Dirty Dozen*). **16** Chesney Hawkes.
17 1960s. **18** Fisher. **19** Branagh. **20** Ball. **21** Gary. **22** Nicolas Cage.
23 1970s. **24** Carrey. **25** *House*.

Answers – see page 49

1   *West Side Story* was based on which Shakespeare play about star-crossed lovers?

2   *Lawrence of Arabia* was set during which world conflict?

3   In *The Day of the Triffids*, what were Triffids?

4   Which 'Baby' was played by Bette Davis in 1962?

5   What colour 'Panther' was a film with Peter Sellers?

6   *A Fistful of Dollars* was the first western to be successful in the USA which was made where?

7   Which duo sang the songs on the soundtrack of *The Graduate*?

8   Which Faye Dunaway/Warren Beatty movie would have been called *Parker and Barrow* if the characters' surnames had been used?

9   Which year was in the title of 'A Space Odyssey' released in 1968?

10   *Guess Who's Coming to Dinner?* was the last film to star Spencer Tracy opposite whom?

11   'The Man Who Shot' whom starred James Stewart and Lee Marvin?

12   What 'Flower' gave Goldie Hawn her first big screen hit?

13   How many 'Magnificent' heroes were there in the 1960s classic?

14   Where was *Doctor Zhivago* set?

15   In which capital city was *La Dolce Vita* set?

16   Which Hitchcock movie featured aggressive feathered friends?

17   *Bullitt* featured a famous car chase in which city?

18   Where in the motel was Janet Leigh when she met her death in *Psycho*?

19   Which movie about a queen of Egypt starred Elizabeth Taylor and Richard Burton?

20   *The Americanization of Emily* was the first non-singing film for which actress who had previously made *Mary Poppins*?

21   'Breakfast at' which jewellers' was the title of an Audrey Hepburn film?

22   How many 'Years BC' were there in the movie with Raquel Welch?

23   Which Jack Lemmon/Shirley MacLaine film is the name of a place to live?

24   *The Longest Day* was about the Allied invasion in which war?

25   Which Iron Curtain country was in the title of the second Bond movie?

Answers Classics (see Quiz 41)
1 *Bonnie and Clyde*. **2** Chariot. **3** Clark Gable. **4** *Sunset Boulevard*. **5** 1960s.
6 Teacher. **7** New York. **8** *My Fair Lady*. **9** *Citizen Kane*. **10** Dog. **11** 1930s.
12 Marilyn Monroe. **13** Stewart. **14** Julie Andrews. **15** New York. **16** *Who's Afraid of Virginia Woolf?*. **17** *Casablanca*. **18** 1930s. **19** *The Graduate*. **20** Yul Brynner **21** Rathbone. **22** Ben Kingsley. **23** *Butch Cassidy and the Sundance Kid*. **24** *Casablanca*. **25** 1930s.

Answers – see page 50

1   What is Goldie Hawn's real name?

2   Which Linda starred in the *Terminator* movies?

3   Which movie did the song 'Take My Breath Away' come from?

4   *Lethal Weapon, Ransom* and *Maverick* all feature which actor?

5   In the *Die Hard* movies what is the job of the Bruce Willis character?

6   Who played the Count in *Bram Stoker's Dracula*?

7   In which TV cop series did movie actor Telly Savalas find fame?

8   Which William starred in *Star Trek: The Motion Picture*?

9   Was Disney's *Snow White* released before, after or during World War II?

10   Which Jodie starred in *Bugsy Malone*?

11   Who played C. S. Lewis in *Shadowlands*?

12   Which creature was 'Called Wanda' in a movie title?

13   Which superhero battles against Lex Luther?

14   Who went on to *Hannah and Her Sisters* from TV's *Peyton Place*?

15   Lee Marvin headed a 'Dirty' cast of how many in a 60s movie?

16   Who sang the title song of *The One and Only*?

17   In which decade of the 20th century was Helena Bonham-Carter born?

18   Which Carrie starred in *The Empire Strikes Back*?

19   Which Kenneth was dubbed 'the new Olivier'?

20   Which actress Lucille did Desi Arnaz marry twice?

21   Frank J. Cooper took on which first name in Hollywood?

22   Which actor links *The Rock, Moonstruck* and *Leaving Las Vegas*?

23   In which decade was *Grease* released?

24   Which Jim starred in *The Mask*?

25   Which word completes the film title, *The Old Dark ___*?

Answers Pot Luck 17 (see Quiz 42)

1 Robin Hood. **2** Anthony Hopkins. **3** 3 hours. **4** Meg Ryan. **5** 1970s. **6** Tandy.
7 Reynolds. **8** Dracula. **9** The Kennedy family. **10** *Oliver!* **11** 1990s.
12 New York. **13** Sylvester Stallone. **14** Liza Minnelli. **15** Lynn. **16** 451
(*Fahrenheit 451*). **17** 1950s. **18** Wales. **19** Lemmon. **20** Elizabeth Taylor.
21 Saturday. **22** Rudolph Valentino. **23** 'Live and Let Die'. **24** 1980s.
25 *General Hospital*.

Answers – see page 55

1	What was the nickname of the westerns he made in Italy?
2	What type of ape features in *Every Which Way But Loose*?
3	*In the Line of Fire* is about a security agent haunted by his failure to prevent which US President's assassination?
4	Who directed him in *Unforgiven*?
5	'A Fistful of' what was the title of his first Italian-made western?
6	He played opposite Meryl Streep in 'The Bridges of' which county?
7	With which Kevin did he co-star in *A Perfect World*?
8	'Escape from' which prison was the title of a 1979 movie?
9	In which decade was Clint Eastwood born?
10	*Any Which Way You Can* was the sequel to what?
11	Whose 'Bluff' was the title of a 60s movie?
12	In which TV series was he famous in the 50s and 60s?
13	What went with 'The Good' and 'The Bad' in the 1966 movie?
14	Eastwood won an Oscar for *Unforgiven* in what category?
15	Which Sondra was Eastwood's co-star in *Every Which Way But Loose* and his partner off screen?
16	Which Tyne of *Cagney and Lacey* fame appeared in the Dirty Harry movie *The Enforcer*?
17	In which decade was his first spaghetti western made?
18	He was elected to which role in Carmel, California in 1986–88?
19	In which western musical starring Lee Marvin did he sing in 1969?
20	*Bird* was about Charlie Parker, famous for what type of music?
21	'Play Misty for' whom was the name of the first movie he directed?
22	What was his nickname in the spaghetti westerns?
23	Which Gene was his co-star in *Unforgiven*?
24	What was the surname of 'The Outlaw – Josey'?
25	Which 'Dirty' character did he play in 1971?

Answers – see page 56

1   Which former 007 appeared in *Spiceworld: The Movie*?
2   How is John Cheese better known?
3   Which Elizabeth won the Best Actress Oscar for *Butterfield 8*?
4   Which actress Janet is Jamie Lee Curtis's mother?
5   Cate Blanchett played English queen Elizabeth, but where does she hail from?
6   In which continent was Richard E. Grant born?
7   Which cosmetics house did Madonna advertise in the late 1990s?
8   What was the name of the town where Winona Ryder was born?
9   What is the name of Laura Dern's father?
10   Who said, 'Having a double barrelled name makes it hell to sign autographs'?
11   What is Liam Neeson's real first name?
12   In which decade of the 20th century was Julia Roberts born?
13   How is *M*A*S*H* actor Elliott Goldstein better known?
14   Which Sean played the condemned man in *Dead Man Walking*?
15   How is Virginia Davis of *Thelma and Louise* better known?
16   How was Farrah Fawcett known during her marriage to actor Lee Majors?
17   Which brother of Ralph Fiennes starred in *Shakespeare in Love*?
18   Who won the Best Actor Oscar for *Ben Hur*?
19   Which French actress said, 'The more I see of men, the more I like dogs'?
20   Actress Nancy Davis married which actor and US President?
21   Which member of the Fonda family starred in *Single White Female* in 1992?
22   Which country shares its name with actor Gooding who starred in *Jerry Maguire*?
23   Which singer and pianist appeared in *Spiceworld: The Movie*?
24   How is Britt-Maria Eklund better known?
25   What was Barbra Streisand's first film, in 1966?

Answers Directors (see Quiz 48)
1 Cameron. **2** Coppola. **3** Anthony. **4** *The Dirty Dozen*. **5** Blake Edwards.
6 1930s. **7** Czechoslovakia. **8** Mel Gibson. **9** Vadim. **10** Charlie Chaplin.
11 *Apocalypse Now*. **12** Charlie Chaplin. **13** Alfred Hitchcock. **14** *M*A*S*H*.
15 Rosemary's. **16** Stone. **17** Cubby Broccoli. **18** Bo Derek. **19** Capra.
20 Mendes. **21** Woody Allen. **22** Federico. **23** Huston. **24** Steven Spielberg.
25 Frank.

Answers – see page 53

1   Which day of the week links 'Thirteenth' and 'Freaky' in movie titles?
2   In which decade of the 20th century was Brooke Shields born?
3   Which star actress was in *The Pelican Brief, Six Days Seven Nights* and *Stepmom*?
4   Which Woody Allen film title includes a reference to a feline?
5   Which singer played the tough guy captain in *Von Ryan's Express*?
6   Which 80s film was the most profitable in Australian history?
7   Which sequel had the subtitle 'Judgment Day'?
8   Who played the lead in *Casablanca* after George Raft turned it down?
9   Which actress links *Eyes Wide Shut* and *Practical Magic*?
10   What kind of fruit can you get at the Whistle Stop Café, according to the film title?
11   Where was Gary Oldman 'Lost' in the 1998 hit movie?
12   Which movie veteran Katharine was the first actress to win four Oscars?
13   Which word follows 'Trading' in an Eddie Murphy movie title?
14   Bing Crosby had just finished a round of what when he died?
15   Which Rick starred in *Honey, I Shrunk the Kids*?
16   Which brothers starred in *Monkey Business*?
17   *Patriot Games, Pulp Fiction* and *Sphere* all feature which actor?
18   Which direction completes this film title, *North By ___*?
19   In which decade was *One Flew Over the Cuckoo's Nest* released?
20   Which singer/actress won the Best Actress Oscar for *Moonstruck*?
21   Which time period completes the film title, *Saturday Night and Sunday ___*?
22   In which decade of the 20th century was Lucille Ball born?
23   To the nearest hour, how long does *The Sound of Music* last?
24   Which Dustin starred in *Tootsie*?
25   What did Nicole Kidman forecast in *To Die For*?

Answers Clint Eastwood (see Quiz 45)
1 Spaghetti westerns. **2** Orang Utan. **3** J.F. Kennedy. **4** He did. **5** Dollars.
6 Madison County. **7** Costner. **8** Alcatraz. **9** 1930s. **10** *Every Which Way But Loose*. **11** Coogan's. **12** *Rawhide*. **13** The Ugly. **14** Best Director. **15** Locke.
16 Daly. **17** 1960s. **18** Mayor. **19** *Paint Your Wagon*. **20** Jazz. **21** Me.
22 The Man with No Name. **23** Hackman. **24** Wales. **25** Harry.

Answers – see page 54

1   On accepting a Golden Globe for *Titanic*, which James said, 'Does this prove that size does matter?'?

2   Which Francis Ford is the uncle of actor Nicolas Cage?

3   What is the first name of Minghella, who made *The English Patient*?

4   Which 'Dirty' film led Robert Aldrich to founding his own studio?

5   Which director's real name is William Blake McEdwards?

6   In which decade of the 20th century was Woody Allen born?

7   In which country was Milos Forman born?

8   Who won the Best Director Oscar for *Braveheart*?

9   Which director Roger did Brigitte Bardot marry?

10   Which superstar of the silent screen was the subject of a biopic directed by Richard Attenborough in 1992?

11   In which of his own movies did Francis Ford Coppola appear in 1979?

12   Who directed and starred in *The Great Dictator* in 1940?

13   Who said, 'If I made *Cinderella* the audience would be looking for a body in the coach'?

14   Robert Altman directed which movie about a Mobile Army Hospital in Korea, later a TV series?

15   Whose 'Baby' was the Hollywood debut for Roman Polanski, in a movie which starred Mia Farrow?

16   Which Oliver directed *Platoon*?

17   How was Albert Broccoli better known?

18   Who was John Derek's wife whom he directed in *Bolero* in 1984?

19   Which Frank won the Best Director Oscar for *It Happened One Night*?

20   Which Sam won a Golden Globe for *American Beauty*?

21   Who took his film surname form his real name, Allen Stewart Konigsberg?

22   What was the first name of Italian director Fellini?

23   Which John won Best Director Oscar for *The Treasure of the Sierra Madre*?

24   Who funded the Survivors of the Shoah Visual History Foundation after making a Holocaust movie?

25   What was the first name of Hollywood director Capra, of *It's a Wonderful Life* fame?

Answers Who's Who? (see Quiz 46)
1 Roger Moore. 2 John Cleese. 3 Taylor. 4 Leigh. 5 Australia. 6 Africa. 7 Max Factor. 8 Winona. 9 Bruce. 10 Helena Bonham Carter. 11 William. 12 60s. 13 Elliott Gould. 14 Penn. 15 Geena Davis. 16 Farrah Fawcett-Majors. 17 Joseph. 18 Charlton Heston. 19 Brigitte Bardot. 20 Ronald Reagan. 21 Bridget. 22 Cuba. 23 Jools Holland. 24 Britt Ekland. 25 *Funny Girl.*

Answers – see page 59

1   Which Katharine's book was subtitled *How I Went to Africa with Bogart, Bacall and Huston and Almost Lost My Mind*?
2   Which Robert turned down Dustin Hoffman's role in *The Graduate*?
3   In which movie did Tom Hanks say, 'Life is like a box of chocolates'?
4   Which Deborah rolled in the sand with Burt Lancaster in *From Here to Eternity*?
5   In which decade was Jack Nicholson born?
6   Which band's music made *Saturday Night Fever* a success?
7   Which English 007 said, 'You're not a star till they can spell your name in Vladivostok'?
8   Which double Oscar-winner became a Dame in 2000 partly for her work with AIDS sufferers?
9   Which Christopher's autobiography was called *Still Me*?
10 Which Peter said, 'My idea of heaven is moving from one smoke filled room to another'?
11 Who won the Best Actress Oscar for *Funny Girl*?
12 Who made a fortune out of a recipe for salad dressing?
13 Which Scots star was at the top of the money-making lists of 1966?
14 Which painter Vincent did Kirk Douglas play in *Lust for Life*?
15 Which lady was the US's top money-maker with Rock Hudson in 1962?
16 Who changed his name after seeing an advertising hoarding for *The Caine Mutiny*?
17 Which Katharine tested for the role of Scarlett O'Hara?
18 Omar Sharif's affair with Barbra Streisand began on the set of which movie?
19 Which Michael's autobiography was called *What's It All About*?
20 What was Julie Andrews's first film, in 1964?
21 How is Doris Kapelhoff better know?
22 Where was Bob Hope born?
23 Which cartoon character did Robin Williams play?
24 Who directed and starred in *Yentl* in 1983?
25 Which tough guy's real name is Charles Buchinski?

Answers Fred Astaire (see Quiz 51)
1 Frederick. **2** Ginger Rogers. **3** Sister. **4** *Top Hat*. **5** Garland. **6** *Towering Inferno*. **7** *Finian's Rainbow*. **8** Dance. **9** Feathers. **10** Rio. **11** Hayworth. **12** Once. **13** Dramatic role. **14** 1890s. **15** *Sergeant Pepper's Lonely Hearts Club Band*. **16** Legs. **17** 1980s. **18** Gene. **19** Tails. **20** Bing Crosby. **21** Fleet. **22** Divorcee. **23** *Swing Time*. **24** 1930s. **25** Audrey.

Answers – see page 60

1	Who partners Turner in a Tom Hanks movie?
2	Which Jim starred in *The Truman Show*?
3	How often are the Oscars presented?
4	Which star actress was in *Dangerous Minds, Wolf* and *One Fine Day*?
5	Which word completes the film title, *Since You Went* ___?
6	Which Bill starred in *Ghostbusters*?
7	What is the first name of Mr Hytner who directed *The Crucible* and *The Madness of King George*?
8	According to the movie title, what do 'Gentlemen Prefer'?
9	Which British actor Jeremy was an Oscar winner with *Reversal of Fortune*?
10	In which decade was *Thelma and Louise* released?
11	Which Tom was male lead in *Jerry Maguire*?
12	Which word follows 'Jumpin' Jack' in a Whoopi Goldberg movie title?
13	What did Dumbo do immediately before his ears grew so big?
14	Which actress Debra served in the Israeli army?
15	In which decade of the 20th century was Clint Eastwood born?
16	Which Caped Crusader was the subject of one of the top 80s films?
17	Which actor links *Platoon, Donnie Brascoe* and *Nick of Time*?
18	How many gunfighters were hired in the 'Magnificent' film of 1960?
19	Who was Warren Beatty's wife whom he directed in *Bugsy* in 1991?
20	Which word completes the film title, *The Rocky Horror Picture* ___?
21	'Evergreen' won an Oscar when it was used in which movie in 1976?
22	Which Tom won the Best Actor Oscar for *Forrest Gump*?
23	In which decade was *The Spy Who Loved Me* released?
24	Who directed *The Commitments*?
25	Charlie Chaplin was famous for wearing what type of hat?

Answers Pot Luck 21 (see Quiz 52)
1 *Ice Storm*. 2 150 minutes. 3 Colbert. 4 1960s. 5 Crystal. 6 Motorcycle.
7 Sharon Stone. 8 *Titanic*. 9 Cagney. 10 Honor. 11 Sarandon. 12 Paris.
13 Hanna & Barbera. 14 Tchaikovsky. 15 Kiefer Sutherland. 16 Gere. 17 In the
Stone. 18 Fred Flintstone. 19 Cher. 20 King. 21 Tom Cruise. 22 Judy Garland.
23 1930s. 24 James Garner. 25 'From Russia with Love'.

Answers – see page 57

1   What was Fred Astaire's full real first name?
2   Who was Astaire's most famous dancing partner?
3   What relation to Fred was Adele Astaire?
4   Which item of formal dress was the name of a famous Astaire movie?
5   With which co-star Judy did he appear in *Easter Parade*?
6   For which 70s disaster film set in a skyscraper was Astaire Oscar-nominated?
7   Which rainbow was the title of a 1968 movie with Fred Astaire?
8   What completes the quote about an Astaire screen test, 'Can't sing, can't act, can ____ a little'?
9   In the 'Cheek to Cheek' number in *Top Hat* which part of Ginger Rogers's dress kept blowing up Astaire's nose?
10   In their first movie together Astaire and Rogers were 'Flying Down to' where?
11   Which Rita starred with Astaire in *You'll Never Get Rich*?
12   How many times did he receive an Oscar for a specific role?
13   *On the Beach* was what type of 'first' for Astaire in 1959?
14   In which decade of the 19th century was Astaire born?
15   Which classic Beatles album features Fred Astaire – among many others – on the cover?
16   What parts of Fred Astaire were heavily insured?
17   In which decade of the 20th century did Astaire die, aged 88?
18   Which Kelly did he replace in *Easter Parade*?
19   What comes after 'Top hat, white tie' in the song from *Top Hat*?
20   Who was his male co-star in *Holiday Inn* – which introduced 'White Christmas' to audiences?
21   In 1936 Astaire and Rogers starred in 'Follow the' what?
22   In the 1930s Astaire starred in 'The Gay' what?
23   Which 'Swing' film featured 'The Way You Look Tonight'?
24   In which decade did Astaire and Rogers star in their first movie together?
25   Which Hepburn was his co-star in *Funny Face*?

Answers – see page 58

1   What type of 'Storm' starred Sigourney Weaver and Kevin Kline in 1997?
2   Does *Pulp Fiction* last 50, 150 or 250 minutes?
3   Which famous Claudette tested for the role of Scarlett O'Hara?
4   In which decade of the 20th century was Laura Dern born?
5   Which Billy starred in *When Harry Met Sally*?
6   On what vehicle did Steve McQueen try to flee in *The Great Escape*?
7   Which actress links *Basic Instinct* and *Last Action Hero*?
8   Which water-linked film took over from *Waterworld* as the most costly to make?
9   *Yankee Doodle Dandy* starred which James?
10 Kathleen Turner was concerned with Prizzi's what?
11 Which Susan starred in *The Client*?
12 Brigitte Bardot had a theatre named after her in which French city?
13 Who created Tom and Jerry at MGM in the 40s?
14 *The Music Lovers* was about which Russian composer?
15 Which son of a M*A*S*H star starred in *Young Guns II*?
16 Which Richard replaced John Travolta in *American Gigolo*?
17 Where is 'The Sword', according to the Disney film title?
18 Which TV cartoon character did John Goodman play in a movie?
19 Who sang 'The Shoop Shoop Song' in *Mermaids*?
20 Which word follows 'The Fisher' in a Robin Williams movie title?
21 Which star actor was in *Top Gun, Jerry Maguire* and *Born on the Fourth of July*?
22 Who played the lead role in *The Wizard of Oz*?
23 In which decade of the 20th century was Dame Judi Dench born?
24 Whose real name is James Baumgarner?
25 What was the Bond theme for *From Russia with Love* called?

Answers – see page 63

1   Which Sam was the G in MGM?
2   Which company, famous for animation, bought Miramax in 1993?
3   What did R stand for in RKO?
4   What was the amalgamation of the Fox Film Corporation and 20th Century Pictures called?
5   Which Harry founded Columbia?
6   Which Mary was the only female founder member of United Artists in 1919?
7   Whose first classic comedies were put out by Essanay?
8   Which blockbuster from Steven Spielberg revived the fortunes of Universal Pictures in the 80s?
9   Which company merged with Time Inc. in 1989?
10   Which British company had a wild cat in its name?
11   Which Australian-born publishing tycoon bought 20th Century Fox in 1985?
12   Which actor was the Lancaster in the Hecht–Lancaster company?
13   Which former Beatle set up HandMade Films?
14   Which Steven set up Dreamworks?
15   Which Brothers bought out First National in 1929?
16   What sort of movies were Hammer famous for?
17   What did the first M stand for in MGM?
18   Which animal was the symbol of MGM?
19   Which computer-generated 'Story' was created by Pixar?
20   Which Japanese company paid $3.4 billion for Columbia in 1990?
21   Which Howard bought a large share of RKO in 1948?
22   What was the first name of Mayer of MGM fame?
23   Which borough of west London gave its name to comedies in the 40s and 50s made in its studios?
24   What was the surname of father and son Darryl F. and Richard of 20th Century Fox fame?
25   How many Warner Brothers were there?

Answers Pot Luck 22 (see Quiz 55)
1 Lewis. 2 *Female*. 3 Paltrow. 4 *Oklahoma!*. 5 Eddie Murphy. 6 Peck.
7 *Murder on the Orient Express*. 8 Five. 9 Stallone. 10 Barney. 11 Crystal.
12 Gere. 13 1960s. 14 John Travolta. 15 Innocence. 16 Keaton.
17 Madonna's. 18 *Annie Hall*. 19 Hunter. 20 Steel. 21 1940s. 22 Seven.
23 Winona Ryder. 24 Bette Davis. 25 Bacon.

Answers – see page 64

1	Who did Antonio Banderas play in *Il Giovane Mussolini*?
2	In which part of the UK was *Trainspotting* set?
3	Where was *Farewell My Concubine* banned when it was first released?
4	On which romantic day did the action of *Picnic at Hanging Rock* take place?
5	*Les Enfants du Paradis* was shot at the end of which war?
6	Michelangelo Antonioni hails from which European country?
7	Where were the first Mad Max films with Mel Gibson made?
8	Which French film director Roger died in February 2000?
9	Which 1993 film by New Zealander Jane Campion has the name of a musical instrument as its title?
10	Jacques Tati hails from country?
11	Which British film magnate had the name and initial J. Arthur?
12	What is the first name of Greek actress Mercouri?
13	Which country's film industry is referred to as 'Bollywood'?
14	Which Italian director was Giuseppe Bertolucci's elder brother?
15	Who, with 'Jules', is in the title of the 60s Truffaut classic?
16	Which film with Cate Blanchett about an English queen was directed by Indian Shekhar Kapur?
17	Where does Neil Jordan hail from?
18	Which French actress was often known by her initials B.B.?
19	*Abba the Movie* was a collaboration between Australia and where?
20	Which Italian actress played opposite Marcello Mastroianni 12 times?
21	Where was *The Seven Samurai* made?
22	How was Czech-born actress Hedy Kielser known when she moved to Hollywood?
23	In which capital city were the Cinecitta Studios founded?
24	Ingmar Bergman hails from which Scandinavian country?
25	What is the first name of Finnish-born Hollywood director Harlin?

Answers 1940s Stars (see Quiz 56)
1 Hayworth. 2 England. 3 Ginger Rogers. 4 Bob Hope. 5 Tracy. 6 Henry.
7 Ingrid Bergman. 8 Ronald Reagan. 9 John Wayne. 10 Costello. 11 Davis.
12 Cole Porter. 13 Lombard. 14 Fruit. 15 Cagney. 16 Sweden. 17 Humphrey
Bogart. 18 Fred Astaire. 19 Taylor. 20 Priest. 21 Hepburn. 22 Robert. 23 Red.
24 Rooney. 25 Legs.

Answers – see page 61

1   Which Juliette starred in *Natural Born Killers*?
2   Which word completes the film title *Single White ____*?
3   Which Gwyneth starred in the 1998 *Great Expectations*?
4   The song 'Oh What a Beautiful Morning' features in which musical movie?
5   Which actor links *Beverly Hills Cop*, *Harlem Nights* and *Boomerang*?
6   Which Gregory starred in *The Omen*?
7   Which 70s Agatha Christie movie was about a murder on a train?
8   Which number completes the film title *Slaughterhouse ____*?
9   Which Sylvester starred in *Judge Dredd*?
10   Which friend of Fred Flintstone was played by Rick Moranis?
11   *City Slickers* starred which Billy?
12   Which Richard starred in *An Officer and a Gentleman*?
13   In which decade was Disney's *Jungle Book* released?
14   Which *Grease* and *Saturday Night Fever* actor is a qualified pilot?
15   Which word follows 'The Age of' in a Michelle Pfeiffer movie title?
16   Which Diane starred in *The Godfather*?
17   Whose black bra made £4,600 at auction in 1997?
18   Which Annie features in a Woody Allen movie title?
19   Which Holly won the Best Actress Oscar for *The Piano*?
20   What metal are 'Magnolias' made from, according to the film title?
21   In which decade of the 20th century was Richard Gere born?
22   How many Mr Olympia titles did Arnold Schwarzenegger win – five, seven or nine?
23   Which star actress was in *Mermaids, Little Women* and *Alien:Resurrection*?
24   How was Ruth Elizabeth Davis better known?
25   Which Kevin starred in *Wild Things*?

Answers – see page 62

1   The Margarita cocktail was named after which Rita, as it was her real first name?
2   In which country was Cary Grant born?
3   Which dancing partner of Fred Astaire won an Oscar for *Kitty Foyle*?
4   Which comedian was Bing Crosby paired with in the *Road* movies?
5   Which Spencer was both Jekyll and Hyde in the 1941 movie?
6   Which Fonda appeared in *The Grapes of Wrath*?
7   If Humphrey Bogart played Rick, who played Ilsa in a 40s classic?
8   Which future politician became president of the Screen Actors Guild?
9   Which western star was nicknamed Duke?
10 Who teamed with Abbott to make them a top money-making duo of the 40s?
11 Which Bette's tombstone said, 'She did it the hard way'?
12 Which Porter did Cary Grant play in *Night and Day*?
13 Which Carole, then Mrs Clark Gable, died in a plane crash in 1942?
14 What sort of organic items did Carmen Miranda wear on her head?
15 Which James, more famous for gangster roles, played George M. Cohan in *Yankee Doodle Dandy*?
16 In which country was Ingrid Bergman born?
17 Who married Lauren Bacall after making *To Have and Have Not* with her?
18 Which dancer, famous for *Top Hat*, appeared with Bing Crosby in *Holiday Inn*?
19 Which Elizabeth played aspiring jockey Velvet Brown in *National Velvet*?
20 What type of role does Bing Crosby play in *The Bells of St Mary's*?
21 Which Katharine played Tracy Lord in *The Philadelphia Story*?
22 Which first name was shared by Mitchum and Taylor?
23 Rita Hayworth was best known for having what colour hair?
24 Which Mickey was the top money-maker as the decade opened?
25 Which part of her did Betty Grable insure for a multimillion-dollar sum?

Answers World Cinema (see Quiz 54)
1 Mussolini. 2 Scotland. 3 China. 4 Valentine's Day. 5 World War II. 6 Italy.
7 Australia. 8 Vadim. 9 *The Piano*. 10 France. 11 Rank. 12 Melina. 13 India.
14 Bernardo Bertolucci. 15 Jim. 16 *Elizabeth*. 17 Ireland. 18 Brigitte Bardot.
19 Sweden. 20 Sophia Loren. 21 Japan. 22 Hedy Lamarr. 23 Rome.
24 Sweden. 25 Renny.

Answers – see page 67

1   Which early 1990s Disney animal cartoon is set in Africa?
2   Who played Princess Leia in *Star Wars*?
3   Which *ER* star played Batman in the 1997 movie?
4   Which Michael Douglas film has the word 'Wall' in the title?
5   In which TV detective series did James Garner find fame after appearing on the big screen?
6   Which silent movie actor was nicknamed the 'Great Stone Face'?
7   Which Patricia wrote the book on which *The Talented Mr Ripley* was based?
8   Which Claire starred in the 90s *Romeo and Juliet*?
9   Who sang 'Call Me' in *American Gigolo*?
10   Which word goes before 'Proposal' in a Demi Moore movie title?
11   What is another name for a horse opera?
12   Which computer company with a fruit logo bought Pixar?
13   What sort of video disc is a DVD?
14   The medium Oda Mae Brown appears in which movie?
15   'Up Where We Belong' was the theme music to which 80s film?
16   Who played Baron von Trapp in *The Sound of Music*?
17   In which decade of the 20th century was Michael J. Fox born?
18   Which keyboard instrument gave its name to a film with Holly Hunter?
19   Which name completes the film title, *Star Trek: The Wrath Of* ____?
20   Which first name goes before 'Valentine' to make a movie title?
21   Which director Blake did Julie Andrews marry?
22   Which Michelle starred in *The Witches of Eastwick*?
23   Which 'Rider' was Clint Eastwood's next western after *The Outlaw Josey Wales*?
24   Which word follows 'Sibling' in a Carrie Fisher movie title?
25   In which movie did Dustin Hoffman play 'Dorothy'?

Answers Judy Garland (see Quiz 59)
1 'Over the Rainbow'. 2 Fred Astaire. 3 Vincente Minnelli. 4 1920s. 5 Ziegfeld.
6 Mason. 7 Dorothy. 8 Gable. 9 Rooney. 10 *The Wizard of Oz*. 11 Bogarde.
12 St Louis. 13 Frances. 14 1960s. 15 Liza Minnelli. 16 *Annie Get Your Gun*.
17 Ira. 18 Star. 19 Shirley Temple. 20 Kelly. 21 *Babes in Arms*.
22 Nuremberg. 23 *Easter Parade*. 24 Lorna. 25 1960s.

Answers – see page 68

1   Which romantic Rudolph did Rudolph Nureyev play on film in 1977?
2   Which 'Story' had the ad line, 'Love means never having to say you're sorry'?
3   Willy Wonka was in charge of what type of factory?
4   The movie *Rocky* was about what type of sportsman?
5   Which dance was 'The Last in Paris' with Marlon Brando?
6   In which decade was *Grease* set?
7   Which cult sci-fi series came to the big screen with *The Motion Picture* in 1979?
8   Which puppets including Kermit and Miss Piggy had their own big screen hit?
9   Which instrumentalist was 'on the Roof' in 1971?
10   Which night of the week suffered 'Night Fever'?
11   Which US city was named twice in the 1977 hit with Robert De Niro?
12   What followed 'What's Up' in the title of the move with Barbra Streisand and Ryan O'Neal?
13   Which gangster movie was based on Mario Puzo's novel?
14   Where did the action of *The Poseidon Adventure* take place?
15   What nationality of 'Graffiti' was directed by George Lucas in 1973?
16   In which country was *The Three Musketeers* set?
17   Which fruit was 'Clockwork' in 1971?
18   Which King's court was included – loosely – in *Monty Python and the Holy Grail*?
19   Which precious gems were in the title of the 1971 Bond movie?
20   How were 'Saddles' described in the 1974 movie with Gene Wilder?
21   What was the sequel to *The Godfather* called?
22   Which Korean War movie spawned a TV series which lasted 11 years?
23   Whose 'Daughter' starred Robert Mitchum and Sarah Miles?
24   Which Warren Beatty movie had the title of a hair-care item as its title?
25   Which 'Connection' starred Gene Hackman?

Answers Pot Luck 24 (see Quiz 60)
1 Nick Park. **2** 1950s. **3** Hercule Poirot. **4** Thompson. **5** Nicholson. **6** Julie Andrews. **7** *Bismarck*. **8** Cliffhanger. **9** Robin Williams. **10** 33⅓. **11** Alfred Hitchcock. **12** Dry ice. **13** Reed. **14** Moore. **15** Goldwyn. **16** Jeff Goldblum. **17** *M*A*S*H*. **18** 1960s. **19** Michael Caine. **20** The cold (*The Spy Who Came in from the Cold*). **21** Ginger Rogers. **22** *Walking*. **23** Mozart. **24** Arnold Schwarzenegger. **25** 'Over the Rainbow'.

Answers – see page 65

1 Which Garland song from *The Wizard of Oz* won an Oscar?
2 Which dancer replaced Gene Kelly in *Easter Parade* after he hurt his ankle?
3 Which husband of Garland's, of Italian descent, directed her in *Meet Me in St Louis*?
4 In which decade was she born?
5 Which 'Girl' was in the title of a 1941 movie?
6 Which James was Garland's co star in *A Star Is Born*?
7 What was the name of her famous character in *The Wizard of Oz*?
8 To which Clark did she sing 'You Made Me Love You' in *Broadway Melody of 1938*?
9 With which Mickey did she first star in 1937?
10 For which famous movie did she receive a special juvenile Oscar?
11 Which Dirk was her co-star in *I Could Go On Singing*?
12 Where did Judy sing 'Meet Me' in the 1944 movie?
13 What was her first name when she was part of the Gumm Sisters Kiddie Act?
14 In which decade did she make her last film?
15 What is the name of her daughter with Vincente Minnelli?
16 On which movie about the wild west's Annie Oakley was she replaced by Betty Hutton in 1950?
17 Which Gershwin wrote the lyrics of Garland's classic 'The Man That Got Away' from *A Star Is Born*?
18 In *Babes in Arms* Garland sang 'You Are My Lucky' what?
19 Which child star did she replace in *The Wizard of Oz*?
20 Which Gene debuted with her in *For Me and My Gal* in 1942?
21 *Babes on Broadway* was a sequel to which movie also with Mickey Rooney?
22 'Judgment at' where, the location for war crime trials, was a 1961 dramatic role for Garland?
23 Which 'Parade' was a 1948 hit musical for her?
24 What is the name of her daughter with producer Sid Luft?
25 In which decade of the 20th century did Judy Garland die?

Answers Pot Luck 23 (see Quiz 57)
1 *The Lion King*. 2 Carrie Fisher. 3 George Clooney. 4 *Wall Street*. 5 *The Rockford Files*. 6 Buster Keaton. 7 Highsmith. 8 Danes. 9 Blondie. 10 Indecent. 11 Western. 12 Apple. 13 Digital. 14 *Ghost*. 15 *An Officer and a Gentleman*. 16 Christopher Plummer. 17 1960s. 18 The piano. 19 *Khan*. 20 Shirley. 21 Edwards. 22 Pfeiffer. 23 *Pale Rider*. 24 Rivalry. 25 *Tootsie*.

Answers – see page 66

1   Who directed *A Close Shave*?
2   In which decade of the 20th century was Carrie Fisher born?
3   Which sleuth features in Agatha Christie's *Murder on the Orient Express*?
4   Which Emma won the Best Actress Oscar for *Howard's End*?
5   Which Jack starred in *Wolf*?
6   Who was the female lead in *Mary Poppins*?
7   Which word completes the film title, *Sink the ____*?
8   What name is given to a situation in film where a suspense scene is temporarily left unresolved?
9   Which actor links *The Birdcage* and *Patch Adams*?
10 What number completes the title, *Naked Gun ____: The Final Insult*?
11 Who directed *To Catch a Thief* and *North by Northwest*?
12 What sort of ice was used to give a misty effect in movie making?
13 Which Oliver played Bill Sikes in *Oliver!*?
14 Which Dudley portrayed Arthur?
15 What does the G stand for in MGM studios?
16 Who played the wisecracking mathematician in *Jurassic Park*?
17 The character Trapper John featured in which war-based movie?
18 In which decade was *True Grit* released?
19 Who played the lead in *Alfie* after Laurence Harvey turned it down?
20 According to the film title, where did the spy come in from?
21 Who danced in high heels in the Astaire/Rogers movies?
22 What completes the film title, *Dead Man ___*?
23 *Amadeus* told the story of which classical composer?
24 Which star actor was in *Junior* and *Terminator 2: Judgment Day*?
25 Which song from *The Wizard of Oz* won an Oscar?

Answers 1970s (see Quiz 58)
1 Valentino. **2** *Love Story*. **3** Chocolate. **4** Boxer. **5** Tango. **6** 1950s. **7** *Star Trek*. **8** The Muppets. **9** Fiddler. **10** Saturday. **11** New York. **12** Doc. **13** *The Godfather*. **14** At sea. **15** American. **16** France. **17** Orange. **18** Arthur. **19** Diamonds (*Diamond Are Forever*). **20** Blazing. **21** *The Godfather Part II*. **22** M*A*S*H. **23** *Ryan's Daughter*. **24** *Shampoo*. **25** *The French Connection*.

Answers – see page 71

1	What was Leonardo DiCaprio's first major movie after *Titanic*?
2	Where does Robert Carlyle hail from?
3	Which major US university did Matt Damon attend?
4	Which star of *The Talented Mr Ripley* was engaged to Brad Pitt?
5	What type of 'Voice' did Jane Horrocks have in the 1998 movie?
6	Which actor links *The Phantom Menace* and *Trainspotting*?
7	What sort of 'Inspector' did Matthew Broderick become?
8	Which Kate found fame in *Sense and Sensibility* when only 20?
9	Which Ms Moore was Ralph Fiennes's co-star in *The End of the Affair*?
10	Which Jennifer provided a voice in *Antz* and starred in *Anaconda*?
11	In which movie did Mena Suvari star with Kevin Spacey?
12	What is the first name of British actress Ms Swinton who appears in *The Beach*?
13	Tom Hanks, Tim Allen and Kelsey Grammer were heard but not seen in which cartoon sequel?
14	Which Jennifer from *Friends* was one of the voices in *The Iron Giant*?
15	Which TV star Alex divorced Ralph Fiennes in 1997?
16	Which Annette starred in *American Beauty*?
17	What day of the week was *Sleepy Hollow*'s Christina Ricci's name in the *Addams Family* movies?
18	Which Jeanne's movies include *Sliding Doors* and *Mickey Blue Eyes*?
19	Which English actor played opposite Gwyneth Paltrow in *The Talented Mr Ripley*?
20	Which Matthew married Sarah Jessica Parker in 1997?
21	Who was the star and executive producer of *Onegin*?
22	Which Anna played opposite Ewan McGregor in *Rogue Trader*?
23	What was Leonardo DiCaprio's first film released in the 21st century?
24	Which star of *There's Something About Mary* was described as 'something of a Jean Harlow of the 90s'?
25	If Jodie Foster was Anna, who was Chow Yun-Fat?

Answers – see page 72

1   What were her real first names?
2   The title of her 1953 movie was 'How to Marry' who?
3   In which film which mentioned blondes did she play Lorelei Lee?
4   In the 1957 movie Olivier played 'The Prince'; who was Monroe?
5   *Some Like It Hot*, about the aftermath of the St Valentine's Day Massacre, is set in which decade?
6   Monroe had a minor role in a Bette Davis movie, 'All About' whom?
7   To which US President did she famously sing 'Happy Birthday'?
8   Which Billy directed her in *The Seven Year Itch*?
9   Which classic Beatles album features Marilyn Monroe – among many others – on the cover?
10 In *Some Like It Hot* which stringed musical instrument does she play?
11 Which Ethel was her leading co-star in *There's No Business Like Show Business*?
12 What was the official cause of her death?
13 What type of sportsman was her second husband, Joe Di Maggio?
14 Which Jack and Tony were her co-stars in *Some Like It Hot*?
15 Which star of *Evita* has a tattoo of Marilyn Monroe on her body?
16 What was her first name as Miss Kane in *Some Like It Hot*?
17 Which brunette Jane was her co-star in *Gentlemen Prefer Blondes*?
18 What sort of 'Business' was the title of a 1952 movie?
19 Which 1953 movie took its name from some Canadian falls?
20 What was the name of the Elton John song about Marilyn Monroe?
21 Which 1955 Monroe movie featured Tom Ewell?
22 What were 'a Girl's Best Friend' in the title of one her songs?
23 Which playwright Arthur was her third and last husband?
24 With which King of Hollywood did she make her last completed film – which was also his final movie?
25 In which decade did Marilyn Monroe die?

Answers – see page 69

1   Which film earned James Cameron a 1997 Oscar?
2   *Home Alone* made which child into a worldwide star?
3   *Platoon* was about which a war in which country?
4   Who was US President when *Air Force One* was released?
5   Which brothers featured in *Animal Crackers*?
6   What name is given to a filming site away from the studio?
7   Which word completes the film title, *The Shop Around the ___*?
8   What is the name of the film about the writer C. S. Lewis?
9   What name is given to a movie which follows up on events of a previous film?
10 In which decade was *The Empire Strikes Back* released?
11 Which Richard starred in *American Graffiti*?
12 What happened at Morgan's Creek, according to the film title?
13 Who insured her legs for a million dollars in the 1940s?
14 Which musical based on *Romeo and Juliet* was a 60s Oscar winner?
15 What natural disaster is at the heart of *Dante's Peak*?
16 What won the Best Film Oscar at the first ceremony of the new Millennium?
17 Which Joan starred in *Whatever Happened to Baby Jane?*?
18 Bugsy Malone features what particular type of performers?
19 What sort of farm animal was Babe?
20 Which Swedish tennis star appeared in *Racquet* in 1979?
21 Which word completes the film title, *Sister Act 2: Back in the ___*?
22 In which decade of the 20th century was Jodie Foster born?
23 Does *A Close Shave* last under an hour, one hour or two hours?
24 Which Tom sang 'It's Not Unusual' in *Mars Attacks!*?
25 Dad Henry and children Jane and Peter are from which family?

Answers – see page 70

1	Which German-born actress was the star of *The Blue Angel*?
2	Which scandal-seeking blonde appeared in *I'm No Angel* and *She Done Him Wrong*?
3	Which Swedish star's first spoken line was, 'Gimme a visky with a ginger ale on the side'?
4	Which middle initial did Edward Robinson use?
5	How many Marx Brothers remained silent on screen?
6	Which first name was shared by actors Stewart and Cagney?
7	Which Johnny took the title role in *Tarzan the Ape Man*?
8	Which Mary, a founder of United Artists, retired in 1933?
9	Actor Fields appeared in *Six of a Kind*; what were his initials?
10	Which Nelson partnered Jeanette Macdonald for the first time in *Naughty Mariette*?
11	Which child star topped the list of US money-makers in 1935?
12	Which Gary appeared in *Mr Deeds Goes to Town*?
13	Did Laurel or Hardy or both of them have a moustache?
14	Which Charles played Quasimodo in *The Hunchback of Notre Dame*?
15	What was Tyrone Power's father called?
16	Which star of *The Wizard of Oz* was born Frances Gumm?
17	Hedy Kiesler found fame swimming nude in a Czech movie; how was she renamed in Hollywood?
18	How many Oscars did Chaplin win in the 1930s?
19	Which star of *Gone with the Wind* was dubbed the King of Hollywood?
20	Margaret Dumont made seven films with which comedy brothers?
21	What colour was Jean Harlow's hair?
22	Which actress with the initials C.C. was Clark Gable's co-star in *It Happened One Night*?
23	Which 30s actress Barbara found fame in the 80s soap *The Colbys*?
24	Which Joan was the subject of a 1970s biography *Mommie Dearest*?
25	Which actress said 'Tomorrow is another day' at the end of *Gone with the Wind*?

Answers Marilyn Monroe (see Quiz 62)
1 Norma Jean. 2 A Millionaire. 3 *Gentlemen Prefer Blondes*. 4 The Showgirl.
5 1920s. 6 Eve. 7 Kennedy. 8 Wilder. 9 *Sergeant Pepper's Lonely Hearts Club Band*. 10 Ukelele. 11 Merman. 12 Drugs overdose. 13 Baseball player.
14 Lemmon & Curtis. 15 Madonna. 16 Sugar. 17 Russell. 18 *Monkey Business*.
19 *Niagara*. 20 'Candle in the Wind'. 21 *The Seven Year Itch*. 22 Diamonds.
23 Miller. 24 Clark Gable – *The Misfits*. 25 1960s.

Answers – see page 75

1   Which star actor was in *As Good as it Gets* and *The Shining*?
2   The original 'Candle in the Wind' was about which movie icon?
3   Which Jim starred in *Ace Ventura, Pet Detective*?
4   What do the male leads do in both *Mrs Doubtfire* and *Tootsie*?
5   Which actress links *Sister Act* and *Ghost*?
6   What sort of store does Hugh Grant own in *Notting Hill*?
7   *Air Force One* starred which Glenn?
8   In which decade was *Aladdin* released?
9   Who played the lead roles in *Butch Cassidy and the Sundance Kid*?
10   Which Terence starred in *The Adventures of Priscilla, Queen of the Desert*?
11   Which word follows 'Presumed' in a Harrison Ford movie title?
12   What name is given to a movie which shows events which happened before a
     previously known story?
13   Which Kevin starred in *Waterworld*?
14   Which role did Mark Hamill play in *Star Wars*?
15   Which early rocker Bill was in the movie *Rock around the Clock*?
16   Who shared the title with Thelma in the 1991 movie?
17   Who won the Best Actress Oscar for *Sophie's Choice*?
18   *Indecent Proposal* and *A Few Good Men* both feature which actress?
19   What sort of movie did a scream queen appear in?
20   Which James starred in *The Philadelphia Story*?
21   In which decade was *The Omen* released?
22   Which movie did the song 'Night Fever' come from?
23   Which word completes the movie title *Honey, I Shrunk The ____*?
24   In which decade of the 20th century was Winona Ryder born?
25   Which Tom starred in *A League of their Own*?

Answers Heroes & Villains (see Quiz 67)
1 Keach. **2** Canada. **3** Arnold Schwarzenegger. **4** Oskar. **5** Pesci. **6** Lee Harvey
Oswald. **7** *The Birds*. **8** Telly Savalas. **9** Shaw. **10** 1970s. **11** Pearl Harbor.
12 Bates. **13** Paris. **14** Jeremy Irons. **15** *The Silence of the Lambs*. **16** Ivy (Uma
Thurman). **17** Caan. **18** Jack Nicholson. **19** Stephen King. **20** John Travolta.
21 The Penguin. **22** *The Terminator*. **23** Sophia Loren. **24** Jodie Foster.
25 Woody Allen.

Answers – see page 76

1   What was the name of Gene Autry's 'Wonder Horse'?
2   Who played Cruella De Vil in the real-life version of *101 Dalmatians*?
3   Which animal played the title role in *Babe*?
4   What type of animal was Rin Tin Tin?
5   What was Dumbo?
6   Which Doctor could 'talk to the animals'?
7   What was unusual about Clarence the Lion's eyes?
8   What did Fritz and Felix have in common?
9   What was Roy Rogers's horse called?
10   Which 70s blockbuster was about a man-eating shark?
11   What breed of lugubrious dog featured in *Turner and Hooch*?
12   *International Velvet* was about what type of animal?
13   What types of animal were to be found in Jurassic Park?
14   What sort of creatures were Leonardo, Michelangelo, Raphael and Donatello?
15   In which decade was the real-life version of *101 Dalmatians* released?
16   What sort of creature was Tarka?
17   What type of animal was Gentle Ben?
18   Cheta was a chimp in which jungle movie series?
19   What name went after 'Free' in the movie about a whale?
20   Which composer shared a name with a St Bernard dog in the movies?
21   In *101 Dalmatians* Cruella De Vil wanted the puppies in order to make what?
22   What sort of animals were the stars of *Born Free*?
23   Which film featured Mufasa the lion?
24   Which animal featured in the Sherlock Holmes story which has been filmed most?
25   What breed of dog was Lassie?

Answers – see page 73

1	Which Stacy spent nine months in Britain's Reading Gaol?
2	Leslie Nielsen was a member of which country's air force?
3	Which bodybuilder was Mr Freeze in *Batman and Robin*?
4	What was the first name of Schindler in the movie with Liam Neeson?
5	Which Joe tries to burgle Macaulay Culkin when he's *Home Alone*?
6	Which real-life villain did Gary Oldman play in *JFK*?
7	What are the villains in the 1963 movie with Tippi Hedren and Rod Taylor?
8	In *On Her Majesty's Secret Service* which smooth-headed TV detective played Blofeld?
9	Which Robert was the cheating gangster in *The Sting*?
10	In which decade did Christopher Reeve first play superhero Superman?
11	Burt Lancaster joined the US army after which major action in the Pacific?
12	Which Kathy played the villainous Annie in *Misery*?
13	Brigitte Bardot was awarded the freedom of which French city?
14	Which British actor played Claus von Bulow in *Reversal of Fortune*?
15	Mega-villain Hannibal Lecter appeared in which 1990s movie?
16	Who was 'Poison' in *Batman and Robin*?
17	Which James played Sonny Corleone in *The Godfather*?
18	Who was the villainous Joker in *Batman* in 1989?
19	Who wrote the novel on which *The Green Mile* was based?
20	Who played the Clintonesque character in *Primary Colors*?
21	Which villain did Danny DeVito play in a Batman movie?
22	In which movie did Arnold Schwarzenegger first say, 'I'll be back'?
23	Which Italian actress was jailed in 1962 for tax evasion?
24	John Hinckley shot Ronald Reagan because of his obsession with which former child star?
25	Which film director married the adopted daughter of his former partner?

Answers Pot Luck 26 (see Quiz 65)
1 Jack Nicholson. **2** Marilyn Monroe. **3** Carrey. **4** Dress in drag. **5** Whoopi Goldberg. **6** Bookshop. **7** Close. **8** 1990s. **9** Paul Newman and Robert Redford. **10** Stamp. **11** Innocent. **12** Prequel. **13** Costner. **14** Luke Skywalker. **15** Haley. **16** Louise. **17** Meryl Streep. **18** Demi Moore. **19** Horror. **20** Stewart. **21** 1970s. **22** *Saturday Night Fever.* **23** *Kids.* **24** 1970s. **25** Hanks.

Answers – see page 74

1   Which star actor was in *Pulp Fiction* and *Look Who's Talking*?
2   Which Gwyneth starred in *Emma*?
3   Which word goes before 'Attraction' in a Michael Douglas movie title?
4   In which decade was *Who Framed Roger Rabbit?* released?
5   Who sang the title song of 'Stand By Me'?
6   Which metal links 'Bullet' and 'Streak' to give two film titles?
7   Which Mel went classical and appeared as Hamlet?
8   In which film did a character named John Dunbar appear?
9   *A Fish Called Wanda* featured which Michael?
10 Which Katharine had both an on- and off-screen relationship with Spencer Tracy?
11 The song 'You Must Love Me' came from which movie?
12 In a Clint Eastwood title, which word follows 'Every Which Way But'?
13 Orson Welles' first film was about which 'Citizen'?
14 *Batman Forever*, *The Wedding Singer* and *Wayne's World 2* all feature which actress?
15 Which name completes the film title, *The Seventh Voyage of ___*?
16 Who played Sally Bowles in *Cabaret*?
17 Which Mr Ford starred in *The Empire Strikes Back*?
18 Which famous Tallulah tested for the role of Scarlett O'Hara?
19 Which woman's name connects with 'Sid' to give a film title?
20 Which plant was Uma Thurman's character named after in *Batman and Robin*?
21 Which Gillian starred in *The X-Files*?
22 Who directed the movie *Bram Stoker's Dracula*?
23 In which TV soap did Charlton Heston find fame after appearing on the big screen?
24 In which decade of the 20th century was Patrick Swayze born?
25 To the nearest hour, how long does the 60s movie *Cleopatra* last?

Answers Animal Movies (see Quiz 66)
1 Champion. **2** Glenn Close **3** Pig. **4** Dog. **5** Elephant. **6** Dolittle. **7** He was cross-eyed. **8** They were cats. **9** Trigger. **10** *Jaws*. **11** Bloodhound. **12** Horses. **13** Dinosaurs. **14** Turtles. **15** 1990s. **16** Otter. **17** Bear. **18** *Tarzan*. **19** Willy. **20** Beethoven. **21** Coat. **22** Lions. **23** *The Lion King*. **24** Hound (of the Baskervilles). **25** Collie.

Answers – see page 79

1   Which aunt of George Clooney starred in *White Christmas*?
2   Who died in his car before his movie *Rebel Without a Cause* was released?
3   Which swashbuckling star, never far away from scandal, died in 1959?
4   Which blonde singer/actress first starred opposite Rock Hudson in *Pillow Talk*?
5   Which singer famous for his blue eyes starred in *From Here to Eternity*?
6   Who famously sang 'The Man that Got Away' in *A Star Is Born*?
7   Which Christopher first played Dracula in 1958?
8   Who, with Lady, was in the second most successful 50s movie?
9   Which Ben won most Oscars in the 1950s?
10   Which Jack was Oscar-nominated for *Some Like It Hot*?
11   Which Danny played Hans Christian Andersen in the 50s biopic?
12   Which star of horror movies starred in *The Fly*?
13   Which Kim appeared opposite James Stewart in *Vertigo*?
14   What was the nationality of Maurice Chevalier who starred in *Gigi*?
15   Which singer, real name Dino Crocetti, starred with John Wayne in *Rio Bravo*?
16   Who was the most famous blonde in *Gentlemen Prefer Blondes*?
17   Which Elizabeth was the *Cat on a Hot Tin Roof*?
18   Which Gregory won an Oscar for *To Kill a Mockingbird*?
19   What does Gene Kelly carry while he is *Singin' in the Rain*?
20   Which 50s star became Princess Grace of Monaco?
21   Which singer joined Frank Sinatra to be in *High Society*?
22   In which country was Sophia Loren born?
23   Which Doris played Calamity Jane?
24   Who did Charlton Heston play in *The Ten Commandments*?
25   Which pop idol appeared in *Jailhouse Rock*?

Answers Pot Luck 28 (see Quiz 71)
1 *All the President's Men.* **2** Hopkins. **3** 1950s. **4** *Buster.* **5** Bacall. **6** Johnny
Depp. **7** *The Lost World.* **8** Kelly. **9** Norman Bates. **10** Carnal. **11** Chimney
sweep. **12** Steve Martin. **13** Oprah Winfrey. **14** Emma Thompson. **15** Edinburgh.
16 Picnic. **17** *The Wizard of Oz.* **18** Zorro. **19** *Funny Girl.* **20** Johnny. **21** To
Town. **22** *Carousel.* **23** England. **24** Bryan Adams. **25** 1980s.

Answers – see page 80

1   Who won Best Director for *Braveheart* which Mel Gibson starred in?
2   Who played the title role in *Evita* whose only Oscar was for the song 'You Must Love Me'?
3   Who was the youngest Oscar nominee at the year 2000 ceremony?
4   Who won Best Actress for *Kitty Foyle* after finding fame as Fred Astaire's dancing partner?
5   Who won a Special Oscar for Outstanding Contribution aged six?
6   Which cat and mouse won Best Short Cartoon in 1943?
7   Which Bob received an honorary award in 1952 for his contribution to comedy?
8   Who played Maria von Trapp in the highest-grossing Oscar-winning musical of the 1960s?
9   'The Madness of' which king earned a nomination for Alan Bennett?
10   Who refused to attend the Oscar ceremony to receive his Best Actor award for *The Godfather*?
11   For playing which Shirley was Pauline Collins Oscar-nominated?
12   Who won Best Supporting Actress for one of the Kramers?
13   Mickey Rooney won an honorary award in 1982 for two, three, four or five decades of movie making?
14   Who starred with Gromit in *A Close Shave*?
15   Which Extra Terrestrial won a Best Visual Effects award for its creators?
16   What sort of worker's daughter gave Sissy Spacek a 1980 Oscar?
17   In which decade did John Williams win for the score of *Star Wars*?
18   Who was Oscar-nominated for his first movie *Citizen Kane*?
19   Ingrid Bergman was a winner for 'Murder on' which luxury train?
20   Which moustache-wearing Marx won an honorary award in 1973?
21   Which George, famous for *Star Wars*, won a special award in 1991?
22   Which Steven directed *Schindler's List*?
23   Which Quentin contributed to the original screenplay of *Pulp Fiction*?
24   Whose 'Ragtime Band' was nominated in 1938?
25   Which shark movie won a music Oscar for composer John Williams?

Answers 1980s (see Quiz 72)
1 *Arthur*. 2 Chelsea. 3 Private. 4 *Return of the Jedi*. 5 Wall Street. 6 Eastwick.
7 American. 8 China. 9 Lethal. 10 French. 11 Twins. 12 Vietnam.
13 *Superman II*. 14 Australia. 15 Three. 16 *9 to 5*. 17 Conan. 18 Twice.
19 Beverley Hills. 20 Cambodia (Kampuchea). 21 Blues Brothers. 22 Prizzi's.
23 Bull. 24 Susan. 25 The Empire.

Answers – see page 77

1   Reporters Woodward and Bernstein featured in which movie?
2   Which Anthony starred in *The Elephant Man*?
3   In which decade was *Room at the Top* released?
4   Which movie did the song 'A Groovy Kind of Love' come from?
5   Which Lauren was married to Humphrey Bogart?
6   *Edward Scissorhands* and *What's Eating Gilbert Grape?* both feature which actor?
7   What was Steven Spielberg's follow-up to *Jurassic Park* called?
8   Which Gene starred in *Singin' in the Rain*?
9   What is the name of the psychopath in *Psycho*?
10   Which word goes before 'Knowledge' in a Jack Nicholson movie title?
11   What was the profession of Dick van Dyke in *Mary Poppins*?
12   Which actor links *Parenthood* and *Father of the Bride*?
13   Which chat show presenter was Oscar-nominated for *The Color Purple*?
14   Who was the female star of *Junior*?
15   In which city was *Trainspotting* set?
16   In the movie title, what was held 'at Hanging Rock'?
17   Which musical movie features a dog called Toto?
18   Which hero left a trademark letter Z behind him?
19   Fanny Brice is a character in which 60s Barbra Streisand movie?
20   In a Michelle Pfeiffer movie title, who partnered Frankie?
21   Where does Mr Deeds go, according to the film title?
22   The song 'You'll Never Walk Alone' features in which musical movie?
23   In which country was Cary Grant born?
24   Who sang 'Everything I Do (I Do it for You)' in *Robin Hood: Prince of Thieves*?
25   In which decade was *Arthur* released?

Answers 1950s Stars (see Quiz 69)
1 Rosemary Clooney. 2 James Dean. 3 Errol Flynn. 4 Doris Day. 5 Frank Sinatra.
6 Judy Garland. 7 Lee. 8 The Tramp. 9 *Ben Hur*. 10 Lemmon. 11 Kaye.
12 Vincent Price. 13 Novak. 14 French. 15 Dean Martin. 16 Marilyn Monroe.
17 Taylor. 18 Peck. 19 Umbrella. 20 Grace Kelly. 21 Bing Crosby. 22 Italy.
23 Day. 24 Moses. 25 Elvis Presley.

Answers – see page 78

1   What was the name of the Dudley Moore movie where he played womanizer Arthur Bach?

2   Which daughter of Bill Clinton shares her name with Jane Fonda's character in *On Golden Pond*?

3   What rank was Goldie Hawn as army recruit Judy Benjamin?

4   The film originally called *Revenge of the Jedi* was changed to what?

5   On which famous financial New York thoroughfare does the movie with Michael Douglas and Charlie Sheen take place?

6   Where were 'The Witches' in the film with Michelle Pfeiffer and Cher?

7   What nationality 'Gigolo' was Richard Gere in 1980?

8   *The Last Emperor* is set in which now-communist Asian country?

9   What type of 'Weapon' did Mel Gibson wield in the movie with Danny Glover?

10   Which 18th century revolution was the setting for *Dangerous Liaisons*?

11   What close relations were Arnold Schwarzenegger and Danny De Vito in the 1988 hit movie?

12   Which country follows 'Good Morning' in the title of the Robin Williams movie?

13   What was the sequel to *Superman* called?

14   Crocodile Dundee comes to New York from which country?

15   How many men looked after the baby in the Tom Selleck hit of 1987?

16   Which hours were Jane Fonda and Dolly Parton working in 1980?

17   Who was 'the Barbarian' played by Arnold Schwarzenegger in 1981?

18   'The Postman Always Rings' how many times in the Jack Nicholson/Jessica Lange movie?

19   Where did Eddie Murphy's Detroit cop operate in the 1984 movie?

20   *The Killing Fields* were in which South-East Asian country?

21   What sort of 'Brothers' were Dan Aykroyd and John Belushi in 1980?

22   Which family's 'Honor' is the subject of a John Huston movie with Jack Nicholson and John's daughter Anjelica?

23   Jake La Motta's story was told in 'Raging' what?

24   A hit man is 'Desperately Seeking' whom in 1985?

25   What 'Strikes Back' in the sequel to *Star Wars*?

Answers Oscars – Who's Who? (see Quiz 70)

1 Mel Gibson. 2 Madonna. 3 Haley Joel Osment. 4 Ginger Rogers. 5 Shirley Temple. 6 Tom & Jerry. 7 Hope. 8 Julie Andrews. 9 George. 10 Marlon Brando. 11 Valentine. 12 Meryl Streep. 13 Five. 14 Wallace. 15 *E.T.* 16 *The Coal Miner's Daughter*. 17 1970s. 18 Orson Welles. 19 Orient Express. 20 Groucho. 21 Lucas. 22 Spielberg. 23 Tarantino. 24 Alexander's. 25 *Jaws*.

Answers – see page 83

1   What colour was Uma Thurman's hair in *Pulp Fiction*?
2   In which decade was *Doctor Zhivago* released?
3   Which Rob starred in *Wayne's World*?
4   Who is the central character in *Good Will Hunting*?
5   *Face/Off*, *Snake Eyes* and *Honeymoon in Vegas* all feature which actor?
6   W. C. Dunkenfield kept his first two initials to become who?
7   Which Hitchcock-directed movie had 'Window' in the title?
8   Which John starred in *The Blues Brothers*?
9   In a musical movie, which number links brides and brothers?
10 Which 1998 movie featured a giant lizard and Matthew Broderick?
11 Which actor was the father of Jeff and Beau Bridges?
12 Which actress Jane married CNN chief Ted Turner?
13 In which animated film does Shere Khan appear?
14 How many millimetres was the standard film gauge width?
15 What was the nationality of Ingrid Bergman?
16 *Lady Sings the Blues* told the life of which Billie?
17 Which Ralph was an *English Patient* Oscar nominee?
18 In which decade was *Indiana Jones and the Last Crusade* released?
19 Who was the male lead in *Casablanca*?
20 Which Hepburn had a cameo role in Spielberg's *Always*?
21 Which Antonio starred in *Evita*?
22 Does *The Color Purple* last between 1 and 2, 2 and 3, or 3 and 4 hours?
23 Who played the lead role in *Lawrence of Arabia* after Albert Finney turned it down?
24 *Look Who's Talking Too* was a sequel to which movie?
25 In which decade of the 20th century was Kurt Russell born?

Answers – see page 84

1   Which Michael won the Best Actor Oscar for *Wall Street*?
2   Who did Stanley Kaufmann say should be called Barbra Strident?
3   What is the name of Casey Affleck's actor brother?
4   Who was Shirley MacLaine named after?
5   Which surname was shared by dad Lloyd and sons Beau and Jeff?
6   Which 'Poison' plant name did Uma Thurman have in *Batman and Robin*?
7   Which Richard played the Spice Girls' manager in *Spiceworld: The Movie*?
8   Who played his namesake Woody Boyd in *Cheers*?
9   How is Mary Elizabeth Spacek better known?
10 Who did Al Pacino play in *Frankie and Johnny*?
11 What was the name of Jane Fonda's actor father?
12 Which Elizabeth – as famous for her frocks as for her films – starred in *Austin Powers, International Man of Mystery*?
13 How is Edward Bridge Danson III better known?
14 Which Daniel won an Oscar for *My Left Foot* in 1989?
15 What is the name of the actress daughter of actor Bruce Dern?
16 Which Danny, of *Junior* and *Twins* fame, married Rhea Perlman?
17 In which decade of the 20th century was Tom Cruise born?
18 What colour did Yul Brynner wear for the last 40 years of his life, to make shopping easier?
19 Who did Vanessa Redgrave play in the biopic *Agatha*?
20 What was the first name of Abbott, of Abbott and Costello fame?
21 Which Rebecca was the nanny from hell in *The Hand that Rocks the Cradle*?
22 In which country was Catherine Deneuve born?
23 How is Alicia Foster better know?
24 Which surname is shared by actors Rosanna, Patricia, David and Alexis?
25 At what sport did Arnold Schwarzenegger excel?

Answers Pot Luck 30 (see Quiz 76)
1 Steven Spielberg. **2** Scott Thomas. **3** 1970s. **4** Elvis Presley. **5** Mary Shelley. **6** Dalmatians. **7** Humphrey Bogart. **8** Meg Ryan. **9** Dr Dolittle. **10** B. **11** The Riddler. **12** *Romeo and Juliet*. **13** *Nashville*. **14** Al Pacino. **15** *The Boston Strangler*. **16** 2001. **17** Keaton. **18** Itch. **19** Body builder. **20** Prisoner (*The Prisoner of Zenda*). **21** 1960s. **22** *Mad Max Beyond The Thunderdome*. **23** John Travolta. **24** Nanny. **25** Barrymore.

Answers – see page 81

1. Robert Redford won a university scholarship in which American sport?
2. Which Jeremiah was the subject of a 1972 film?
3. Which Katharine was a co-star in *Butch Cassidy*?
4. What sort of 'People' were in the title of his directorial debut in 1980?
5. In which gambling capital is *Indecent Proposal* set?
6. How many 'Days of the Condor' were in the title of the 1975 film?
7. In which state, capital Salt Lake City, is his Sundance Institute?
8. In which movie with Paul Newman did Redford first find fame?
9. He was 'Out of' where in the 1985 movie with Meryl Streep?
10. Redford was born in Santa Monica in which west-coast state?
11. Which Barbra played opposite Redford in *The Way We Were*?
12. In which decade did he make *The Candidate*?
13. Which animal is named in the 'Whisperer' title of his 1998 success?
14. In *All the President's Men* which President is being referred to?
15. In which decade of the Depression was *The Sting* set?
16. To which Moore did he make an *Indecent Proposal* in 1993?
17. In 1996 Redford was 'Up Close and' what in the movie?
18. Which Mary did he direct in *Ordinary People*?
19. In *Butch Cassidy and the Sundance Kid* which part did Redford play?
20. In *All the President's Men* the journalists worked for which Washington newspaper?
21. Which 1974 movie saw him as Jay Gatsby?
22. What colour is Redford's hair?
23. Redford was 'Barefoot in the' what in the movie with Jane Fonda based on a Neil Simon play?
24. What sort of 'Show 'earned him an Oscar-nomination in 1994?
25. Which 'Legal' birds were in the title of his 1986 movie?

Answers Pot Luck 29 (see Quiz 73)
1 Black. **2** 1960s. **3** Lowe. **4** Will Hunting. **5** Nicolas Cage. **6** W. C. Fields.
7 *Rear Window*. **8** Belushi. **9** Seven (*Seven Brides for Seven Brothers*). **10** *Godzilla*.
11 Lloyd Bridges. **12** Fonda. **13** *Jungle Book*. **14** 35. **15** Swedish. **16** Holliday.
17 Fiennes. **18** 1980s. **19** Humphrey Bogart. **20** Audrey. **21** Banderas.
22 2 and 3. **23** Peter O'Toole. **24** *Look Who's Talking*. **25** 1950s.

Answers – see page 82

1   Who directed *Schindler's List*?
2   Which Kristin starred in *The Horse Whisperer*?
3   In which decade was *Moonraker* released?
4   Who sang the title song of *Jailhouse Rock*?
5   Which writer created the character Frankenstein?
6   In a movie title there were 101 what?
7   Who won the Best Actor Oscar for *The African Queen*?
8   Which star actress was in *When Harry Met Sally*, *Courage Under Fire* and *French Kiss*?
9   The song 'Talk to the Animals' features in which movie?
10   Which initial featured in Cecil de Mille's name?
11   In *Batman Forever* which villain was played by Jim Carrey?
12   Which 90s film of a Shakespeare play starred Leonardo DiCaprio?
13   Which 70s film was also the name a Tennessee town famous for its music?
14   Which Al won Best Actor Oscar for *Scent of a Woman*?
15   The character Albert DeSalvo appeared in which murder movie?
16   What year was 'A Space Odyssey' for Stanley Kubrick?
17   Which Michael starred in *Batman Returns*?
18   Marilyn Monroe starred in 'The Seven Year' what?
19   What did Arnold Schwarzeneger play in *Stay Hungry*?
20   In a movie title, what type of person was found in Zenda?
21   In which decade of the 20th century was Keanu Reeves born?
22   Which mid 80s film did rock star Tina Turner star in?
23   *Saturday Night Fever*, *Get Shorty* and *Phenomenon* all feature which actor?
24   What was the profession of Mrs Doubtfire?
25   Which Drew starred in *E.T.*?

Answers Famous Names (see Quiz 74)
1 Douglas. 2 Barbra Streisand. 3 Ben. 4 Shirley Temple. 5 Bridges. 6 Ivy. 7 E. Grant. 8 Woody Harrelson. 9 Sissy Spacek. 10 Johnny. 11 Henry. 12 Hurley. 13 Ted Danson. 14 Day-Lewis. 15 Laura Dern. 16 DeVito. 17 1960s. 18 Black. 19 Agatha Christie. 20 Bud. 21 De Mornay. 22 France. 23 Jodie Foster. 24 Arquette. 25 Weightlifting.

Answers – see page 87

1	What was the highest grossing film of the 1990s?
2	Who wrote the first *Rocky* movie as well as starring in it?
3	Which member of the Sheen family was Bud Fox in *Wall Street*?
4	Which 1977 smash hit was re-released 20 years later?
5	*Goodfellas* was about which organization?
6	*Babe* was the tale of a pig which wanted to be a what?
7	Which Cecil directed *The Greatest Show on Earth*?
8	Which British Bob found himself with a cartoon rabbit co-star in 1988?
9	Which Tom Hanks movie was the fourth most successful in the US in 1994?
10	Which 'Day' took $104.3 million in its first week in 1996?
11	Which Spielberg war movie was the most successful of the 1990s?
12	The *Men in Black* operated in which city?
13	Who wrote the George Lucas-directed *Star Wars*?
14	Which movie about the Kennedy assassination has just three letters in its title?
15	Which film set in Africa was Disney's most successful ever when it was released in 1994?
16	R2-D2 and C-3PO were in which film series?
17	*The Longest Day* was about which landings?
18	Which 1930s movie has been showing in Atlanta ever since it was released?
19	What colour suit did John Travolta wear in the disco in *Saturday Night Fever*?
20	Which character looks back in *Titanic*?
21	Lara's Theme was from which movie set in Russia?
22	Which Robert Altman movie was a smash, though set in the dark days of the Korean War?
23	Which movie included 'A Spoonful of Sugar' and 'Feed the Birds'?
24	Which Newman/Redford hit used Scott Joplin ragtime tunes?
25	Sensurround was used to add impact to which natural disaster movie?

Answers – see page 88

1   Which actor Reeves starred in *Bill and Ted's Excellent Adventure*?
2   What sort of creatures run amok in *Jurassic Park*?
3   *E.T.* arrived in a suburb of which Californian city?
4   Where were Gary Oldman and William Hurt 'Lost' in 1998?
5   Which Bruce faced *Armageddon* in 1998?
6   Which 1998 movie featured TV's Mulder and Scully?
7   What sort of giant reptile was Godzilla?
8   Which special day in the USA was the subject of a 1996 movie with Will Smith?
9   Which Judge was played by Sylvester Stallone in 1995?
10 Which Rick 'Shrunk the Kids'?
11 'Close Encounters of' which kind were a 1977 Spielberg success?
12 What was the name of the Princess in *Star Wars*?
13 'The Planet of' which creatures starred Charlton Heston in 1968?
14 The time-travelling hero of the *Highlander* movies came from which part of the UK?
15 *Aliens* was the sequel to which 1979 movie?
16 Which pop superstar David starred in *Labyrinth*?
17 In which decade was *Jurassic Park* released?
18 Which 1985 Terry Gilliam movie takes its name from a South American country famous for its coffee?
19 Which 'Runner' starred Harrison Ford?
20 Which Barrymore played Gertie in *E.T.*?
21 Which Lois is played by Margot Kidder in *Superman*?
22 Tommy Lee Jones and Will Smith were 'Men in' what colour?
23 In which 'Motion Picture' did Mr Spock get a big-screen outing?
24 What colour is Superman's cape in the movies with Christopher Reeve?
25 Which Matthew played Dr Niko Tatopoulos in *Godzilla*?

Answers 1970s Stars (see Quiz 80)
1 Bo Derek. **2** Reynolds. **3** Carrie Fisher. **4** Clint Eastwood. **5** Mental hospital.
6 *Jaws 2*. **7** Ross. **8** Lee. **9** Sutherland. **10** Harvey. **11** McQueen. **12** Marlon Brando. **13** Dustin Hoffman. **14** Woody Allen. **15** Superman. **16** Taxi.
17 Newton-John **18** Tatum O'Neal. **19** Martin. **20** Australia **21** De Niro.
22 Sigourney Weaver. **23** Monty Python. **24** Michael Douglas. **25** Moore.

Answers – see page 85

1   Which former partner of Mick Jagger appeared in *Batman*?
2   Which John starred in *Face/Off*?
3   Which word completes the film title, *Monty Python's the ___ of Life*?
4   Which Zorro film was released in 1998?
5   What was Richard Curtis's next Hugh Grant movie after *Four Weddings and a Funeral*?
6   Which Jessica starred in *Tootsie*?
7   Which Randy wrote the music for *James and the Giant Peach*?
8   Who was 'Versus the Volcano' in a Meg Ryan movie?
9   Which Olivia, star of *Grease*, appeared in the less successful *Xanadu*?
10 *The Nutty Professor* and *Doctor Dolittle* both feature which actor?
11 Was Irving Thalberg in his 20s, 30s or 40s when he died in the 1930s?
12 Which brothers enjoyed *A Night at the Opera*?
13 In which decade of the 20th century was Meg Ryan born?
14 In which decade was *Terminator 2: Judgment Day* released?
15 Which actress links *E.T.* and *Scream*?
16 Which word follows 'Tequila' in a Michelle Pfeiffer movie title?
17 Which former 007 played a Scottish villain in *The Avengers*?
18 Who directed *Blazing Saddles*?
19 What is the popular name of the annual awards presented by the Academy of Motion Picture Arts and Sciences?
20 Who played the female lead in *Sophie's Choice*?
21 In *The Pink Panther*, Peter Sellers is an inspector in which country?
22 Ingrid Bergman and Judy Garland have had what type of flower named after them?
23 What did the man do to Liberty Valance, according to the film title?
24 Which Leonard starred in *Star Trek: The Motion Picture*?
25 In which decade was *Bullitt* released?

Answers Box Office Successes (see Quiz 77)
1 *Titanic*. 2 Sylvester Stallone. 3 Charlie. 4 *Star Wars*. 5 The Mafia. 6 Sheepdog. 7 B. de Mille. 8 Hoskins. 9 *Forrest Gump*. 10 *Independence Day*. 11 *Saving Private Ryan*. 12 New York. 13 George Lucas. 14 *JFK*. 15 *The Lion King*. 16 *Star Wars*. 17 D-Day Landings. 18 *Gone with the Wind*. 19 White. 20 Rose. 21 *Dr Zhivago*. 22 *M*A*S*H*. 23 *Mary Poppins*. 24 *The Sting*. 25 *Earthquake*.

Answers – see page 86

1   Which actress starred in *10* with Dudley Moore?

2   Which Burt was a 70s hit star but filed for bankruptcy 20 years later?

3   Which daughter of Eddie Fisher and Debbie Reynolds found fame in *Star Wars*?

4   Which star of spaghetti westerns appeared as *The Outlaw Josey Wales*?

5   In what type of hospital is *One Flew over the Cuckoo's Nest* set?

6   What was the sequel to *Jaws* called?

7   Which Supreme Diana starred in *Lady Sings the Blues*?

8   Which horror movie star Christopher played Scaramanga in *The Man with the Golden Gun*?

9   Which Donald, father of Kiefer, played opposite Julie Christie in *Don't Look Now*?

10   What is the first name of Mr Keitel who played Charlie in *Mean Streets*?

11   Which Steve starred opposite future real-life wife Ali McGraw in *Getaway*?

12   Who played the head of the Corleone family in *The Godfather*?

13   Which actor suffers in the dentist's chair in *Marathon Man*?

14   Which bespectacled American directed and starred in *Annie Hall*?

15   Which cartoon character was played by Christopher Reeve?

16   What type of 'Driver' was Robert De Niro in 1976?

17   Which Olivia played Sandy in *Grease*?

18   Which child star was dubbed 'Tantrum' O'Neal?

19   Which member of the Sheen family starred in *Apocalypse Now* in '79?

20   In which country was US-born Mel Gibson brought up?

21   Which New Yorker Robert famously said, 'You talkin' to me?'?

22   Who was the lead actress in *Alien*?

23   Which comedy team which included John Cleese made the *Life Of Brian*?

24   Which son of actor Kirk starred in *The China Syndrome*?

25   Which Roger was the most frequent James Bond in the 70s?

Answers – see page 91

1   Which Anne starred in the 1998 *Great Expectations*?
2   *The Witches of Eastwick* and *Up Close and Personal* both feature which actress?
3   Which Shirley won an Oscar at the age of five?
4   In which show is Mr Burbank a popular character?
5   Which word follows 'Last Action' in a Sharon Stone movie title?
6   What is the nationality of Brigitte Nielsen, Sylvester Stallone's second wife?
7   Which Joe starred in *Home Alone*?
8   What is the name of the male cub in *The Lion King*?
9   Marni Nixon dubbed whose singing voice in *My Fair Lady*?
10   Which word follows 'Dog Day' in an Al Pacino movie title?
11   Which Gary starred in *High Noon*?
12   Which crime writer did Vanessa Redgrave play in *Agatha*?
13   Which Richard starred in *Close Encounters of the Third Kind*?
14   The song 'If I Were a Rich Man' features in which musical movie?
15   In which decade was *Raiders of the Lost Ark* released?
16   Commandant Goeth appears in which movie?
17   Which superhero gets involved with Lois Laine?
18   Which actress links *The Rose* and *Get Shorty*?
19   *Braveheart* was set in which country?
20   Which Donald starred in *Halloween*?
21   Who played the lead role in *My Fair Lady* after Cary Grant refused it?
22   Which actress co-launched the Planet Hollywood restaurant chain?
23   Which word completes the film title *The Shawshank ___*?
24   In which decade of the 20th century was Roger Moore born?
25   Which Sally featured in *Forrest Gump*?

Answers Musicals (see Quiz 83)
1 Argentina. **2** Travolta. **3** Gene. **4** Penguins. **5** Pink Floyd. **6** *West Side Story*.
7 *Grease*. **8** *The Rocky Horror Picture Show*. **9** *Paint Your Wagon*. **10** Louis
Armstrong. **11** John Travolta. **12** Yellow. **13** Omar Sharif. **14** The Beatles.
15 *Calamity Jane*. **16** *Mary Poppins*. **17** *The King and I*. **18** New York.
19 Harrison. **20** Maurice Chevalier. **21** Austria. **22** *Funny Girl*. **23** Ross.
24 Show Business. **25** The Bee Gees.

Answers – see page 92

1   Chaplin said all he needed to make a movie was a park, a policeman and a pretty what?

2   What type of hat did the Little Tramp wear?

3   Which company famous for its crazy cops was Chaplin invited to join?

4   What was the first name of Mr Karno, with whose troupe Chaplin first went to the USA?

5   What was Chaplin's middle name, shared by Winston Churchill?

6   Which Mack first employed Chaplin in the movies?

7   Chaplin's debut movie was called 'Making a' what?

8   Which United company did he found in 1919 with three other stars of the silent movie era?

9   Which 'Rush' did he film in 1925?

10   Which actress Paulette did he marry in 1933?

11   Of his four wives, how many were in their teens when he married them?

12   Where was Chaplin referring to when he said 'I'd never go back there if Jesus Christ was President.'?

13   What was the name of the biopic directed by Richard Attenborough?

14   'A Countess from' where was the title of a 60s Chaplin movie?

15   Who wrote most of the musical score for *City Lights*?

16   *The Great Dictator* was made during which conflict?

17   Which Buster teamed up with Chaplin in *Limelight*?

18   What relation is actress Geraldine Chaplin to Charlie?

19   In which decade of the 20th century did Chaplin die at the age of 88?

20   Which 'Modern' film was a satire on the industrialization of society?

21   In which British city was Chaplin born?

22   Which name is shared by his half-brother and his son – both performers?

23   Which member of his family played the part of his mother in the 1992 movie about his life?

24   What did the Tramp carry and twirl in his hand?

25   His fourth wife Oona O'Neill was the daughter of which playwright?

Answers Pot Luck 33 (see Quiz 84)
1 Arnold Schwarzenegger. 2 The Muppets. 3 Foster. 4 *America*. 5 New York. 6 'Colors of the Wind'. 7 *Waterworld*. 8 Field. 9 Lon Chaney. 10 A London tube train. 11 Barbra Streisand. 12 Francis Ford Coppola. 13 King Arthur. 14 Dead. 15 TV journalist. 16 In Paris. 17 Brooks. 18 1960s. 19 Astaire. 20 Marilyn Monroe. 21 Nicholson. 22 'Goldeneye'. 23 The Righteous Brothers. 24 1970s. 25 The Flintstones.

Answers – see page 89

1. In which country does the action of *Evita* take place?
2. Which John starred in *Grease* in 1978?
3. Which Kelly directed *Hello Dolly*?
4. Which Antarctic creatures feature in *Mary Poppins*?
5. Which 'Pink' band made the movie *The Wall*?
6. In which movie based on *Romeo and Juliet* did Richard Beymer play Tony?
7. Which movie featured the song 'Greased Lightning'?
8. In which 'Picture Show' does Frank N. Furter appear?
9. In which western musical did Lee Marvin sing 'Wandrin' Star'?
10. Which jazz trumpeter nicknamed Satchmo appeared in *High Society*?
11. Who played Tony Manero in *Saturday Night Fever*?
12. What colour submarine was a Beatles classic?
13. Which bridge-playing actor played Mr Arnstein in *Funny Girl*?
14. Which 60s pop band's second movie was *Help!*?
15. 'Secret Love' won Best Song Oscar from which 'Calamity' film?
16. 'Chim Chim Cheree' came from which movie about a super-nanny?
17. Which musical was banned in Thailand for most of the latter half of the 20th century?
18. *West Side Story* takes place on the west side of which city?
19. Which Rex reprised his Broadway role as Professor Higgins in the movie *My Fair Lady*?
20. Which French star wrote an autobiography called *I Remember It Well*?
21. *The Sound of Music* was set in which country?
22. Which 1968 film with Barbra Streisand was about Fanny Brice?
23. Which Diana played Dorothy in *The Wiz*?
24. According to Irving Berlin's musical 'There's No Business Like' what?
25. Which pop brothers wrote the music for *Saturday Night Fever*?

Answers – see page 90

1. *Eraser*, *The Terminator* and *Last Action Hero* all feature which actor?
2. Which band of puppets featured in their own *Christmas Carol*?
3. Which Jodie starred in *Silence of the Lambs*?
4. Which country completes the film title, *Once Upon a Time in ____*?
5. In which city was Robert De Niro a sinister *Taxi Driver*?
6. Which song won Best Song Oscar for *Pocahontas*?
7. In which ill-fated movie did Kevin Kostner play Mariner?
8. Which Sally featured in *Smokey and the Bandit*?
9. Which horror film actor was nicknamed 'the man of a thousand faces'?
10. In *Sliding Doors* the sliding doors were part of what?
11. Who got her first starring role in *Funny Girl*?
12. Who won the Best Director Oscar for *The Godfather, Part II*?
13. The film musical *Camelot* involves which King?
14. In a movie title which word goes in front of 'Poets' Society'?
15. What was the profession of Schwarzenegger's wife?
16. In a movie title, where did the 'Last Tango' take place?
17. Which director Mel did Anne Bancroft marry?
18. In which decade of the 20th century was Eddie Murphy born?
19. Which famous movie Fred is on the cover of *Sergeant Pepper*?
20. Who was the most famous blonde in *Gentlemen Prefer Blondes*?
21. Which Jack starred in *A Few Good Men*?
22. What was the Bond theme for *Goldeneye* called?
23. Who sang 'Unchained Melody' in *Ghost*?
24. In which decade was *Love Story* released?
25. Which family lives in Bedrock?

Answers Charlie Chaplin (see Quiz 82)
1 Girl. **2** Bowler. **3** Keystone. **4** Fred. **5** Spencer. **6** Sennett. **7** Living. **8** United Artists. **9** *The Gold Rush*. **10** Goddard. **11** All four. **12** America. **13** *Chaplin*. **14** Hong Kong. **15** Chaplin himself. **16** World War II. **17** Keaton. **18** Daughter. **19** 1970s. **20** *Modern Times*. **21** London. **22** Sydney. **23** His daughter Geraldine. **24** Cane. **25** Eugene O'Neill.

Answers – see page 95

1	Which Katharine won most Best Actress Oscars in the 20th century?
2	Which Gwyneth dissolved in tears at the 1998 ceremony?
3	Which Jessica was the oldest Best Actress of the 20th century?
4	What was the first 1990s movie which made Jodie Foster a winner?
5	Which pop star won with *Moonstruck*?
6	Whose 'Choice' made Meryl Streep a 1982 winner?
7	Which Kathy played the crazed fan from hell in *Misery*?
8	Which British politician Glenda won two Oscars?
9	Which child star won a special award in 1934 aged six?
10	Which daughter of Ryan O'Neal was the first 10-year-old to win a Best Supporting award in her own right?
11	Which daughter of Judy Garland won for *Cabaret* in 1972?
12	In which decade did Louise Fletcher win for *One Flew Over the Cuckoo's Nest*?
13	Which Jane won twice in the 70s for *Klute* and *Coming Home*?
14	Was Katharine Hepburn in her 50s, 60s, 70s or 80s when she won for *On Golden Pond*?
15	Which star of *Sister Act* was Best Supporting Actress for *Ghost*?
16	In *Dead Man Walking* what was Susan Sarandon's profession?
17	How many times was Jodie Foster Best Supporting Actress in the 90s?
18	Who won for her title role in *Mary Poppins*?
19	Which Ellen was a winner for *Alice Doesn't Live Here Any More*?
20	Which musical instrument gave Holly Hunter a 1993 award?
21	What colour 'Sky' was the title of Jessica Lange's 1994 winner?
22	What is the nationality of Juliette Binoche, a winner for *The English Patient*?
23	Who got a Best Actress Oscar in the 90s without speaking?
24	Which member of the Huston dynasty won Best Supporting role for *Prizzi's Honor*?
25	For which movie did Vivien Leigh win Best Actress and Hattie McDaniel win Best Supporting Actress?

Answers Pot Luck 34 (see Quiz 87)
1 Gwyneth Paltrow. 2 Foster. 3 1960s. 4 A nun. 5 Francis Ford Coppola.
6 Humphrey Bogart. 7 Bank clerk. 8 Bridget. 9 Elizabeth I. 10 Pierce Brosnan.
11 *Annie Get Your Gun.* 12 Archaeologist. 13 Instinct. 14 Tatum O'Neal.
15 Turtles. 16 Madonna. 17 Willis. 18 Jodie Foster. 19 1960s. 20 Her hair.
21 Stephen Fry. 22 His valet. 23 James Cagney. 24 George Clooney. 25 *Wax.*

Answers – see page 96

1   How was Alonzo Chaney, the man with a thousand faces, better known?
2   Which Mary was one of the first female film stars?
3   Which child star Jackie starred with Chaplin in *The Kid*?
4   Where was Rudolph Valentino born?
5   What was the first name of British-born actor Colman?
6   What was the surname of Pearl who appeared in *The Perils of Pauline*?
7   What was larger-than-life Roscoe Arbuckle's nickname?
8   What was the first name of actor Von Stroheim?
9   Although born in Canada, Mary Pickford was known as which country's sweetheart?
10 What was the surname of John, Ethel and Lionel?
11 How was Joseph Francis Keaton better known?
12 Which United company did Chaplin, Griffith, Fairbanks and Pickford found?
13 What type of star was Rin Tin Tin?
14 Which John partnered Garbo on and off screen?
15 Which Clara was called the 'It' Girl?
16 Which Charlie was discovered by Mack Sennett?
17 Which part of the skyscraper tower did Harold Lloyd hang from in the famous *Safety Last*?
18 Which Mack helped set up the Keystone Company?
19 Which master of animation founded Laugh O Gram Films in 1922?
20 What was the first name of the high-living actress Miss Normand?
21 Which Joan made her screen debut in 1925?
22 Who was born Greta Louisa Gustaffson?
23 Which Douglas made his screen debut in 1915?
24 Which Stan and Ollie graduated to sound after success in the silent era?
25 What was the first name of Miss Gish who starred in *The White Sister*?

Answers 1990s (see Quiz 88)
1 Will. 2 *Ace Ventura*. 3 Fortune. 4 Louise. 5 Robin Hood. 6 Dracula.
7 Swayze. 8 Dogs. 9 *Jurassic Park*. 10 Indecent. 11 Seattle. 12 World War II.
13 *Peter Pan*. 14 Roberts. 15 Antonio Banderas. 16 Innocent. 17 Elizabeth.
18 *Terminator 2*. 19 President Kennedy. 20 *Look Who's Talking Too*. 21 Addams
family. 22 Scissorhands. 23 Tomatoes. 24 The Edge. 25 *The Doors*.

Answers – see page 93

1   Which star actress was in *Hook, Great Expectations* and *Emma*?
2   Which Jodie starred in *Nell*?
3   In which decade of the 20th century was Demi Moore born?
4   In *Sister Act* what was Whoopi Goldberg disguised as?
5   Who directed *Apocalypse Now*?
6   *Bogey's Baby* was a biography of the wife of which movie star?
7   In *The Mask* the central character worked as what type of clerk?
8   Which Fonda is Peter's daughter?
9   Which Queen appears in *Shakespeare in Love*?
10   Which James Bond actor starred in *Dante's Peak*?
11   Which musical was sharpshooter Annie Oakley the subject of?
12   What is the profession of Indiana Jones in the adventure movies?
13   Which word follows 'Basic' in a Michael Douglas movie title?
14   Which actress became Mrs John McEnroe in the 1980s?
15   What type of creatures were Donatello, Raphael, Michaelangelo and Leonardo?
16   Which singer/actress married Sean Penn in 1985?
17   Which Bruce starred in *The Fifth Element*?
18   Who won the Best Actress Oscar for *The Silence of the Lambs*?
19   In which decade was *My Fair Lady* released?
20   What did Demi Moore have removed to make *G.I. Jane*?
21   Who played the title role in the 1997 movie *Wilde*?
22   Which member of Arthur's staff was played by John Gielgud in *Arthur*?
23   Who won the Best Actor Oscar for *Yankee Doodle Dandy*?
24   Who starred in *Batman and Robin* after finding fame in TV's *ER*?
25   Which word completes the film title, *Mystery of the ____ Museum*?

Answers Oscars – Best Actresses (see Quiz 85)
1 Hepburn. **2** Paltrow. **3** Tandy. **4** *The Silence of the Lambs*. **5** Cher. **6** Sophie's.
7 Bates. **8** Jackson. **9** Shirley Temple. **10** Tatum O'Neal. **11** Liza Minnelli.
12 1970s. **13** Fonda. **14** 70s. **15** Whoopi Goldberg. **16** Nun. **17** Never.
18 Julie Andrews. **19** Burstyn. **20** *The Piano*. **21** Blue. **22** French. **23** Holly
Hunter (*The Piano*). **24** Anjelica. **25** *Gone with the Wind*.

Answers – see page 94

1   Which 'Good' person was 'Hunting' in the movie with Matt Damon?
2   Which 'Pet Detective' movie was Jim Carrey's big break?
3   Jeremy Irons starred in 'Reversal of' what?
4   Who hits the road with Thelma in the 1991 movie?
5   Which hero was 'Prince of Thieves' in the Kevin Costner movie?
6   Which Bram Stoker story was filmed by Francis Ford Coppola in 1992?
7   Which Patrick was the murder victim in *Ghost*?
8   Which animal follows 'Reservoir' in the title of the movie with Harvey Keitel?
9   Which 'Park' was home to dinosaurs in 1993?
10   What type of 'Proposal' did Robert Redford make to Demi Moore?
11   Where was Tom Hanks 'Sleepless' in the romantic movie?
12   The action of *Saving Private Ryan* takes place during which war?
13   *Hook* was based on which J.M. Barrie children's story?
14   Which Julia was the *Pretty Woman* of the film with Richard Gere?
15   Which Spanish star was Che in *Evita* opposite Madonna in 1996?
16   In 1990 Harrison Ford is 'Presumed' what in the 1990 thriller?
17   Which English queen won awards for Cate Blanchett in 1999?
18   Which 1991 *Terminator* film had the subtitle 'Judgment Day'?
19   Who was the subject of the movie *JFK*?
20   What was the first sequel to *Look Who's Talking*?
21   Which ghoulish family had their own movie after first appearing in a cartoon
     strip?
22   What type of hands did Edward have in the movie with Johnny Depp?
23   What were 'Fried Green' at the Whistle Stop Café?
24   Where were 'Postcards From' in the title of the 1990 movie?
25   What was the name of the 1991 movie about The Doors and its lead singer Jim
     Morrison?

Answers Stars of The Silent Years (see Quiz 86)
1 Lon Chaney. **2** Pickford. **3** Coogan. **4** Italy. **5** Ronald. **6** White. **7** Fatty
Arbuckle. **8** Erich. **9** America's. **10** Barrymore. **11** Buster Keaton. **12** United
Artists. **13** Dog. **14** Gilbert. **15** Bow. **16** Chaplin. **17** Clock face. **18** Sennett.
19 Walt Disney. **20** Mabel. **21** Crawford. **22** Greta Garbo. **23** Fairbanks.
24 Laurel and Hardy. **25** Lilian.

Answers – see page 99

1   In which decade was *Home Alone* released?
2   What was Boris Karloff's role in *Frankenstein*?
3   Which Denise starred in *Wild Things*?
4   *Misery* is based on the novel by which writer?
5   Which word completes the film title, *Sense and ____*?
6   What is the first name of Mrs Peel in *The Avengers*?
7   Which Alec featured in *Working Girl*?
8   Which Oscar-winner based in India set a record for most extras?
9   *Saving Private Ryan* and *Philadelphia* both feature which actor?
10   Who won the Best Actress Oscar for *Klute*?
11   Which middle initial did director Alan Pakula use?
12   Michael Palin is the voice of which rodent in *The Wind in the Willows*?
13   Who are the stars of *A Grand Day Out*?
14   What were the first names of *Abbott and Costello*?
15   In which decade of the 20th century was Rob Lowe born?
16   The song 'Get Me to the Church on Time' features in which musical movie?
17   Which famous Lana tested for the role of Scarlett O'Hara?
18   According to the film title, what happened on 34th Street?
19   Who played the lead in *The Graduate* after Robert Redford refused it?
20   Which Donald starred in *Singin' in the Rain*?
21   *Enter the Dragon* was the first US kung fu film of which Mr Lee?
22   Charlie Chaplin was a founder of which United film studio?
23   In which decade was *M*A*S*H* released?
24   Which John starred in *A Fish Called Wanda*?
25   Which word completes the film title, *See No Evil, Hear No ____*?

Answers Pot Luck 36 (see Quiz 91)
1 Jack Nicholson. 2 Martin. 3 Vanities. 4 Landau. 5 Chocolates. 6 1990s.
7 Hepburn. 8 *Staircase*. 9 Winger. 10 *The Wrong Trousers*. 11 Glover.
12 King. 13 Russell. 14 1940s. 15 Cruise. 16 File. 17 Spielberg. 18 Demi
Moore. 19 Batman. 20 River Phoenix. 21 Sarandon. 22 Chicago. 23 Day.
24 *Lady*. 25 Fisher.

Answers – see page 100

1   Which movie featured Jim Carrey as Truman Burbank?
2   Which comic star Ellen starred in *Doctor Dolittle* with Eddie Murphy?
3   Which Austin was the 'International Man of Mystery'?
4   Which Mr was the subject of the 'Ultimate Disaster Movie', with Rowan Atkinson?
5   In which 1997 movie did Jim Carrey promise to tell the truth for a whole day?
6   In which Yorkshire steel town was *The Full Monty* set?
7   Which zany Jerry made the 60s version of *The Nutty Professor*?
8   Which cartoon family from Bedrock hit the big screen in 1994?
9   Who found fame as Charles in *Four Weddings and a Funeral*?
10   Which day was the subject of a 1993 movie with Bill Murray and Andie MacDowell?
11   What job does Mrs Doubtfire take on to look after 'her' own children?
12   Who received $8 million for making the sequel to *Sister Act, Sister Act 2*?
13   In 1963 what sort of precious gem was 'The Pink Panther'?
14   Whose 'World' starred Mike Myers and Dana Carvey?
15   What sort of reptiles were Donatello and Leonardo?
16   Which Morgan was *Driving Miss Daisy* in 1989?
17   The *Sliding Doors* of Gwyneth Paltrow's movie are on which type of train?
18   Who was Michelle Pfeiffer 'Married to' in the movie with Matthew Modine?
19   Who played the title role in *Tootsie*?
20   Which star of *Cabaret* appeared with Dudley Moore in *Arthur*?
21   Which country singer appeared in *9 to 5*?
22   Which 'Brothers' played by John Belushi and Dan Aykroyd were Jake and Elwood?
23   Which 1979 Woody Allen movie shares its name with a rich part of New York?
24   Which Jack was one half of *The Odd Couple*?
25   'A Funny Thing Happened on the Way to' where in 1966?

Answers Film Festivals (see Quiz 92)
1 France. **2** Berlin. **3** *Pulp Fiction*. **4** Sliding. **5** Gene. **6** Cannes. **7** Redford.
8 Golden Palm. **9** Edinburgh. **10** *Spiceworld: The Movie*. **11** *Rain Man*. **12** Hitler
invaded Poland. **13** *Michael Collins*. **14** 1960s. **15** Grand Prix. **16** Europe.
17 *Barton Fink*. **18** Collins. **19** May. **20** Grant. **21** Golden. **22** Stoppard.
23 *Pulp Fiction*. **24** Venice. **25** Burke.

Answers – see page 97

1   *A Few Good Men* and *One Flew Over the Cuckoo's Nest* featured which actor?
2   The 90s version of *Sergeant Bilko* featured which Steve?
3   Which word follows 'The Bonfire of the' in a Bruce Willis movie title?
4   Which Martin featured in *The X-Files*?
5   Forrest Gump declared that life was like a box of what?
6   In which decade was *Groundhog Day* released?
7   Which Audrey starred in *Breakfast at Tiffany's*?
8   Which word completes the film title, *The Spiral ___*?
9   Which Debra starred in *An Officer and a Gentleman*?
10 Which trousers won Nick Park an Oscar?
11 Which Danny starred in *The Color Purple*?
12 Which word title links 'Creole' and 'The Fisher' in movie titles?
13 *Backdraft* starred which Kurt?
14 In which decade of the 20th century was Goldie Hawn born?
15 Which Tom starred in *The Firm*?
16 In a movie title which word goes after 'The Ipcress'?
17 Which Steven directed *Saving Private Ryan*?
18 Which star actress was in *G.I. Jane*, *Striptease* and *Disclosure*?
19 Which character battles against The Penguin?
20 Who was the late brother of Joaquin Phoenix, known in some movies as Leaf?
21 Which Susan won the Best Actress Oscar for *Dead Man Walking*?
22 *The Sting* took place in which gangster city?
23 Which Doris starred in romantic films with Rock Hudson?
24 Which word completes the film title, *The ___ Vanishes*?
25 Which Carrie featured in *When Harry Met Sally*?

Answers Pot Luck 35 (see Quiz 89)
1 1990s 2 The monster. 3 Richards. 4 Stephen King. 5 *Sensibility*. 6 Emma.
7 Baldwin. 8 *Gandhi*. 9 Tom Hanks. 10 Jane Fonda. 11 J. 12 Rat.
13 Wallace and Gromit. 14 Bud, Lou. 15 1960s. 16 *My Fair Lady*. 17 Turner.
18 A Miracle. 19 Dustin Hoffman. 20 O'Connor. 21 Bruce. 22 United Artists.
23 1970s. 24 Cleese. 25 *Evil*.

Answers – see page 98

1 Which country hosts the Cannes Film Festival?
2 Which German festival gives an award of a Golden Bear?
3 Which 'Fiction' movie won a prize at Cannes in 1994?
4 What sort of 'Doors' won Peter Howitt a screenwriter award in 1998?
5 Which Kelly was a winner with *Invitation to the Dance* in 1956?
6 Which festival was the subject of a book called *Hollywood on the Riviera*?
7 Which Robert founded the Sundance Festival?
8 What does Palme d'Or mean in the award from the Cannes Film festival?
9 Which Scottish city hosts a film festival and an arts festival in August?
10 Which Spice Girls movie was launched at the Cannes Film Festival?
11 Which Dustin Hoffman/Tom Cruise movie won a Golden Bear in 1989?
12 Why was the first Cannes Film Festival abandoned in 1939?
13 Which 'Michael' won a Golden Lion for Neil Jordan in 1996?
14 In which decade was the Cannes Film Festival disrupted due to nationwide demonstrations in France?
15 Which term, often used in motor racing, was used as the name of the main prize at Cannes just after World War II?
16 Which continent has awards called Felixes?
17 Which movie with 'Barton' in the title found success at Cannes?
18 Which Michael did Liam Neeson play in the title role of Neil Jordan's movie which won in Venice in 1996?
19 In which month of the year does the Cannes Festival take place?
20 Which Hugh won Best Actor at Venice for his debut movie *Maurice*?
21 What colour Lion is the name of the award at Venice?
22 Which Tom won in Venice for *Rosencrantz and Guildenstern Are Dead*?
23 Which Quentin Tarantino film won a Palme d'Or in 1994?
24 Which Italian city famous for its canals hosts a film festival?
25 Which Kathy won for *Nil by Mouth* at Cannes in 1998?

Answers Comedy (see Quiz 90)
1 *The Truman Show*. 2 DeGeneres. 3 Powers. 4 Bean. 5 *Liar Liar*. 6 Sheffield.
7 Lewis. 8 The Flintstones. 9 Hugh Grant. 10 Groundhog Day. 11 Nanny.
12 Whoopi Goldberg. 13 Diamond. 14 *Wayne's World*. 15 Turtles.
16 Freeman. 17 Underground. 18 The Mob 19 Dustin Hoffman. 20 Liza Minnelli.
21 Dolly Parton. 22 Blues Brothers. 23 *Manhattan*. 24 Lemmon. 25 The Forum.

Answers – see page 103

1   In which decade was Jodie Foster born?
2   Which Richard was her co star in *Sommersby*?
3   Who spoke her lines in the French film *Moi, Fleur Bleue*?
4   In which city was her film *Taxi Driver* set?
5   For which movie did she win her first 90s Oscar?
6   In which decade did she win her first ever Oscar for *The Accused*?
7   Which Liam was her co-star in *Nell*?
8   In which 1994 gambling movie did she star with James Garner?
9   In which movie with only children in the cast did she play a gangster's moll?
10 Which Martin directed her with Robert de Niro in *Taxi Driver*?
11 Who won the Best Actor Oscar when Foster won for *The Silence of the Lambs*?
12 In which Californian city was she born?
13 Who owns the production company Egg which made *Nell*?
14 Which 'Freaky' day was in the title of a 1977 Disney film?
15 Which Cybill appeared with Foster in *Taxi Driver* as campaign worker Betsy?
16 What is the name of Foster's first son?
17 What did she advertise as a child as The Coppertone Girl?
18 What is her real first name?
19 Which President suffered an assassination attempt by a stalker obsessed by Foster?
20 In which country did she advertise Honda cars, where they were first made?
21 In which movie did she win an Oscar as federal agent Clarice Starling?
22 Who 'Doesn't Live Here Any More' according to her 1974 movie?
23 In which film did she play Anna in a *King and I*-style remake?
24 Which 'Little Man' saw her major feature film directing debut?
25 In which Woody's film *Shadows and Fog* did she have a cameo role?

Answers 1990s Stars (see Quiz 95)
1 Affleck. 2 Spanish. 3 *The Truman Show*. 4 Costner. 5 Whoopi Goldberg.
6 Drew. 7 Mike Myers. 8 Leonardo DiCaprio. 9 Madonna. 10 Five. 11 Kate
Winslet. 12 Pitt. 13 Animals. 14 Canada. 15 Gerard. 16 Hugh Grant.
17 Jodie Foster. 18 Robin Williams. 19 Anderson. 20 The Mohicans. 21 Depp.
22 Tom Cruise's. 23 Alec. 24 English. 25 Keanu.

Answers – see page 104

1	Which word follows 'Pale' in a Clint Eastwood movie title?
2	Which Jack starred in *The Witches of Eastwick*?
3	In which decade was *The Birds* released?
4	Who played the lead role in *The King and I* after James Mason turned it down?
5	Who played the baddie Pierce Brosnan was up against in *The World is Not Enough*?
6	Which colour completes the film title *The Solid ____ Cadillac*?
7	Who was Adele Austerlitz's famous brother?
8	*The Sunshine Boys* starred which George?
9	What sort of column did Hedda Hopper write about Hollywood?
10	Which blonde country star appeared in *The Best Little Whorehouse in Texas*?
11	Which important person is held to ransom in *Air Force One*?
12	Which actress took the lead in *The Avengers*?
13	Which word completes the film title *A Star Is ____*?
14	For which film did Julie Andrews win her first Oscar?
15	Which Hollywood star was nicknamed 'The Look'?
16	The Von Trapp family featured in which musical movie?
17	Who played Tinkerbell in *Hook*?
18	Which Burt starred in the 50s movie *From Here to Eternity*?
19	What is the name of the chief male character in *The Avengers*?
20	Who sang the title song of *A Hard Day's Night*?
21	Who plays Deloris in *Sister Act*?
22	In the film title, what goes with 'Kind Hearts'?
23	In which decade of the 20th century was Melanie Griffith born?
24	Who starred in *Private Benjamin* after finding fame in TV's *Laugh In*?
25	*Mermaids* and *Edward Scissorhands* featured which actress?

Answers Pot Luck 38 (see Quiz 96)
1 The Big. **2** Kate Winslet. **3** Foot (*My Left Foot*). **4** Tom Cruise. **5** *The Graduate*. **6** Gwyneth Paltrow. **7** 20s. **8** The Mob. **9** *The Sound of Music*. **10** Judi Dench. **11** London. **12** Spaghetti. **13** Gotham. **14** Jeff Bridges. **15** *Dr No*. **16** St Bernard. **17** Spielberg. **18** 1980s. **19** *Mermaids*. **20** Kiss. **21** *The Bodyguard*. **22** Georgia. **23** Carlyle. **24** Gangsters. **25** Ingrid Bergman.

Answers – see page 101

1	Which Ben co-wrote and starred in *Good Will Hunting* with Matt Damon?
2	What is the nationality of Antonio Banderas?
3	Which 'Show' was a big hit for Jim Carrey?
4	Which Kevin played John Dunbar in *Dances with Wolves*?
5	Which African-American actress played the medium in *Ghost*?
6	Which member of the Barrymore acting dynasty appeared in *The Wedding Singer*?
7	Who played the spoof spy Austin Powers in the late 1990s movies?
8	Which heart-throb played Romeo opposite Claire Danes in *Romeo and Juliet*?
9	Which future star of *Evita* played Breathless Mahoney in *Dick Tracy*?
10	How many Spice Girls star in *Spiceworld: The Movie*?
11	Who played Rose in the blockbuster *Titanic*?
12	Which Brad became engaged to Jennifer Aniston after breaking off his engagement to Gwyneth Paltrow?
13	Eddie Murphy as Dr Doolittle could talk to whom in the 1998 hit?
14	In which part of North America was Dan Aykroyd born?
15	What is the first name of French actor Depardieu?
16	Liz Hurley was the long-time partner of which *Four Weddings and a Funeral* star?
17	Who played the female FBI agent in *The Silence of the Lambs*?
18	Who played the title role in *Mrs Doubtfire*?
19	Which Gillian played Scully in the movie version of *The X-Files*?
20	Daniel Day-Lewis is the 'Last of' which people in the 1992 movie?
21	Which Johnny was nearly 30 when he played teenager Gilbert in *What's Eating Gilbert Grape*??
22	Whose 'Mission' was 'Impossible' in 1996?
23	Who is oldest of the Baldwin brothers, who married Kim Basinger?
24	American Gwyneth Paltrow adopted what national accent for *Sliding Doors* and *Emma*?
25	What is Keanu Reeves's real first name?

Answers Jodie Foster (see Quiz 93)
1 1960s. 2 Gere. 3 She did. 4 New York. 5 *The Silence of the Lambs*.
6 1980s. 7 Neeson. 8 *Maverick*. 9 *Bugsy Malone*. 10 Scorsese. 11 Anthony Hopkins. 12 Los Angeles. 13 Jodie Foster. 14 Friday. 15 Shepherd. 16 Charles. 17 Suntan lotion. 18 Alicia. 19 Reagan. 20 Japan. 21 *The Silence of the Lambs*. 22 Alice. 23 *Anna and the King*. 24 Tate. 25 Allen.

Answers – see page 102

1   In movie titles which two words go in front of 'Chill', 'Heat' and 'Lebowski'?
2   Which leading actress was Oscar-nominated for *Titanic*?
3   Which left part of the body is named in the title of a movie with Daniel Day-Lewis?
4   *Rain Man, The Firm* and *Cocktail* all feature which actor?
5   Middle-aged seductress Mrs Robinson features in which movie?
6   Who won the Best Actress Oscar for *Shakespeare in Love*?
7   In which decade of the 20th century was Audrey Hepburn born?
8   Who was Michelle Pfeiffer 'Married to' in a movie title?
9   The song 'Climb Every Mountain' features in which musical movie?
10   Which English actress was the first to play M in the Bond movies?
11   Bob Hope was born in which European capital city?
12   What's the Italian food often linked with westerns?
13   In which city does the action of *Batman* take place?
14   What's the name of the actor brother of Beau Bridges?
15   What was the first Bond movie with Sean Connery?
16   What breed of dog is Beethoven?
17   Which director Steven did Amy Irving marry?
18   In which decade was *Wall Street* released?
19   Which movie featured 'The Shoop Shoop Song'?
20   Which word completes the film titles, ____ *Me Deadly* and ____ *Me Kate*?
21   Which film saw Whitney Houston's acting debut?
22   *Gone with the Wind* is set in which American state?
23   Which Robert starred in *The Full Monty*?
24   What is the main 'occupation' of the characters in *Bugsy Malone*?
25   Who was the female lead in *Casablanca*?

Answers Pot Luck 37 (see Quiz 94)
1 Rider. 2 Nicholson. 3 1960s. 4 Yul Brynner. 5 Robert Carlyle. 6 *Gold*.
7 Fred Astaire. 8 Burns. 9 Gossip. 10 Dolly Parton. 11 US President. 12 Uma
Thurman. 13 *Born*. 14 *Mary Poppins*. 15 Lauren Bacall. 16 *The Sound of Music*.
17 Julia Roberts. 18 Lancaster. 19 Steed. 20 The Beatles. 21 Whoopi Goldberg.
22 Coronets. 23 50s. 24 Goldie Hawn. 25 Winona Ryder.

Answers – see page 107

1 In which city did Hugh Grant make the headlines for 'lewd conduct'?
2 Where was Elizabeth Taylor born?
3 Who died two days after finishing *Giant*?
4 Which Julie's voice was damaged after a minor op went wrong?
5 Michael J. Fox hit the headlines after disclosing he was suffering from which disease?
6 Which Sidney was the first black actor to top the money making list?
7 In *All the President's Men* Redford and Hoffman play journalists investigating which break-in?
8 Which Mr Moore scored 10 before disclosing he had an incurable disease?
9 Which Sharon had the famous leg-crossing scene in *Basic Instinct*?
10 Which 'Heavenly' Michael Cimino movie nearly destroyed United Artists?
11 Who hit the headlines by receiving $8.5 million for the sequel to *Sister Act*?
12 Who starred in a TV remake of *Rear Window* after becoming paralysed after a fall from a horse?
13 In the1940s which Flynn was acquitted of assault charges on his yacht?
14 Which star of *Saturday Night Fever* famously danced with Diana, Princess of Wales at a White House reception?
15 Which Liz went to a premiere in a dress held together by safety pins?
16 Which Richard married and divorced supermodel Cindy Crawford?
17 Which husband and wife starred in *Shanghai Surprise* in 1986?
18 Which silent star sold his Hollywood home to move to Switzerland in 1953?
19 Which Jack played The Joker in a Batman movie?
20 In what type of crash did Grace Kelly meet her death?
21 The relationship between Richard Burton and Elizabeth Taylor began on the set of which movie?
22 Which Julia married Lyle Lovett after leaving Kiefer Sutherland at the altar?
23 Which cosmetics house did Liz Hurley advertise?
24 Which daughter of Henry was known as Hanoi Jane for her anti-Vietnam War actions?
25 Warren Beatty's affair with Madonna began on the set of which movie?

Answers Pot Luck 39 (see Quiz 99)
1 1990s. **2** Aykroyd. **3** Marilyn Monroe. **4** Quiet. **5** De Niro. **6** World War II.
7 Jodie Foster. **8** *Mission: Impossible.* **9** *Entrapment.* **10** *The Wizard of Oz.*
11 Daniel Day-Lewis. **12** Bruce Willis. **13** A woman. **14** Ship. **15** Canada.
16 50s. **17** LeBlanc. **18** Dredd. **19** Meet Me. **20** Nicolas Cage. **21** None.
22 1970s. **23** The Bee Gees. **24** Roberts. **25** Green.

Answers – see page 108

1	Where was *The Beach* made?
2	In which country was *Angela's Ashes* set?
3	Which member of the Arquette family appeared in *Stigmata*?
4	Johnny Depp starred in what type of 'Hollow'?
5	What sort of 'Collector' was played by Denzel Washington?
6	What was the first Bond movie showing in the new millennium?
7	Who was Bicentennial Man?
8	What sort of 'Sense' did Bruce Willis have in the screen ghost story?
9	In which north of England city was *East Is East* set?
10	What colour 'Streak' features in the title of the Martin Lawrence movie?
11	Which Tommy was the pursuer in *Double Jeopardy*?
12	Which Mr was 'Talented' in the movie with Matt Damon?
13	Which Ralph Fiennes movie had the ad line, 'The end was just the beginning'?
14	Which 'Orchard' came to the big screen with Charlotte Rampling and Alan Bates?
15	Where was 'The House' in the movie directed by William Malone?
16	Which *Scream* movie appeared at the start of Y2K?
17	What was the sequel to *Toy Story*?
18	Which Martin directed *Bringing Out the Dead*?
19	Which G & S were the subjects of *Topsy Turvy*?
20	*Music of the Heart* was about what type of musician?
21	Which Emily plays Angela in *Angela's Ashes*?
22	Which Matt and Ben starred in *Dogma*?
23	Which Kevin starred in *American Beauty*?
24	Who was Johnny Depp's co-star in *Sleepy Hollow*?
25	What type of 'Giant' was the name of an animated movie hit?

Answers Action (see Quiz 100)

1 *Dr No.* **2** Leonardo DiCaprio. **3** Fiennes. **4** Batman. **5** Pryce. **6** Pierce Brosnan. **7** Tornado. **8** 1970s. **9** Kidman. **10** *Braveheart.* **11** Jamie Lee Curtis. **12** *The Fugitive.* **13** Seymour. **14** D-Day landings. **15** 1990s. **16** James Bond. **17** Ursula Andress. **18** Izzard **19** A POW camp. **20** Burton. **21** Telly Savalas **22** Three. **23** Arthur. **24** Pizza. **25** Pierce Brosnan.

Answers – see page 105

1   In which decade was *Misery* released?
2   Which Dan starred in *Ghostbusters*?
3   Who was the lead actress in *Some Like It Hot*?
4   According to the film title, it was all what on the Western Front?
5   Which Robert starred in the 1998 *Great Expectations*?
6   During which war was *Land Girls* set?
7   Which star actress was in *Contact, The Accused* and *Sommersby*?
8   The spy Ethan Hunt appears in which movie with a Mission?
9   In which 1999 film did Sean Connery star with Catherine Zeta Jones?
10   A cowardly lion appears in which musical movie?
11   Who played Hawkeye in the 90s movie *The Last of the Mohicans*?
12   Who went on to the *Die Hard* movies from TV's *Moonlighting*?
13   In *Tootsie* what does the Dustin Hoffman character pretend to be to get a part in a soap?
14   *The Poseidon Adventure* is about a disaster on what type of vehicle?
15   In which country on the American continent was Donald Sutherland born?
16   In which decade of the 20th century was Michael Keaton born?
17   Which Matt starred in *Lost in Space*?
18   Which Judge from *2000 AD* comic appeared on film in 1995?
19   In a movie title, what will you do to me in St Louis?
20   Which actor was in *Con Air, City of Angels* and *It Could Happen to You*?
21   How many Oscar nominations did Madonna get for *Evita*?
22   In which decade was *Cabaret* released?
23   Who sang 'Night Fever' in *Saturday Night Fever*?
24   Which Julia starred in *Pretty Woman*?
25   Which colour goes before 'Card' and 'Pastures' in film titles?

Answers Headline Makers (see Quiz 97)
1 Los Angeles. 2 England. 3 James Dean. 4 Andrews. 5 Parkinson's Disease.
6 Poitier. 7 Watergate. 8 Dudley. 9 Stone. 10 *Heaven's Gate*. 11 Whoopi
Goldberg. 12 Christopher Reeve. 13 Errol. 14 John Travolta. 15 Hurley.
16 Gere. 17 Sean Penn & Madonna. 18 Charlie Chaplin. 19 Nicholson. 20 Car.
21 *Cleopatra*. 22 Roberts. 23 Estee Lauder. 24 Jane Fonda. 25 *Dick Tracy*.

QUIZ 100 ACTION ···LEVEL ONE

Answers – see page 106

1 Which Bond movie was shown in Japan as *No Need for a Doctor*?
2 Which star of *Titanic* was King Louis XIV in *The Man in the Iron Mask*?
3 Which Ralph starred as Steed in *The Avengers*?
4 Which comic-book character was played by George Clooney of *ER* fame in 1997?
5 Which Jonathan, a star of *Evita*, played villain Elliott Carver in *Tomorrow Never Dies*?
6 Which 90s 007 starred as Harry Dalton in *Dante's Peak*?
7 What type of natural disaster is the setting for *Twister*?
8 In which decade did the action of *Apollo 13* take place?
9 Which Mrs Cruise, Nicole, starred in *Batman Forever*?
10 Which 1995 Mel Gibson movie told the story of Scot, William Wallace?
11 Which daughter of Tony Curtis played Arnold Schwarzenegger's wife in *True Lies*?
12 In which movie – from the classic TV series of the same name – did Harrison Ford play Richard Kimble?
13 Which British-born Jane was Roger Moore's first Bond girl in *Live and Let Die*?
14 Which Landings feature in the action of *Saving Private Ryan*?
15 In which decade was *The Lost World: Jurassic Park* released?
16 Which role did Timothy Dalton play in *The Living Daylights*?
17 Who played the Bond girl in *Dr No*?
18 Which comedian Eddie appeared in *The Avengers*?
19 *The Great Escape* was an escape from what?
20 Which Richard, husband of Elizabeth Taylor, starred in *Where Eagles Dare*?
21 Which TV Kojak played Blofeld in *On Her Majesty's Secret Service*?
22 How many 'Days of the Condor' feature in the title of the 70s Robert Redford movie?
23 *Excalibur* featured action at the court of which legendary King?
24 What type of Italian food was a Turtles' favourite?
25 Who succeeded Timothy Dalton as 007 in *GoldenEye*?

Answers The 21st Century (see Quiz 98)
1 Thailand. **2** Ireland. **3** Patricia. **4** *Sleepy Hollow*. **5** Bone. **6** *The World Is Not Enough*. **7** Robin Williams. **8** Sixth. **9** Manchester. **10** Blue. **11** Lee Jones. **12** Ripley. **13** *The End of the Affair*. **14** *The Cherry Orchard*. **15** On Haunted Hill. **16** *Scream 3*. **17** *Toy Story 2*. **18** Scorsese. **19** Gilbert & Sullivan. **20** Violinist. **21** Watson. **22** Damon & Affleck. **23** Spacey. **24** Christina Ricci. **25** *The Iron Giant*.

Answers – see page 110

1	What colour is an Oscar?
2	In which decade were the Oscars first presented?
3	What was the last movie of the 1990s to win more than nine Oscars?
4	Which theme park founder won 20 Oscars?
5	In which season does the Oscars ceremony usually take place?
6	At which home of the film industry was the first Oscar ceremony held?
7	Which rodent won Walt Disney a Special Award in 1932?
8	Which Mickey won a 1938 Oscar for 'bringing the spirit of youth to the screen'?
9	Which Maggie won an Oscar for playing an Oscar-nominee in *California Suite*?
10	Whose Oscar sold for $510,000 for her role in *Gone with the Wind*?
11	Which Vanessa won Best Supporting Actress for *Julia*, even though she played the title role?
12	In *Sleuth*, there were two characters; how many were nominated?
13	Which 'Color' in 1985 had 11 nominations and not a single win?
14	What relation were winners Olivia de Havilland and Joan Fontaine?
15	How many times did Alfred Hitchcock win an Oscar for which he was nominated?
16	What relation was Oscar-winner Walter to Oscar-winner John Huston?
17	Which wife of Paul Newman has also been Oscar-nominated?
18	Which song from *The Wizard of Oz* won the Best Song Oscar?
19	Richard Burton was Oscar-nominated in three successive years; how many times did he win?
20	'The Cool Cool Cool' of which part of the day won a songwriting Oscar for Hoagy Carmichael?
21	In *Who's Afraid of Virginia Woolf*, there were four characters; how many were Oscar-nominated?
22	Which Anthony Hopkins and Jodie Foster film won for them both?
23	'Days of Wine and Roses' won best song, from which movie?
24	Which Civil War movie was the last winner before the outbreak of World War II?
25	How many actors shared the Best Actor Award in 1932?

Answers Partnerships (see Quiz 103)
1 Ginger Rogers. **2** Gershwin. **3** Spencer Tracy. **4** Demi Moore. **5** Garth.
6 Streisand. **7** Helen Mirren. **8** *Dangerous Liaisons*. **9** Nicole Kidman. **10** Nelson.
11 Chaplin. **12** Bruce Willis & Demi Moore. **13** Paul Newman & Joanne Woodward.
14 Richard Burton & Elizabeth Taylor. **15** Lauren Bacall. **16** Oldman. **17** Michael
Douglas. **18** Wayne. **19** Kline. **20** Griffith. **21** Frank Sinatra. **22** *Crocodile
Dundee*. **23** Brother, Eric. **24** Brooks. **25** Kenneth Branagh & Emma Thompson.

Answers – see page 111

1   Which word goes in front of 'Morning, Vietnam' and 'Will Hunting' in film titles?
2   *Air Force One* starred which Harrison?
3   About which film was it said, 'It's light years ahead'?
4   Which Matt co-wrote *Good Will Hunting*?
5   *Interview with the Vampire, Twelve Monkeys* and *The Devil's Own* all feature which actor?
6   Which Michelle playted Titania in the 1990s *A Midsummer Night's Dream*?
7   What is the first name of Macaulay Culkin's character in *Home Alone*?
8   In which decade was *Heat* released?
9   Which Gene starred in *The French Connection*?
10 The character Eliza Doolittle appears in which musical movie?
11 Which name completes the title *Whatever Happened to Baby ____*??
12 Who played Obi-Wan Kenobi in the *Star Wars* trilogy?
13 The song 'Tonight' features in which musical movie?
14 Which poison goes with 'Old Lace'?
15 What was Best Picture when Tom Hanks won Best Actor Oscar for *Forrest Gump*?
16 Who went on to star in *Entrapment* after appearing on UK TV's *The Darling Buds of May*?
17 Which famous Norma tested for the role of Scarlett O'Hara?
18 Which Michelle starred in *Wolf*?
19 Did Clark Gable die during the1950s, 1960s or 1970s?
20 Who directed *Alien*?
21 Which Helen won the Best Actress Oscar for *As Good as it Gets*?
22 In which decade was *Thunderball* released?
23 The character Mrs Doubtfire supposedly came from which country?
24 Who sang the title song of *Three Coins in the Fountain*?
25 In which decade of the 20th century was Deborah Kerr born?

Answers Oscar Trivia (see Quiz 101)
1 Gold. 2 1920s. 3 *Titanic*. 4 Walt Disney. 5 Spring. 6 Hollywood. 7 Mickey Mouse. 8 Rooney. 9 Smith. 10 Vivien Leigh. 11 Redgrave. 12 Two. 13 *The Color Purple*. 14 Sisters. 15 Never. 16 Father. 17 Joanne Woodward. 18 'Over the Rainbow'. 19 Never. 20 Evening. 21 Four. 22 *The Silence of the Lambs*. 23 *Days of Wine and Roses*. 24 *Gone with the Wind*. 25 Two.

Answers – see page 109

1 Who was the screen partner of the dancer whose real name was Frederick Austerlitz?

2 Which brothers George and Ira wrote the music for 'Someone to Watch Over Me'?

3 Who played opposite Katharine Hepburn 10 times?

4 Who was the actress who launched Planet Hollywood with actors Willis, Schwarzenegger and Stallone?

5 Who is Wayne's sidekick in *Wayne's World*?

6 Which Barbra did actor James Brolin marry in 1998?

7 Which star of *Prime Suspect* was Liam Neeson's co star in *Excalibur*?

8 Michelle Pfeiffer's affair with John Malkovich began on the set of which movie?

9 Which wife of Tom Cruise has also been Oscar-nominated?

10 What was the first name of actor Eddy who had an on-screen partnership with Jeanette MacDonald?

11 Paulette Goddard was the co-star and third wife of which Charlie?

12 Who are the parents of Rumer, Scout and Tallulah Willis?

13 Which husband and wife starred in *Mr and Mrs Bridge* in 1994?

14 Which husband and wife were Oscar-nominated together in 1966?

15 Humphrey Bogart's affair with which actress started in real life while they were making *To Have and Have Not*?

16 Which Gary was married to Uma Thurman?

17 Who announced his engagement to Catherine Zeta Jones in 2000?

18 Which John first starred with Maureen O'Hara in *Rio Grande*?

19 Which Kevin did Phoebe Cates marry in 1989?

20 Which actress Melanie did Don Johnson marry twice?

21 Which singer/actor was the first husband of Mia Farrow?

22 The relationship between Paul Hogan and Linda Koslowski began on the set of which movie?

23 Julia Roberts make her screen debut opposite which family member?

24 Which Mel did Anne Bancroft marry in 1964?

25 Which husband and wife were the subject of the biography *Ken and Em*?

Answers Pot Luck 40 (see Quiz 102)

1 Good. **2** Ford. **3** *Toy Story*. **4** Damon. **5** Brad Pitt. **6** Pfeiffer. **7** Kevin. **8** 1990s. **9** Hackman. **10** *My Fair Lady*. **11** *Jane*. **12** Alec Guinness. **13** *West Side Story*. **14** Arsenic. **15** *Forrest Gump*. **16** Catherine Zeta Jones. **17** Shearer. **18** Pfeiffer. **19** 1960s. **20** Ridley Scott. **21** Hunt. **22** 1960s. **23** Scotland. **24** Frank Sinatra. **25** 20s.

Things are hotting up. The easy questions are behind you and you will have to test those brain cells just a little bit more with this section.

Once again it is questions on worldwide cinema and famous people which make up most of this level of *The Best Movie Quiz Book Ever!*. Highly complex and mind-blowingly obscure questions are still to come! There will be a fair number of the-answer's-on-the-tip-of-my-tongue type questions as well. You can remember who won the Best Supporting Actress Oscar for *Shakespeare in Love* just after the event but can you remember who won it a couple of years later? This is how the questions are getting that little bit harder.

In most public quizzes the majority of your questions will be at this level. You've had the easy questions to get them in the mood and the difficult questions are just around the corner. If you are setting topic sections in groups of ten for a general audience, perhaps give two easy questions, two difficult ones and six medium ones. You should know your audience. If you have quiz rookies then increase the number of easy questions. If they're real quiz experts then reduce the number of medium questions and increase the difficulty quotient. The more quizzes you run the more experienced you will become and the balance of levels will become simpler to estimate.

A quick word of advice about the Pot Luck sections here. Genuine movie buffs can bone up on their specialist subjects but with the Pot Luck sections they have no idea at all what is going to be thrown at them. They may be experts on the films of Arnold Schwarzenegger but ask them a question on weepies and they could be stumped. Use these sections frequently!

Answers – see page 115

1   Who turned down Eddie Murphy's role in *Beverly Hills Cop*?
2   Who directed *Thelma and Louise*?
3   How is Caryn Johnson better known?
4   In which decade was *Mr Smith Goes to Washington* released?
5   *Indiana Jones and the Last Crusade* and *Speakers* both feature which actor?
6   Who won the Best Actor Oscar for *La Vita E Bella* (*Life is Beautiful*)?
7   Which Madeleine starred in *The Last of the Mohicans*?
8   To the nearest hour, how long does *The Birds* last?
9   Which Elisabeth starred in *Leaving Las Vegas*?
10 Which poet's life story is told in *Tom and Viv*?
11 What was the name of Tom Hanks's character in *Saving Private Ryan*?
12 What is actress Drew Barrymore's real first name?
13 Who played Anita in *West Side Story*?
14 What nationality does Juliette Binoche play in *The English Patient*?
15 What was the name of Tom Hanks's character in *Big*?
16 Who directed *The Piano* and *The Portrait of a Lady*?
17 *International Velvet* and *Dreamscape* both featured which actor?
18 Which song won Best Song Oscar for *The Man Who Knew Too Much*?
19 Anthony Minghella won his first Best Director Oscar for which movie?
20 Who won the Best Actress Oscar for *The Accused*?
21 *Goodfellas* was released in which decade?
22 Which Jenny starred in *Logan's Run*?
23 Who directed *The Truman Show*?
24 Who played George III's consort in *The Madness of King George*?
25 Which baseball star did Marilyn Monroe marry in 1954?

Answers Partnerships (see Quiz 3)
1 *Eyes Wide Shut*. **2** Ewan McGregor. **3** Renny Harlin. **4** Martin Scorsese.
5 Joanne Whalley-Kilmer. **6** *The Misfits*. **7** Ethan Hawke. **8** Tom & Jerry. **9** Tom
Cruise. **10** Kelly Preston. **11** Jane Seymour. **12** Kristin Scott Thomas. **13** Rhea
Perlman. **14** Charles Bronson. **15** *One Night in the Tropics*. **16** Demi Moore.
17 Jeff & Beau Bridges. **18** Ava Gardner. **19** Whitney Houston. **20** Bogart &
Bacall. **21** Paul Simon. **22** Orson Welles. **23** Gwyneth Paltrow. **24** *Camelot*.
25 Diandra.

Answers – see page 116

1   In which movie did Errol Flynn say, 'It's injustice I hate, not the Normans'?
2   What was the Marx Brothers' first film for MGM?
3   Who found fame in *Public Enemy*?
4   Which subject of the 90s movie *Gods and Monsters* directed *Frankenstein*?
5   Which movie was about Longfellow Deeds?
6   Which famous Robert Louis Stevenson personality was the subject of a 1932 movie with Fredric March?
7   The star of many Tarzan movies had been an accomplished Olympian in which sport?
8   Who played Elizabeth I in *Elizabeth and Essex* opposite Errol Flynn?
9   In which movie did Bela Lugosi say, 'Listen to them, children of the night. What music they make'?
10   Who choreographed *Forty-Second Street*?
11   In which 1934 Oscar-winning movie did Clark Gable famously say, 'Behold the walls of Jericho'?
12   Which movie made a star of Claude Rains, though he was only seen for a few moments?
13   Which 'Bride' was Elsa Lanchester in a 1935 classic?
14   Who did Charles Laughton play in *Mutiny on the Bounty*?
15   Which studio filmed *Goodbye Mr Chips* in England?
16   Which British star of *Gone with the Wind* was 'The Scarlet Pimpernel'?
17   Which city was terrorized by *King Kong*?
18   To the nearest hour, how long does *Monkey Business* last?
19   Who starred as 'Camille'?
20   Who was the French star of *Love Affair* in 1939?
21   In which movie did Chaplin satirize the mechanical society?
22   Which youthful duo starred in *Babes in Arms*?
23   How was song-and-dance director William Berkeley Enos better known?
24   Which British-born director made *Sabotage*?
25   In which 1934 movie did Astaire and Rogers dance 'The Continental'?

Answers Pot Luck 2 (see Quiz 4)
1 Anthony Perkins. **2** William. **3** Crowe. **4** Victor Fleming. **5** Tatiana Romanova.
6 Denys Finch-Hatton. **7** Ming the Merciless. **8** 1970s. **9** Bean. **10** Los Angeles.
11 Jason Gould (her real-life son). **12** 139 minutes. **13** Malcolm McDowell.
14 John Lasseter. **15** Bowie. **16** *The Avengers*. **17** Three. **18** Howard Keel.
19 Dr Evil. **20** Tomlinson. **21** Tony Curtis. **22** Tony Scott. **23** Claudette Colbert.
24 1940s. **25** Joe Pesci.

Answers – see page 113

1	In which 1999 movie wer Harvey Keitel and Jennifer Jason Leigh replaced by Tom Cruise and Nicole Kidman?
2	Who did Danny Boyle direct in both *Trainspotting* and *Shallow Grave*?
3	Which director was Geena Davis's third husband?
4	Harvey Keitel is particularly known for his work with which director?
5	How did Joanne Whalley style herself during her 1988–1996 marriage?
6	Marilyn Monroe divorced Arthur Miller a week after the premiere of which movie?
7	Who was Uma Thurman's on- and off-screen partner in *Gattaca*?
8	Fred Quimby was partly responsible for bringing which duo to the big screen?
9	Mimi Rogers was the first wife of which superstar of the 80s and 90s?
10	Which star of *Twins* married John Travolta?
11	Which wife of director James Keach was a Bond girl in *Live and Let Die*?
12	Which star of *The Horse Whisperer* married a French doctor?
13	Who married Danny DeVito during a break on *Cheers*?
14	Which tough guy played opposite Jill Ireland 12 times?
15	What was Abbot and Costello's first feature film?
16	Who played the mother of her daughter Rumer in *Striptease* in 1996?
17	Which brothers appeared in *The Fabulous Baker Boys*?
18	Which wife of Frank Sinatra was Oscar-nominated at the same time as him?
19	Which singer/actress was Mrs Bobby Brown?
20	*Dark Passage* featured which couple?
21	Who married Debbie Reynolds's daughter in 1983?
22	Which director did Rita Hayworth marry?
23	Who was Brad Pitt's on- and off-screen partner while they were making *Se7en*?
24	Vanessa Redgrave's affair with Franco Nero began on the set of which musical movie?
25	What was the name of Mrs Michael Douglas who divorced him in 1995?

Answers Pot Luck 1 (see Quiz 1)

1 Sylvester Stallone. **2** Ridley Scott. **3** Whoopi Goldberg. **4** 1930s. **5** River Phoenix. **6** Roberto Benigni. **7** Stowe. **8** 2 hours. **9** Shu. **10** T.S. Eliot. **11** Captain John Miller. **12** Andrew. **13** Rita Moreno. **14** Canadian. **15** Josh. **16** Jane Campion. **17** Christopher Plummer. **18** 'Whatever Will Be, Will Be' ('Que Sera, Sera'). **19** *The English Patient*. **20** Jodie Foster. **21** 1990s. **22** Agutter. **23** Peter Weir. **24** Helen Mirren. **25** Joe DiMaggio.

Answers – see page 114

1   *Desire under the Elms* and *Psycho III* both feature which actor?
2   What is the first name of Brad Pitt, who uses his middle name in the movies?
3   Which Russell starred in *LA Confidential*?
4   Who won the Best Director Oscar for *Gone with the Wind*?
5   What was the name of the Bond girl in *From Russia with Love*?
6   What was the name of Robert Redford's character in *Out of Africa*?
7   What was the name of the villain in *Flash*?
8   In which decade was *Mean Streets* released?
9   Which Sean starred in *GoldenEye*?
10   Where does Rowan Atkinson's *Bean* take place?
11   Who played Barbra Streisand's son in *The Prince of Tides*?
12   Within twenty minutes, how long does *Apocalypse Now* last?
13   Who did Stanley Kubrick cast in the lead role in *A Clockwork Orange*?
14   Who directed *Toy Story*?
15   Which David starred in *Labyrinth*?
16   A character named Sir August de Wynter appeared in which film?
17   How many Oscars did Woody Allen win for *Annie Hall*?
18   Who played opposite Betty Hutton in *Annie Get Your Gun*?
19   Who is the bad character in *Austin Powers: International Man of Mystery*?
20   Which David featured in *Mary Poppins*?
21   Who played Albert DeSalvo in *The Boston Strangler*?
22   Who directed *Top Gun*?
23   Who won the Best Actress Oscar for *It Happened One Night*?
24   In which decade was Disney's *Pinocchio* released?
25   *Home Alone* and *Lethal Weapon 3* both feature which actor?

Answers 1930s (see Quiz 2)
1 *The Adventures of Robin Hood*. **2** *A Night at the Opera*. **3** James Cagney.
4 James Whale. **5** *Mr Deeds Goes to Town*. **6** *Dr Jekyll and Mr Hyde*.
7 Swimming. **8** Bette Davis. **9** *Dracula*. **10** Busby Berkeley. **11** *It Happened One Night*. **12** *The Invisible Man*. **13** Bride of Frankenstein. **14** Captain Bligh. **15** MGM.
16 Leslie Howard. **17** New York. **18** 1 hour (78 mins). **19** Greta Garbo.
20 Charles Boyer. **21** *Modern Times*. **22** Mickey Rooney & Judy Garland.
23 Busby Berkeley. **24** Alfred Hitchcock. **25** *The Gay Divorcee*.

Answers – see page 119

1   Who or what was Andre in the film of the same name?
2   What sort of whale was Willy?
3   Which movie saw a creature threatening Amity off the Long Island coast?
4   What was the sequel to *Beethoven* called?
5   On whose novel was *101 Dalmatians* based?
6   Which creatures predominate in *Deep Blue Sea*?
7   Which actress founded the Born Free Foundation after appearing in the movie?
8   What sort of animal was the star of *Gus*?
9   In which film does Tom Hanks use the help of a dog to solve a murder?
10 Which veteran, and former child star, was one of the voices in the 80s *The Fox and the Hound*?
11 What sort of star was Rhubarb?
12 Which *X-Files* star played a villain in *Beethoven*?
13 Which animals were the stars of *Ring of Bright Water*?
14 What was Tom Mix's horse called?
15 The first dog to play which big-screen star was really called Pal?
16 What was the name of the basketball-playing golden retriever in *Air Bud* in 1997?
17 How many horses did Gene Autry have called Champion?
18 In which musical does Bill have a dog called Bullseye?
19 What type of animal was Digby in the Peter Sellers movie?
20 What breed of dog was K9 in the John Belushi movie?
21 How many dogs and cats make *The Incredible Journey*?
22 Which little girl had a dog as a nanny, called Nana?
23 What sort of animal featured in *My Friend Flicka*?
24 What was the cat called in *Breakfast at Tiffany's*?
25 What was the sequel to *The Incredible Journey* called?

Answers Pot Luck 3 (see Quiz 7)
1 William. **2** Motor Racing. **3** William Holden. **4** Ang Lee. **5** 1940s. **6** Liotta.
7 Burns. **8** Bob Hoskins. **9** Louisiana. **10** Kevin Bacon. **11** 2 hours. **12** John and
Anjelica Huston. **13** Sean Penn. **14** *The Wedding Singer*. **15** Lee. **16** Ethel
Merman. **17** Mozart. **18** Preston. **19** Scott Hicks. **20** West Germany. **21** *A Bill of
Divorcement*. **22** 1980s. **23** McDormand. **24** William Wyler. **25** Ward.

Answers – see page 120

1   What was his nickname?

2   In which classic western did he play the Ringo Kid?

3   Which sport did he play competitively when he was at college?

4   Which wife of Charlie Chaplin was his co-star in *Reap the Wild Wind*?

5   What was the first movie in which he starred with Maureen O'Hara?

6   Which singer was his drunken assistant in *Rio Bravo*?

7   What type of sportsman did he pay in *The Quiet Man*?

8   Which Hollywood great was his female co-star in *The Shootist*?

9   In which movie did he famously say, 'Truly this man was the son of God'?

10   Which role did he play in *The Alamo*?

11   In which 1975 movie did he reprise his role from *True Grit*?

12   What was his real name?

13   He starred in and directed *The Green Berets* during which war?

14   What was the first movie for which he received an Oscar?

15   Which movie earned him his first Oscar nomination?

16   Which TV western series did he introduce the first episode of on camera?

17   Which legendary ruler did he play in *The Conqueror*?

18   What was the name of his first major movie?

19   Which director gave him the role in *She Wore a Yellow Ribbon*?

20   In which city was *Brannigan* set?

21   On what occasion was his last public appearance?

22   What was his directorial debut?

23   In which movie did he play Civil War veteran Ethan Edwards?

24   *El Dorado* was a virtual remake of which 1959 hit movie?

25   What was the name of his final movie?

Answers Oscars – Best Actors (see Quiz 8)
1 George Burns. **2** *Wall Street*. **3** *The English Patient*. **4** Ben Kingsley. **5** Jude Law.
6 Priest. **7** Emil Jannings. **8** Manservant. **9** Daniel Day-Lewis. **10** *The People versus Larry Flint*. **11** None. **12** Rex Harrison. **13** *Midnight Cowboy*. **14** None.
15 *Wall Street*. **16** George III. **17** *Amistad*. **18** *Chinatown*. **19** James Dean.
20 Daniel Day-Lewis. **21** Marlon Brando. **22** *The Elephant Man*. **23** Don Corleone. **24** *Schindler's List*. **25** Rex Harrison.

Answers – see page 117

1   What is Liam Neeson's real first name?
2   At what sport did Paul Newman excel?
3   Who won the Best Actor Oscar for *Stalag 17*?
4   Who directed *Sense and Sensibility*?
5   In which decade was the epic *Samson and Delilah* released?
6   Which Ray starred in *Field of Dreams*?
7   What is Harry's surname in *When Harry Met Sally*?
8   Who played Smee in *Hook*?
9   In which state is *The Green Mile* set?
10   Which actor links *Tremors* and *Flatliners*?
11   To the nearest hour, how long does *The Blues Brothers* last?
12   Which father and daughter respectively directed and starred in *Prizzi's Honor*?
13   *Taps* and *We're No Angels* featured which actor?
14   In which film did a character named Robbie Hart appear?
15   Which Bernard featured in *Moonraker*?
16   Whose real name was Ethel Zimmerman?
17   Which composer did Tom Hulce play in a 1984 Milos Forman film?
18   What is the last name of Bill from *Bill and Ted's Excellent Adventure*?
19   Who directed *Shine*?
20   In which country was Bruce Willis born?
21   What was Katharine Hepburn's first film, in 1932?
22   In which decade was *Raging Bull* released?
23   Which Frances starred in *Fargo*?
24   Who won the Best Director Oscar for *Ben Hur*?
25   Which Stephen did John Hurt play in *Scandal*?

Answers Animals On Screen (see Quiz 5)
1 Seal. 2 Orca (Killer Whale). 3 *Jaws*. 4 *Beethoven's Second*. 5 Dodie Smith.
6 Sharks. 7 Virginia McKenna. 8 Mule. 9 *Turner and Hooch*. 10 Mickey Rooney.
11 Cat. 12 David Duchovny. 13 Otters. 14 Tony. 15 Lassie. 16 Buddy.
17 Three. 18 *Oliver!*. 19 Dog. 20 German Shepherd. 21 Two dogs, one cat.
22 Wendy (*Peter Pan*). 23 Horse. 24 Cat. 25 *Homeward Bound: The Incredible Journey*.

Answers – see page 118

1 Who was 80 when he won for *The Sunshine Boys*?
2 What was Michael Douglas's first nomination as performer?
3 For which movie did Ralph Fiennes receive his second nomination?
4 How is 1982 winner, Krishna Bahji, better known?
5 Which 1999 Oscar nominee played Lord Alfred Douglas in *Wilde*?
6 What was Bing Crosby's profession in *Going My Way*?
7 Who won the first Oscar for Best Actor?
8 What was John Gielgud's profession in the movie *Arthur* for which he won an award?
9 When Brenda Fricker first won as Best Actress which winner played her son?
10 For which movie did Woody Harrelson receive his first nomination?
11 What is the total number of Oscars won by Errol Flynn, Peter Cushing and Richard Burton?
12 Who was nominated for *Cleopatra* but won a year later as Professor Higgins?
13 Jon Voight's first nomination was for which X-rated movie?
14 How many Oscars did Sean Connery win for James Bond?
15 What was Michael Douglas's first win as Actor?
16 Which King gave Nigel Hawthorne a nomination?
17 For which Spielberg movie was Anthony Hopkins nominated in 1997?
18 What was the second of Jack Nicholson's three nominations between 1973 and 1975?
19 Who was the first actor to be awarded two posthumous Oscars?
20 Which 80s winner and 90s nominee is the son of Jill Balcon and a poet laureate?
21 Whose first award was for playing Terry Malloy in a 50s classic?
22 For which movie did John Hurt receive a nomination after *Midnight Express*?
23 Who did Robert De Niro play in *The Godfather Part II*?
24 Which Spielberg movie gave Liam Neeson his first nomination?
25 Which Brit won Best Actor in a musical the same year that Julie Andrews won for *Mary Poppins*?

Answers John Wayne (see Quiz 6)
1 Duke. **2** *Stagecoach*. **3** (American) Football. **4** Paulette Goddard. **5** *Rio Grande*. **6** Dean Martin. **7** Boxer. **8** Lauren Bacall. **9** *The Greatest Story Ever Told*. **10** Davy Crockett. **11** *Rooster Cogburn*. **12** Marion Morrison. **13** Vietnam. **14** *True Grit*. **15** *Sands of Iwo Jima*. **16** *Gunsmoke*. **17** Genghis Khan. **18** *The Big Trail*. **19** John Ford. **20** London. **21** 1979 Oscar ceremony. **22** *The Alamo*. **23** *The Searchers*. **24** *Rio Bravo*. **25** *The Shootist*.

Answers – see page 123

1   Who directed *Scream*?
2   How is Joyce Frankenberg better known?
3   In which decade was *Gigi* released?
4   Which Linda starred in *Dante's Peak*?
5   Who won the Best Actress Oscar for *Misery*?
6   In which film did Roger Moore first play 007?
7   What was the name of Tommy Lee Jones's character in *Men in Black*?
8   Who won the Best Director Oscar for *The Apartment*?
9   Used in *Breakfast at Tiffany's*, 'Moon River' is the theme music from which film?
10 Who was 'La Lollo'?
11 Who co-starred with Meryl Streep in *A Cry in the Dark*?
12 Who received her first Oscar nomination for *Silkwood*?
13 Which song won Best Song Oscar for *The Towering Inferno*?
14 In which film did a character named Johnny Castle appear?
15 Who replaced George Segal in Blake Edwards's comedy *10*?
16 Who directed Anthony Hopkins in *Shadowlands*?
17 What was Marilyn Monroe's last film?
18 Who plays the title role in *Michael Collins*?
19 To the nearest hour, how long does *The Bodyguard* last?
20 Which actor links the films *Alice* and *Malice*?
21 Who directed *Romeo + Juliet*?
22 In which decade was *Willy Wonka and the Chocolate Factory* released?
23 Who won the Best Actor Oscar for *Leaving Las Vegas*?
24 Which Toni starred in *Emma*?
25 Who played the Bond girl in *Live and Let Die*?

Answers Robin Williams (see Quiz 11)
1 *Mork & Mindy.* **2** Sally Field. **3** Robert De Niro. **4** 1980s. **5** Nixon. **6** Pierce
Brosnan. **7** *The World According to Garp.* **8** Popeye. **9** Kenneth Branagh. **10** *Mrs
Doubtfire.* **11** Lawyer. **12** Jeff. **13** The genie. **14** Peter Pan. **15** Shelley Duvall.
16 Aberdeen. **17** *Jumanji.* **18** Disc jockey. **19** *Moscow on the Hudson.*
20 Gilliam. **21** *Good Morning, Vietnam.* **22** *Dead Poets Society.* **23** Levinson.
24 *Cadillac Man.* **25** 1960s.

Answers – see page 124

1	In which classic did Paul Heinreid play Victor Laszlo?
2	Which animal sings 'We're off to see the wizard, the wonderful Wizard of Oz' with Dorothy and co.?
3	In which movie did Trevor Howard play Alec Harvey?
4	What was deemed the cinema's first epic?
5	Which 50s movie told of Moses leading the children of Israel to the Promised Land?
6	'All right, Mr de Mille, I'm ready for my close-ups now' is the last line of which movie?
7	In which movie did Debra Winger begin with, 'Anyone here named Loowis?'?
8	Was Debbie Reynolds 18, 20 or 22 when she made *Singin' in the Rain*?
9	Which inventor did Michael Redgrave play in *The Dam Busters*?
10	Which of the stars of *The Philadelphia Story* donated his salary for the movie to war relief?
11	Who was Spade in *The Maltese Falcon*?
12	In *The Third Man* who had Joseph Cotten come to Vienna to meet?
13	Which movie had the ad line, 'Meet Benjamin. He's a little worried about his future'?
14	*A Man for All Seasons* is about whom?
15	Which 1946 Frank Capra movie with James Stewart became a Christmas classic?
16	Who did Marlene Dietrich play in *The Blue Angel*?
17	Who does James Cagney play in *White Heat*?
18	Which movie opens with the line, 'What can you say about a 25-year-old girl who died'?
19	Which member of the Corleone family did Al Pacino play in the *Godfather* trilogy?
20	In which movie did Rita Hayworth remove a glove to 'Put the Blame on Mame'?
21	What was Lauren Bacall's first film, in 1943?
22	In *Genevieve* who or what was Genevieve?
23	Which movie did Elvis Presley make next after *King Creole*?
24	Who played opposite Lana Turner in the original *The Postman Always Rings Twice*?
25	In which 1954 movie did Marlon Brando play a boxer?

Answers – see page 121

1   In which TV series did Robin Williams find fame in the 70s/80s?
2   Who played his ex-wife in *Mrs Doubtfire*?
3   Who was his male co-star in *Awakenings*?
4   In which decade did he make his first major movie?
5   In *Good Morning, Vietnam*, which President does Cronauer alias Williams impersonate?
6   Which 007 starred in *Mrs Doubtfire*?
7   Which 80s movie saw co-star Glenn Close win an Oscar nomination?
8   Which cartoon character did he play in a 1980 Robert Altman movie?
9   Which then-husband of Emma Thompson directed *Dead Again*?
10 In which movie does he play Daniel Hilliard?
11 What is the occupation of the grown-up Peter Pan in *Hook*?
12 Which member of the Bridges family was a co-star in *The Fisher King*?
13 Whose voice did he provide in *Aladdin*?
14 Who did he play in *Hook*?
15 Who played Olive to his Popeye?
16 Where in Scotland is the 'nanny' from in *Mrs Doubtfire*?
17 In which film was he 'released' from a board game after 26 years?
18 What was his job in *Good Morning, Vietnam*?
19 In which early film did he play a Russian saxophonist?
20 Which former Python Terry directed him in *The Fisher King*?
21 Which movie gave him his first Oscar nomination?
22 In which movie did he play an unorthodox prep school teacher?
23 Which Barry directed him in *Good Morning, Vietnam*?
24 In which film is he a car salesman held hostage by a jealous husband?
25 The 80s *Good Morning, Vietnam* featured songs from which decade on its soundtrack?

Answers Pot Luck 4 (see Quiz 9)
1 Wes Craven. **2** Jane Seymour. **3** 1950s. **4** Hamilton. **5** Kathy Bates. **6** *Live and Let Die*. **7** K. **8** Billy Wilder. **9** *Days of Wine and Roses*. **10** Gina Lollobrigida. **11** Sam Neill. **12** Cher. **13** 'We May Never Love Like This Again'. **14** *Dirty Dancing*. **15** Dudley Moore. **16** Richard Attenborough. **17** *The Misfits*. **18** Liam Neeson. **19** 2 hours. **20** Alec Baldwin. **21** Baz Luhrmann. **22** 1970s. **23** Nicolas Cage. **24** Collette. **25** Jane Seymour.

QUIZ 12 POT LUCK 5 ···LEVEL TWO

Answers – see page 122

1   On whose book was the River Phoenix film *Stand By Me* based?
2   Who won the Best Actor Oscar for *The Color of Money*?
3   Which Linda starred in *Crocodile Dundee*?
4   Who recorded the title song of *The Good, the Bad and the Ugly*?
5   Who starred opposite Nicole Kidman in *The Peacemaker*?
6   Who won the Best Director Oscar for *On the Waterfront*?
7   *Tootsie* and *Scrooged* both feature which actor?
8   A character named Charlie Babbitt appeared in which film?
9   Which Lionel featured in *New York, New York*?
10   Who played Cosmo Brown in *Singin' in the Rain*?
11   Which actor's split from long-time partner Michelle introduced the word 'palimony'?
12   *Ghostbusters* and *Parenthood* both feature which actor?
13   Who did John Cleese play in *A Fish Called Wanda*?
14   In which decade was *Bus Stop* released?
15   In which film was Laurence Olivier teamed with Marilyn Monroe?
16   Which actor links *In the Bleak Mid-Winter* and *Othello*?
17   Who directed Mel Gibson in *Hamlet*?
18   To the nearest hour, how long does *Alien* last?
19   Which Marx brother was born Julius?
20   What was the Bond theme for *The Spy Who Loved Me* called?
21   Who directed *A River Runs Through It*?
22   Who won the Best Actress Oscar for *Dangerous*?
23   Which John starred in *Con Air*?
24   Which singer appeared in *The Wall*?
25   In which decade was *Pygmalion* released?

Answers Classics (see Quiz 10)
1 *Casablanca*. 2 Lion. 3 *Brief Encounter*. 4 *Birth of a Nation*. 5 *The Ten Commandments*. 6 *Sunset Boulevard*. 7 *Shadowlands*. 8 20. 9 Barnes Wallis. 10 Cary Grant. 11 Humphrey Bogart. 12 Harry Lime. 13 *The Graduate*. 14 Thomas More. 15 *It's a Wonderful Life*. 16 Lola Lola. 17 Cody Jarrett. 18 *Love Story*. 19 Michael. 20 *Gilda*. 21 *To Have and Have Not*. 22 Car. 23 *GI Blues*. 24 John Garfield. 25 *On the Waterfront*.

124

Answers – see page 127

1   Who was the voice of the dragon in *Mulan*?
2   Which 1997 movie featured the voices of Meg Ryan and John Cusack?
3   What was the first full-length animated movie to be Oscar-nominated for Best Film?
4   Whose songs feature in *Toy Story*?
5   Where do the characters live in *Who Framed Roger Rabbit*?
6   Which 1945 Gene Kelly movie featured an animation sequence by Hanna and Barbera?
7   Which movie features Jiminy Cricket and Figaro?
8   *The Land Before Time* features an orphaned what?
9   Which 1995 movie saw Robin Williams being rescued from a board game?
10   Hakuna Matata is in which movie?
11   What are the Siamese cats called in *Lady and the Tramp*?
12   What was the name of the wicked uncle in *The Lion King*?
13   What is the name of the dinosaur in *Toy Story*?
14   *The Return of Jafar* was the sequel to which movie?
15   Which classic film has a rabbit called Thumper?
16   Which director provided a voice in *Antz*?
17   Which star of *Friends* provides a voice in *The Iron Giant*?
18   Who was the voice of John Smith in *Pocahontas*?
19   Who was the voice of Jessica in *Who Framed Roger Rabbit*?
20   Which studio, famous for musicals, did Hanna and Barbera work for in the 40s?
21   Which 1999 movie featured the voices of Minnie Driver and Tony Goldwyn?
22   Which duo's first movie was in *Puss Gets the Boot*?
23   Lea Salonga sang on the soundtrack of *Aladdin* after making her name in which musical?
24   In *The Lion King* what sort of animal was Shenzi?
25   What is the name of 'the king of the swingers' in Disney's *Jungle Book*?

Answers Pot Luck 6 (see Quiz 15)
1 Johnny Depp. **2** Lithgow. **3** 87 minutes. **4** Jonathan Demme. **5** 1940s. **6** Lane.
7 Brad Pitt. **8** Barry Levinson. **9** *The Deer Hunter*. **10** *Scream*. **11** 1970s.
12 Moorehead. **13** Sharon and Susan. **14** Groucho Marx. **15** *Crocodile Dundee*.
16 Kelly McGillis. **17** Dan Aykroyd. **18** Mel Gibson. **19** Holly Goodhead.
20 Broderick. **21** Mrs Pearce. **22** Jack Lemmon. **23** *Blind Date*. **24** Katharine
Hepburn. **25** 1950s.

Answers – see page 128

1   What sort of accent does Meryl Streep have in *Out of Africa*?
2   Who was described as the Buster Keaton of Hong Kong?
3   Which star of *Chariots of Fire* and *Gandhi* died of AIDS in 1990?
4   Where does Rutger Hauer hail from?
5   Which Oscar-winner from *Ordinary People* was married to Debra Winger for three years?
6   What was Diane Keaton's next Oscar nomination after *Annie Hall*?
7   Kevin Kline appeared in the movie of which Gilbert & Sullivan opera which he had starred in on Broadway?
8   What sort of musician was Sigourney Weaver in *Ghostbusters*?
9   Which outspoken talk-show hostess made her movie debut in *Hairspray*?
10   Which widow of Kurt Cobain was a star of *Sid and Nancy*?
11   In which film did Jack Nicholson say, 'Here's Johnny'?
12   Which star of TV's *Cheers* is famous on the big screen for *Look Who's Talking*?
13   Who won the National Society of Film Critics award in the US for playing the ghoul in *Beetlejuice*?
14   Who was the aerobics instructor in *Perfect*?
15   Who gained notoriety for her 'you like me, you really like me' Oscar acceptance speech in 1984?
16   Who had his wife as co-star in *Shanghai Surprise*?
17   Which father and son appeared in *Wall Street*?
18   Who played Loretta Lynn in *Coal Miner's Daughter*?
19   For which movie was Julie Walters Oscar-nominated on her film debut?
20   Which husband and wife starred in *DOA* in 1988?
21   Who played two parts in *Dead Ringers* in 1988?
22   In which movie did Debra Winger play an angel?
23   Who played Sid Vicious in *Sid and Nancy*?
24   Which writer did Jack Nicholson play in *Reds*?
25   Who married Melanie Griffith twice?

Answers Dustin Hoffman (see Quiz 16)
1 *Kramer versus Kramer.* 2 Two. 3 *Papillon.* 4 Journalist. 5 Broderick. 6 *The Merchant of Venice.* 7 Jessica Lange. 8 1930s. 9 Nichols. 10 *Little Big Man.* 11 Los Angeles. 12 *Billy Bathgate.* 13 *The Graduate.* 14 *Tootsie.* 15 Willy Loman. 16 Raymond. 17 *Midnight Cowboy.* 18 *Marathon Man.* 19 *Ishtar.* 20 Carl Bernstein. 21 *Agatha.* 22 Lenny Bruce. 23 Sean Connery. 24 *Dick Tracy.* 25 Captain Hook in *Hook.*

Answers – see page 125

1	Which movie star had 'Winona Forever' tattooed on his arm?
2	Which John starred in *Cliffhanger*?
3	Within fifteen minutes, how long does *The Blair Witch Project* last?
4	Who won the Best Director Oscar for *The Silence of the Lambs*?
5	In which decade of the 20th century was Chevy Chase born?
6	Which Diane featured in *Rumble Fish*?
7	Who played JD in *Thelma and Louise*?
8	Who directed *Rain Man*?
9	Which Michael Cimino film about Vietnam won five Oscars in the 70s?
10	In which film did a character named Gale Weathers first appear?
11	In which decade was *Chinatown* released?
12	Which Agnes appeared in *Citizen Kane* and *Jane Eyre*?
13	What are the names of the twins in *The Parent Trap*?
14	Margaret Dumont was which comedian's most famous film stooge?
15	In which 80s action comedy did the character Sue Charlton appear?
16	Who was Tom Cruise's leading lady in *Top Gun*?
17	Which actor links *The Couch Trip* and *Sergeant Bilko*?
18	Which actor's middle names are Columcille Gerard?
19	What was the name of the Bond girl in *Moonraker*?
20	Which Matthew starred in *The Cable Guy*?
21	Who is Professor Higgins's housekeeper in *My Fair Lady*?
22	Who won the Best Actor Oscar for *Save the Tiger*?
23	What was Bruce Willis's first film, in 1987?
24	Who won the Best Actress Oscar for *Morning Glory*?
25	In which decade was *Around the World in Eighty Days* released?

Answers Cartoons (see Quiz 13)
1 Eddie Murphy. **2** *Anastasia*. **3** *Beauty and the Beast*. **4** Randy Newman.
5 Toontown. **6** *Anchors Aweigh*. **7** *Pinocchio*. **8** Dinosaur. **9** *Jumanji*. **10** *The Lion King*. **11** Si & Am. **12** Scar. **13** Rex. **14** *Aladdin*. **15** *Bambi*. **16** Woody Allen. **17** Jennifer Aniston. **18** Mel Gibson. **19** Kathleen Turner. **20** MGM. **21** *Tarzan*. **22** Tom & Jerry. **23** *Miss Saigon*. **24** Hyena. **25** King Louie.

Answers – see page 126

1   Which 70s weepie saw Meryl Streep as his co-star?
2   How many 20th century Oscars did he win?
3   In which movie did he play a prisoner on Devils' Island?
4   What was his occupation in *All the President's Men*?
5   Which Matthew played his son in *Family Business*?
6   Which Shakespeare play did he appear in on Broadway and in London in 1989 and 1990 respectively?
7   Who was his female co-star in *Tootsie*?
8   In which decade was he born?
9   Which Mike directed him in *The Graduate*?
10   In which western did he age from 12 to 121?
11   In which city was he born?
12   In which 1991 movie did he play gangster Dutch Schultz?
13   For which movie did he receive his first Oscar nomination?
14   Which movie saw him as a female soap star?
15   Which character did he play on stage in *Death of a Salesman*?
16   What was his character called in *Rain Man*?
17   In which movie did he play Ratso Rizzo?
18   For which 1976 role did he famously keep himself awake for seven days to look the part?
19   For which flop did he team up with Warren Beatty?
20   What was the name of his character in *All the President's Men*?
21   In which 1979 biopic did he receive mixed reviews?
22   Who did he portray in *Lenny*?
23   Which superstar played his father in *Family Business*?
24   In which Warren Beatty movie did he play Mumbles in 1990?
25   Which character was he in a 1991 film based on a children's classic?

Answers 1980s Stars (see Quiz 14)
1 Danish. **2** Jackie Chan. **3** Ian Charleson. **4** Holland. **5** Timothy Hutton.
6 *Reds.* **7** *Pirates of Penzance.* **8** Cellist. **9** Ricki Lake. **10** Courtney Love. **11** *The Shining.* **12** Kirstie Alley. **13** Michael Keaton. **14** Jamie Lee Curtis. **15** Sally Field.
16 Sean Penn. **17** Martin & Charlie Sheen. **18** Sissy Spacek. **19** *Educating Rita.*
20 Dennis Quaid & Meg Ryan. **21** Jeremy Irons. **22** *Made in Heaven.* **23** Gary Oldman. **24** Eugene O'Neill. **25** Don Johnson.

Answers – see page 131

1   Who described himself as Mr Average Joe American?

2   Which silent star's name was an anagram of 'Arab death'?

3   Who was the sister of Olivia De Havilland?

4   About whom did Elia Kazan say, 'He was sad and sulky. You kept expecting him to cry'?

5   Whose biography was called *Blonde Venus*?

6   Which 30s star famous for his dislike of children said, 'I am free of all prejudices, I hate everybody equally'?

7   How many times did Alan Hale play Little John in a Robin Hood movie?

8   Which director was the subject of *Gods and Monsters*, played on screen by Sir Ian McKellen?

9   Who said, 'There are two reasons I'm in showbusiness and I'm standing on both of them'?

10 What colour was Danny Kaye's hair before Goldwyn made him dye it blond?

11 Who said, 'Astaire represents the aristocracy when he dances. I represent the proletariat'?

12 Whose photo in a swimsuit was pinned to the atomic bomb dropped on Bikini?

13 Who did Goldwyn mean when he said, 'It took longer to make one of Mary's contracts than to make one of Mary's pictures'?

14 In *Casablanca* which British actor said, 'I'm only a poor corrupt official'?

15 Which Tex sang the title song from *High Noon*?

16 Which creator of *Star Trek* was executive producer on the early *Star Trek* movies?

17 Who was the mother of actress Isabella Rossellini?

18 Which French actor's body was exhumed in 1997 because of a paternity suit?

19 Who died shortly after finishing *Network*?

20 In which decade did Jean Harlow die?

21 Whose marriage to Ava Gardner lasted just seven months?

22 Anthony Perkins died during the making of which movie?

23 Who played opposite Olivia De Havilland eight times?

24 Where was Audrey Hepburn born?

25 Whose autobiography was called *Back in the Saddle Again*?

Answers 1940s (see Quiz 19)

1 Little John. 2 Rita Hayworth. 3 Jo. 4 Betty Grable. 5 Aldous Huxley. 6 *It's a Wonderful Life*. 7 Larry Parks. 8 *Brigadoon*. 9 *Miracle on 34th Street*. 10 Maxim De Winter. 11 James Cagney. 12 Gene Autry. 13 *Casablanca*. 14 Charles Foster. 15 Bra. 16 Heinreid. 17 Spencer Tracy. 18 Betty Grable. 19 Bing Crosby. 20 *Pimpernel Smith*. 21 *Great Expectations*. 22 World War I. 23 *The Magnificent Ambersons*. 24 Judy Garland. 25 Jennifer Jones.

Answers – see page 132

1   What was the name of Nicolas Cage's character in *Con Air*?
2   In which decade was *Driving Miss Daisy* released?
3   Which movie star released a single called 'A Distant Star' in 1986?
4   Which suave actor turned down Robert Preston's role in *The Music Man*?
5   Which Elizabeth starred in *Big*?
6   Who won the Best Actor Oscar for *Dr Jekyll and Mr Hyde*?
7   What is Richard Gere's middle name?
8   Who was the youngest Marx brother?
9   What is Schindler's nationality in *Schindler's List*?
10   Who did Louise Fletcher play in *One Flew over the Cuckoo's Nest*?
11   For which film did Gregory Peck win his first Oscar?
12   Which Kevin featured in *Se7en*?
13   Who was Paul Newman's second wife?
14   Who played Renton in *Trainspotting*?
15   Which film features the song 'Brush Up Your Shakespeare'?
16   In which decade was *El Dorado* released?
17   Which actress is Mrs Carlo Ponti?
18   Who sang the Bond theme 'From Russia with Love'?
19   Who won the Best Actress Oscar for *Jezebel*?
20   What was the name of Jack Nicholson's character in *Prizzi's Honor*?
21   Which Shelley starred in *The Brady Bunch Movie*?
22   Who played the devious US Senator in *GI Jane*?
23   Which type of disability affects Tom Cruise and Susan Hampshire?
24   In the 1980s who bought the screen rights to *Dick Tracy* and made a film from it?
25   Who is Mrs Danny DeVito?

Answers – see page 129

1   Which Merry Man did Alan Hale play in *The Adventures of Robin Hood*?
2   Which redhead played Virginia Brush in *Strawberry Blonde*?
3   Which sister did June Allyson play in *Little Women*?
4   Which blonde replaced Alice Faye in *Down Argentina Way*?
5   Which author of *Brave New World* wrote screenplays for *Pride and Prejudice* and *Jane Eyre*?
6   In which movie did Henry Travers play an angel?
7   Who played Al Jolson in *The Jolson Story*?
8   What was the first musical hit in 1947 of Lerner and Loewe, which became a movie hit seven years later?
9   In which classic movie did Edward Gwenn play Kris Kringle?
10 Who did Laurence Olivier play in *Rebecca*?
11 Who played George M. Cohan in *Yankee Doodle Dandy*?
12 Which cowboy was high up in the money-making lists in 1940?
13 Which movie had the line, 'We'll always have Paris'?
14 What were Citizen Kane's first names?
15 Which garment did Howard Hughes develop for Jane Russell in *The Outlaw*?
16 Which Paul was one of Bette Davis's co-stars in *Now Voyager*?
17 Who played two parts in *Dr Jekyll and Mr Hyde* in 1941?
18 Who was the star of the 40s version of *Million Dollar Legs*?
19 Who was Father O'Malley to Ingrid Bergman's Sister Benedict in 1945?
20 What was the Leslie Howard version of *The Scarlet Pimpernel* called?
21 Which Dickens novel was successfully adapted for the big screen by David Lean in 1946?
22 *Sergeant York* was about a hero from which conflict?
23 Which Orson Welles movie was given its final edit without his approval?
24 Who was Fred Astaire's co-star in *Easter Parade*?
25 Which real-life Jennifer starred in *Portrait of Jennie*?

Answers Late Greats (see Quiz 17)
1 Gary Cooper. **2** Theda Bara. **3** Joan Fontaine. **4** James Dean. **5** Marlene Dietrich. **6** W.C. Fields. **7** Three. **8** James Whale. **9** Betty Grable. **10** Red. **11** Gene Kelly. **12** Betty Grable. **13** Mary Pickford. **14** Claude Rains. **15** Ritter. **16** Gene Roddenberry. **17** Ingrid Bergman. **18** Yves Montand. **19** Peter Finch. **20** 1930s. **21** Artie Shaw. **22** *Psycho V*. **23** Errol Flynn. **24** Belgium. **25** Gene Autry.

Answers – see page 130

1. A character named Dan Gallagher appears in which film?
2. Which Helen starred in *As Good as it Gets*?
3. How is Maurice Micklewhite better known?
4. In which decade was *Planet of the Apes* released?
5. Who won the Best Actress Oscar for *The Song of Bernadette*?
6. What was the name of the Bond girl in *Diamonds Are Forever*?
7. Who directed *Philadelphia*?
8. *A Star Is Born* and *The Verdict* featured which actor?
9. Jabba the Hutt is a villain in which 1983 movie sequel?
10. Which Simon featured in *Four Weddings and a Funeral*?
11. Which actor links *Hannah and Her Sisters* and *Mighty Aphrodite*?
12. Which actor's first two wives were Judy Carne and Loni Anderson?
13. Who played Oscar Madison in *The Odd Couple*?
14. Who was Alain Delon's *Girl on an Motorcycle* in 1968?
15. A character named Fletcher Reede appeared in which film?
16. Which song won Best Song Oscar for *The Woman in Red*?
17. Which Kelly featured in *Jerry Maguire*?
18. Who played opposite Dustin Hoffman in *Tootsie*?
19. In which decade was *Annie Hall* released?
20. Who won the Best Actor Oscar for *Elmer Gantry*?
21. What did the second M stand for in MGM?
22. Which Lynn featured in *Shine*?
23. *Cat Ballou* and *Paint Your Wagon* both featured which actor?
24. Who won the Best Director Oscar for *Midnight Cowboy*?
25. Which Annette starred in *The American President*?

Answers – see page 135

1	Which actress was Oscar-nominated for *The End of the Affair*?
2	What nationality are Jennifer Lopez's parents?
3	Who was Valerie Edmond's male co-star in *One More Kiss*?
4	Which actress voices Jessie in *Toy Story 2*?
5	Which actor links *Sleepy Hollow* and *Starship Troopers*?
6	Who links the films *Now and Then* and *American Beauty*?
7	Who does Virginie Ledoyden play in *The Beach*?
8	Who starred opposite Johnny Depp in *Devil's Advocate*?
9	Who played the law officer in *Double Jeopardy*?
10	Who plays Toni Collette's son in *The Sixth Sense*?
11	Which actress links *Romeo + Juliet* and *Little Women*?
12	What name links *Stigmata* and *Scream 3*?
13	Who has been Oscar-nominated for *Being John Malkovich*?
14	Who was 'the next best thing' for Madonna in the movie of the same name?
15	Which actor links *The Beach* and *Angela's Ashes*?
16	Which actress links *Elizabeth* and *The Talented Mr Ripley*?
17	Who voices the Rooster in *Chicken Run*?
18	Which actress links *Pleasantville* and *Dangerous Liaisons*?
19	Who links *Trainspotting* and *Star Wars: The Phantom Menace*?
20	Which actress links *Leon* and *Star Wars: The Phantom Menace*?
21	Who played the young temptress in *American Beauty*?
22	Who links *Picture Perfect* and *The Iron Giant*?
23	What was the name of DiCaprio's character in *The Beach*?
24	Who was Oscar-nominated for *The Talented Mr Ripley*?
25	Which actress links *The Ice Storm* and *The Opposite of Sex*?

Answers – see page 136

1   What is Macaulay Culkin's brother called who starred in *Father of the Bride*?
2   Which former child star became Mrs Andre Agassi?
3   Who played the Artful Dodger in *Oliver!*?
4   In which movie, remade in 1998, did Hayley Mills sing 'Let's Get Together'?
5   Whose autobiography was called *Little Girl Lost*?
6   Who played the possessed child in *The Exorcist*?
7   Which Oscar winner from *As Good as it Gets* was a child star on US TV?
8   In which Bruce Willis movie did Haley Joe Osment star?
9   Mark Lester played the title role in which 60s musical?
10   How many movies had Macaulay Culkin made before *Home Alone*?
11   Was Judy Garland 13, 15 or 17 when she played Dorothy in *The Wizard of Oz*?
12   In which 1993 dinosaur film did Joseph Mazello star?
13   Lisa Jakub ended up having her father disguised as a nanny in which movie?
14   Rumer Willis appeared with Mum in *Striptease*; who is she?
15   Which child star appeared in *Mermaids*, aged 10, and moved on to *The Ice Storm*?
16   Was Jodie Foster 12, 14 or 16 when she starred in *Taxi Driver*?
17   Who was Macaulay Culkin's first wife?
18   Who said, 'I was a 16-year-old boy for 30 years'?
19   Former child star Richard Beymer starred in which 60s musical opposite Natalie Wood?
20   In which country was Deanna Durbin born?
21   Which star of *Chasing Amy* started acting at the age of eight?
22   What was Hayley Mills's first film, in 1959?
23   How many times did Judy Garland marry?
24   Who played two parts in *The Prince and the Pauper* in 1977?
25   Who played opposite Judy Garland 10 times?

Answers Directors (see Quiz 24)
1 Finland. **2** Cecil B. de Mille. **3** Charlton Heston. **4** Christopher Guest. **5** *Cry Freedom*. **6** *Heaven's Gate*. **7** *Pulp Fiction*. **8** Kenneth Branagh. **9** Alan Parker. **10** Julie Andrews. **11** Ireland. **12** Blount. **13** Geena Davis. **14** John. **15** Cuba. **16** Kirk. **17** Kenneth Branagh. **18** Roman Polanski. **19** *Poetic Justice*. **20** *Jurassic Park*. **21** Antonio Banderas. **22** Robert Wise. **23** *The Horse Whisperer*. **24** Frank Sinatra. **25** *Bruno*.

Answers – see page 133

1   Which Kathy featured in *Sister Act*?
2   At what sport did Robert De Niro excel?
3   Which Mary starred in *The Abyss*?
4   Who won the Best Actress Oscar for *Gaslight*?
5   *The Muppet Movie* and *The Man with Two Brains* link which actor?
6   Who directed *Mrs Doubtfire*?
7   What was the name of John Travolta's character in *Face/Off*?
8   William Hurt and Marlee Matlin's relationship began on the set of which movie?
9   Which classical composer's music features in *Brief Encounter*?
10   In which decade was *An Affair to Remember* released?
11   Who won the Best Director Oscar for *Patton*?
12   Which classic musical charts the careers of Lockwood and Lamont?
13   In which film did the character President James Marshall appear?
14   What was the name of Helena Bonham Carter's character in *A Room with a View*?
15   Who directed the 1938 version of *The Lady Vanishes*?
16   For which film was Vincente Minnelli awarded his only Oscar?
17   Who played Seward in the 90s *Bram Stoker's Dracula*?
18   *The Blob* and *Le Mans* both featured which actor?
19   Sisters named Celie and Nettie appeared in which film?
20   Who wrote the book on which *Jaws* was based?
21   Who played Heinrich Himmler in *The Eagle Has Landed*?
22   Which British actor won an Oscar for *Reversal of Fortune*?
23   Which Courtney starred in *Ace Ventura, Pet Detective*?
24   In which decade was *Airplane!* released?
25   Who won the Best Actor Oscar for *Judgment at Nuremberg*?

Answers Stars of the 21st Century (see Quiz 21)
1 Julianne Moore. **2** Puerto Rican. **3** Gerry Butler. **4** Joan Cusack. **5** Casper Van Dien. **6** Thora Birch. **7** Francoise. **8** Charlize Theron. **9** Tommy Lee Jones. **10** Haley Joel Osment. **11** Claire Danes. **12** Arquette (Patricia and David). **13** Spike Jonze. **14** Rupert Everett. **15** Robert Carlyle. **16** Cate Blanchett. **17** Mel Gibson. **18** Reese Witherspoon. **19** Ewan McGregor. **20** Natalie Portman. **21** Mena Suvari. **22** Jennifer Aniston. **23** Richard. **24** Jude Law. **25** Christina Ricci.

Answers – see page 134

1   Where does Renny Harlin hail from?
2   About which producer/director did his brother say, 'Cecil always bites off more than he can chew, then chews it'?
3   Who directed and starred in *Antony and Cleopatra* in 1973?
4   Which director did Jamie Lee Curtis marry?
5   Which movie did Richard Attenborough direct about a journalist's escape from South Africa?
6   Which flop was Michael Cimino's next film after *The Deer Hunter*?
7   In which of his own movies did Quentin Tarantino appear in 1994?
8   Which British director's autobiography was called *In the Beginning*?
9   Who directed *Angela's Ashes*?
10   Which movie star is Blake Edwards married to?
11   John Ford was from a family which originally came from which country?
12   What did the B stand for in Cecil B. de Mille's name?
13   Who was Renny Harlin's wife when he directed her in *The Long Kiss Goodnight*?
14   Which Boulting brother was the director?
15   Director Tomas Gutierrez Alea hails from which island?
16   Which Douglas made his directorial debut in *Posse*?
17   Who directed his then mother-in-law in *Much Ado About Nothing* in 1993?
18   Which director, whose mother perished in Auschwitz, subsequently fled the USA on an assault charge?
19   What was John Singleton's follow-up to *Boyz N the Hood*?
20   Which movie was Spielberg editing by satellite while filming *Schindler's List*?
21   Whose directorial debut was *Crazy in Alabama*?
22   Who replaced William Wyler as director of *The Sound of Music*?
23   What was Robert Redford's first attempt at directing himself?
24   Which singer/actor's only foray behind the camera was in *None But the Brave*?
25   What was Shirley MacLaine's first film in full charge as director?

Answers Child Stars (see Quiz 22)
1 Kieran. 2 Brooke Shields. 3 Jack Wild. 4 *The Parent Trap.* 5 Drew Barrymore.
6 Linda Blair. 7 Helen Hunt. 8 *The Sixth Sense.* 9 *Oliver!.* 10 Three. 11 17.
12 *Jurassic Park.* 13 *Mrs Doubtfire.* 14 Demi Moore. 15 Christina Ricci. 16 14.
17 Rachel Miner. 18 Mickey Rooney. 19 *West Side Story.* 20 Canada. 21 Ben
Affleck. 22 *Tiger Bay.* 23 Five. 24 Mark Lester. 25 Mickey Rooney.

Answers – see page 139

1   Which song won an Oscar for *Evita*, although it did not feature in the original stage show?

2   When Mary Poppins lands to take over the Banks household, what does she carry in her right hand?

3   Who was Fred Astaire's partner in *The Band Wagon*?

4   Which 80s movie has the song 'I Had The Time of My Life'?

5   Which fading movie star is played by Jean Hagen in *Singin' in the Rain*?

6   Which *Mary Poppins* song won the Academy Award?

7   Who played Eva's lover Magaldi in *Evita*?

8   Which musical featured the song 'Hopelessly Devoted to You'?

9   Who directed the musical *New York, New York*?

10   In which musical did Albert Finney play Daddy Warbucks?

11   Which Nellie sang 'I'm Gonna Wash That Man Right Out of My Hair'?

12   Which member of Procul Harum sang about the 'Rainbow Tour' in *Evita*?

13   Who climbed the walls singing 'Make 'em Laugh' in *Singin' in the Rain*?

14   'The Rhythm of Life' came from which musical?

15   What is the plant's catchphrase in *Little Shop of Horrors*?

16   Which musical ends with the line, 'Where the devil are my slippers'?

17   Which musical was a remake of *The Philadelphia Story*?

18   How many Oscars did *West Side Story* win?

19   What is the song played at the end of *The Sound of Music*?

20   Who was the Famous Five's manager in *Spiceworld*?

21   In which 50s musical did Fred Astaire dance on the walls and ceiling of a hotel?

22   Who won an Oscar for his role as Master of Ceremonies in *Cabaret*?

23   In *My Fair Lady* Jeremy Brett sings 'On the Street Where You Live' as which character?

24   Who sang 'Did You Ever' in *High Society*?

25   In which musical did Judy Garland sing 'Have Yourself a Merry Little Christmas'?

Answers   Marlon Brando (see Quiz 27)
1 Motorcycles. **2** *A Streetcar Named Desire*. **3** Mexico. **4** Cannes. **5** 1920s.
6 Vito Corleone. **7** *On the Waterfront*. **8** Manslaughter. **9** *The Wild One*.
10 *Brando: Songs My Mother Never Taught Me*. **11** Frank Sinatra. **12** *Guys and Dolls*. **13** *A Dry White Season*. **14** *The Men*. **15** *Last Tango in Paris*. **16** *One Eyed Jacks*. **17** Tahiti. **18** Vivien Leigh. **19** *On the Waterfront*. **20** *A Countess from Hong Kong*. **21** Francis Ford Coppola. **22** *A Streetcar Named Desire*. **23** *The Teahouse of the August Moon*. **24** *The Godfather*. **25** Mark Antony.

Answers – see page 140

1   A character named Dr Sherman Klump appeared in which film?
2   Which actress links *Torn Curtain* and *Star!*?
3   In which decade was *Porky's* released?
4   Which actor had siblings called Leaf, Rainbow, Summer and Liberty?
5   Who won the Best Director Oscar for *A Man for All Seasons*?
6   Which film musical features Nellie Forbush?
7   Which Denise featured in *Starship Troopers*?
8   What was the name of the Bond girl in *Octopussy*?
9   In which city does the action of *Godzilla* take place?
10 In which decade of the 20th century was Geena Davis born?
11 Which Mary featured in *Independence Day*?
12 Who won the Best Actress Oscar for *Mildred Pierce*?
13 Who played General Ben Vandervoort in *The Longest Day*?
14 To the nearest hour, how long does *Spartacus* last?
15 In which movie was Whoopi Goldberg the voice of hyena Shenzi?
16 Which writer directed *Rosencrantz and Guildenstern Are Dead* in 1990?
17 The character Martin Riggs appeared in which film?
18 Which actor is the grandson of producer Michael Balcon?
19 *Local Hero* is set on the west coast of which country?
20 *Planet of the Apes* and *The Poseidon Adventure* featured which actor?
21 Which redhead sang 'Bewitched, Bothered and Bewildered' in *Pal Joey*?
22 Which Sam featured in *The Hunt for Red October*?
23 In which decade was *The Bells of St Mary's* released?
24 *Top Gun* and *Cat Chaser* both feature which actress?
25 What's Arnold Schwarzenegger's job in *Total Recall*?

Answers – see page 137

1   What modes of transport dominate *The Wild One*?
2   Which Oscar-nominated movie had Brando previously done as a play on Broadway?
3   Where was *Viva Zapata* set?
4   At which European film festival did he win with *On the Waterfront*?
5   In which decade was he born?
6   Which character did he play in *The Godfather*?
7   For which movie did he receive his first Oscar?
8   His son Christian was jailed on what charge?
9   Which movie had the ad line, 'That streetcar man has a new desire'?
10   What was his autobiography called?
11   Which singer was earmarked for Brando's role in *On the Waterfront*?
12   In which musical did he play Sky Masterson?
13   For which 1989 movie did he receive an Oscar nomination?
14   In which movie did he make his screen debut?
15   For which 70s Bernardo Bertolucci film was he Oscar-nominated?
16   Which movie saw his directorial debut?
17   Near which South Sea island is his home Tetiaroa?
18   Who played Blanche opposite Brando in *A Streetcar Named Desire*?
19   In which movie did he famously say, 'I coulda had class. I coulda been a contender'?
20   Which Chaplin movie did he make in 1967?
21   Who directed Brando in *The Godfather*?
22   For which movie did he receive his first Oscar nomination?
23   In which 1956 movie did he play a Japanese interpreter?
24   He sent a native American Indian to pick up his Oscar for which film?
25   Which role earned him a 1953 Oscar nomination in *Julius Caesar*?

Answers Musicals (see Quiz 25)
1 'You Must Love Me'. **2** Umbrella. **3** Cyd Charisse. **4** *Dirty Dancing*. **5** Lina Lamont. **6** 'Chim Chim Cheree'. **7** Jimmy Nail. **8** *Grease*. **9** Martin Scorsese. **10** *Annie*. **11** Forbush (*South Pacific*). **12** Gary Brooker. **13** Donald O' Connor. **14** *Sweet Charity*. **15** 'Feed Me'. **16** *My Fair Lady* **17** *High Society*. **18** 10. **19** 'Climb Every Mountain'. **20** Richard E. Grant. **21** *Royal Wedding*. **22** Joel Grey. **23** Freddie Eynsford-Hill. **24** Bing Crosby & Frank Sinatra. **25** *Meet Me in St Louis*.

Answers – see page 138

1	What was the name of Jimmy Workman's character in *The Addams Family*?
2	Who won the Best Director Oscar for *Amadeus*?
3	Which Catherine featured in *Home Alone*?
4	Who played Victor Laszlo in *Casablanca*?
5	In which decade was *Blade Runner* released?
6	Cher won her first Oscar for which film?
7	Which Michael featured in *The Terminator*?
8	Who sang the Bond theme from 'You Only Live Twice'?
9	Who starred as Eliot Ness in *The Untouchables* in 1987?
10	Who directed *The Mask*?
11	Who did Julie Christie play in the 1975 film *Nashville*?
12	In which country did Charlie Chaplin spend the final years of his life?
13	Who won the Best Actress Oscar for *A Streetcar Named Desire*?
14	*An Officer and a Gentleman* and *Big* both feature which actor?
15	How is Lee Yuen Kam better known in western movies?
16	In which decade was *The Longest Day* released?
17	Tony Manero was a character in a movie about which day?
18	Which 1982 film did rock star Debbie Harry star in?
19	In which film did a character named Paul Varjak appear?
20	*El Cid* and *The Millionairess* both featured which actress?
21	In which film did a character named Max Cody appear?
22	Who won the Best Actor Oscar for *Kiss of the Spider Woman*?
23	Who directed *The X-Files*?
24	What was Charlton Heston's first film, in 1950?
25	Which actor is the son of a British Poet Laureate?

Answers Pot Luck 10 (see Quiz 26)
1 *The Nutty Professor*. **2** Julie Andrews. **3** 1980s. **4** River Phoenix. **5** Fred Zinnemann. **6** *South Pacific*. **7** Richards. **8** Octopussy. **9** New York. **10** 1950s. **11** McDonnell. **12** Joan Crawford. **13** John Wayne. **14** 3 hours. **15** *The Lion King*. **16** Tom Stoppard. **17** *Lethal Weapon*. **18** Daniel Day-Lewis. **19** Scotland. **20** Roddy McDowall. **21** Rita Hayworth. **22** Neill. **23** 1940s. **24** Kelly McGillis. **25** Construction worker.

Answers – see page 143

1	In which movie did Robert Duvall say, 'I love the smell of napalm in the morning'?
2	In *Tomorrow Never Dies*, who played M?
3	Which singer appeared in *Mad Max Beyond Thunderdome*?
4	What was the third *Die Hard* movie called?
5	Which French city was the location for *French Connection II*?
6	What was the name of Sean Connery's villain in *The Avengers*?
7	Who was Harrison Ford's male co-star in *The Devil's Own*?
8	Which tunnel is the location for a helicopter pursuit in *Mission: Impossible*?
9	What was Serpico's first name, as played by Al Pacino?
10	Ian Fleming's Jamaican home gave its name to which Bond movie?
11	Which actor plays the head of the crew in *Armageddon*?
12	Which 007 starred in *Dante's Peak*?
13	What came number three in Oliver Stone's Vietnam trilogy?
14	Which 70s movie with Jack Lemmon was about a cover-up over a nuclear accident?
15	In *Day of the Jackal* who was the leader who was to be assassinated?
16	What was the name of Eddie Murphy's character in *48 Hours*?
17	*Courage under Fire* was about which conflict?
18	Who was the star of *Last Action Hero*?
19	Who sang the Bond theme from *For Your Eyes Only*?
20	What was Leonardo Di Caprio's first film after *Titanic*?
21	Where was *Apocalypse Now* filmed?
22	Who played the pregnant police chief in *Fargo*?
23	Which movie had the ad line, 'They came too late and stayed too long'?
24	*Patriot Games* was the sequel to which movie?
25	Who played Danny Velinski in *The Great Escape*?

Answers Pot Luck 12 (see Quiz 31)
1 3 hours. **2** 1980s. **3** Julie Andrews. **4** Judd. **5** Paul Robeson. **6** Warren Beatty. **7** Tom Mullen. **8** Julia Roberts. **9** Honor Blackman. **10** Emily Lloyd. **11** 1920s. **12** *One Flew over the Cuckoo's Nest*. **13** Robertson. **14** Edward G. Robinson. **15** Moore. **16** *The Rock*. **17** Colin Firth. **18** Tippi Hedren. **19** Jon Voight. **20** 1950s. **21** Alan Rickman. **22** Arthur Hiller. **23** Modine. **24** Audrey Hepburn. **25** Christopher Lloyd.

Answers – see page 144

1. Who received her first Best Actress nomination for *The English Patient*?
2. Who was the female singer on 'Hopelessly Devoted (to You)' from a winning soundtrack?
3. Which screenwriter was nominated for *Four Weddings and a Funeral*?
4. Who was Oscar-nominated for the music for *Angela's Ashes*?
5. What nationality is director Ang Lee?
6. In which movie did Al Pacino play Frank Slade?
7. For which Cher/Meryl Streep movie did Nora Ephron receive her first nomination?
8. How many nominations had Helen Hunt received before winning for *As Good as it Gets*?
9. Who first sang 'The Way We Were' in the movie of the same name?
10. In 1981 who shouted 'The British are coming' at the Oscars ceremony?
11. Who has sung two 1990s Oscar-winning songs?
12. Which Brit made the animated Oscar-winner in 1993 and 1995?
13. Who shared a best screenplay Oscar for *Pygmalion*?
14. What was the nationality of the actor who won for *Life Is Beautiful*?
15. Who directed Gary Cooper to an Oscar in *Sergeant York*?
16. Who earned a nomination for the theme song from *9 to 5*?
17. Who, in addition to Cher, won an Oscar for *Moonstruck*?
18. Who designed the Oscar?
19. Which actress criticized the US government over Haiti before announcing the nominees at the 1992 Oscar ceremony?
20. Who has hosted the Oscars ceremony most often?
21. Which two British stars were nominated for *Gods and Monsters*?
22. Who was Oscar-nominated for *Twelve Monkeys*?
23. Who was 80 when she won an Oscar?
24. Who received a Special Award for *Pollyanna* aged 13?
25. Which Italian director received an honorary award in 1995?

Answers Stars of the 50s (see Quiz 32)
1 Gene Kelly. 2 Claire Bloom. 3 Jean Hagen (as Lina Lamont). 4 Mario Lanza.
5 Christopher Lee. 6 Ethel Merman. 7 Kim Novak. 8 James Dean. 9 Jayne
Mansfield. 10 Pal Joey. 11 Alistair Sim. 12 Harry. 13 Fred Astaire. 14 World
War I. 15 *North by Northwest*. 16 Brigitte Bardot. 17 Yul Brynner. 18 Paul
Newman & Joanne Woodward. 19 Richard Burton. 20 Pearl Bailey. 21 *Roman
Holiday*. 22 James Stewart. 23 *Witness for the Prosecution*. 24 Burl Ives. 25 Gene
Kelly.

Answers – see page 141

1   To the nearest hour, how long does *Braveheart* last?
2   In which decade was *Trading Places* released?
3   How is Julia Wells better known?
4   Which Ashley featured in *Heat*?
5   In the 1930s who sang 'Old Man River' in *Showboat*?
6   Who won the Best Director Oscar for *Reds*?
7   What was the name of Mel Gibson's character in *Ransom*?
8   Who married Lyle Lovett instead of Kiefer Sutherland?
9   Who played the Bond girl in *Goldfinger*?
10 *Wish You Were Here* and *The Real Thing* featured which actress?
11 Was *The Untouchables* with Kevin Costner set in the 1920s, 40s or 60s?
12 In which film did a character named Randle P. McMurphy appear?
13 Which Cliff featured in *Three Days of the Condor*?
14 Which screen gangster was born Emmanuel Goldenberg in Rumania in 1893?
15 Which Julianne starred in *The Lost World: Jurassic Park*?
16 A character named John Mason appeared in which film?
17 Who played Kristin Scott Thomas's husband in *The English Patient*?
18 Who was the blonde female star in *Marnie* and *The Birds*?
19 Who won the Best Actor Oscar for *Coming Home*?
20 In which decade was *The Greatest Show on Earth* released?
21 Who played the villain in *Robin Hood: Prince of Thieves*?
22 Who directed *Love Story*?
23 Which Matthew starred in *Married to the Mob*?
24 Who won the Best Actress Oscar for *Roman Holiday*?
25 *Who Framed Roger Rabbit?* and *Back to the Future III* featured which actor?

Answers Action (see Quiz 29)
1 *Apocalypse Now.* 2 Judi Dench. 3 Tina Turner 4 *Die Hard with a Vengeance.*
5 Marseilles. 6 Sir August De Wynter. 7 Brad Pitt. 8 Channel Tunnel. 9 Frank.
10 *GoldenEye.* 11 Bruce Willis. 12 Pierce Brosnan. 13 *Platoon.* 14 *The China Syndrome.* 15 Charles de Gaulle. 16 Reggie Hammond. 17 Gulf War. 18 Arnold Schwarzenegger. 19 Sheena Easton 20 *The Man in the Iron Mask.* 21 The Philippines. 22 Frances McDormand. 23 *The Wild Bunch.* 24 *The Hunt for Red October.* 25 Charles Bronson.

Answers – see page 142

1   In *An American in Paris* who said, 'That's quite a dress you almost have on'?
2   Which unknown was chosen by Chaplin to star with him in *Limelight*?
3   In *Singin' in the Rain*, who said, 'we feel all our hard work ain't been in vain for nothin'!'?
4   How was Alfredo Cocozza who starred in *The Great Caruso* better known?
5   Who was the monster in *The Curse of Frankenstein*?
6   Which lady with a massive voice was the star of *Call Me Madam*?
7   Who was the blonde James Stewart had to follow in *Vertigo*?
8   Who died while filming *Giant* in 1955?
9   Which blonde starred in *Will Success Spoil Rock Hunter*??
10 In which movie did Rita Hayworth sing 'Bewitched, Bothered and Bewildered'?
11 Who played Scrooge in the classic movie, with George Cole as his younger self?
12 'The Trouble with' whom was a movie debut for Shirley MacLaine?
13 Which dancer did Danny Kaye replace in *White Christmas*, a remake of *Holiday Inn*?
14 *The African Queen* is about events in which war?
15 Which Hitchcock/Cary Grant film has its climax on Mount Rushmore?
16 Who was described as France's most ogled export in 1956?
17 Which Russian-born star played the Pharaoh in *The Ten Commandments*?
18 Which husband and wife first appeared together in *The Long Hot Summer*?
19 Which Welsh actor wins Jesus' robe in a dice game in *The Robe*?
20 Whose autobiography was called *The Raw Pearl*?
21 For what was Audrey Hepburn Oscar-nominated on her film debut?
22 Who played Glenn Miller in *The Glenn Miller Story*?
23 In which movie did Tyrone Power have his final completed role?
24 Who played Big Daddy in *Cat on a Hot Tin Roof*?
25 Which dancer discovered Leslie Caron?

Answers – see page 147

1   In which state does the action of *The Blair Witch Project* take place?
2   How old was Regan MacNeil when she was possessed in *The Exorcist*?
3   What is the name of the film in *Scream 2* based on the murders in *Scream*?
4   Who plays Sergeant Neil Howie in *The Wicker Man*?
5   What is John Cassavetes's occupation in *Rosemary's Baby*?
6   What type of bird is the first to attack Melanie in *The Birds*?
7   Who played Dr Seward in *Bram Stoker's Dracula*?
8   Who wrote the score for *Psycho*?
9   What does Mike throw into the river in *The Blair Witch Project*?
10   What is the name of the lead character in *Night of the Living Dead*?
11   Who plays 'Leatherface' in the film *The Texas Chainsaw Massacre*?
12   Who produced *Poltergeist*?
13   Who was the star of *The House of Wax*?
14   Who directed *Psycho III*?
15   In which horror movie did Johnny Depp make his debut?
16   What is the name of Danny's imaginary friend in *The Shining*?
17   In which movie does Anjelica Houston say, 'Don't torture yourself, Gomez. That's my job'?
18   Which Mrs Charles Laughton played the title role in *The Bride of Frankenstein*?
19   Who directed *The Evil Dead*?
20   In which state is *Halloween* set?
21   Brad Pitt stayed in Peter Cushing's house while making which movie?
22   Who has the double role in *Mary Reilly*, based on *Dr Jekyll and Mr Hyde*?
23   Upon whose novel is *Carrie* based?
24   What was the first Sherlock Holmes Hammer horror movie in colour?
25   What was the name of Richard Dreyfuss's character in *Jaws*?

Answers – see page 148

1 In which film does a character named Rod Tidwell appear?
2 The song 'Unchained Melody' was revived by featuring in which movie?
3 Which Alan featured in the 1991 movie *Hamlet*?
4 Who won the Best Director Oscar for *Forrest Gump*?
5 Who played Susie Diamond in *The Fabulous Baker Boys*?
6 Who won the Best Actress Oscar for *The Three Faces of Eve*?
7 Who played Cruella De Vil's sidekick Jasper in *101 Dalmatians*?
8 Which veteran starred with Burt Lancaster in *Tough Guys* in 1986?
9 What was the name of the Keir Dullea character in *2001: A Space Odyssey*?
10 In which decade was *Romancing the Stone* released?
11 Who directed *Lethal Weapon*?
12 Which early screen comedian's real name was Louis Cristillo?
13 Which soap did Hollywood star Alec Baldwin star in?
14 In which film did Clint Eastwood first play 'The man with no name'?
15 Who was the US teacher in *To Sir with Love*?
16 In which decade was *Fahrenheit 451* released?
17 Who played King Arthur in the film musical *Camelot*?
18 *Dracula* and *The Man with the Golden Gun* both featured which actor?
19 From 1990 to 1997 every movie that got the Best Picture Oscar also got an Oscar in which other category?
20 *Dances with Wolves* concerns a soldier from which war?
21 Who played Doug Roberts in *The Towering Inferno*?
22 *2010* and *Memphis Belle* both feature which actor?
23 Who won the Best Actor Oscar for *The Private Life of Henry VIII*?
24 What was the Bond girl's name in *The Man with the Golden Gun*?
25 Which Burt appeared in *Bean –The Ultimate Disaster Movie*?

Answers Meryl Streep (see Quiz 36)
1 Clint Eastwood. **2** *Silkwood*. **3** Jeremy Irons. **4** Linda. **5** Karen Blixen. **6** Taken by a dingo. **7** *Dancing at Lughnasa*. **8** *Julia*. **9** Australian. **10** Alan Alda.
11 Carrie Fisher. **12** *The River Wild*. **13** *The French Lieutenant's Woman*. **14** *Evita*.
15 John Cazale. **16** Bruce Willis. **17** *Manhattan*. **18** *The Deer Hunter*. **19** Jack Nicholson. **20** *Sophie's Choice*. **21** Shirley Maclaine. **22** *Silkwood*. **23** *Kramer versus Kramer*. **24** Robert De Niro. **25** Goldie Hawn.

Answers – see page 145

1	Who was the villainous Sheriff in *Robin Hood: Prince of Thieves*?
2	Which tough guy directed *Christmas in Connecticut*?
3	Which movie featured Jack Torrance?
4	Which actor kidnapped Harrison Ford in *Air Force One*?
5	Which horror star did Martin Landau play in *Ed Wood*?
6	Which star of *Goodfellas* was a child star on radio?
7	*The Clan*, with Sinatra, Martin & Co. was also known as what?
8	In which movie did Diana Rigg play Mrs 007?
9	Which sportsman-turned-actor whose journey in a white truck was real-life drama had the nickname 'The Juice'?
10	Whose first major movie as director was *Reservoir Dogs*?
11	How many Batman films did Michael Keaton appear in?
12	Who played outlaw Rob Roy in the 90s film of the same name?
13	Who was Sharon Tate married to at the time of her murder?
14	Which villain's name appeared in the title of a 1999 film with Cher and Maggie Smith?
15	Who won an Oscar for *Coming Home* after missing out for *Midnight Cowboy*?
16	Oliver Reed died during the making of which movie?
17	Who was nicknamed 'The Muscles from Brussels'?
18	Who was in *Batman Returns* 14 years after playing the crazed POW in *The Deer Hunter*?
19	Which Hitchcock villain said, 'A boy's best friend is his mother'?
20	Who played Colonel Nicholson in *Bridge on the River Kwai* after Bogart and Olivier rejected it?
21	Who is associated with the role of Ripley in *Aliens*?
22	Which 30s sex symbol replied to 'I've heard so much about you' with 'You can't prove a thing!'?
23	Which member of the Rat Pack was a Kennedy brother-in-law?
24	Who did James Mason play in *The Desert Fox*?
25	Which screen villain was born Hans Erich Maria Stroheim von Nordenwall?

Answers Horror (see Quiz 33)
1 Maryland. **2** 12. **3** *Stab*. **4** Edward Woodward. **5** Actor. **6** Seagull.
7 Richard E. Grant. **8** Bernard Herrmann. **9** The map. **10** Barbara. **11** Gunner Hansen. **12** Steven Spielberg. **13** Vincent Price. **14** Anthony Perkins. **15** *A Nightmare on Elm Street*. **16** Tony. **17** *The Addams Family*. **18** Elsa Lanchester. **19** Sam Raimi. **20** Illinois. **21** *Interview with the Vampire*. **22** John Malkovich. **23** Stephen King. **24** *The Hound of the Baskervilles*. **25** Hooper.

Answers – see page 146

1   Who was her co-star in *The Bridges of Madison County*?
2   Which of her films was about a nuclear nightmare?
3   Who was her English co-star in *The French Lieutenant's Woman*?
4   What was the name of her character in *The Deer Hunter*?
5   Which Danish author did she play in *Out of Africa*?
6   In *A Cry in the Dark* how did she say her baby had died in the Australian outback?
7   In which 90s movie did she master an Irish accent?
8   In which movie with Vanessa Redgrave and Jane Fonda did she make her screen debut?
9   What was the nationality of her character in *A Cry in the Dark*?
10   Which M*A*S*H star was her co-star in *The Seduction of Joe Tynan*?
11   Her role in *Postcards from the Edge* was based on the life of which actress who wrote the book?
12   What was her first action film in 1994?
13   In which film did she play an actress and the Victorian character she plays?
14   Which musical role eluded her in the mid-90s after she had impressed with her singing in *Postcards from the Edge*?
15   *The Deer Hunter* was the last film for which actor who was her then partner?
16   Who was her male co-star in *Death Becomes Her*?
17   In which Woody Allen film did she appear in 1979?
18   Which 70s movie about Vietnam won her her first Oscar nomination?
19   Who was her co-star in *Ironweed*?
20   In which movie did she win an Oscar for her portrayal of a Polish holocaust victim?
21   Who played her mother in *Postcards from the Edge*?
22   In which movie did she play a factory worker opposite Cher?
23   Which divorce drama won her her first Oscar?
24   Who was her co-star in the unsuccessful *Falling in Love* in 1984?
25   Which blonde actress was her co-star in *Death Becomes Her*?

Answers Pot Luck 13 (see Quiz 34)
1 *Jerry Maguire.* 2 *Ghost.* 3 Bates. 4 Robert Zemeckis. 5 Michelle Pfeiffer.
6 Joanne Woodward. 7 Hugh Laurie. 8 Kirk Douglas. 9 Dave Bowman.
10 1980s. 11 Richard Donner. 12 Lou Costello. 13 *The Doctors.* 14 *A Fistful of Dollars.* 15 Sidney Poitier. 16 1960s. 17 Richard Harris. 18 Christopher Lee.
19 Best Director. 20 American Civil War. 21 Paul Newman. 22 John Lithgow.
23 Charles Laughton. 24 Mary Goodnight. 25 Reynolds.

Answers – see page 151

1   *King Kong* and *Cape Fear* both featured which actress?

2   Who played the journalist loosely based on Carl Bernstein in *Heartburn*?

3   Which Ben featured in *The Truth about Cats and Dogs*?

4   In which decade was *Oklahoma!* first released?

5   What was the name of Will Smith's character in *Independence Day*?

6   Who won the Best Actress Oscar for *Darling*?

7   Which poet's name was the middle name of James Dean?

8   Which Kevin featured in *A Few Good Men*?

9   Who played Jack Lemmon's daughter in *Grumpy Old Men*?

10   In which decade of the 20th century was Sally Field born?

11   A character named John Doherty appeared in which film?

12   Who played Susan Sarandon's husband in *Lorenzo's Oil*?

13   Who won the Best Director Oscar for *The Sound of Music*?

14   Who played Rudyard Kipling in *The Man Who Would Be King*?

15   Who beat Meryl Streep for the lead role in *The Horse Whisperer*?

16   Which animals feature in *Oliver and Company*?

17   *The Killers* and *Field of Dreams* both feature which actor?

18   Who directed *LA Confidential*?

19   How were producers Harry, Albert, Sam and Jack known collectively?

20   In which category did Joel Gray win an Oscar for *Cabaret*?

21   Which Michelle featured in *Tomorrow Never Dies*?

22   Who directed *Labyrinth*?

23   Who played the wistful widowed father in *Sleepless in Seattle*?

24   In which decade was *Witness* released?

25   Who won the Best Actor Oscar for *The Lost Weekend*?

Answers The Silent Years (see Quiz 39)

1 12. **2** Samuel Goldfish. **3** United Artists. **4** *The Mark of Zorro*. **5** Irving Thalberg. **6** Pickfair. **7** Keystone. **8** William. **9** Universal. **10** Mabel Normand. **11** Potemkin. **12** Clara Bow. **13** Roscoe. **14** William Randolph Hearst. **15** Censorship and self-regulation of the movie industry. **16** Very large eyes. **17** Mack Sennett. **18** Glasses. **19** Buster Keaton. **20** Pauline. **21** New York. **22** Edison. **23** Keystone. **24** Davis. **25** Adolph Zukor.

QUIZ 38 BLOCKBUSTERS

Answers – see page 152

1   *Titanic* overtook which movie as the most costly ever made?
2   On whose books was *Mary Poppins* based?
3   Upon which day do the characters in *Independence Day* launch a nuclear attack on the alien mother ship?
4   Who plays Alfred in *Batman*?
5   What number in the series of Bond films is *GoldenEye*?
6   Against which king is Mel Gibson fighting in *Braveheart*?
7   In what year is *Apollo 13* set?
8   What is the name of Andy's sister in *Toy Story*?
9   What is Harry Tasker's fake job in *True Lies*?
10   What is the last sin to be executed in *Se7en*?
11   Who voiced Shenzi in *The Lion King*?
12   What speed must the bus keep above to stop it from exploding in *Speed*?
13   Who was the female lead in *Raiders of the Lost Ark*?
14   Where do Fred and Barney work in *The Flintstones*?
15   In which state is *Nell* set?
16   Which character is played by Gary Sinise in *Forrest Gump*?
17   Which character did Ben Kingsley play in *Schindler's List*?
18   In which city is *The Firm* set?
19   In which movie did Bette Davis say, 'Fasten your seatbelts. It's going to be a bumpy night'?
20   What nationality is Holly Hunter's character in *The Piano*?
21   In *Jurassic Park* the DNA of which creature is mixed with dinosaur DNA?
22   What city is *Judge Dredd* set in?
23   Who kills Vincent in *Pulp Fiction*?
24   What is the last image we see in *Forrest Gump*?
25   Who is the evil kid next door in *Toy Story*?

Answers Pot Luck 15 (see Quiz 40)
1 Chewbacca. 2 Warren Beatty. 3 Wrestling. 4 1980s. 5 White. 6 John Ford.
7 Babcock. 8 Vivien Leigh. 9 Christopher Lambert. 10 *Independence Day*.
11 'Streets of Philadelphia'. 12 Nora Ephron. 13 Susan George. 14 Cameron
Crowe. 15 Ingrid Bergman. 16 Al Pacino. 17 Judy Garland. 18 1940s.
19 *Splendor in the Grass*. 20 Ben Kingsley. 21 Dennis Quaid. 22 *The Sting*.
23 Mel Gibson. 24 Anne Bancroft. 25 Brolin.

Answers – see page 149

1	How many reels were there in D.W. Griffith's *Birth of a Nation*?
2	Who founded Goldwyn Pictures with Archibald & Edgar Selwyn in 1916?
3	The quote, 'The lunatics have taken over the asylum' referred to the founding of which company, by actors?
4	What was Douglas Fairbanks's first movie in his famous swashbuckling role?
5	Who was in charge of production when MGM was first formed?
6	What was the name of the home Douglas Fairbanks shared with Mary Pickford?
7	Which company founded in 1912 was famous for its slapstick comedies?
8	What was the first name of Fox of 20th Century Fox fame?
9	Which company did Carl Laemmle found in 1912?
10	Who was the most famous female star of Mack Sennett's Keystone movies?
11	Which 'Battleship' was the subject of a 20s movie by Eisenstein?
12	Who acquired her nickname after starring in the movie *It*?
13	What was Fatty Arbuckle's real first name?
14	On which newspaper tycoon's yacht was director Thomas Ince murdered?
15	What was the Hays Office set up to do after the death of starlet Virginia Rappe?
16	Which of Eddie Cantor's physical attributes was particularly unusual?
17	Who founded Keystone in 1912?
18	Which accessory was Harold Lloyd's trademark?
19	Who directed and starred in *The General* in 1929?
20	In 1914 Pearl White starred in 'The Perils of' whom?
21	In which US city did *Birth of a Nation* open in 1915?
22	Which prolific US inventor co-founded the Motion Picture Patents Company?
23	Which studio was famous for its Bathing Beauties?
24	Which star Mildred did Harold Lloyd marry?
25	Who founded the Famous Players Film Company?

QUIZ 40 POT LUCK 15 ························· LEVEL TWO

Answers – see page 150

1   What was the name of Peter Mayhew's character in *Star Wars*?
2   Who turned down Al Pacino's role in *The Godfather*?
3   At what sport did Kirk Douglas excel?
4   In which decade was *Field of Dreams* released?
5   Mickey Mouse's gloves are what colour?
6   Who won the Best Director Oscar for *The Grapes of Wrath*?
7   Which Barbara featured in *Far and Away*?
8   Who won an Oscar as Blanche in *A Streetcar Named Desire*?
9   *Subway* and *Highlander* both featured which actor?
10 A character named President Whitmore appears in which film?
11 Which song from *Philadelphia* won an Oscar?
12 Which writer directed *Sleepless in Seattle*?
13 Who played Dustin Hoffman's wife in *Straw Dogs*?
14 Who directed *Jerry Maguire*?
15 In the 1940s who was shunned by Hollywood when she left her husband for Roberto Rossellini?
16 Who won the Best Actor Oscar for *Scent of a Woman*?
17 Who was the most famous member of the Gumm Sisters Kiddie Act?
18 In which decade was *Song of the South* released?
19 What was Warren Beatty's first film, in 1961?
20 *Testimony* and *Schindler's List* both featured which actor?
21 Who played Jerry Lee Lewis in *Great Balls of Fire*?
22 For which film did Robert Redford win his first Oscar nomination?
23 Who played Fletcher Christian in *The Bounty* in 1984?
24 Who won the Best Actress Oscar for *The Miracle Worker*?
25 Which James featured in *Westworld*?

Answers Blockbusters (see Quiz 38)
1 *Waterworld*. 2 P.L. Travers. 3 July 4th. 4 Michael Gough. 5 17th. 6 Edward I.
7 1970. 8 Emily. 9 Computer salesman. 10 Wrath. 11 Whoopi Goldberg.
12 50 mph (80 km/h). 13 Karen Allen. 14 Slate gravel quarry. 15 North
Carolina. 16 Lieutenant Dan Taylor. 17 Itzhak Stern. 18 Memphis. 19 *All About Eve*.
20 Scottish. 21 Frog. 22 Mega City One. 23 Butch (Bruce Willis). 24 A feather.

Answers – see page 155

1   Who plays the neighbour James Stewart suspects of murder in *Rear Window*?

2   Which composer was Oscar-nominated for *On the Waterfront* seven years before making *West Side Story*?

3   What is the 'Green Fire' in the title of the movie with Grace Kelly and Stewart Granger?

4   Which Brando movie was banned in the UK for 15 years?

5   In which movie did Marilyn Monroe sing 'That Old Black Magic'?

6   Who played Captain Ahab in *Moby Dick*?

7   Who was Judy Garland's British co-star in *A Star Is Born*?

8   Which daughter of Hitchcock appeared in *Strangers on a Train*?

9   In *Guys and Dolls* where does Sarah go with Sky to find 12 sinners?

10   Who played Eloise Kelly in *Mogambo*?

11   Norman Maine in *A Star Is Born* is based on which silent movie star?

12   What was Tony Curtis and Cary Grant's only movie together?

13   Who played Al Capone in *Al Capone*?

14   Which movie was about the island which won a George Cross in World War II?

15   What was Elvis Presley's third movie?

16   *The Forbidden Planet* was loosely based on which Shakespeare play?

17   In which city is *Limelight* set?

18   Who played Jesse James in *Kansas Raiders*?

19   *White Christmas* was a partial remake of which classic?

20   In which movie did Gloria Swanson say, 'I am big. It's the pictures that got small'?

21   What was the sequel to the first *Godzilla* movie called?

22   Who played Moses in *The Ten Commandments*?

23   What was James Stewart's profession in *Rear Window*?

24   What name did Jack Lemmon adopt when disguised in drag in *Some Like It Hot*?

25   To the nearest twenty minutes, how long does *Ben Hur* last?

Answers Behind the Camera (see Quiz 43)
1 Jim Threapleton. **2** *Charlie's Angels*. **3** Alec Baldwin. **4** John Dykstra. **5** Cecil Beaton. **6** Alan Bennett. **7** *A Room with a View*. **8** Kenneth Branagh. **9** Cubby Broccoli. **10** Coco Chanel. **11** Warhol. **12** Roddy Doyle. **13** Demi Moore. **14** Todd AO. **15** Roy. **16** Nora Ephron. **17** Elton John. **18** Stephen King. **19** *Taxi Driver*. **20** Balmain. **21** Jodie Foster. **22** David Wark. **23** Frank McCourt. **24** Selznick Independent Pictures. **25** *Close Encounters of the Third Kind*.

Answers – see page 156

1   In which decade was *The Shining* released?
2   How is Bernard Schwarz better known?
3   What was the name of Brad Pitt's character in *Se7en*?
4   Who played the man in the wheelchair in Hitchcock's *Rear Window*?
5   Who directed *Independence Day*?
6   Which Juliette featured in *The English Patient*?
7   Which song won Best Song Oscar for *Evita*?
8   Who played the sadistic sheriff in Eastwood's *Unforgiven*?
9   Who won the Best Director Oscar for *All About Eve*?
10   *Clean and Sober* and *Batman Returns* both featured which actor?
11   The Bogart and Bacall relationship began on the set of which movie?
12   Who played Christy Brown's mother in *My Left Foot*?
13   Who won the Best Actress Oscar for *Room at the Top*?
14   Who was married to Debbie Reynolds and Elizabeth Taylor?
15   Who directed *Jackie Brown*?
16   What did the W stand for in W.C. Fields's name?
17   Which musical gangster movie features 'bullets' of whipped cream?
18   What was the name of the villain in *Diamonds Are Forever*?
19   In which decade was Disney's *Peter Pan* released?
20   Which horror writer directed the film *Maximum Overdrive*?
21   Who won the Best Actor Oscar for *The Goodbye Girl*?
22   *Kiss of the Spider Woman* and *The Addams Family* both feature which actor?
23   Who played the surprise guest in *Guess Who's Coming to Dinner*?
24   Which Yale graduate was known as the King of the Horror Movie?
25   Which Kenneth featured in *What's Up, Doc?*?

Answers Space & Sci-Fi (see Quiz 44)
1 *Apollo 13*. 2 Superman. 3 Rollerball. 4 *Star Trek*. 5 George Lucas. 6 Ewan McGregor. 7 Bees. 8 Ray Bradbury. 9 Robby. 10 Saul David. 11 Red Leader. 12 1997. 13 Hoth. 14 The Eiffel Tower. 15 A V-8. 16 Shepperton studios. 17 California. 18 Walter Seltzer. 19 Douglas Trumbull. 20 James Earl Jones. 21 *The Sentinel*. 22 Otis. 23 Michael Hutchence. 24 Cave. 25 J.

Answers – see page 153

1	Which director did Kate Winslet marry?
2	What was Drew Barrymore's debut as producer?
3	Which Mr Kim Basinger became a partner in Eldorado Pictures?
4	Who was the computer-controlled Dykstraflex camera named after?
5	Who designed the stunning costumes in *Gigi* and *My Fair Lady*?
6	Which British playwright was Oscar-nominated for *The Madness of King George*?
7	What was Merchant Ivory's first film, an adaptation of an E.M. Forster novel?
8	Who set up the Shakespeare Film Company in 1998?
9	Who was producer of the first James Bond movies and *Chitty Chitty Bang Bang*?
10	Which French fashion designer designed for several films in the 30s and 40s, including *La Marseillaise*?
11	Joe Dallesandro found fame in which Andy's movies?
12	Who was the original author on whose novel *The Commitments* was based?
13	Who starred in and also co-produced *Now and Then....*?
14	Which wide-screen system was promoted by Mike Todd?
15	Which Boulting brother was the producer?
16	Who wrote *Sleepless in Seattle*?
17	Which singer produced *Women Talking Dirty*?
18	Who wrote the novel on which *The Shawshank Redemption* was based?
19	In which of his own movies did Martin Scorsese appear in 1976?
20	Which French designer Pierre founded his own couture house in the 50s and contributed to over 70 movies?
21	Who directed and starred in *Little Man Tate* in 1991?
22	What did the D.W. stand for in D.W. Griffith's name?
23	On whose book is *Angela's Ashes* based?
24	What was David O. Selznick's independent production company called?
25	Which 70s sci-fi blockbuster got Frank Warner a Special Award for sound effects editing?

Answers 1950s (see Quiz 41)
1 Raymond Burr. **2** Leonard Bernstein. **3** Emeralds. **4** *The Wild One*. **5** *Bus Stop*.
6 Gregory Peck. **7** James Mason. **8** Patricia. **9** Havana. **10** Ava Gardner.
11 John Gilbert. **12** *Operation Petticoat*. **13** Rod Steiger. **14** *The Malta Story*.
15 *Jailhouse Rock*. **16** *The Tempest*. **17** London. **18** Audie Murphy. **19** *Holiday Inn*. **20** *Sunset Boulevard*. **21** *Godzilla Raids Again*. **22** Charlton Heston.
23 Photographer. **24** Daphne. **25** 212 minutes.

Answers – see page 154

1	Which film has the line, 'Houston, we have a problem'?
2	Who had a father called Jor-El?
3	What sport did James Caan play as Jonathan E?
4	Which sci-fi series did De Forrest Kelly star in?
5	Who did Spielberg describe as 'Walt Disney's version of a mad scientist'?
6	Who replaced Alec Guinness in *The Phantom Menace*?
7	What type of creature carries the disease in *The X-Files*?
8	Who wrote the novel *Fahrenheit 451*?
9	What is the name of the robot in *Forbidden Planet*?
10	Who produced *Logan's Run*?
11	Who is Luke Skywalker's squadron commander in the final battle in *Star Wars*?
12	In what year is *Escape from New York* set?
13	What planet were the rebels on before Darth Vader destroyed their base in *The Empire Strikes Back*?
14	For which monument is an H-bomb intended in *Superman II*?
15	What does Mel Gibson drive in the film *Mad Max*?
16	In which British studios was *Alien* filmed?
17	In which state does the *Invasion of the Body Snatchers* take place?
18	Who produced *The Omega Man*?
19	Who created the special effects for *Star Trek: The Motion Picture*?
20	Who was the voice of Darth Vader in the *Star Wars* trilogy?
21	*2001: A Space Odyssey* is based on which Arthur C. Clarke story?
22	What is the name of Lex Luthor's henchman in *Superman*?
23	Which member of INXS appeared in *Dogs in Space* in 1986?
24	In what sort of dwelling does Ben Kenobi live?
25	What is the name of Will Smith's character in *Men in Black*?

Answers – see page 159

1   Which star of *Look Who's Talking Too* was a TV regular on 'Cheers'?
2   Who sang the Bond theme from *GoldenEye*?
3   *Mermaids* and *Hook* featured which actor?
4   Who won the Best Director Oscar for *Lawrence of Arabia*?
5   Which Dianne featured in *Edward Scissorhands*?
6   A character named Sister Helen Prejean appeared in which film?
7   Which Jon featured in *Mission: Impossible*?
8   Who directed *The Ice Storm*?
9   Who played the title role in *Goldfinger*?
10   In which decade was *From Here To Eternity* released?
11   Which British actor won an Oscar for *My Left Foot*?
12   In which film did a character named Farmer Hoggett appear?
13   How was Hollywood's Joan de Beauvoir de Havilland better known?
14   Who won Best Supporting Actor Oscar for *Ryan's Daughter*?
15   Who was the first Jane to Johnny Weissmuller's *Tarzan*?
16   Who achieved notoriety by directing *Women In Love* in 1969?
17   Dietrich appeared in the German *The Blue Angel*, but who starred in the US version?
18   Who won the Best Actress Oscar for *I Want To Live*?
19   Which was the first animated film in the 90s for which Tim Rice won an Oscar?
20   *The Third Man* and *My Fair Lady* featured which British actor?
21   Which star of *The Godfather* bought an island called Tetiaroa?
22   In which film did a character named Oliver Barrett IV first appear?
23   In which film did Reynolds, Kelly and O'Connor sing 'Good Morning'?
24   *Lovesick* and *Santa Claus* featured which actor?
25   In which decade was *Dead Poets Society* released?

Answers 1930s Stars (see Quiz 47)
1 Bert Lahr. 2 Lucille Ball. 3 Charles Boyer. 4 The Dionne Quins. 5 Carole Lombard. 6 Alice Faye. 7 Australian. 8 Tallulah Bankhead. 9 Claudette Colbert. 10 Peter Lorre. 11 Laurel & Hardy. 12 Jean Harlow. 13 *The Private Life of Henry VIII*. 14 Gypsy Rose Lee. 15 Mickey Rooney. 16 Myrna Loy. 17 Jimmy Durante. 18 Paulette Goddard. 19 Bela Lugosi. 20 White. 21 John Gilbert. 22 W.C. Fields. 23 Mary Pickford. 24 Joan Crawford. 25 Gary Cooper.

Answers – see page 160

1   What was the last film personally produced by Walt Disney?
2   Which vehicle chased Cary Grant in *North by Northwest*?
3   Which movie persuaded everyone to 'Phone home'?
4   Which lizard first appeared in the Japanese movie *Gojira*?
5   Who painted the Picasso picture used in *Titanic* which was owned by Kate Winslet's character Rose?
6   Which 90s musical saw the most costume changes of any movie?
7   Which *Gone with the Wind* character has her baby while Atlanta is burning?
8   In which movie did Burt Lancaster have his most memorable scene with Deborah Kerr?
9   In which Joan Fontaine/Laurence Olivier movie does Mrs Van Hopper stub out her cigarette in the face cream?
10 Which Oliver Reed/Alan Bates movie was the first to feature male nudity?
11 Which movie with David Niven and Cantinflas boasted an all-star cast?
12 Which 30s horror classic had the ad line, 'A love story that lived for a thousand years'?
13 Who played the Jewish accountant in *Schindler's List*?
14 In which 90s movie is Clarice on the trail of Buffalo Bill?
15 Which actor played the mad scientist who created Edward Scissorhands?
16 Which movie introduced words such as 'Cowabunga' into the juvenile vocabulary?
17 Where does the most memorable scene in *When Harry Met Sally* take place?
18 Which movie about the Cambodian war introduced the expression for scenes of wartime atrocities?
19 Which movie did John Hurt make which required him to spend hours each day in make-up?
20 In which movie was Clint Eastwood first in danger of being upstaged by Clyde?
21 Which boy is on stage with Carrie in the gory finale to the movie?
22 Who plays the forger who goes blind in *The Great Escape*?
23 On which date does the movie *Independence Day* begin?
24 Where does *The Fantastic Voyage* take place?
25 What does Rita Hayworth peel off as she sings 'Put the Blame on Mame' in *Gilda*?

Answers Pot Luck 18 (see Quiz 48)
1 *Nutcracker Suite*. 2 Chris Columbus. 3 Meg Ryan. 4 Sutherland. 5 Cop.
6 (Sir) Anthony Hopkins. 7 John Carpenter. 8 *Braveheart*. 9 Peter Finch.
10 *Popeye*. 11 1960s. 12 Twiggy. 13 Coco. 14 Gordon Macrae. 15 Sir
Anthony Hopkins. 16 James Garner. 17 Barry Levinson. 18 *The Seven Year Itch*.
19 Margaret Rutherford. 20 *Dirty Harry*. 21 John Malkovich. 22 Diana Rigg.
23 Jane Fonda. 24 Macchio. 25 1940s.

Answers – see page 157

1   Who said, 'After *The Wizard of Oz* I was typecast as a lion, and there aren't many parts for lions'?

2   Which former Goldwyn Girl went on to TV superstardom as comedienne and producer?

3   Which French actor did not say, 'Come with me to the Casbah' in *Algiers*?

4   Which quintet were the star of *Five of a Kind*?

5   How was Jane Peters better known?

6   Which blonde sang the title song in *Alexander's Ragtime Band*?

7   In 1942 Errol Flynn changed to US citizenship from what?

8   Which star of the 20s and 30s said, 'I'm as pure as the driven slush'?

9   Who played Cleopatra in de Mille's 1934 classic?

10 Who starred as the murderer in *M*?

11 Which comedy duo were the stars of *Way Out West*?

12 In *Hell's Angels* which blonde asked if she could slip into something more comfortable?

13 In which movie did Charles Laughton say, 'Am I a king or a breeding bull?'?

14 Which famous striptease artist was born Louise Hovick?

15 Which child star played Puck in *A Midsummer Night's Dream*?

16 Who was dubbed the Queen of Hollywood in the 30s?

17 Whose catchphrase was 'Everyone wants to get into de act!'?

18 How was Marion Levy, a.k.a. Mrs Chaplin, better known?

19 Who played Igor in *Son of Frankenstein* in 1939?

20 What colour suit and boots did Tom Mix famously wear?

21 Who was Garbo's co-star in *Queen Christina*?

22 Which noted enemy of 'animals and children' played Mr Micawber in *David Copperfield*?

23 Which silent movie star announced her retirement in 1933?

24 Which Lucille changed her name to Joan and found fame playing strong roles?

25 Who links *Beau Geste*, *City Streets* and *The Lives of a Bengal Lancer*?

Answers Pot Luck 17 (see Quiz 45)
1 Kirstie Alley. **2** Tina Turner. **3** Bob Hoskins. **4** David Lean. **5** Wiest. **6** *Dead Man Walking*. **7** Voight. **8** Ang Lee. **9** Gert Frobe. **10** 1950s. **11** Daniel Day Lewis. **12** *Babe*. **13** Joan Fontaine. **14** John Mills. **15** Maureen O'Sullivan. **16** Ken Russell. **17** Dietrich. **18** Susan Haywood. **19** *Aladdin*. **20** Wilfrid Hyde-White. **21** Marlon Brando. **22** *Love Story*. **23** *Singin' In the Rain*. **24** Dudley Moore. **25** 1980s.

Answers – see page 158

1	Which Tchaikovsky ballet piece features in Disney's *Fantasia*?
2	Who directed *Home Alone*?
3	Which actress played Jim Morrison's girlfriend in *The Doors*?
4	Which Donald featured in *Disclosure*?
5	What was Michael Douglas's profession in *Basic Instinct*?
6	*Magic* and *Desperate Hours* both feature which actor?
7	Who directed the 70s movie *Halloween*?
8	Which 90s film was about William Wallace?
9	Who won the Best Actor Oscar for *Network*?
10	What was Robin Williams's first film, in 1980?
11	In which decade was *Sink the Bismarck* released?
12	Who played the female lead role in *The Boyfriend* in 1971?
13	What was the name of Irene Cara's character in *Fame*?
14	Who played Curly in the 1955 musical *Oklahoma!*?
15	Which knighted Welsh actor was born on New Year's Eve?
16	Which star of *Maverick* played Brett Maverick in the TV series?
17	Who won the Best Director Oscar for *Rain Man*?
18	The character Richard Sherman is in which time-linked film?
19	Which Dame played Agatha Christie's Miss Marple in four 60s whodunnits?
20	A serial killer named Scorpio appears in which film?
21	Who played the Vicomte de Valmont in *Dangerous Liaisons*?
22	Who played the first Mrs James Bond?
23	Who won the Best Actress Oscar for *Coming Home* in 1978?
24	Which Ralph featured in *My Cousin Vinny*?
25	In which decade was *Bambi* released?

Answers Memorable Movie Moments (see Quiz 46)
1 *The Happiest Millionaire.* 2 Plane. 3 *E.T.* 4 Godzilla. 5 They used the original.
6 *Evita.* 7 Melanie. 8 *From Here to Eternity.* 9 *Rebecca.* 10 *Women in Love.*
11 *Around the World in Eighty Days.* 12 *The Mummy.* 13 Ben Kingsley.
14 *Silence of the Lambs.* 15 Vincent Price. 16 *Teenage Mutant Ninja Turtles.*
17 Restaurant. 18 *The Killing Fields.* 19 *The Elephant Man.* 20 *Every Which Way But Loose.* 21 Tommy. 22 Donald Pleasence. 23 2nd July. 24 In a scientist's bloodstream. 25 Glove.

Answers – see page 163

1   Which Bond film was released on the same day as the Beatles' first single?
2   Which Latvian ballet dancer made his movie debut in *The Turning Point*?
3   Who was chief artist on the very first Mickey Mouse cartoon?
4   What was Michael Jackson's first movie?
5   How was 'famous first' Asa Yoelson better known?
6   What was Hitchcock's first talkie?
7   Which ground-breaking animation film was developed by Silicon Graphics Inc.?
8   Which movie pioneer said, 'I moved the whole world on to a 20-foot screen'?
9   What was Hitchcock's first film in colour?
10 Which Shakespeare play was the first British movie to win a BAFTA, in 1948?
11 What was Tatum O'Neal's first movie, which won her an Oscar?
12 What was the first movie shown in Cinemascope?
13 Which Richard Burton/Elizabeth Taylor movie was Mike Nichols's directorial debut and won him an Oscar nomination?
14 Which James's screen debut was in a Pepsi commercial?
15 Which Janet was the first Best Actress Oscar winner?
16 Which Irish novelist opened Dublin's first cinema?
17 In which movie did Elizabeth Taylor first act with Richard Burton?
18 Mike Nichols won the first director's BAFTA for which Dustin Hoffman classic?
19 Glenn Close made her film debut as whose mother in *The World According to Garp*?
20 In which movie did pop star Tommy Steele make his Hollywood debut?
21 What was the first movie shown at the White House?
22 *Broken Arrow* was the first western made from which perspective?
23 Who was the first British winner of a Best Actress BAFTA for *The Prime of Miss Jean Brodie*?
24 Whose made his screen debut aged 13 with father John in *Tiger Bay*?
25 Which 'Express' was Spielberg's debut as a feature film director?

Answers Who's Who? (see Quiz 51)
1 Ralph Fiennes. 2 Granddaughter. 3 Air Force. 4 Fred Flintstone. 5 Eric.
6 George Clooney. 7 Joseph Fiennes. 8 Jason Gould. 9 William Hurt. 10 Susan
Sarandon. 11 Jacqueline Du Pré. 12 Sonny. 13 Faye Dunaway. 14 Morgan
Freeman. 15 John Thaw. 16 Diane Ladd. 17 Nine. 18 Milan. 19 Bruce Willis.
20 Yardley. 21 Timothy Leary. 22 Jane Wyman. 23 Janet. 24 Ewan McGregor.
25 Gertrude Lawrence.

Answers – see page 164

1   In which film did King Jaffe Joffer appear?
2   Which Alan featured in *Die Hard*?
3   In which decade was *Rebecca* released?
4   In which movie did Winona Ryder play Cher's daughter?
5   Who won the Best Director Oscar for *One Flew over the Cuckoo's Nest*?
6   Which actor married US journalist Maria Shriver, one of the Kennedy clan?
7   Which character did Anthony Hopkins play in *Legends of the Fall*?
8   To the nearest hour, how long does *Dances with Wolves* last?
9   'King of the Cowboys' Leonard Slye was better known as whom?
10 Who directed *Goodfellas*?
11 A character named Rooster Cogburn first appeared in which film?
12 Who played Dolly in the 60s *Hello Dolly*?
13 In which decade was *A Streetcar Named Desire* released?
14 Which James was Professor Lindenbrook in *Journey to the Centre of the Earth*?
15 Who won the Best Actress Oscar for *Children of a Lesser God*?
16 *Anna and the King of Siam* and *Cleopatra* featured which Rex?
17 Who played Blofeld in *On Her Majesty's Secret Service*?
18 In which decade of the 20th century was Danny Glover born?
19 Which pop veteran featured in *The Man Who Fell to Earth*?
20 Who was Roger Moore's first Bond girl?
21 At what sport did Warren Beatty excel?
22 Who won the Best Actor Oscar for *Captains Courageous*?
23 Which conductor is Woody Allen's father in law?
24 Who directed *The Full Monty*?
25 Who played Lieutenant Schaffer in *Where Eagles Dare*?

Answers Box Office Successes (see Quiz 52)
1 Maize. **2** Demolitions expert. **3** Detective. **4** John Ford. **5** Elvis. **6** Boston.
7 Goldfish. **8** *Ben Hur*. **9** Miranda Richardson. **10** 85. **11** Desert explorer.
12 Lester. **13** Alexis Arquette. **14** Qantas. **15** Peter Weir. **16** Jenny.
17 Tiberius. **18** Jerry Hall. **19** 3. **20** Dewey. **21** James Cameron. **22** *Revenge of the Jedi*. **23** Mike Todd. **24** Sofia Coppola. **25** *Licence Revoked*.

Answers – see page 161

1   Who starred in, and was executive producer of, *Onegin*?
2   What relation, if any, is Bridget Fonda to Henry?
3   Morgan Freeman was in which branch of the services before he became an actor?
4   Which comic-strip character did John Goodman play on screen?
5   What is the name of Julia Roberts's estranged brother?
6   Who replaced Val Kilmer as Batman?
7   Who found fame in *Shakespeare in Love* and *Elizabeth* in 1998?
8   What is the actor son of Barbra Streisand called?
9   Which actor links *Broadcast News* and *Lost in Space*?
10 Who was originally known as Susan Tomalin?
11 Who did Emily Watson play in *Hilary and Jackie*?
12 What is Al Pacino's nickname?
13 Who was in both the 60s and 90s versions of *The Thomas Crown Affair*?
14 Who played Red in the 90s version of *The Shawshank Redemption*?
15 In the 1992 biopic *Chaplin*, who played Fred Karno?
16 Who played the mother of real-life daughter Laura in *Wild at Heart*?
17 How many times did Zsa Zsa Gabor marry?
18 In which Italian city was Greta Scacchi born?
19 Which actor had a hit with 'Under the Boardwalk'?
20 Which cosmetics house did Helena Bonham Carter advertise?
21 Which hippie guru was Winona Ryder's godfather?
22 Who was the only actress to divorce a future US president?
23 Which Jackson starred in *Poetic Justice*?
24 Which *Phantom Menace* actor's uncle is fellow actor Denis Lawson?
25 Who did Julie Andrews play in *Star!*?

Answers – see page 162

1. What type of crops grow in the field in which Mulder and Scully are chased across in *The X-Files*?
2. What is Harry Stamper's occupation in *Armageddon*?
3. What is Kevin Spacey's job in *LA Confidential*?
4. Which director links *Prizzi's Honor* and *The African Queen*?
5. Which famous rocker is said to have been an alien in *Men in Black*?
6. In which city is *Good Will Hunting* set?
7. In *Titanic*, what does Rose bring aboard the salvage boat, other than her luggage?
8. Which 50s film cost $4million, twice the maximum cost of the time?
9. Who plays Christina Ricci's stepmother in *Sleepy Hollow*?
10. How many changes of costume does Madonna have in *Evita*?
11. What is *The English Patient*'s occupation?
12. Which character is played by Kevin Spacey in *American Beauty*?
13. Which actor wears a single white glove in *The Wedding Singer*?
14. According to Charles in *Rain Man*, which airline has never had a crash?
15. Who directed *The Truman Show*?
16. What is the name of Tea Leoni's character in *Deep Impact*?
17. What does the 'T' stand for in James T. Kirk?
18. Who plays Alicia in *Batman*?
19. How many brothers did Private Ryan have?
20. Which character is played by David Arquette in *Scream 2*?
21. Who directed the first *Terminator* films?
22. What was *Return of the Jedi* originally called?
23. Which husband of Elizabeth Taylor produced *Around the World in Eighty Days* before his early death?
24. Who appeared in dad's *Godfather Part III*?
25. What was the original title of *Licence to Kill*?

Answers Pot Luck 19 (see Quiz 50)
1 *Coming to America*. 2 Rickman. 3 1940s. 4 *Moonstruck*. 5 Milos Forman.
6 Arnold Schwarzenegger. 7 Colonel Ludlow. 8 3 hours. 9 Roy Rogers.
10 Martin Scorsese. 11 *True Grit*. 12 Barbra Streisand. 13 1950s. 14 Mason.
15 Marlee Matlin. 16 Harrison. 17 Telly Savalas. 18 1940s. 19 David Bowie.
20 Jane Seymour. 21 American Football. 22 Spencer Tracy. 23 Andre Previn.
24 Peter Cattaneo. 25 Clint Eastwood.

Answers – see page 167

1	Which Jessica featured in *Play Misty for Me*?
2	How is Margaret Hyra better known?
3	In which decade was *All Quiet on the Western Front* released?
4	Who won the Best Actor Oscar for *Goodbye Mr Chips*?
5	What is Charlie Sheen's real name?
6	Omar Sharif is an expert at which card game?
7	Which Aidan featured in *Desperately Seeking Susan*?
8	Who played Scrooge in the 1951 *A Christmas Carol*?
9	A character named Harry Tasker appeared in which film?
10	Who won the Best Director Oscar for *Mr Deeds Goes to Town*?
11	Which actress links *High Noon* and *Rear Window*?
12	What was the name of Indiana Jones's sidekick in *The Temple of Doom*?
13	Who was Isabella Rossellini's mother?
14	Which song won Best Song Oscar for *The Sandpiper*?
15	The character named Charlie Croker is in which comedy/thriller film?
16	Which veteran actress said, 'I acted vulgar, Madonna *is* vulgar'?
17	Which surname was shared by John, Lionel, Ethel and Drew?
18	To the nearest hour, how long does *Doctor Zhivago* last?
19	Which actor's films include *Big Jim McLain*, *McLintock* and *McQ*?
20	Who directed *A Few Good Men*?
21	Which actress links *Love on the Dole* and *An Affair to Remember*?
22	In which decade was *The Driver* released?
23	What was the name of the villain in *Moonraker*?
24	Who won the Best Actress Oscar for *Guess Who's Coming to Dinner*?
25	In which film did a character named Horace Vendergelder appear?

Answers Pot Luck 21 (see Quiz 55)
1 *The Bodyguard*. 2 1950s. 3 Walken. 4 Frank Sinatra. 5 *The Third Man*.
6 *Out of Africa*. 7 Jennifer Jones. 8 *Schindler's List*. 9 Betty Grable. 10 Maggie
Smith. 11 Katz. 12 1 hour. 13 Normandy. 14 *Dick Tracy*. 15 Mark Lester.
16 David Lynch. 17 Nicholson. 18 Los Lobos. 19 *The Search for Spock*. 20 Mike
Nichols. 21 Boxing. 22 1960s. 23 Ernest Hemingway. 24 *The Client*.
25 Tomlin.

Answers – see page 168

1   In which decade was she born?

2   Which play, in which she played Tracy Lord, did she buy the film rights for and then sell to MGM?

3   Which John was her father in her first movie, *Bill of Divorcement*?

4   How many times was she Oscar-nominated in the 20th century?

5   Which American First Lady did she model herself on for *The African Queen*?

6   Which star of westerns was her co-star in *Rooster Cogburn*?

7   What was the name of her autobiography?

8   For which movie did she receive her first Oscar?

9   In which movie did she say, 'Nature, Mr Allnut, is what we are put in this world to rise above'?

10   In 1938 she was referred to as 'box office' what?

11   What part did Ludlow Ogden Smith play in her life?

12   For which 1962 Eugene O'Neill movie was she Oscar-nominated and a winner at the Cannes Film Festival?

13   For which film with Spencer Tracy did she win her second Oscar?

14   Which actor's aunt did she play in *Love Affair* in 1994?

15   How many films did she make with Spencer Tracy?

16   Which acerbic critic said, 'She ran the gamut of emotions from A to B'?

17   Who, with Cary Grant, was her male co-star in *The Philadelphia Story*?

18   With which star of the musical *Funny Girl* did she share an Oscar in 1968?

19   Who was her co-star in *Bringing Up Baby*?

20   Which 1933 movie, based on a novel by Louisa M. Alcott, did she star in?

21   Which French woman did she play in *The Lion in Winter*?

22   For which film did she win her third Oscar?

23   In which 1951 movie did she play a spinster opposite Humphrey Bogart?

24   For which film with Henry Fonda did she win her fourth Oscar?

25   In which US state was she born?

Answers Music On Film (see Quiz 56)

1 Richard Rodgers. 2 Burt Bacharach. 3 Shirley Bassey. 4 Quincy Jones. 5 Bill Haley and the Comets. 6 *South Park Bigger, Longer & Uncut.* 7 George Harrison. 8 'You'll Be in My Heart'. 9 Burt Bacharach. 10 *Toy Story 2.* 11 Beethoven. 12 'A Spoonful of Sugar'. 13 Harry Connick Jr. 14 Cole Porter. 15 Stephen Sondheim. 16 Ennio Morricone. 17 *The Deer Hunter.* 18 Donny Osmond. 19 James Horner. 20 *Let's Make Love.* 21 Eric Clapton. 22 Isaac Hayes. 23 A-ha. 24 Stephen Sondheim. 25 Leopold Stokowski.

Answers – see page 165

1   A character named Frank Farmer appeared in which film?
2   In which decade was *Father of the Bride* first released?
3   Which Christopher featured in *The Deer Hunter*?
4   Who won an Oscar as Maggio in *From Here to Eternity*?
5   'I never knew the old Vienna' is the first line of which movie?
6   Which film was about Danish author Karen Blixen?
7   Which actress links the 1950s *Carrie* and *Towering Inferno*?
8   Which movie gave Steven Spielberg his first Oscar?
9   Who was voted No. 1 pin-up by US soldiers in World War II?
10   Which English actress played an elderly Wendy in *Hook*?
11   Which Mike featured in *Pumping Iron*?
12   To the nearest hour, how long does *Dumbo* last?
13   *Saving Private Ryan* dealt with events in which part of France?
14   The relationship between Warren Beatty and Madonna began on the set of which movie?
15   Who played the title role in *Oliver!*?
16   Who directed *The Elephant Man*?
17   In *The Bridge on the River Kwai*, Alec Guinness was which Colonel?
18   Who sang the title song of *La Bamba*?
19   What is the subtitle of *Star Trek III*?
20   Who directed *The Birdcage*?
21   Before entering films which sport did Mickey Rourke practise?
22   In which decade was *If...* released?
23   Which author appeared in *The Old Man and the Sea*?
24   In which film did a character named Reggie Love appear?
25   Which Lily featured in *Nashville*?

Answers – see page 166

1   Who worked with Oscar Hammerstein II on *South Pacific* and *Oklahoma*?
2   Who was Oscar-nominated for *What's New Pussycat?*?
3   Who sang the Bond theme from *Moonraker*?
4   Who wrote the soundtrack for *The Italian Job*?
5   Who provided the music for *The Blackboard Jungle*?
6   'Blame Canada' came from which movie?
7   Which Beatle was responsible for the music in *Shanghai Surprise*?
8   Which *Tarzan* song was Oscar-nominated?
9   Who scored *Butch Cassidy and the Sundance Kid*?
10   'When She Loved Me' came from which animated movie?
11   Which classical composer's music did Malcolm McDowell like in *A Clockwork Orange*?
12   Which song is played over the opening credits in *Mary Poppins*?
13   Whose music features on the soundtrack of *When Harry Met Sally*?
14   Whose music was used in *Anything Goes* and *High Society*?
15   Who wrote the *West Side Story* lyrics to Leonard Bernstein's music?
16   Who wrote the music for *The Good, the Bad and the Ugly*?
17   'Cavatina' was the theme music for which 70s movie?
18   Who provided the songs in *Mulan*?
19   Who wrote the music for the Oscar-winning song from *Titanic*?
20   In which movie did Marilyn Monroe sing 'My Heart Belongs to Daddy'?
21   Which UK guitarist and singer wrote the soundtrack for *Rush*?
22   Who won an Oscar for *Shaft*?
23   Who sang the Bond theme from *The Living Daylights*?
24   Which composer provided the music for *Reds*?
25   Who led the Philadelphia Orchestra in *Fantasia*?

Answers Katharine Hepburn (see Quiz 54)
1 1900s. **2** *The Philadelphia Story*. **3** Barrymore. **4** Eight. **5** Eleanor Roosevelt.
6 John Wayne. **7** Me. **8** *Morning Glory*. **9** *The African Queen*. **10** Poison.
11 She married him. **12** *Long Day's Journey into Night*. **13** *Guess Who's Coming to Dinner?* **14** Warren Beatty's. **15** Nine. **16** Dorothy Parker. **17** James Stewart.
18 Barbra Streisand. **19** Cary Grant. **20** *Little Women*. **21** Eleanor of Aquitaine.
22 *The Lion in Winter*. **23** *The African Queen*. **24** *On Golden Pond*.
25 Connecticut.

Answers – see page 171

1   Which star of *Gone with the Wind* was shot down by German fighter planes in 1943?

2   Who was Olivia De Havilland's sister?

3   Who was the US's highest paid woman star of the 1940s?

4   Who played Elsa Bannister in *The Lady from Shanghai*?

5   How is Betty Thornberg, who starred in *Annie Get Your Gun*, better known?

6   Which star of *Brief Encounter* made her debut in *In Which We Serve*?

7   To the nearest two inches, how tall was Alan Ladd?

8   Who was famous for her long blonde hair which hung over one eye?

9   Who co-wrote and sang the songs in *Lady and the Tramp*?

10 Who was called 'The Hunk'?

11 Who played Bill Walker in *GI Joe*?

12 Which duo were reunited in 1949 after a 10-year gap in *The Barkleys of Broadway*?

13 Which redhead said, 'I never thought of myself as a sex symbol, more a comedienne who could dance'?

14 Ingrid Bergman's romance with which Italian director forced her to leave Hollywood for Europe?

15 Who played the title role in *Mr Skeffington* opposite Bette Davis?

16 Which Victor said, 'I'm no actor and I've 64 films to prove it'?

17 Which star of *Song of Bernadette* married David O. Selznick?

18 Which *Gone with the Wind* nominee's 40s films included *The Dark Mirror* and *The Snake Pit*?

19 Whose role in *Odd Man Out* took him to Hollywood?

20 Who was Bill Sikes when Alec Guinness starred as Fagin?

21 Whose death in 1942 persuaded Clark Gable to join the US Air Corps?

22 Which actress links Hitchcock's *Spellbound* and *The Bells of St Mary's*?

23 Which 40s star was famous for her sarong?

24 Who was described as 'Slinky! Sultry! Sensational!' in a promotion poster before *To Have and Have Not*?

25 Who was dubbed the 'Brazilian Bombshell'?

Answers 1960s (see Quiz 59)
1 *Whatever Happened to Baby Jane?* 2 Helen Keller. 3 Jerry Lewis. 4 *Darling*. 5 Jackie Gleason. 6 Glenn Campbell. 7 Henry Fonda. 8 Givenchy. 9 Howard Hughes. 10 *Paint Your Wagon*. 11 Paris & New York. 12 Bolivia. 13 Sidney Poitier. 14 *Winning*. 15 Turin. 16 *Hud*. 17 *Oliver!*. 18 *Alfie*. 19 *Tom Jones*. 20 Charlton Heston. 21 2 hours. 22 D-Day landings. 23 Ursula Andress. 24 *The Greatest Story Ever Told*. 25 *Hello Dolly*.

Answers – see page 172

1   What was Mel Gibson's job in the 1997 thriller *Conspiracy Theory*?
2   Which George turned down Bogart's role in *The Maltese Falcon*?
3   The character Catherine Tramell appeared in which movie?
4   Who won the Best Actor Oscar for *Patton*?
5   Which Arsenio featured in *Coming to America*?
6   Who starred opposite Mickey Rooney in *National Velvet* in 1944?
7   Which Karen featured in *Raiders of the Lost Ark*?
8   Who directed *Dead Man Walking*?
9   Who played the title role in *The Bachelor*?
10   Pearl Slaghoople is mother-in-law to which fictional character?
11   Which comedian played opposite Jane Russell in *The Paleface*?
12   Who played the Bond girl in *Never Say Never Again*?
13   Who is Pongo's mate in *101 Dalmatians*?
14   Which former child star became ambassador to Ghana and Czechoslovakia?
15   Which actress links *A Streetcar Named Desire* and *Planet of the Apes*?
16   Who won the Best Actress Oscar for *Mrs Miniver*?
17   What was the first Monty Python film for the cinema?
18   In which movie did Gregory Peck play James McKay?
19   To the nearest fifteen minutes, how long does *Fantasia* last?
20   A character named Rachel Marron appeared in which film?
21   In which decade was Disney's *Sleeping Beauty* released?
22   Which brothers starred in *Young Guns*?
23   *The Sting* and *Sneakers* both featured which actor?
24   Which Henry turned down Peter Finch's role in *Network*?
25   What was the name of Tommy Lee Jones's character in *The Fugitive*?

Answers Superstars (see Quiz 60)
1 Demi Moore. 2 Richard Gere. 3 *Book*. 4 Alfredo James. 5 Julie Andrews.
6 *Daylight*. 7 Michael Douglas. 8 Canada. 9 Michelle Pfeiffer. 10 Uma Thurman.
11 *Pulp Fiction*. 12 Dolly Parton. 13 Brad Pitt. 14 Sharon Stone. 15 Brad Pitt.
16 Enzio. 17 26. 18 Leonardo DiCaprio. 19 Eight. 20 *Taxi Driver*. 21 Michelle
Pfeiffer. 22 Robin Williams. 23 Whoopi Goldberg. 24 Kathleen Turner. 25 Emma
Thompson.

Answers – see page 169

1   In which movie did Bette Davis and Joan Crawford play two old ladies with murder in mind?

2   Which blind and deaf lady was the subject of *The Miracle Worker*?

3   Who played two parts in *The Nutty Professor* in 1963?

4   In which movie did Dirk Bogarde say to Julie Christie, 'Your idea of fidelity is not having more than one man in bed at the same time'?

5   Who played Minnesota Fats in *The Hustler*?

6   Which gentle-voiced country singer appeared in *True Grit*?

7   Who played against type in *Once Upon a Time in the West*?

8   Which French fashion designer Hubert worked on *Breakfast at Tiffany's*?

9   Which eccentric recluse and film-maker was the basis for a character played by George Peppard in *The Carpetbaggers*?

10   What was the last of Lerner and Loewe's 60s musicals?

11   Between which two cities is *The Great Race* set?

12   In which South American country were Butch Cassidy and Sundance finally tracked down?

13   Who played the guest in *Guess Who's Coming to Dinner*?

14   Paul Newman has motor-raced professionally since starring in which movie?

15   In which city was *The Italian Job* filmed?

16   Which movie had the ad line, 'The man with the barbed wire soul'?

17   For which movie was Jack Wild Oscar-nominated on his film debut?

18   Which 1966 movie made Brit Michael Caine an international star?

19   In which of his own movies did Tony Richardson appear in 1963?

20   Who played Michelangelo in *The Agony and the Ecstasy*?

21   To the nearest hour, how long does *A Man for All Seasons* last?

22   Which event was *The Longest Day* about?

23   Which Bond girl appeared in *What's New Pussycat?*?

24   In which movie did Donald Pleasence play the devil?

25   Which musical movie featured the character Horace Vandergelder?

Answers 1940s Stars (see Quiz 57)

1 Leslie Howard. 2 Joan Fontaine. 3 Betty Grable. 4 Rita Hayworth. 5 Betty Hutton. 6 Celia Johnson. 7 5 feet 5 inches. 8 Veronica Lake. 9 Peggy Lee. 10 Victor Mature. 11 Robert Mitchum. 12 Fred Astaire & Ginger Rogers. 13 Rita Hayworth. 14 Roberto Rossellini. 15 Claude Rains. 16 Mature. 17 Jennifer Jones. 18 Olivia De Havilland. 19 James Mason. 20 Robert Newton. 21 His wife, Carole Lombard's. 22 Ingrid Bergman. 23 Dorothy Lamour. 24 Lauren Bacall. 25 Carmen Miranda.

Answers – see page 170

1   Which star of *St Elmo's Fire* was the voice of Esmerelda in the cartoon *Hunchback of Notre Dame*?

2   Who published the book *Pilgrim* containing photos he had taken in Tibet?

3   What simple title did Whoopi Goldberg's autobiography have?

4   What are Al Pacino's real first names?

5   About whom did Christopher Plummer say, 'Working with her is like being hit over the head with a Valentine card'?

6   Which 1996 disaster movie starred Sylvester Stallone?

7   Michael Keaton shares his real name with another superstar; whom?

8   Where was Rick Moranis born?

9   Which actress links Susie in *The Fabulous Baker Boys* and Countess Ellen in *The Age of Innocence*?

10   Whose first two husbands were Gary Oldman and Ethan Hawke?

11   Which 90s movie got John Travolta's career back on track after a series of flops?

12   Which country star was in the list of top movie money-makers in 1981?

13   Who was Richard Gere's younger male co-star in *Seven Years In Tibet*?

14   Which star of *Basic Instinct* provided a voice in *Antz*?

15   In 1999 who in the US was voted 'the man you would most like to repopulate the world with after a Martian invasion'?

16   What is Sylvester Stallone's middle name?

17   How old was Barbra Streisand when she made her screen debut?

18   Who played Meryl Streep's son in *Marvin's Room*?

19   How many times did Elizabeth Taylor marry in the 20th century?

20   In which movie did Robert De Niro say, 'You talkin' to me?'?

21   Which star of *The Witches of Eastwick* was the voice of Tzipporah in *Prince of Egypt*?

22   Who has children called Zachary and Zelda?

23   Which film star wrote the novel *Alice*?

24   Whose first Oscar nomination was for *Peggy Sue Got Married*?

25   Which English actress was John Travolta's co-star in *Primary Colors*?

Answers Pot Luck 22 (see Quiz 58)
1 Cabbie. 2 Raft. 3 *Basic Instinct*. 4 George C. Scott. 5 Hall. 6 Elizabeth Taylor.
7 Allen. 8 Tim Robbins. 9 Chris O'Donnell. 10 Fred Flintstone. 11 Bob Hope.
12 Kim Basinger. 13 Perdita. 14 Shirley Temple. 15 Kim Hunter. 16 Greer
Garson. 17 *And Now for Something Completely Different*. 18 *The Big Country*.
19 115 minutes. 20 *The Bodyguard*. 21 1950s. 22 Charlie Sheen, Emilio Estevez.
23 Robert Redford. 24 Fonda. 25 Sam Gerard.

Answers – see page 175

1   In which film did Michael Douglas declare that 'Greed is good'?
2   Within fifteen minutes, how long does *The Elephant Man* last?
3   Who played Bernardo in *The Magnificent Seven*?
4   Who won the Best Actor Oscar for *Sergeant York*?
5   Which John featured in *Carrie*?
6   Who was the voice of Jessica Rabbit in *Who Framed Roger Rabbit*?
7   In which movie does Sugar Kane appear?
8   In which decade was *On the Town* released?
9   A character named Mitch McDeere appeared in which film?
10   Which director Roger links Bardot, Deneuve and Fonda?
11   Which actress links *Hannah and Her Sisters* and *Beaches*?
12   Which Oscar did Kevin Costner win for *Dances with Wolves*?
13   Which George featured in *Look Who's Talking*?
14   Within thirty minutes, how long does *Reservoir Dogs* last?
15   Which 1973 film did rock star Bob Dylan star in?
16   Which notorious 1943 movie had the advertising tag, 'Mean, moody, magnificent'?
17   *The Bostonians* and *Superman* featured which actor?
18   Who won the Best Director Oscar for *Gigi*?
19   In which film did a character named Madeleine Elster appear?
20   Who won the Best Actress Oscar for *Kitty Foyle*?
21   What was the name of Herbert Lom's character in *A Shot in the Dark*?
22   Who directed *Dead Poets Society*?
23   Which Steven featured in *Rambo: First Blood, Part II*?
24   In which decade was *Harvey* released?
25   Who won an Oscar as Margaret Schlegel in *Howard's End* in 1992?

Answers Sequels & Remakes (see Quiz 63)
1 *The Godfather*. 2 *A Perfect Murder*. 3 *The Jewel of the Nile*. 4 *Anna and the King*. 5 *Indiana Jones and the Last Crusade*. 6 *Oliver's Story*. 7 *Cabaret*. 8 One. 9 *Another 48 Hours*. 10 *One Million Years BC*. 11 *Patriot Games*. 12 *The Return of Jafar*. 13 Deloris (*Sister Act II*). 14 *Return of the Jedi*. 15 Eric Clapton. 16 Val Kilmer. 17 One. 18 Clouseau. 19 *Alien³*. 20 Paul Hogan. 21 *The Lost World*. 22 30. 23 New York. 24 *The Hustler*. 25 Ripley.

Answers – see page 176

1   Who played the White House PR guru in *Wag the Dog*?
2   Who played two parts in *The Man in the Iron Mask* in 1998?
3   What is the name of Susan Sarandon's character in *Dead Man Walking*?
4   In which movie did Gwyneth Paltrow first practise her English accent?
5   Who was Drew Barrymore's co-star in *The Wedding Singer*?
6   Who play the undercover cops in *Rush*?
7   Whose first movie was *Kiss Daddy Goodnight*?
8   Which musician did Geoffrey Rush play in *Shine*?
9   Which member of the Arquette family married the nephew of Francis Ford
     Coppola?
10   What was Antonio Banderas's follow-up to *Evita*?
11   Whose first major follow-up to *Another Country* was *My Friend's Wedding*?
12   Who was the SAS man who escaped from Alcatraz in *The Rock*?
13   In which movie did Al Pacino play the devil?
14   Who played two parts in *Meet Joe Black* in 1998?
15   What was the name of Robert Carlyle's character in *Trainspotting*?
16   Who played Anthony Hopkins's daughter in *The Mask of Zorro*?
17   What is the name of Morgan Freeman's detective in *Se7en*?
18   Which British actor played the villain in the third *Die Hard* movie?
19   In which movie did John Travolta play an angel?
20   Which husband and wife starred in *Too Much* in 1996?
21   In which movie did Susan Sarandon play Michaela Odone, the mother of a
     dying child?
22   Who played Leonardo DiCaprio's stepfather in *This Boy's Life*?
23   What is the name of Gwyneth Paltrow's character in *Shakespeare in Love*?
24   Who played Tina Turner in *What's Love Got to Do With It*??
25   Which low-budget 1999 thriller starred Joseph Leonard?

Answers Pot Luck 24 (see Quiz 64)
1 Blanche. 2 Allen. 3 Shirley MacLaine. 4 1940s. 5 Brigitte Bardot. 6 Caan.
7 *The Thomas Crown Affair*. 8 Annie Wilkes. 9 *The Fugitive*. 10 Chico.
11 Goldie Hawn. 12 Neil Simon. 13 Peggy Lee. 14 Petula Clark. 15 1930s.
16 Harold Hill. 17 Jerome Robbins & Robert Wise. 18 Lauren Bacall. 19 Sean
Bean. 20 1930s. 21 *The Lion in Winter*. 22 *Kiss Me Kate*. 23 115 minutes.
24 Keanu Reeves. 25 *Gone with the Wind*.

Answers – see page 173

1   What was the first sequel to an Oscar-winner to win an Oscar?

2   Which 90s movie was a remake of *Dial M for Murder* with Grace Kelly?

3   What was the sequel to *Romancing the Stone*?

4   Which Jodie Foster movie was a remake of a 50s music classic with Deborah Kerr?

5   Which movie announced, 'The man with the hat is back. And this time he's bringing his dad'?

6   What was the follow up to *Love Story*?

7   Which 70s musical was based on *I Am a Camera*?

8   How many *Terminator* films were made before the one called *Judgment Day*?

9   What was the sequel to *48 Hours* called?

10   *When Dinosaurs Ruled the Earth* was the sequel to which Raquel Welch movie?

11   *Clear and Present Danger* was the sequel to which 'Games'?

12   Which follow-up to Disney's *Aladdin* was released soon after the original?

13   Which heroine came 'Back in the Habit'?

14   What was the second sequel to *Star Wars*?

15   Which guitarist nicknamed Slowhand provided the music for *Lethal Weapon* and its first two sequels?

16   Who succeeded Michael Keaton as Batman?

17   How many sequels to *Die Hard* did Bonnie Bedelia star in?

18   *A Shot in the Dark* was one of the sequels about which Inspector?

19   Which sequel was criticized with the comment, 'In space no one can hear you snore'?

20   Who wrote and starred in *Crocodile Dundee II*?

21   What was the sequel to *Jurassic Park* called?

22   To the nearest million dollars, how much did *Rambo III* lose?

23   Where was Kevin lost in *Home Alone II*?

24   *The Color of Money* recreated the main character from which film?

25   What was the name of the only crew member to survive in *Alien*?

Answers – see page 174

1   What was the name of Baby Jane's sister in *Whatever Happened to Baby Jane*?
2   Which Nancy featured in *Robocop*?
3   Who won the Best Actress Oscar for *Terms of Endearment*?
4   In which decade was *His Girl Friday* released?
5   How is Camille Javal better known?
6   Which James featured in *A Bridge Too Far*?
7   'The Windmills of Your Mind' won an Oscar when it was used in which movie?
8   What was the name of the lady 'gaoler' in *Misery*?
9   In which film did a character named Dr Richard Kimble appear?
10 Who was the oldest Marx brother?
11 Which actress links *Shampoo* and *Overboard*?
12 Who wrote the play on which *The Odd Couple* was based?
13 Who sings 'He's a Tramp' in *Lady and the Tramp*?
14 Who played opposite Peter O'Toole in the 1960s *Goodbye Mr Chips*?
15 In which decade of the 20th century was Christopher Lloyd born?
16 What was the name of Robert Preston's character in *The Music Man*?
17 Who won the Best Director Oscar for *West Side Story*?
18 Who was the female lead actress in the 1940s *The Big Sleep*?
19 Which movie star has '100% Blade' tattooed on his arm?
20 In which decade was *Hell's Angels* released?
21 What was Anthony Hopkins's first film, in 1968?
22 Which musical film is based on *The Taming of the Shrew*?
23 Within fifteen minutes, how long does *E.T.* last?
24 *River's Edge* and *The Night Before* both feature which actor?
25 In which classic did Olivia de Havilland play Melanie Wilkes?

Answers 1990s Stars (see Quiz 62)
1 Anne Heche. **2** Leonardo DiCaprio. **3** Sister Helen Prejean. **4** *Emma*. **5** Adam
Sandler. **6** Jennifer Jason Leigh & Jason Patric. **7** Uma Thurman. **8** David Helfgott.
9 Patricia (Mrs Nicolas Cage). **10** *The Mask of Zorro*. **11** Rupert Everett. **12** Sean
Connery. **13** *The Devil's Advocate*. **14** Brad Pitt. **15** Begbie. **16** Catherine Zeta
Jones. **17** Somerset. **18** Jeremy Irons. **19** Michael. **20** Antonio Banderas &
Melanie Griffith. **21** *Lorenzo's Oil*. **22** Robert De Niro. **23** Viola De Lessops.
24 Angela Bassett. **25** *The Blair Witch Project*.

Answers – see page 179

1	In which film did he fall for a mermaid?
2	In which US state was he born?
3	In *Forrest Gump* he tours China playing which game?
4	In which movie was he the subject of a radio phone-in?
5	*Volunteers* is about volunteers in which corps?
6	In *Turner and Hooch*, who or what is his detective partner?
7	What is his real name in *Sleepless in Seattle*?
8	For which movie was he Oscar-nominated for playing a boy trapped in a man's body?
9	Who played his mother in *Philadelphia*?
10	In which decade is *That Thing You Do!* set?
11	Who played his partner in *Philadelphia*?
12	Whom did he play in *Apollo 13*?
13	In which movie did he play Captain John Miller?
14	What was his first Oscar-winner in the title role?
15	He met his wife Rita Wilson on the set of which movie?
16	In which movie did he play a lawyer dying from AIDS?
17	In what year did the real action of *Apollo 13* take place?
18	Whom did he marry after his divorce from Samantha Lewes?
19	Who plays the only lawyer willing to take on his case in *Philadelphia*?
20	Who was his co-star in *Splash*?
21	Which sport was featured in *A League of their Own*?
22	Who played Annie in *Sleepless in Seattle*?
23	Which 1996 movie saw him as director as well actor?
24	Who played his mother in *Forrest Gump*?
25	Which future Mrs Antonio Banderas was his co-star in *Bonfire of the Vanities*?

Answers Pot Luck 25 (see Quiz 67)
1 Roth. 2 100 minutes. 3 Daniel Hillard. 4 1960s. 5 *Postcards from the Edge.*
6 John Ford. 7 *Scent of a Woman.* 8 Gladys Knight. 9 Robert Wagner.
10 Sonja Henie. 11 Michael Crichton. 12 Charlie Allnutt. 13 Diane Keaton.
14 Jeff Bridges. 15 1940s. 16 Tim Robbins. 17 Orson Welles. 18 *A River Runs Through It.* 19 Fox. 20 *Amistad.* 21 2 hours. 22 Whoopi Goldberg. 23 John Landis. 24 Paul Scofield. 25 Marceau.

Answers – see page 180

1   Who was Frank Sinatra's second wife to be a professional actress?

2   Which actor, who died in 1997, was famous for his slow drawl and slow walk?

3   By what single name was Harris Glenn Milstead better known?

4   Which voluptuous blonde was Miss Photoflash 1952?

5   What was Bob Hope's theme song?

6   On what island did Oliver Reed die?

7   Where was Anthony Quinn born?

8   Leonard Slye was better known as which cowboy star?

9   Which husband of Ava Gardner said of her, 'a lady of strong passions, one of them rage'?

10   Which godfather of Jennifer Aniston was Oscar-nominated for *The Birdman of Alcatraz*?

11   Which king did Robert Shaw play in *A Man for All Seasons*?

12   Who was head of Universal at 21, MGM at 25 and died aged 37 in 1936?

13   Which of Spencer's famous co-stars said to him, 'I'm a little tall for you, Mr Tracy'?

14   Whose funeral in the USA in 1926 was a national event and prompted a number of suicides?

15   Lee Van Cleef found fame in what type of movies?

16   Otto Preminger was from which country before settling in the USA?

17   Who was originally billed as 'Oklahoma's Yodeling Cowboy'?

18   Which husband of Barbara Stanwyck had the real name of Spangler Arlington Brugh?

19   Which French writer/director's second wife was Jane Fonda?

20   Which wife of Roman Polanski was murdered by the Charles Manson Family?

21   How many times did Lana Turner marry?

22   William Powell was engaged to which blonde actress at the time of her untimely death?

23   Whose marriage to Ethel Merman lasted just three weeks?

24   Whose only Oscar nomination was for *Running on Empty* before his early death?

25   In a difficult dance sequence in *Top Hat*, Fred Astaire broke many what?

Answers Children's Films (see Quiz 68)
1 Kermit & Miss Piggy. **2** Dustbin. **3** Jasmine. **4** Pongo & Perdita. **5** Rick Moranis. **6** *The Hunchback of Notre Dame*. **7** Robin Williams. **8** Gertie. **9** The garden. **10** Danny DeVito. **11** *Hook*. **12** Ralph. **13** California. **14** Harry Connick Jr **15** *Bugsy Malone*. **16** Baloo. **17** Blue. **18** Danny Kaye. **19** Rowan Atkinson. **20** *Jurassic Park*. **21** *Pig in the City*. **22** Woody. **23** Disney. **24** Gene Wilder. **25** Anne Bancroft.

Answers – see page 177

1   Which Tim featured in *Reservoir Dogs*?
2   Within fifteen minutes, how long does *Edward Scissorhands* last?
3   What was the name of Robin Williams's character in *Mrs Doubtfire*?
4   In which decade was the biker classic *Easy Rider* released?
5   The character named Suzanne Vale appeared in which film?
6   Who won the Best Director Oscar for *How Green Was My Valley*?
7   In which film did a character named Colonel Frank Slade appear?
8   Who sang the Bond theme from *Licence to Kill*?
9   Which actor was married twice to Natalie Wood?
10   Which Norwegian skater starred in *Thin Ice*?
11   Which writer directed *Westworld* in 1973?
12   What was the name of Humphrey Bogart's character in *The African Queen*?
13   Who won the Best Actress Oscar for *Annie Hall*?
14   *Starman* and *The Fisher King* starred which actor?
15   In which decade was *Rope* released?
16   *Bull Durham* and *Bob Roberts* featured which actor?
17   Who played Harry Lime in *The Third Man*?
18   In which movie did Brad Pitt play the character *Paul MacLean*?
19   Which animal is Robin Hood in the Disney film?
20   Which Spielberg film was about slavery?
21   To the nearest hour, how long does *The Last of the Mohicans* last?
22   Which actress links *Burglar* and *Ghost*?
23   Who directed *Coming to America*?
24   Who won the Best Actor Oscar for *A Man for All Seasons*?
25   Which Sophie featured in *Braveheart*?

Answers Tom Hanks (see Quiz 65)
1 *Splash*. 2 California. 3 Ping Pong. 4 *Sleepless in Seattle*. 5 Peace Corps.
6 Dog. 7 Sam. 8 *Big*. 9 Joanne Woodward. 10 1960s. 11 Antonio Banderas.
12 Jim Lovell. 13 *Saving Private Ryan*. 14 *Forrest Gump*. 15 *Volunteers*.
16 *Philadelphia*. 17 1970. 18 Rita Wilson. 19 Denzel Washington. 20 Daryl
Hannah. 21 Baseball. 22 Meg Ryan. 23 *That Thing You Do!*. 24 Sally Field.
25 Melanie Griffith.

Answers – see page 178

1   Who were the Cratchits in *The Muppet Christmas Carol*?
2   Where does Beethoven hide when he first escapes from the puppy robbers' truck?
3   What is the name of the princess in *Aladdin*?
4   Who were responsible for setting up the 'Twilight Bark'?
5   Who plays the inventor in *Honey, I Shrunk the Kids*?
6   Kevin Kline provided a voice in which Disney movie set in France?
7   Who was the Prof in the remake of *The Absent Minded Professor*?
8   Who did Drew Barrymore play in *E.T.*?
9   Where does the professor dump the kids in *Honey, I Shrunk the Kids*?
10   Who starred in and directed *Matilda*?
11   In which 1991 children's movie did Glenn Close appear uncredited as a pirate?
12   Which Fiennes was a voice in *The Prince of Egypt*?
13   Where did 'The Karate Kid' move to?
14   Which musician who found fame with *When Harry Met Sally* contributes to *The Iron Giant*?
15   Which children's gangster movie marked Alan Parker's directorial debut?
16   Who teaches Mowgli 'The Bare Necessities of Life'?
17   At the Mad Hatter's tea party in *Alice in Wonderland* what colour is Alice's dress?
18   Who played the title role in *Hans Christian Andersen*?
19   Which British comedian was the voice of Zazu in *The Lion King*?
20   What was an adventure '65 million years in the making'?
21   What was the sequel to *Babe* called?
22   Who becomes a collector's item in *Toy Story 2*?
23   Which studio made the end-of-millennium *Tarzan*?
24   Which Gene played the owner of the factory in *Willy Wonka and the Chocolate Factory*?
25   Which Mrs Mel Brooks can be heard in *Antz*?

Answers Unforgettables (see Quiz 66)
1 Mia Farrow. 2 James Stewart. 3 Divine. 4 Jayne Mansfield. 5 'Thanks for the Memory'. 6 Malta. 7 Mexico. 8 Roy Rogers. 9 Mickey Rooney. 10 Telly Savalas. 11 Henry VIII. 12 Irving Thalberg. 13 Katharine Hepburn. 14 Rudolph Valentino. 15 Spaghetti westerns. 16 Austria. 17 Gene Autry. 18 Robert Taylor. 19 Roger Vadim. 20 Sharon Tate. 21 Seven. 22 Jean Harlow. 23 Ernest Borgnine. 24 River Phoenix. 25 Canes.

Answers – see page 183

1	A character named Dr Ellie Sattler appeared in which film?
2	*Rich and Famous* and *Top Gun* both feature which actress?
3	Which actress links *Meet Me in St Louis* and *Easter Parade*?
4	In a 1990 film which heroes lived in the sewers?
5	In which decade was *Monkey Business* first released?
6	In which film does Mark Renton appear?
7	Which actress links *Lady Jane* and *Howard's End*?
8	In which film did a character named Julian Kaye appear?
9	What was the name of the Bond girl in *Goldfinger*?
10	Who played Cal in *East of Eden*?
11	Who won the Best Director Oscar for *My Fair Lady*?
12	A character named Maggie Pollitt appeared in which 1950s film?
13	Within fifteen minutes, how long does *The English Patient* last?
14	Which Gary featured in *Lethal Weapon*?
15	Who directed *Casablanca*?
16	Which Julie featured in *Shampoo*?
17	Which movie did the song 'Call Me' come from?
18	How was Natasha Gurdin better known?
19	Which movie gave Steven Spielberg his first Oscar nomination?
20	Which fairy tale became a movie with the song 'Bibbidy Bobbidy Boo'?
21	Who founded the Sundance Festival for independent film makers?
22	Which Ted featured in *Body Heat*?
23	In which decade was *Monty Python's Life of Brian* released?
24	Who won the Best Actor Oscar for *Going My Way*?
25	A character named Holly Golightly appeared in which film?

Answers Tony Curtis (see Quiz 71)
1 1920s. **2** Bernard. **3** New York. **4** Navy. **5** Five. **6** Saxophonist. **7** *The Last Tycoon.* **8** Ali Baba. **9** Painting. **10** *Houdini.* **11** Cary Grant. **12** Malibu. **13** *Tony Curtis.* **14** *Some Like It Hot.* **15** *Trapeze.* **16** Janet Leigh. **17** *Boeing Boeing.* **18** Albert De Salvo. **19** *The Defiant Ones.* **20** *Kid Andrew Cody & Julie Sparrow.* **21** Cary Grant. **22** Kelly Curtis. **23** Joe. **24** Kirk Douglas. **25** Natalie Wood.

Answers – see page 184

1   In 1913 who did Fatty Arbuckle sign up with to make comedies?
2   Which Chaplin movie made a star of Jackie Coogan?
3   Who was the star of *Grandma's Boy*?
4   Who shot to stardom with *The Miracle Man*?
5   Who starred in *Sherlock Junior* and *The Navigator*?
6   Who did Garbo sign up with in 1925?
7   Which Louise was the star of *Lulu*?
8   Whose biography was subtitled *The Woman Who Made Hollywood*?
9   Which comedy star was arrested on charges of rape and manslaughter in 1920?
10 Who was the Mabel in the title of the Jerry Herman musical about her and Mack Sennett?
11 Where was Erich von Stroheim born?
12 Marion Davies was the protégée of which newspaper magnate?
13 Which deadpan comic made films with Fatty Arbuckle from 1917?
14 Which British-born comic starred in Mack Sennett's *Tillie's Punctured Romance*?
15 Which comedy group's debut was *The Cocoanuts*?
16 Who starred in the epic *The Wind*?
17 Which actress starred in D.W. Griffith's *The Violin Maker of Cremona* after being an extra just a few months before?
18 Who was considered the first vamp?
19 In which decade did Laurel team up with Hardy?
20 Which bespectacled comic was famous for his *Lucky Luke* two-reelers?
21 Who made his screen debut in *Making a Living* in 1914?
22 What relation was Dorothy to Lillian Gish?
23 Which frequent leading lady of Chaplin's starred with him in *The Kid*?
24 What was Mack Sennett's real first name?
25 Which four-legged star made his debut in *The Man from Hell's River*?

Answers Pot Luck 27 (see Quiz 72)
1 *White Hunter, Black Heart.* 2 Gregory Peck. 3 Goldblum. 4 Jake and Elwood.
5 Bette Midler. 6 Lauren Bacall. 7 O'Toole. 8 1940s. 9 Louise Fletcher.
10 Wendy Torrance. 11 John Landis. 12 *South Pacific.* 13 Little Richard. 14 Ally
Sheedy. 15 Heche. 16 *Flubber.* 17 Jenny. 18 James Cagney. 19 Mick Jackson.
20 Mickey Rooney. 21 Robert Redford. 22 Berkley. 23 1960s. 24 Peter Banning.
25 *Young Guns.*

Answers – see page 181

1   In which decade was Tony Curtis born?
2   What is his real first name?
3   In which city was he born?
4   In which branch of the services did he serve in World War II?
5   How many wives had he had by the end of the 20th century?
6   What type of instrumentalist was he in *Some Like It Hot*?
7   In which 70s movie were Robert De Niro and Robert Mitchum his co-stars?
8   Who was he 'Son of' in a 1952 film?
9   In which branch of the arts did he also achieve success in later life?
10 In which biopic did he star with Janet Leigh in 1953?
11 Which Hollywood great did he parody in *Some Like It Hot*?
12 On which famous beach is *Don't Make Waves* set?
13 What was the name of his autobiography?
14 In which movie does he end up with Marilyn Monroe in a motorboat?
15 Which 1956 movie was about the circus?
16 Which star of *Psycho* was he married to?
17 In which jet-age comedy did he star with Jerry Lewis in 1965?
18 What was the name of his character in *The Boston Strangler*?
19 Which movie with Sidney Poitier gave him his first Oscar nomination?
20 What was the name of the novel he wrote in 1977?
21 Who was his male co-star in *Operation Petticoat*?
22 Who is his other famous actress daughter along with Jamie Lee?
23 What was the name of his character in *Some Like It Hot*?
24 Who played the title role in *Spartacus* in which he starred?
25 Which late star was his co-star in *The Great Race*?

Answers Pot Luck 26 (see Quiz 69)
1 *Jurassic Park*. 2 Meg Ryan. 3 Judy Garland. 4 Teenage Mutant Ninja Turtles.
5 1930s. 6 *Trainspotting*. 7 Helena Bonham Carter. 8 *American Gigolo*. 9 Pussy
Galore. 10 James Dean. 11 George Cukor. 12 *Cat on a Hot Tin Roof*. 13 155
minutes. 14 Busey. 15 Michael Curtiz. 16 Christie. 17 *American Gigolo*.
18 Natalie Wood. 19 *Close Encounters of the Third Kind*. 20 Cinderella. 21
Robert Redford. 22 Danson. 23 1970s. 24 Bing Crosby. 25 *Breakfast at Tiffany's*.

Answers – see page 182

1   Which Clint Eastwood movie was based on the screenwriter Peter Viertel's experiences while shooting *The African Queen*?
2   Who won the Best Actor Oscar for *To Kill a Mockingbird*?
3   Which Jeff featured in *The Big Chill*?
4   What were the names of the 'Blues Brothers'?
5   *The Rose* and *Scenes from a Mall* starred which actress?
6   Which actress links *Misery* and *The Mirror Has Two Faces*?
7   Which Peter featured in *The Last Emperor*?
8   In which decade was *Great Expectations* first released?
9   Who won the Best Actress Oscar for *One Flew over the Cuckoo's Nest*?
10   What was the name of Shelley Duvall's character in *The Shining*?
11   Who directed *The Blues Brothers*?
12   In which film did a nurse named Nellie Forbush appear?
13   Who married Bruce Willis and Demi Moore?
14   *Short Circuit* and *Betsy's Wedding* featured which actress?
15   Which Anne featured in *Six Days, Seven Nights*?
16   What was the 90s remake of *The Absent Minded Professor* called?
17   What was the name of Robin Wright's character in *Forrest Gump*?
18   Which famous gangster actor was a founder of the Screen Actors' Guild?
19   Who directed *The Bodyguard*?
20   *National Velvet* and *Breakfast at Tiffany's* both featured which actor?
21   Who won the Best Director Oscar for *Ordinary People*?
22   Which Elizabeth featured in *Showgirls*?
23   In which decade was *Spartacus* released?
24   What was the name of Robin Williams's character in *Hook*?
25   Which 80s teenage western starred actors known as the Brat Pack?

Answers Stars of the Silent Years (see Quiz 70)
1 Mack Sennett. **2** *The Kid*. **3** Harold Lloyd. **4** Lon Chaney. **5** Buster Keaton.
6 MGM. **7** Brooks. **8** Mary Pickford. **9** Fatty Arbuckle. **10** Normand.
11 Austria. **12** William Randolph Hearst. **13** Buster Keaton. **14** Charlie Chaplin.
15 The Marx Brothers. **16** Lillian Gish. **17** Mary Pickford. **18** Theda Bara.
19 1920s. **20** Harold Lloyd. **21** Charlie Chaplin. **22** Sisters. **23** Edna Purviance.
24 Michael. **25** Rin Tin Tin.

Answers – see page 187

1   Who said in *The Times*, 'We take our commitment to each other very seriously' just before splitting up?

2   Who directed and starred in *Chinese Coffee*?

3   Which much-married actress was Miss Hungary 1936?

4   Who was paid $6 million to play 'The Saint' in 1996?

5   Who founded Maverick with Time Warner to make records and movies?

6   For which movie did Demi Moore become Hollywood's highest paid actress?

7   Who did Barbra Streisand replace Dudley Moore with in *The Mirror Has Two Faces*?

8   In which of his own movies did Roman Polanski appear in 1974?

9   What was Michael J. Fox's follow-up to *Back to the Future III*?

10   Who was Carrie Fisher's first husband?

11   Which movie did Jonathan Pryce make after *Carrington*?

12   Which singer/actor was deemed head of the 'Rat Pack'?

13   Which TV remake of a Hitchcock movie did Christopher Reeve make after his riding accident?

14   Which female member of the Fiennes family is famous as a director?

15   About whom did Howard Hughes say, 'There are two reasons why men will go to see her'?

16   Why will Winona Ryder never forget the name of the place she was born?

17   Leading lady Jean Peters retired from movies to marry which millionaire recluse?

18   How many times did Brigitte Bardot marry?

19   Which film star wrote the novel *Prime Time*?

20   Whose legs were insured for most, Fred Astaire's, Betty Grable's or Ginger Rogers's?

21   Which actress's official title is Lady Haden-Guest?

22   Who said the famous line, 'Win one for the Gipper', which he used in a different context in a later career?

23   Which Batman movie did Mrs Tom Cruise star in?

24   Which 60s model did Ken Russell cast in *The Boyfriend*?

25   Which star of *Friends* appeared in *Six Days Seven Nights*?

Answers Studios & Companies (see Quiz 75)
1 1950s. **2** Keystone. **3** Mountain. **4** Oliver. **5** Richard Burton. **6** New York.
7 *Alien Resurrection*. **8** Coca Cola. **9** Hammer. **10** Arnold Schwarzenegger.
11 *Saturday Night Live*. **12** Louis B. Mayer. **13** Fox; 20th Century Pictures.
14 Miramax. **15** MGM. **16** 20th Century Fox. **17** Pillow Talk. **18** *E.T.*
19 Hammer. **20** Gene Kelly. **21** Keystone. **22** David O. Selznick. **23** United
Artists. **24** *Antz*. **25** *A Bug's Life*.

QUIZ 74 POT LUCK 28 ·· LEVEL TWO

Answers – see page 188

1   What was the name of Julia Roberts's character in *The Pelican Brief*?
2   Who won the Best Actress Oscar for *Alice Doesn't Live Here Any More*?
3   How is Ramon Estevez better known?
4   In which decade was *Adam's Rib* released?
5   In which film did the characters Doralee and Violet appear?
6   To the nearest hour, how long does *Marnie* last?
7   Who played the villain in the 80s movie *Flash Gordon*?
8   'For All We Know' won an Oscar when used in which movie in 1970?
9   Who starred opposite Liza Minnelli in *New York, New York*?
10 Who played the ageing Zorro in the 1998 movie?
11 How is Mary Cathleen Collins better known?
12 Who was Richard Hannay in the original *The Thirty-Nine Steps*?
13 Which veteran won an Oscar in 1981, two years after his daughter?
14 Which was the next 14-Oscar-nominated film after *All About Eve*?
15 *Where Eagles Dare* and *1984* starred which actor?
16 Who directed *Blade Runner*?
17 *The Man with the Golden Arm* and *Pal Joey* both featured which actor?
18 Who played the Bond girl in *Moonraker*?
19 To the nearest hour, how long does *The King and I* last?
20 Which comedies was Michael Balcon responsible for?
21 Who won the Best Director Oscar for *The Sting*?
22 Which Alec featured in *Beetlejuice*?
23 In which decade was *Peyton Place* released?
24 What was Kirk Douglas's first film, in 1946?
25 Which actress links *Logan's Run* and *The Cannonball Run*?

Answers 1970s (see Quiz 76)
1 *Lady Sings the Blues.* 2 *The Devils.* 3 Four. 4 Carrie Fisher. 5 Robin Givens.
6 *Live and Let Die.* 7 *All the President's Men.* 8 Transylvania. 9 *Monty Python and the Holy Grail.* 10 *The Champ.* 11 Dustin Hoffman. 12 Tchaikovsky. 13 *Ryan's Daughter.* 14 *Vampira.* 15 *M*A*S*H.* 16 *Day for Night.* 17 Billie Holiday.
18 *Alien.* 19 *Prime Cut.* 20 *Tommy.* 21 Scott Joplin's. 22 Roger Moore. 23 *Ode to Billie Joe.* 24 *Play Misty for Me.* 25 *That's Entertainment.*

Answers – see page 185

1   In which decade did Hammer make the first of its Dracula series?
2   Which US company was famous for its slapstick comedy?
3   What was the logo of Paramount Pictures?
4   What did the O stand for in David O. Selznick's name?
5   Which Welsh actor first went to 20th Century Fox when he moved to Hollywood in the early 50s?
6   Where is the Actors' Studio which was founded in 1947?
7   Which sequel to *Alien* was made by Amalgamated Dynamics Inc. in 1997?
8   Which drinks company bought Columbia in 1982?
9   Which company's famous horror movies were made at Bray Studios?
10   Who starred in *Last Action Hero*, which was a flop for Columbia?
11   Which late-night US comedy show spawned movies such as *Wayne's World*?
12   Who was head of MGM for 25 years from 1925?
13   Which companies merged to make 20th Century Fox in 1935?
14   Which company did Disney acquire in 1993, which went on to make *Sliding Doors*?
15   Which company made *Singin' in the Rain*?
16   Which of the big five movie companies had Darryl F. Zanuck as its head, on and off, until the 60s?
17   What was the first singing comedy Doris Day made for Universal?
18   Which Spielberg movie was Universal's then biggest ever hit?
19   Which company made *When Dinosaurs Ruled the Earth*?
20   MGM lent Columbia which dancer for *Cover Girl*?
21   Which company foundered when Mack Sennett left for Paramount?
22   Who became head of RKO in 1931?
23   Which company made the first Bond movies?
24   Which computer-generated movie was made by Dreamworks in 1998?
25   What was Disney's answer to *Antz*?

Answers Headline Makers (see Quiz 73)
1 Richard Gere & Cindy Crawford. **2** Al Pacino. **3** Zsa Zsa Gabor. **4** Val Kilmer.
5 Madonna. **6** *Striptease*. **7** George Segal. **8** *Chinatown*. **9** *Doc Hollywood*.
10 Paul Simon. **11** *Evita*. **12** Frank Sinatra. **13** *Rear Window*. **14** Martha.
15 Jane Russell. **16** Born in Winona, Minnesota. **17** Howard Hughes. **18** Five.
19 Joan Collins **20** Betty Grable's. **21** Jamie Lee Curtis. **22** Ronald Reagan.
23 *Batman Forever*. **24** Twiggy. **25** David Schwimmer.

Answers – see page 186

1   For which movie was Diana Ross Oscar-nominated on her film debut?
2   Which Ken Russell movie was an adaptation of *The Devils of Loudun*?
3   How many years were there between *The French Connection* and *French Connection II*?
4   Who did Brian De Palma originally want for the title role in *Carrie*?
5   Which star of *The Wiz* married Mike Tyson?
6   What was Roger Moore's first Bond movie as 007?
7   Which Alan Pakula movie was about Watergate?
8   Where is Tim Curry's character from in *The Rocky Horror Picture Show*?
9   Which Monty Python movie was very loosely based on the Arthurian legend?
10 In which 1979 movie did Jon Voight play a boxer?
11 Who accidentally shot himself making *Little Big Man*?
12 Which composer did Richard Chamberlain play in *The Music Lovers*?
13 Which movie set in Ireland was David Lean's follow up to *Dr Zhivago*?
14 In which movie did David Niven play Dracula?
15 Which Korean War film gave Sally Kellerman an Oscar nomination?
16 In which of his own movies did Francois Truffaut appear in 1973?
17 *Lady Sings the Blues* was about which singer?
18 Which movie had the ad line, 'In space no one can hear you scream'?
19 In which movie did Sissy Spacek make her film debut?
20 Which rock opera did Ann Margret star in?
21 Whose piano rags were used in *The Sting*?
22 Who starred with Richard Harris and Richard Burton in *The Wild Geese*?
23 Which movie took its name and plot from a Bobbie Gentry song?
24 In which movie did Clint Eastwood play DJ Dave Garland?
25 Which movie was a compilation of MGM musicals?

Answers Pot Luck 28 (see Quiz 74)
1 Darby Shaw. **2** Ellen Burstyn. **3** Martin Sheen. **4** 1940s. **5** *9 to 5*. **6** 2 hours.
7 Max von Sydow. **8** *Lovers and Other Strangers*. **9** Robert de Niro. **10** Anthony
Hopkins. **11** Bo Derek. **12** Robert Donat. **13** Henry Fonda. **14** *Titanic*.
15 Richard Burton. **16** Ridley Scott. **17** Frank Sinatra. **18** Lois Chiles. **19** 2 hours.
20 Ealing comedies. **21** George Roy Hill. **22** Baldwin. **23** 1950s. **24** *The Strange
Love of Martha Ivers*. **25** Farah Fawcett.

Answers – see page 191

1   *Mad Max* was released in which decade?
2   At what sport did Liam Neeson excel?
3   Marlon Brando and who else turned down Robert Redford's role in *Butch Cassidy and the Sundance Kid*?
4   Which Tommy featured in *Batman Forever*?
5   Who won the Best Actor Oscar for *The Best Years of Our Lives*?
6   In which film did a character named Snake Plissken appear?
7   Who won the Best Director Oscar for *Out of Africa*?
8   Which actor links *Dragnet* and *A League of Their Own*?
9   Who played Melanie Wilkes in *Gone with the Wind*?
10   Who played Oscar's mother in *Wilde*?
11   In which decade was *Holiday Inn* released?
12   *Police Academy IV* and *Total Recall* both feature which actress?
13   Who married her co-star Alec Baldwin after they starred in *Too Hot to Handle*?
14   Who adapted Arthur Miller's *The Crucible* for the 90s film?
15   In which country was *The Good, the Bad and the Ugly* made?
16   Which animal is Little John in the Disney film *Robin Hood*?
17   What relation is Bridget Fonda to Jane?
18   Within fifteen minutes, how long does *National Velvet* last?
19   A character named Captain Ross appeared in which 1990s film?
20   Who won the Best Actress Oscar for *Coal Miner's Daughter*?
21   *Peggy Sue Got Married* and *The Rock* starred which actor?
22   Who directed *Barry Lyndon*?
23   Which Jonathan featured in *Star Trek: First Contact*?
24   Who played the Bond girl in *Octopussy*?
25   What was the name of Donald Sutherland's character in *Ordinary People*?

Answers Pot Luck 30 (see Quiz 79)
1 *Jaws*. 2 Linney. 3 1940s. 4 Gene Hackman. 5 *The Dirty Dozen*. 6 Billy Wilder. 7 *Alien*. 8 *An Officer and a Gentleman*. 9 *On the Waterfront* . 10 Robert Zemeckis. 11 Georg. 12 Katharine Hepburn. 13 Sam. 14 Honey Rider. 15 *Edward Scissorhands*. 16 David Niven. 17 Hobson. 18 Amanda Donohoe. 19 *Snow White and the Seven Dwarfs*. 20 Rod Steiger. 21 Mexico. 22 1950s. 23 Timothy Dalton. 24 *Unforgiven*. 25 1940s.

Answers – see page 192

1   What was the second of Meryl Streep's three nominations between 1981 and 1983?
2   Who was nominated for *Secrets and Lies*?
3   Which former Mrs Harvey Keitel was nominated for *Goodfellas*?
4   Which 80s winner has children called Chastity and Elijah Blue?
5   Who had a nomination for *The Wings of the Dove*?
6   For which movie did Mrs Antonio Banderas receive her first nomination?
7   Who was nominated for *Tumbleweeds*?
8   What was the name of Kate Winslet's character in *Titanic*?
9   Who was nominated for *Grifters* and *American Beauty*?
10   Which 60-something won in the 1990s after her second nomination in successive years?
11   Which one-time presidential candidate's cousin won for *Moonstruck*?
12   Who was the first English winner of the 1990s?
13   Sean Ferrer was the son of which 60s Best Actress?
14   For which movie did Holly Hunter win without speaking?
15   Who was the only female winner for *One Flew over the Cuckoo's Nest*?
16   For which movie was Glenn Close Oscar-nominated on her film debut?
17   Who won her first Oscar for *LA Confidential*?
18   Which Best Actress said, 'Women get all excited about nothing – then marry him'?
19   Marlee Matlin played someone coming to terms with deafness in which movie?
20   For which 1990s film was Julie Christie Oscar-nominated?
21   Who was Oscar-nominated for playing Tina Turner in the biopic?
22   What is the nationality of Brenda Fricker who won for *My Left Foot*?
23   Who was the older winner of the shared Best Actress Oscar in 1968?
24   Which TV personality was nominated for *The Color Purple*?
25   Who received her last Oscar for *The Trip to Bountiful*?

Answers Living Legends (see Quiz 80)
1 Ghana. 2 *Klute*. 3 Charlton Heston. 4 Luciano Pavarotti. 5 Joan Plowright.
6 Sister. 7 Rocky & Rambo. 8 Rod Steiger. 9 Robin Williams. 10 Micheline.
11 Jane Wyman. 12 Egypt. 13 Dustin Hoffman. 14 Walter Matthau. 15 Jack
Nicholson. 16 Howard Keel. 17 H. 18 Bob Hope. 19 *Planet of the Apes*.
20 Jason Robards. 21 Gregory Peck. 22 Spartan. 23 Robert De Niro. 24 Kirk
Douglas. 25 Julie Andrews.

Answers – see page 189

1   *A Stillness in the Water* was eventually released as which ripping blockbuster?
2   Which Laura featured in *The Truman Show*?
3   In which decade was *The Grapes of Wrath* released?
4   Which actor links *Bonnie and Clyde* and *Superman*?
5   The character John Cassavetes appeared in which action film?
6   Who won the Best Director Oscar for *The Lost Weekend*?
7   The spacecraft Nostromo featured in which movie?
8   'Up Where We Belong' won an Oscar when used in which movie?
9   A character named Terry Malloy appeared in which gritty film?
10 Who directed *Back to the Future*?
11 In *The Sound of Music* what is Baron von Trapp's first name?
12 Who won the Best Actress Oscar for *On Golden Pond*?
13 What was the name of Patrick Swayze's character in *Ghost*?
14 What was the name of the Bond girl in *Dr No*?
15 In which film did a character named Kim Boggs appear?
16 Which actor's autobiography was called *The Moon's a Balloon*?
17 What was the name of the butler, played by John Gielgud, in *Arthur*?
18 Who played Lucy Irvine in *Castaway*?
19 Which Disney film got a special Academy Award for 'a significant screen innovation'?
20 Who won the Best Actor Oscar for *In the Heat of the Night*?
21 In which country is the village where the action of *The Magnificent Seven* takes place?
22 In which decade of the 20th century was Bill Murray born?
23 Which James Bond played Heathcliff in the 1970 *Wuthering Heights*?
24 The character Will Munny appeared in which film?
25 In which decade was Orson Welles's *Jane Eyre* released?

Answers – see page 190

1 In the 1970s Shirley Temple was made US Ambassador to which West African country?
2 Jane Fonda's affair with Donald Sutherland began on the set of which movie?
3 Who said, 'It's hard living up to Moses'?
4 Which tenor's only movie was *Yes Giorgio* in 1982?
5 How is Lady Olivier, star of *Tea with Mussolini*, better known?
6 What relation to Francis Ford Coppola is actress Talia Shire?
7 Which two characters did Sylvester Stallone say were 'money-making machines that could not be switched off'?
8 Which one-time husband of Claire Bloom appeared in *Mars Attacks*?
9 Starting with *Good Morning, Vietnam*, who made seven films which took over $100m at the US box office?
10 What is the first name of Mrs Sean Connery?
11 Who, when asked why she divorced Ronald Reagan, said, 'He talked too much'?
12 Where was Omar Sharif born?
13 Which superstar played Sean Connery's son in *Family Business*?
14 Who starred as a 'grumpy old man' with Jack Lemmon?
15 Which star was born in Neptune, New Jersey, in 1937?
16 Which musical star of *Annie Get Your Gun* and *Kiss Me Kate* also found TV fame in *Dallas*?
17 Which letter does Paul Newman say all his best movies begin with?
18 Who won three Special Oscars in over 60 years, partly for work entertaining US troops?
19 In which movie did Charlton Heston say, 'Take your paws off me, you dirty ape'?
20 Who was Lauren Bacall's second husband?
21 Who was Ambrose Pierce to Jane Fonda's schoolteacher in *Old Gringo*?
22 What was the name of Stallone's character in *Demolition Man*?
23 Who directed and starred in *A Bronx Tale* in 1993?
24 Whose autobiography was called *The Ragman's Son*?
25 Which film star wrote the novel *The Last of the Really Great Whangdoodles*?

QUIZ 81 WESTERNS

Answers – see page 195

1   Which Irishman plays English Bob in *Unforgiven*?
2   Which western film title links Randolph Scott and Daniel Day-Lewis?
3   Which member of the Brat Pack played Billy the Kid in *Young Guns*?
4   Which western superstar's son directed him in *The Train Robbers*?
5   Which brothers played Frank and Jesse James in *Long Riders*?
6   Kris Kristofferson and John Hurt were graduates from where in *Heaven's Gate*?
7   'For a minute there I thought we were in trouble' is the last line of which movie?
8   Who narrated *How the West Was Won*?
9   Which star played the title role in *Billy the Kid Returns* in 1939?
10 Which country was the location for *A Fistful of Dollars*?
11 Who was the Quaker bride of Gary Cooper in *High Noon*?
12 Who sang the title song for *Gunfight at the OK Corral*?
13 Who was the subject of the autobiographical *To Hell and Back*?
14 *Pale Rider* was a remake of which classic western?
15 What was the third of Sergio Leone's trio of spaghetti westerns?
16 Who directed the Civil War sequences of *How the West Was Won*?
17 Who was Clint Eastwood's co-star on and off screen in *Bronco Billy*?
18 What was the 50s remake of *Destry Rides Again* called?
19 In which movie did John Wayne play Tom Dunson?
20 Who played Sheriff Garrett in *Pat Garrett and Billy the Kid*?
21 Who was the star of *Jeremiah Johnson*?
22 What is the name of Gene Hackman's sheriff in *Unforgiven*?
23 In which western did Jodie Foster play a poker player?
24 In which 1953 classic did Alan Ladd face Jack Palance?
25 Which Huston played Wyatt Earp in *Law and Order* in the 30s?

Answers – see page 196

1   Characters named Gertie and Elliot appeared in which film?
2   In which decade was *National Velvet* first released?
3   What was the first name of Schindler of *Schindler's List*?
4   What is the name of the Eddie Murphy character in the *Beverly Hills Cop* films?
5   Within fifteen minutes, how long does *My Fair Lady* last?
6   Robin Williams's *The Birdcage* was a remake of which film?
7   Who won the Best Actress Oscar for *Suspicion*?
8   Which Helen featured in *Twister*?
9   What is the name of Audrey Hepburn's cat in *Breakfast at Tiffany's*?
10   *Hot Shots!* and *Honey, I Blew Up the Kids* starred which actor?
11   Who directed *Babe*?
12   Which actress was Oscar-nominated for *Starting Over*?
13   Which Miriam tested for the role of Scarlett O'Hara?
14   *Young Blood* and *Dirty Dancing* both feature which actor?
15   Who won the Best Director Oscar for *The Best Years of Our Lives*?
16   Heinrich Harrer is a character in a film with which country in the title?
17   Who sang the Bond theme from *The Spy Who Loved Me*?
18   Which actor links *Witness* and *Predator 2*?
19   In *Singin' in the Rain* who danced with Gene Kelly in the Broadway Ballet scene?
20   To the nearest hour, how long does *The Apartment* last?
21   Which British actor won an Oscar for *A Man for All Seasons*?
22   Which Bond girl starred with Elvis Presley in *Fun in Acapulco*?
23   Which Sean featured in *The Avengers*?
24   In which decade was Disney's *Lady and the Tramp* released?
25   Who won the Best Actor Oscar for *Shine*?

Answers World Cinema (see Quiz 84)
1 Deneuve. 2 *Life Is Beautiful*. 3 Gerard Depardieu. 4 Australia. 5 Fellini.
6 Benigni . 7 Brenda Blethyn. 8 Ingmar Bergman. 9 France . 10 Rome (*Roma*).
11 Farces. 12 Charles Aznavour. 13 Sophia Loren. 14 *Il Postino*. 15 *Blow Up*.
16 Jeremy Irons. 17 Jeanne Moreau. 18 *Seven Samurai*. 19 1900s.
20 *Emmanuelle*. 21 Australia. 22 Fernando Rey. 23 Rome. 24 Gerard
Depardieu. 25 *Eight and a Half*.

Answers – see page 193

1 In which movie with Audrey Hepburn did Cary Grant take a shower – fully clothed?
2 Which Scottish pop star sang the title song from *To Sir with Love*?
3 Who played two parts in *Cat Ballou* in 1965?
4 Which future wife of Frank Sinatra failed an audition to play one of the children in *The Sound of Music*?
5 Which horror movie star found fame in *The House of Usher*?
6 Which duo topped the money-making list of movie stars after starring in a string of light comedies together?
7 Who co-starred with Peter Fonda in *Easy Rider*?
8 For which movie was Richard Burton Oscar-nominated for playing an Archbishop of Canterbury?
9 Who starred in *To Kill a Mockingbird* and *The Guns of Navarone*?
10 Who made his directorial debut with the second sequel to *Psycho*?
11 Who was Dustin Hoffman's male co-star in *Midnight Cowboy*?
12 Who was Anita in *West Side Story*?
13 Who starred opposite Peter Finch and Alan Bates in *Far from the Madding Crowd* in 1967?
14 Who was directed by her then husband in the futuristic *Barbarella*?
15 Who was the star of *Our Man Flint*?
16 Which George was the star of *The Blue Max*?
17 Leonard Whiting and Olivia Hussey were the unknowns chosen by Franco Zeffirelli to make which movie?
18 Peggy Wood was Oscar-nominated for which role in *The Sound of Music*?
19 Which one-time girlfriend of Mick Jagger was *The Girl on a Motorcycle*?
20 Who appeared in two major David Lean movies, *Lawrence of Arabia* and *Dr Zhivago*?
21 Which Mrs Cary Grant starred in *Bob and Carol and Ted and Alice*?
22 Whose autobiography was called *Baby Doll*?
23 Which former child star was born Natasha Gurdin?
24 Who was the first black actor to top the poll of movie money-earners?
25 Who was the star of *That Touch of Mink*?

Answers Westerns (see Quiz 81)
1 Richard Harris. **2** *The Last of the Mohicans.* **3** Emilio Estevez. **4** Michael Wayne (son of John). **5** James & Stacy Keach. **6** Harvard. **7** *Butch Cassidy and the Sundance Kid.* **8** Spencer Tracy. **9** Roy Rogers. **10** Mexico. **11** Grace Kelly. **12** Frankie Laine. **13** Audie Murphy. **14** *Shane.* **15** *The Good, the Bad and the Ugly.* **16** John Ford. **17** Sondra Locke. **18** *Destry.* **19** *Red River.* **20** James Coburn. **21** Robert Redford. **22** Sheriff Daggett. **23** *Maverick.* **24** *Shane.* **25**

Answers – see page 194

1   What did Catherine Dorleac change her surname to?
2   Which 1998 movie written by and starring Roberto Benigni won the Grand Jury prize at Cannes?
3   Who played the title role in the 1990 *Cyrano De Bergerac*?
4   Where was *Muriel's Wedding* made?
5   Who directed the 60s hit *La Dolce Vita*?
6   Which Roberto found success in his native Italy with *Johnny Stecchino*?
7   Who won Best Actress at Cannes for *Secrets and Lies*?
8   Which Swedish director won the Palme de Palme D'or at the 50th Cannes Film Festival?
9   Which country did Dirk Bogarde move to in the 60s, which made him a star of many European movies?
10 About which city did Federico Fellini make a 1972 movie?
11 Georges Feydeau was a writer of what type of plays, many of which were made into movies?
12 Which Armenian-born French singer starred in Truffaut's *Shoot the Pianist*?
13 Which actress is Mrs Carlo Ponti?
14 Which 1994 movie was about a postman on an Italian island?
15 What was Michelangelo Antonioni's first English-language film, in 1966?
16 Which English actor played the title role in the US/French movie *Kafka*?
17 Who was the female star of *Jules et Jim*?
18 *The Magnificent Seven* was based on which Japanese classic?
19 In which decade does the action of *Picnic at Hanging Rock* take place?
20 Which 1974 movie went on to make Sylvia Kristel an international star?
21 *Strictly Ballroom* came from which country?
22 How was Fernando Arambillet of *French Connection* fame better known?
23 In which city was *La Dolce Vita* set?
24 Which French actor starred in *The Return of Martin Guerre*?
25 Which number was the name of an Oscar-nominated Fellini movie?

Answers – see page 199

1	How is Allen Konigsberg better known?
2	Which Robert featured in *Austin Powers: International Man of Mystery*?
3	Who won the Best Actor Oscar for *Hamlet* in 1948?
4	*High Society* was a musical remake of which film?
5	Which pianist is the subject of *Shine*?
6	Which actor links *The Great Escape* and *Victor/Victoria*?
7	What was the first name of Demi Moore's character in *Ghost*?
8	In which decade was *A Day at the Races* released?
9	In real life Clint Eastwood became mayor of which town?
10	To the nearest hour, how long does *Napoleon* last?
11	'Say You, Say Me' won an Oscar when it was used in which movie?
12	Who died during the filming of *Dark Blood* in 1993?
13	Who directed *Arsenic and Old Lace*?
14	Which movie was going to be called *The Bride and the Wolf*?
15	The relationship between Steve McQueen and Ali MacGraw began on the set of which movie?
16	Who played contrasting roles of a mechanic in *Mona Lisa*, and Falstaff in *Henry V*?
17	Who was the Doctor in the original musical film *Doctor Dolittle*?
18	Who starred with Bette Davis in *Whatever Happened to Baby Jane?*?
19	Who is Leslie Nielsen in the *Naked Gun* films?
20	Which Eddie turned down Al Jolson's role in *The Jazz Singer*?
21	*The Birds* and *Cocoon* featured which actress?
22	Who won the Best Director Oscar for *Tom Jones* in 1963?
23	In which decade was *Wuthering Heights*, starring Laurence Olivier, released?
24	Who played the villain in the 70s movie *Diamonds are Forever*?
25	*JFK* and *Cool Runnings* starred which actor?

Answers Oscar Trivia (see Quiz 87)

1 *The Rains Came.* **2** Academy of Motion Picture Arts and Sciences. **3** Nine.
4 *Coming Home.* **5** *Midnight Cowboy.* **6** 13. **7** *The Sting.* **8** Woodstock.
9 19th. **10** *The Madness of King George.* **11** *Chariots of Fire.* **12** *Arthur.*
13 Burma. **14** Elizabeth Taylor. **15** 13.5 inches. **16** Haing S. Ngor. **17** 12.
18 Roosevelt Hotel. **19** Eight. **20** David Niven. **21** Diane Ladd & Laura Dern.
22 Six. **23** Christopher Hampton. **24** He died after the film was made. **25** Ben
Kingsley.

Answers – see page 200

1   In which decade was he born?
2   Which movie gave him his first lead role in 1958?
3   What colour were his eyes?
4   Who was his male co-star in *Papillon*?
5   What is his occupation *The Towering Inferno*?
6   Who was his co-star in *The Thomas Crown Affair*?
7   Which branch of the services did he join before going AWOL?
8   What was his first movie, in 1958?
9   What was his job in *Bullitt*?
10   What job did he have on *An Enemy of the People* in addition to acting?
11   In which country did he die?
12   In *The Getaway*, where did he and Ali McGraw get away to?
13   How did he attempt to escape in *The Great Escape*?
14   What was Bullitt's first name in the 1968 hit movie?
15   Which movie was about a famous motor race?
16   Which co-star from *The Getaway* did he marry?
17   In which 1960 classic western was he one of a group of gunmen?
18   Who was his first wife?
19   What was his documentary *On Any Sunday* about?
20   How many children did he have by his first wife?
21   For which 1966 film was he Oscar-nominated?
22   On which island is *Papillon* set?
23   What was the name of his last film?
24   Which film about a millionaire bank robber was a 1968 success?
25   In which decade did he die?

Answers Pot Luck 33 (see Quiz 88)
1 Abba. **2** Baseball. **3** 2 hours. **4** Ron Howard. **5** 1940s. **6** Duvall. **7** Jessica
Tandy. **8** *Goodfellas.* **9** James Cagney. **10** Michael Cimino. **11** Jamie Lee Curtis.
12 Cyd Charisse. **13** Doug Quaid. **14** Marlon Brando. **15** Albert Finney.
16 Hayley Mills. **17** *Thank God It's Friday.* **18** Bronson. **19** The Sex Pistols.
20 1950s. **21** *48 Hours.* **22** Glenda Jackson. **23** Stephen King. **24** Lea
Thompson. **25** Steenburgen.

Answers – see page 197

1   For which movie was the first special effects Oscar awarded?
2   Who owns the Oscar once it has been awarded?
3   How many Oscars did *The English Patient* win?
4   What was the second of Jane Fonda's three nominations between 1977 and 1979?
5   What was the first X-rated film to win an Oscar?
6   How many nominations did *Mary Poppins* have?
7   For which movie did Marvin Hamlisch receive his first nomination?
8   Which pop festival was the subject of a documentary which won an Oscar in 1970?
9   *Topsy Turvy* is set during which century?
10   Which movie had the ad line, 'First he lost America. Now he's losing his mind'?
11   Which movie's title was a quote from Blake's 'Jerusalem'?
12   The hit song 'The Best That You Can Do' came from which movie?
13   In what country is *Bridge on the River Kwai* set?
14   Who won the only Oscar for *Butterfield 8*?
15   Within one inch, how tall is an Oscar?
16   Who was the only Cambodian winner of the 1980s?
17   How many 20th-century Oscar nominations did Meryl Streep have?
18   At which hotel were the first Oscar ceremonies held?
19   *Raging Bull* won two Oscars, but how many nominations did it receive?
20   Who was hosting the 1974 ceremony when it was interrupted by a streaker?
21   Who were the first mother and daughter to be nominated for the same film?
22   How many Oscars did *Oliver!* win?
23   Which dramatist won for *Dangerous Liaisons*?
24   Why did Peter Finch not collect his Oscar for *Network*?
25   Who won Best Actor for his first major role in 1982?

Answers Pot Luck 32 (see Quiz 85)
1 Woody Allen. 2 Wagner. 3 Laurence Olivier. 4 *The Philadelphia Story*.
5 David Helfgott. 6 James Garner. 7 Molly. 8 1930s. 9 Carmel. 10 5 hours.
11 *White Nights*. 12 River Phoenix. 13 Frank Capra. 14 *Moonstruck*. 15 *The Getaway*. 16 Robbie Coltrane. 17 Rex Harrison. 18 Joan Crawford. 19 Frank Drebin. 20 Cantor. 21 Jessica Tandy. 22 Tony Richardson. 23 1930s.
24 Charles Gray. 25 John Candy.

Answers – see page 198

1	Muriel is a fan of which band in *Muriel's Wedding*?
2	At what sport did Billy Crystal excel?
3	To the nearest hour, how long does *Pretty Woman* last?
4	Who directed *Apollo 13*?
5	In which decade was Disney's *Dumbo* released?
6	Which Robert featured in *Apocalypse Now*?
7	Who was the oldest ever Oscar-winner when she won best actress in 1989?
8	In which film did a character named Henry Hill appear?
9	Who played George M. Cohan in *Yankee Doodle Dandy*?
10	Who won the Best Director Oscar for *The Deer Hunter*?
11	*My Girl* and *Forever Young* starred which actress?
12	How was Tula Ellice Finklea better known?
13	What was the name of the Schwarzenegger character in *Total Recall*?
14	Which tough guy played Sky Masterson in *Guys and Dolls*?
15	Which actor links *Annie* and *Miller's Crossing*?
16	Who was awarded a miniature Oscar for her role in *Pollyanna*?
17	The song 'Last Dance' came from which movie?
18	Which Charles thought his face was 'like a rock quarry that somebody has dynamited'?
19	Which band appeared in the movie *The Great Rock 'n' Roll Swindle*?
20	In which decade was *The Robe* released?
21	What was Eddie Murphy's first film, in 1982?
22	Who won the Best Actress Oscar for *A Touch of Class*?
23	Which writer directed *Maximum Overdrive* in 1986?
24	*Back to the Future* and *Space Camp* featured which actress?
25	Which Mary featured in *What's Eating Gilbert Grape*??

Answers Steve McQueen (see Quiz 86)
1 1930s. **2** *The Blob*. **3** Blue. **4** Dustin Hoffman. **5** Fire officer. **6** Faye
Dunaway. **7** Marines. **8** *Somebody Up There Likes Me*. **9** Detective. **10** Executive
Producer. **11** Mexico. **12** Mexico. **13** Motorcycle. **14** Frank. **15** *Le Mans*.
16 Ali McGraw. **17** *The Magnificent Seven*. **18** Neile Adams. **19** Motorcycle
racing. **20** Two. **21** *The Sand Pebbles*. **22** Devil's Island. **23** *The Hunter*. **24** *The Thomas Crown Affair*. **25** 1980s.

Answers – see page 203

1   Which McGann brother co-starred with Richard E. Grant in *Withnail and I*?
2   What was Timothy Dalton's last movie as 007?
3   Who was *The Jazz Singer* in the 1980 movie?
4   In *Scarface*, where did Tony Montana come from?
5   *Coal Miner's Daughter* was about which singer?
6   Whose *Empire of the Sun* was the basis of the hit movie made by Spielberg?
7   In which movie did Sean Connery play monk William of Baskerville?
8   Which future star of *LA Law* was Oliver Reed's co-star in *Castaway*?
9   Which outrageous French fashion designer designed for *The Cook, the Thief, His Wife and Her Lover*?
10   Which Beatle was producer on *Withnail and I*?
11   In which movie based on an Agatha Christie story did Rock Hudson star with Elizabeth Taylor?
12   For playing which composer was Tom Hulce Oscar-nominated in 1984?
13   What was the working title of *Ghostbusters*?
14   Which Woody Allen movie was Sharon Stone's debut?
15   What was the name of Glenn Close's character in *Fatal Attraction*?
16   Whose big break came as Lydia in *Beetlejuice*?
17   Who played Sonny Corleone in the first sequel to *The Godfather*?
18   Which Jack Lemmon movie was about US involvement in the overthrow of Allende's government in Chile?
19   For which movie was Marlee Matlin Oscar-nominated on her film debut?
20   Who played Annette Desoto in *Steel Magnolias*?
21   In which movie did Jessica Lange play an angel?
22   Which actress played two parts in *The French Lieutenant's Woman* in 1981?
23   Which writer did Daniel Day-Lewis play in *My Left Foot*?
24   In which movie did Helena Bonham Carter find fame as Lucy Honeychurch?
25   Who played Joan Crawford in *Mommie Dearest*?

Answers Comedies (see Quiz 91)
1 Seven. 2 Maggie Smith. 3 *Tootsie*. 4 Manhattan. 5 Paris. 6 Adam Sandler.
7 *Some Like It Hot*. 8 Connie Booth. 9 *A Night in Casablanca*. 10 *American Pie*.
11 Steve Martin. 12 *The Runaway Bride*. 13 James Caan. 14 *The Pink Panther Strikes Again*. 15 Leslie Nielsen. 16 Goldie Hawn. 17 Kevin Kline. 18 Seahaven.
19 Alan Alda. 20 Mike Myers. 21 *Fierce Creatures*. 22 Bruce Willis. 23 Marty McFly. 24 Burns. 25 Lee Evans.

Answers – see page 204

1	What is the name of Indiana Jones's father?
2	Who directed *Aliens*?
3	*Jack and Sarah* and *Shakespeare in Love* both starred which actress?
4	Which Bill featured in *While You Were Sleeping*?
5	Who played Kenneth Branagh's wife in *Peter's Friends*?
6	Who or what are Tom, Dick and Harry in *The Great Escape*?
7	Who did Johnny Depp play in *LA Without a Map*?
8	The character Ray Kinsella appeared in which film about 'Dreams'?
9	Who won the Best Director Oscar for *Cabaret*?
10	In which decade was *Sabotage* released?
11	Which movie did the song 'The One and Only' come from?
12	Who was the leading actor in Hitchcock's *Rear Window*?
13	Mia Farrow starred in 'The Purple Rose of' where?
14	Which song from *Dick Tracy* won an Oscar?
15	Who won the Best Actress Oscar for *Anastasia* in 1956?
16	What was the name of the Bond girl in *Never Say Never Again*?
17	'(I've Had) The Time of My Life' won an Oscar when it was used in which movie in 1987?
18	To the nearest hour, how long does *Saving Private Ryan* last?
19	Who directed *Four Weddings and a Funeral*?
20	*Great Expectations* and *The Swiss Family Robinson* both featured which John?
21	Who starred opposite Julia Roberts in *My Best Friend's Wedding*?
22	Which author appeared in *Creepshow*?
23	In which decade was *Rio Bravo* released?
24	Which Jenny featured in *An American Werewolf in London*?
25	What were the first names of Hanna & Barbera?

Answers Kevin Costner (see Quiz 92)
1 Los Angeles. **2** *The Bodyguard*. **3** 1920s. **4** Gary. **5** Morgan Freeman. **6** Eliot Ness. **7** Sioux. **8** Mary Elizabeth Mastrantonio. **9** Clint Eastwood. **10** Robert De Niro. **11** Advertising. **12** 1950s. **13** Oliver Stone. **14** *Bull Durham*. **15** Whitney Houston. **16** Baseball. **17** *Dances with Wolves*. **18** Diana, Princess of Wales. **19** Jim Garrison. **20** *Waterworld*. **21** Wyatt Earp. **22** *Robin Hood*. **23** The corpse. **24** Steve McQueen. **25** *Dances with Wolves*.

Answers – see page 201

1   How many characters does Eddie Murphy play in *The Nutty Professor*?
2   Who played the head of the convent in *Sister Act*?
3   In which of his own movies did Sydney Pollack appear in 1982?
4   Where are the spooks running wild in *Ghostbusters*?
5   In *Home Alone* where have the family gone for the Christmas vacation?
6   Who played singer Robbie Hart in *The Wedding Singer*?
7   'Nobody's perfect' is the last line of which movie?
8   Who played the witch in *Monty Python and the Holy Grail*?
9   Which Marx Brothers movie has an amusing comparison with the Ingrid Bergman/Humphrey Bogart wartime classic?
10 Which 1999 movie shared its name with a Don Maclean classic song?
11 Who wrote and starred in *Bowfinger*?
12 Which 1999 movie re-teamed Richard Gere and Julia Roberts?
13 Who played Hugh Grant's prospective father-in-law in *Mickey Blue Eyes*?
14 What was the name of the fourth Pink Panther film?
15 Who played the title role in Mel Brooks's spoof *Dracula: Dead and Loving It*?
16 Which member of 'The First Wives Club' has the blondest hair?
17 Who played Otto in *A Fish Called Wanda*?
18 What is the name of the idyllic community in *The Truman Show*?
19 Which star of TV's *M*A*S*H* appeared in Woody Allen's *Manhattan Murder Mystery*?
20 Who played Dr Evil in the Austin Powers movie?
21 Which movie was 'an equal not a sequel' to *A Fish Called Wanda*?
22 Who was the voice of Mikey in *Look Who's Talking*?
23 What part did Michael J. Fox play in *Back to the Future*?
24 What was Harry's surname in *When Harry Met Sally*?
25 Which British comic appeared in *There's Something About Mary*?

Answers – see page 202

1   He was born in which city?
2   In which movie did he play Frank Farmer?
3   In which decade did *The Untouchables* take place?
4   Which former pop star Kemp co-stars in *The Bodyguard*?
5   Who was his Moorish sidekick in *Robin Hood: Prince of Thieves*?
6   What was the name of his character in *The Untouchables*?
7   Which tribe features in *Dances with Wolves*?
8   Who was Maid Marian to his Robin Hood in 1991?
9   Who was his co-star and director in *A Perfect World*?
10 Who played Al Capone in his movie *The Untouchables*?
11 Which career did he start out in?
12 In which decade was he born?
13 Who directed him in *JFK*?
14 In which 1988 film did he co-star with Tim Robbins?
15 Who was his female co-star in *The Bodyguard*?
16 *Field of Dreams* was about which sport?
17 Which 1990 movie did he act in, direct and produce?
18 Who was he reputedly in conversation with to make a sequel to *The Bodyguard*?
19 What was the name of his District Attorney in *JFK*?
20 Which 1995 movie is reputedly the biggest flop ever made?
21 Which western hero did he play in 1994?
22 Which English hero did he play in _____ *Prince of Thieves*?
23 Which role did he famously have in the opening sequence of *The Big Chill*?
24 Which 70s star was earmarked for Costner's *Bodyguard* role?
25 In which movie does he play the role of John Dunbar?

Answers Pot Luck 34 (see Quiz 90)
1 Dr Henry Jones. **2** James Cameron. **3** Dame Judi Dench. **4** Pullman. **5** Rita Rudner. **6** Escape tunnels. **7** Himself. **8** *Field of Dreams*. **9** Bob Fosse. **10** 1930s. **11** *Buddy's Song*. **12** James Stewart. **13** Cairo. **14** 'Sooner or Later'. **15** Ingrid Bergman. **16** Domino. **17** *Dirty Dancing*. **18** 3 hours. **19** Mike Newell. **20** Mills. **21** Rupert Everett. **22** Stephen King. **23** 1950s. **24** Agutter. **25** William & Joseph.

Answers – see page 207

1	In *The Seven Year Itch* what colour was Monroe's skirt, blown around by air from a grating?
2	The relationship between Tom Cruise and Nicole Kidman began on the set of which movie?
3	In which decade of the 20th century was Christian Slater born?
4	Which actor links *St Elmo's Fire* and *Young Guns*?
5	What was the name of Richard Gere's character in *Pretty Woman*?
6	In which decade was *The Apartment* released?
7	Who won the Best Actor Oscar for *Boys' Town*?
8	Which Harry is the lead character in *The Ipcress File*?
9	Which song from *Mary Poppins* won an Oscar?
10	In which city is *Bullitt* set?
11	What was the sequel to *Grumpy Old Men* called?
12	The character John Keating was in which Robin Williams film?
13	Who said, 'People think I was born in top hat and tails'?
14	Who played Watson to Rathbone's Holmes in *The Hound of the Baskervilles*?
15	In which decade was *The Bridge on the River Kwai* released?
16	In which film did a lady named Tess Trueheart appear?
17	Who was known as the 'It' girl?
18	Who directed *The Alamo*?
19	For what did Walt Disney win a Special Award in 1931/2?
20	Who won the Best Actress Oscar for *The Country Girl*?
21	To the nearest hour, how long does *Ryan's Daughter* last?
22	What was the name of Arnold Schwarzenegger's character in *Twins*?
23	*The Towering Inferno* and *Superman III* both feature which suave actor?
24	Who sang the Bond theme from *Live and Let Die*?
25	In which film did a character named Vicky Vale appear?

Answers – see page 208

1   What did Johnny Depp change his 'Winona Forever' tattoo to when his relationship with Ms Ryder finished?
2   What is Bonnie Bedelia's real famous surname?
3   Which famous cartoon voice's autobiography was called *That's All Folks!*?
4   What was the name of James Cagney's sister?
5   Who did George Clooney replace as Batman?
6   What is Matt Damon's middle name?
7   What name does the J stand for in Michael J. Fox's name?
8   Whose autobiography was called *Dear Me*?
9   Which famous name did Nancy Davis marry?
10   Rebecca De Mornay was educated at which progressive English school?
11   Who played the mother of real-life daughter Mia in *Hannah and Her Sisters* in 1986?
12   Jamie Lee Curtis was born just before her father was about to shoot which movie?
13   What was Danny DeVito's profession prior to acting?
14   Who played Jerry Lee Lewis in *Great Balls of Fire*?
15   Which comic-strip character did Michelle Pfeiffer play on screen?
16   Where was Julie Christie born?
17   What are Meryl Streep's two real first names?
18   Whose autobiography was called *Absolutely Mahvelous*?
19   In which movie did Clint Eastwood say, 'Go ahead punk. Make my day'?
20   On which special day of the year was Sissy Spacek born?
21   Where was Richard E. Grant born?
22   Who played JD in *Thelma and Louise* after William Baldwin pulled out?
23   What relation is Helena Bonham Carter to former British PM Herbert Asquith?
24   Jeff Goldblum's affair with Laura Dern began on the set of which movie?
25   In which movie did Holly Hunter play an angel?

Answers Pot Luck 36 (see Quiz 96)
1 Hutton. **2** Ruth. **3** 1980s. **4** Oliver Stone. **5** *Pretty Woman.* **6** *Body Heat.*
7 105 minutes. **8** Glenn Close. **9** *Dick Tracy.* **10** Britt Ekland. **11** Mike Nichols.
12 Four. **13** 'Dance of the Hours'. **14** Simon. **15** *Jailhouse Rock.* **16** 1930s.
17 *Mad City.* **18** 'When You Wish Upon a Star'. **19** Gene Wilder. **20** *The Towering Inferno.* **21** Glen Campbell. **22** Katharine Hepburn. **23** Wolfgang Peterson. **24** Richard Dreyfuss. **25** *Wild at Heart.*

Answers – see page 205

1   Who was Ali McGraw's third husband?
2   Who played the lead role in Bob Fosse's *All That Jazz*?
3   Which husband of Susan George starred in *Death on the Nile*?
4   Who was Marian to Sean Connery's Robin in *Robin and Marian*?
5   Who played Elvis Presley in *Elvis: The Movie*?
6   Which TV doctor played Tchaikovsky in *The Music Lovers*?
7   Which *Klute* co-star of Jane Fonda was a member of her anti-war troupe during the Vietnam conflict?
8   Who said he would not accept an Oscar if given one, as the ceremony was a meat parade?
9   In which 70s movie did Elton John appear?
10   Which movie with Tim Curry had wacky songs such as 'Time Warp'?
11   Who was Vanessa Redgrave's hell-raising co-star in *The Devils*?
12   Who was Philip Marlowe in *Farewell My Lovely* in the latter part of his career?
13   Who played the MC of the Kit Kat Club in *Cabaret*?
14   Who played the youth on a killing spree in *Badlands* opposite Sissy Spacek?
15   Who played the first-time bank robber in *Dog Day Afternoon*?
16   Which martial arts hero died suddenly in 1973 aged 33?
17   Which star of *Death Wish* was known in France as *le sacre monstre*?
18   What was Stallone's first Rambo movie?
19   Which French film director did Candice Bergen marry in 1980?
20   What was Roger Moore's last 70s movie as 007?
21   Whose roles included Kay Corleone in *The Godfather* and the heroine of *Looking for Mr Goodbar*?
22   Which Mrs Bronson said, 'I'm in so many Charles Bronson films because no one else will work with him'?
23   Who played Rocky's girlfriend in the first *Rocky* movie?
24   Who played the object of Dudley Moore's fantasies in *10*?
25   Which horror movie star played the villain in *The Man with the Golden Gun*?

Answers Pot Luck 35 (see Quiz 93)
1 White. **2** *Days of Thunder*. **3** 1960s. **4** Emilio Estevez. **5** Edward Lewis.
6 1960s. **7** Spencer Tracy. **8** Palmer. **9** 'Chim Chim Cheree'. **10** San Francisco.
11 *Grumpier Old Men*. **12** *Dead Poets Society*. **13** Fred Astaire. **14** Nigel Bruce.
15 1950s. **16** *Dick Tracy*. **17** Clara Bow. **18** John Wayne. **19** The creation of
Mickey Mouse. **20** Grace Kelly. **21** 3 hours. **22** Julius Benedict. **23** Robert
Vaughn. **24** Wings. **25** *Batman*.

Answers – see page 206

1   Which Lauren featured in *American Gigolo*?
2   What is the first name of Bette Davis, who used her middle name in the movies?
3   In which decade was *The Abyss* released?
4   Who directed the 1996 movie *Nixon*?
5   A character named Vivian Ward appeared in which film?
6   What was Kathleen Turner's first film, in 1981?
7   Within fifteen minutes, how long does *The X-Files* last?
8   *Hook* and *Mars Attacks!* starred which actress?
9   'Sooner or Later (I Always Get My Man)' won an Oscar when it was used in which movie in 1990?
10   Who played the Bond girl in *The Man with the Golden Gun*?
11   Who won the Best Director Oscar for *The Graduate*?
12   How many times did Humphrey Bogart marry?
13   Which Ponchielli piece features in Disney's *Fantasia*?
14   Which Neil wrote *California Suite*?
15   In which film did Elvis play Vince Everett?
16   In which decade was *Scarface* released?
17   In which movie is John Travolta a museum security guard who loses his job?
18   Which song from *Pinocchio* won an Oscar?
19   *Bonnie and Clyde* and *The Woman in Red* both feature which actor?
20   Which disaster movie featured the character Michael O'Hallorhan?
21   Which country singer was in *True Grit*?
22   Who won the Best Actress Oscar for *The Lion in Winter*?
23   Who directed *Air Force One*?
24   Which actor links *Stakeout* and *Always*?
25   In which film did a character named Lula Pace Fortune appear?

Answers Famous Names (see Quiz 94)
1 'Wino Forever'. **2** Culkin. **3** Mel Blanc. **4** Jeanne. **5** Val Kilmer. **6** Paige.
7 Nothing. **8** Peter Ustinov. **9** Ronald Reagan. **10** Summerhill. **11** Maureen
O'Sullivan. **12** *Some Like It Hot*. **13** Hairdresser. **14** Dennis Quaid. **15**
Catwoman. **16** India. **17** Mary Louise. **18** Billy Crystal. **19** *Sudden Impact*. **20**
Christmas Day. **21** Swaziland. **22** Brad Pitt. **23** Great granddaughter. **24** *Jurassic Park*.

Answers – see page 211

1   What was Orson Welles's first movie?
2   In which decade was he born?
3   Which H.G. Wells dramatization caused panic when Welles's production convinced people that aliens were invading?
4   Which film about an American family was a follow up to *Citizen Kane*?
5   Which character from a Charlotte Bronte novel did he play in 1944?
6   Which glamorous redhead did he marry in 1943?
7   Which 'Scottish play' did he release in 1948?
8   What was the name of his character in *The Third Man*?
9   Which newspaper magnate tried to endanger the release of *Citizen Kane*?
10   Who directed him in *The Third Man*?
11   Which Shakespeare play did he make in Morocco with himself in the title role?
12   Within three years, how old was Welles when he made *Citizen Kane*?
13   In which film about Sir Thomas More did he appear in 1966?
14   Which movie did Welles and Rita Hayworth finish immediately before she filed for divorce?
15   Which studio released his first movie?
16   What did he describe as the biggest toy train set a boy ever had?
17   How many Oscars did *Citizen Kane* win?
18   In *Citizen Kane*, what is the tycoon's dying word?
19   Where was Welles working before he went to Hollywood?
20   Which 'Journey' did he film in 1942?
21   Which Bond film did he appear in with David Niven as 007?
22   In which decade did he die?
23   He said he started at the top and worked where?
24   In which European city was *The Third Man* set?
25   Which German actress said of him, 'People should cross themselves when they say his name'?

Answers Pot Luck 37 (see Quiz 99)
1 Matt Dillon. 2 Wrestling. 3 Elvis Presley. 4 Steve Oedekerk. 5 Ricci. 6 Metro.
7 Clint Eastwood. 8 1930s. 9 Garrett Breedlove. 10 95 minutes. 11 Alec
Guinness. 12 John Connor. 13 Geena Davis. 14 *City Slickers*. 15 *Help!*
16 Maggie Smith. 17 *The King and I*. 18 Sara. 19 Jane Russell. 20 John Huston.
21 The Monkees. 22 2 hours. 23 Sir Carol Reed. 24 Bruce Willis. 25 1970s.

Answers – see page 212

1   What is Catherine Zeta Jones's job in *Entrapment*?
2   Which beach is shown in the opening sequence of *Saving Private Ryan*?
3   In which movie does Sean Penn play Matthew Poncelet?
4   Where was *Turtle Beach* filmed?
5   *Brassed Off* takes place in which mining town?
6   Which movie about a US President and a teenage girl was released around the time of the Lewinsky scandal?
7   *Ten Things I Hate About You* was based on which Shakespeare play?
8   Who played Woody Allen's wife in *Mighty Aphrodite*?
9   In which movie did Kathy Burke play opposite Meryl Streep and Emma Thompson?
10 What are the three students called in *The Blair Witch Project*?
11 Which 1995 movie was based on a *2000 AD* comic strip character?
12 Where was *The Rock* set?
13 Which Queen is the subject of *Mrs Brown*?
14 What is the name of John Travolta's president in *Primary Colors*?
15 What was 'an equal not a sequel' to *Four Weddings and a Funeral*?
16 Who plays Charles van Doren in *Quiz Show*?
17 In which movie did Leonardo DiCaprio play Meryl Streep's rebellious son?
18 What was the name of Uma Thurman's character in *Pulp Fiction*?
19 What is the surname of the Jim Carrey character who is part of his own popular TV show?
20 What was the Richard Gere/Julia Roberts follow up to *Pretty Woman*?
21 Which director was played by Ian McKellen in *Gods and Monsters*?
22 Which roles did Leonardo DiCaprio play in *The Man in the Iron Mask*?
23 Who played the title role in *Onegin*?
24 In which movie did Al Pacino play Vincent Hanna?
25 In what month of what year does the action of *Apollo 13* take place?

Answers Oscars – Best Films (see Quiz 100)
1 *Romeo and Juliet.* **2** *Goodfellas.* **3** Cornwall and Monte Carlo. **4** *The Silence of the Lambs.* **5** *Forrest Gump.* **6** Brother. **7** Sioux. **8** World War II. **9** *Gandhi.* **10** *Shakespeare in Love.* **11** *Chariots of Fire.* **12** 1920s. **13** Pennsylvania. **14** *Cabaret.* **15** *My Fair Lady.* **16** Balboa. **17** *In the Heat of the Night.* **18** *Let It Be.* **19** *Dances with Wolves.* **20** Ralph & Joseph Fiennes. **21** 1950s. **22** *Forrest Gump.* **23** Frank Sinatra. **24** *Driving Miss Daisy.* **25** *All About Eve.*

Answers – see page 209

1   Which actor links *The Outsiders* and *Rumble Fish*?
2   At what sport did Tom Cruise excel?
3   Who turned down Kris Kristofferson's role in *A Star Is Born*?
4   Who directed *Ace Ventura: When Nature Calls*?
5   Which Christina featured in *The Addams Family*?
6   What did the first M stand for in MGM?
7   Which movie star released an album called *Cowboy Favorites* in 1959?
8   In which decade was *The Thin Man* released?
9   Who did Jack Nicholson play in *Terms of Endearment*?
10   Within fifteen minutes, how long does *Wayne's World* last?
11   Which British actor won an Oscar for *Bridge on the River Kwai*?
12   What was the name of Edward Furlong's character in *Terminator 2*?
13   *Fletch* and *Beetlejuice* starred which actress?
14   In which film did a character named Mitch Robbins appear?
15   What was the Beatles' second film?
16   Who won the Best Actress Oscar for *The Prime of Miss Jean Brodie*?
17   In which film musical is Mrs Anna Leonowens a lead character?
18   What is the name of the heroine of *A Little Princess*?
19   Who played Rio in *The Outlaw*?
20   *The Maltese Falcon* was whose directorial debut?
21   Which band appeared in the movie *Head*?
22   To the nearest hour, does *Air Force One* last 1, 2 or 3 hours?
23   Who won the Best Director Oscar for *Oliver!*?
24   *Sunset* and *Death Becomes Her* both feature which actor?
25   In which decade was *Catch-22* released?

Answers Orson Welles (see Quiz 97)
1 *Citizen Kane*. 2 1910s. 3 *War of the Worlds*. 4 *The Magnificent Ambersons*.
5 Mr Rochester. 6 Rita Hayworth. 7 *Macbeth*. 8 Harry Lime. 9 William Randolph
Hearst. 10 Carol Reed. 11 *Othello*. 12 25. 13 *A Man for All Seasons*. 14 *The Lady from Shanghai*. 15 RKO. 16 Film studio. 17 Nine. 18 'Rosebud'. 19 New York. 20 *Journey into Fear*. 21 *Casino Royale*. 22 1980s (1985). 23 Down. 24 Vienna. 25 Marlene Dietrich.

Answers – see page 210

1   *Shakespeare in Love* told the story behind the making of which play?
2   Which movie had the ad line, 'Three decades of life in the Mafia'?
3   In which two locations is *Rebecca* set?
4   Which movie had the line, 'I wish we could chat longer, but I'm having an old friend for dinner'?
5   After which film's success was a book of quotes by its hero published?
6   What relation is Tom Cruise to Dustin Hoffman in *Rain Man*?
7   Which tribe is the subject of *Dances with Wolves*?
8   *Mrs Miniver* was set during which conflict?
9   Which 20th century winner had most extras?
10   What was the first Best Film Joseph Fiennes appeared in?
11   Which film was about a Jew and a Scotsman in 1924?
12   In which decade does the action of *Out of Africa* take place?
13   The friends in *The Deer Hunter* are from which state?
14   Which winning film was about Sally Bowles?
15   Which musical *Pygmalion* won in 1964?
16   What was Rocky's surname in *Rocky*?
17   Which Sidney Poitier movie won in 1967?
18   What was the only Beatles movie to receive a nomination?
19   What was the first western to win a Best Picture Oscar after a 60-year gap?
20   Which two brothers appeared in Best Films in the 1990s?
21   In which decade was *Marty* a winner?
22   What was the first 90s Best Film to have 13 nominations?
23   Which singing superstar was one of 44 cameos in *Around the World in Eighty Days*?
24   In which Best Film did Morgan Freeman play a chauffeur called Hoke?
25   Which Best Picture was about Margo Channing?

Answers 1990s (see Quiz 98)
1 Insurance Investigator. **2** Omaha. **3** *Dead Man Walking*. **4** Thailand.
5 Grimley. **6** *Wag the Dog*. **7** *The Taming of the Shrew*. **8** Helena Bonham Carter.
9 *Dancing at Lughnasa*. **10** Michael, Heather & Joshua. **11** *Judge Dredd*.
12 Alcatraz. **13** Victoria. **14** Jack Stanton. **15** *Notting Hill*. **16** Ralph Fiennes.
17 *Marvin's Room*. **18** Mia Wallace. **19** (Truman) Burbank. **20** *The Runaway Bride*. **21** James Whale. **22** Louis XIV & his twin Philippe. **23** Ralph Fiennes.
24 *Heat*. **25** April 1970.

Answers – see page 215

1	Which country did he represent in the Mr Universe contest?
2	What was the name of his first wife?
3	In which branch of the armed forces did he serve?
4	In which 90s film did he play Sir August De Wynter?
5	What is the name of his actor son?
6	Which king did he play in *Robin Hood: Prince of Thieves*?
7	In which movie of an Agatha Christie classic did he appear in 1974?
8	Where in Scotland was he born?
9	In 1951 he appeared in the chorus of which famous Rodgers & Hammerstein musical?
10	In which Hitchcock movie did he star in 1964?
11	Whose names does he have on a tattoo?
12	Who was his female co-star in *The Russia House*?
13	In how many Bond films did he appear in the 60s?
14	In which 80s film did he play Harrison Ford's father?
15	In which 70s film did he play a legendary English hero?
16	Who was his co-star in *Goldfinger*?
17	In which 007 movie did he return in 1983?
18	Which 1990 film was based on a John Le Carré novel?
19	What is his real first name?
20	What was his only Bond movie of the 70s?
21	In which movie did he play a medieval detective?
22	What was he a commander of in *The Hunt for Red October*?
23	What is the name of the second Mrs Connery?
24	Which Welsh actress was his co-star in *Entrapment*?
25	In which 80s film did he play an Irish cop?

Answers Pot Luck 38 (see Quiz 102)
1 *Back to the Future III.* **2** Turner. **3** Solitaire. **4** *Smokey and the Bandit.* **5** 1950s.
6 James Cameron. **7** Logan. **8** 150 minutes. **9** Never. **10** Jim Garrison.
11 *Prince of Eygpt.* **12** John Wayne. **13** *Les Girls.* **14** Laura Dern. **15** Elizabeth
Taylor. **16** Sonny Corleone. **17** Bernstein. **18** *Love Story.* **19** 1950s. **20** *Blade
Runner.* **21** *Beauty and the Beast.* **22** Danny DeVito. **23** Kathy Bates. **24** 1940s.
25 William Wyler.

Answers – see page 213

1   Which *Back to the Future* film returns to the Wild West?
2   Which Kathleen featured in *The Accidental Tourist*?
3   What was the name of the Bond girl in *Live and Let Die*?
4   The relationship between Burt Reynolds and Sally Field began on the set of which movie?
5   *Sunset Boulevard* was released in which decade?
6   Who directed *The Abyss*?
7   What is the last name of Ted from *Bill and Ted's Excellent Adventure*?
8   Is *West Side Story* nearer to 90, 120 or 150 minutes?
9   How many times had James Coburn been Oscar nominated before he won for *Affliction*?
10 What was the name of Kevin Costner's character in *JFK*?
11 'When You Believe' won an Oscar when it was used in which movie in 1998?
12 Who played Genghis Khan in *The Conqueror*?
13 A character named Barry Nichols appeared in which 1950s film?
14 *Blue Velvet* and *Jurassic Park* both starred which actress?
15 Who won the Best Actress Oscar for *Who's Afraid of Virginia Woolf?*?
16 Who did James Caan play in *The Godfather*?
17 Who was Woodward's fellow reporter in *All the President's Men*?
18 A character named Jenny Cavilleri appeared in which film?
19 In which decade does the action of *Grease* take place?
20 In which film does a character named Rick Deckard appear?
21 Characters named Gaston and Belle appeared in which film?
22 Which actor links *Taxi* and *War of the Roses*?
23 Who played the villain in the movie *Misery*?
24 In which decade was Disney's *Cinderella* released?
25 Who won the Best Director Oscar for *Mrs Miniver*?

Answers The 21st Century (see Quiz 103)
1 *House on Haunted Hill.* 2 Limerick. 3 Mike Leigh. 4 Ashley Judd. 5 *Sleepy Hollow.* 6 Ambulance Drivers. 7 American Football. 8 *The Wonder Boys.* 9 *Toy Story 2.* 10 Scotland. 11 *The Sixth Sense.* 12 Angela. 13 Cab driver. 14 Blue. 15 Evil Emperor Zurg. 16 New York City. 17 Madonna. 18 Robin Williams. 19 *The Mikado.* 20 *The Big Tease.* 21 Anthony Minghella. 22 Carolyn. 23 Andy's. 24 To escape from their run. 25 Daffy.

Answers – see page 214

1 Which horror movie was a remake of a 1958 hit?
2 Where in Ireland is *Angela's Ashes* set?
3 Who was Oscar-nominated for the screenplay of *Topsy Turvy*?
4 Who plays the fugitive in *Double Jeopardy*?
5 Which Washington Irving ghost story starred Tim Burton and Johnny Depp?
6 What sort of drivers are the subject of *Bringing Out the Dead*?
7 *Any Given Sunday* is about which sport?
8 In which movie did Michael Douglas play an unkempt, thrice-married professor?
9 Which new millennium movie included the voices of Tom Hanks and Tim Allen?
10 Where is Valerie Edmond's childhood home in *One More Kiss*?
11 Which movie with Haley Joel Osment was Oscar-nominated?
12 What is the name of Mena Suvari's character in *American Beauty*?
13 What is the occupation of the serial killer in *The Bone Collector*?
14 What colour shirt is Bruce Willis wearing in *The Sixth Sense*?
15 Who is Buzz Lightyear's father in *Toy Story 2*?
16 Where does Johnny Depp's character travel from to reach Sleepy Hollow?
17 Who starred in *The Next Best Thing*?
18 Who was 'Bicentennial Man'?
19 *Topsy Turvy* is about the making of which Gilbert and Sullivan opera?
20 Which Craig Ferguson movie was about a hairdressing championship?
21 Which director adapted *The Talented Mr Ripley* for the big screen?
22 What is the name of Kevin Spacey's wife in *American Beauty*?
23 Whose bedroom do the toys inhabit in *Toy Story 2*?
24 What is the chickens' main aim in *Chicken Run*?
25 Which character gives Leonardo DiCaprio the map in *The Beach*?

Answers Sean Connery (see Quiz 101)
1 Scotland. 2 Diane Cilento. 3 Navy. 4 *The Avengers*. 5 Jason. 6 Richard I.
7 *Murder on the Orient Express*. 8 Edinburgh. 9 *South Pacific*. 10 *Marnie*.
11 Mum & Dad. 12 Michelle Pfeiffer. 13 Five. 14 *Indiana Jones and the Last Crusade*. 15 *Robin and Marian*. 16 Honor Blackman. 17 *Never Say Never Again*.
18 *The Russia House*. 19 Thomas. 20 *Diamonds Are Forever*. 21 *The Name of the Rose*. 22 Submarine. 23 Micheline. 24 Catherine Zeta Jones. 25 *The Untouchables*.

LEVEL THREE: THE HARD QUESTIONS

These are the hard questions – and do we mean hard! When we were telling you about the easy questions we suggested you use them so that everyone can answer something. This is the section for those who have found it fairly straightforward so far and need something very challenging indeed. Alternatively, if you're one of those people with an amazing memory for the most obscure bits of information, this could just be the section for you.

You will still find questions on famous movie folk and major movies but this is where we also ask you about the lesser-known happenings in this fascinating industry. The questions may not be straightforward. You may need several bits of information to come up with the correct answer. You may have part of the information but not all of it. There was no limit to our cunning when this section was compiled!

It does happen that when you have a quiz for a prize or prizes you end up with a tie. We suggest that this is the section of the book you use to come up with a tie-breaker. The real subject experts may not be fazed by some of the specialist sections, mind-numbingly difficult though they are, so maybe use a few Pot Luck questions as tie-breakers. In this way you will know they won't have boned up in advance.

If you are reading *The Best Movie Quiz Book Ever!* for your own entertainment and are answering most of the questions in this supremely difficult section then congratulate yourself. John Wayne said, 'Motion pictures are for amusement.' We hope that this quiz book about motion pictures will give you many hours of amusement as well.

Answers – see page 219

1	Who said, 'You can't get spoiled if you do your own ironing'?
2	How is Edna Gilhooley better known?
3	What was the name of the band Johnny Depp played in before turning to acting?
4	At which university did Richard E. Grant study?
5	In which city was Edward G. Robinson born?
6	Who said he would prefer 'animal' on his passport to 'actor'?
7	Who said, 'I look like a quarry someone has dynamited'?
8	How is Francoise Sorya Dreyfus better known?
9	Who was dubbed the '80s Errol Flynn' by *Vanity Fair* magazine?
10	Which star actor was born on exactly the same day as the late Laurence Harvey?
11	Who said, 'I stopped making pictures because I don't like taking my clothes off'?
12	Who played Woody Guthrie in *Bound for Glory*?
13	Which director did Theresa Russell marry?
14	Whose marriage to Michelle Phillips lasted just eight days?
15	Which film star wrote the novel *Adieu Volidia*?
16	About which of his co-stars did Anthony Hopkins say, 'She's serious about her work but doesn't take herself seriously'?
17	What is Michael J. Fox's middle name?
18	Who starred in *Prom Night* and *Terror Train*?
19	Whom did Harrison Ford replace as Indiana Jones in *Raiders of the Lost Ark*?
20	Which actress's father was one of the Dalai Lama's first American Buddhist monks?
21	Which actor played drums in a band called Scarlet Pride?
22	Which actor is Sissy Spacek's cousin?
23	What does Tim Roth have tattooed on his arm?
24	What is Shirley MacLaine's real name?
25	Who played Francis Bacon in *Love Is the Devil*?

Answers Humphrey Bogart (see Quiz 3)
1 DeForest. **2** Surgeon. **3** Leviathan. **4** *Broadway's Like That.* **5** Alexander Woollcott. **6** 28. **7** Mary Philips. **8** Captain Queeg. **9** Warner Brothers. **10** Duke Mantee. **11** John Huston. **12** *Virginia City.* **13** George Raft. **14** Leslie Howard. **15** *The Treasure of the Sierra Madre.* **16** *Casablanca.* **17** General Sternwood (Charles Waldron). **18** *To Have And Have Not.* **19** *The Maltese Falcon.* **20** Santana Pictures. **21** *High Sierra.* **22** Katharine Hepburn. **23** *The Harder they Fall.* **24** Vivian Sherwood Rutledge. **25** *The Big Sleep.*

Answers – see page 220

1   What room number does Norman Bates put Janet Leigh in?
2   What is the profession of Nicole Kidman's father?
3   Which movie star released an album called *Love's Alright* in 1993?
4   Who won the Best Director Oscar for *Kramer versus Kramer*?
5   Which Ann featured in *The Accused*?
6   Within five minutes, how long does *Zulu* last?
7   What was the name of Bruce Willis's character in *Armageddon*?
8   In what year did Tom Cruise and Nicole Kidman supposedly land in Oklahoma in the film *Far and Away*?
9   Which actor links *The Paper* and *The Scarlet Letter*?
10 Who said, 'Universal signed me as a contract player – which is a little lower than working in the mail room'?
11 What colour scarf is Scrooge given in *The Muppets' Christmas Carol*?
12 How old was David Lean when he made *A Passage to India*?
13 Who wrote the screenplay for *The Seven Year Itch* with Billy Wilder?
14 Which 1971 film did pop star James Taylor star in?
15 Which 90s movie featured the voices of Gary Shandling, Chris Reubens and Paul Rock?
16 Which movie gave Carlo Rambaldi a Special Award in 1976 for visual effects?
17 Which Amy featured in *The Accidental Tourist*?
18 Who played the Bond girl in *Diamonds Are Forever*?
19 Within ten minutes, how long does the 1970s version of *Carrie* last?
20 In which movie did Clark Gable play Gay Langland?
21 Who won the Best Actor Oscar for *The Way of All Flesh*?
22 Who was originally set to play Indiana Jones before Harrison Ford?
23 Who directed *Wolf*?
24 How many *Road* films did Crosby, Hope and Lamour make?
25 Which Michael starred in *The Abyss*?

Answers Horror (see Quiz 4)
1 Bela Lugosi. **2** Summer Isle. **3** Corey Haim. **4** TV horror film host. **5** Bodega Bay. **6** *Return of the Fly*. **7** The Arctic. **8** Lon Chaney. **9** Manhattan. **10** George A. Romero. **11** Property developer. **12** Stephen Hopkins. **13** His body is struck by lightning. **14** Billy. **15** *Seizure*. **16** Ellen Burstyn. **17** Daryl Hannah. **18** John Williams. **19** 110 minutes. **20** Friday the 13th. **21** The right hand of Christopher Hart. **22** He did not speak. **23** Ants. **24** Joseph Losey. **25** Neil Jordan.

Answers – see page 217

1   What was his middle name?
2   What was the occupation of his father?
3   On which ship was he serving in World War I when he injured his lip, giving him his characteristic tough look?
4   In which short did he make his screen debut?
5   Which reviewer described his acting as 'what is usually and mercifully described as inadequate'?
6   How many feature films did he make between 1936 and 1940?
7   Who did he marry after Helen Menken?
8   For which character was he Oscar-nominated in *The Caine Mutiny*?
9   Which studio was he working for at the outbreak of World War II?
10 What was the name of the killer he played in *The Petrified Forest*?
11 Who collaborated with W.R. Burnett to write the hit *High Sierra*?
12 In which Errol Flynn western did he play a Mexican bandit?
13 Who turned down the Sam Spade role in *The Maltese Falcon*?
14 Who insisted he get the screen role in *The Petrified Forest* which he had played on Broadway?
15 In which movie did he play Fred C. Dobbs?
16 In which movie did he say, 'I stick my neck out for nobody'?
17 Whose daughter is Philip Marlowe hired to protect in *The Big Sleep*?
18 *The Breaking Point* was a remake of which Bogart movie?
19 Which film starred Bogart in John Huston's directorial debut?
20 Which company did he form in 1947?
21 In which movie did he play Mad Dog Earle?
22 Which of his co-stars said, 'There was no bunkum with Bogart'?
23 What was the name of the film released shortly before his death?
24 What role did Mrs Bogart play in *The Big Sleep*?
25 In which movie did he say, 'I don't mind if you don't like my manners. I don't like them myself'?

Answers Who's Who? (see Quiz 1)
1 Meryl Streep. **2** Ellen Burstyn. **3** The Kids. **4** Cape Town. **5** Bucharest.
6 Mickey Rourke. **7** Charles Bronson. **8** Anouk Aimee. **9** Kevin Kline. **10** George Peppard. **11** Debbie Reynolds. **12** David Carradine. **13** Nicholas Roeg.
14 Dennis Hopper. **15** Simone Signoret. **16** Emma Thompson. **17** Andrew.
18 Jamie Lee Curtis. **19** Tom Selleck. **20** Uma Thurman. **21** Ewan McGregor.
22 Rip Torn. **23** The birthdates of his children. **24** Shirley Maclean Beaty. **25** Derek Jacobi.

Answers – see page 218

Answers – see page 218

1   Which actor was known professionally for a time as Ariztid Olt?
2   What is the name of the island that *The Wicker Man* is set upon?
3   Who played Sam in *The Lost Boys*?
4   What is Peter Vincent's occupation in *Fright Night*?
5   Where does Mitch live in *The Birds*?
6   What was the name of the 1959 sequel to *The Fly*?
7   Where is the action set in 50s classic *The Thing*?
8   Which actor was originally chosen to play Bela Lugosi's role in the 1931 film *Dracula*?
9   Where does Mia Farrow live in *Rosemary's Baby*?
10   Who directed *Night of the Living Dead*?
11   What is the father's occupation in *Poltergeist*?
12   Who directed *A Nightmare on Elm Street 5: The Dream Child*?
13   How is Jason brought back to life in *Friday the Thirteenth Part VI –Jason Lives*?
14   Who receives Gizmo as a gift in *Gremlins*?
15   Which low-budget horror movie did Oliver Stone direct in 1974?
16   Which star of *The Exorcist* is also known by the name Edna Rae?
17   Who starred in *The Final Terror* with then flat-mate Rachel Ward?
18   Who wrote the score for *Jaws*?
19   Within fifteen minutes, how long does *Scream* last?
20   On which day in America did *Bram Stoker's Dracula* open?
21   Who or what plays Thing in *The Addams Family*?
22   What is unusual about Christopher Lee's role in *Dracula – Prince of Darkness*?
23   What creatures were the stars of *Them!*?
24   Who made *The Damned* for Hammer?
25   Who directed *Interview with the Vampire: The Vampire Chronicles*?

Answers – see page 223

1   Which movie star was born on the same day as Quincy Jones?
2   A character named Melvin Udall appeared in which film?
3   Which Martin featured in *All the President's Men*?
4   Within five minutes, how long does *Yellow Submarine* last?
5   Which actor links *Another Country* and *Dance with a Stranger*?
6   Who directed *Batman*?
7   Who was elected President of the Screen Actors Union in 1947 and again in 1959?
8   Which Paul featured in *American Graffiti*?
9   On which Hawaiian island was *Jurassic Park* filmed?
10 After 'Best Boy' appears on the end credits of *Airplane II: The Sequel*, who appears as 'Worst Boy'?
11 A character named Jack Crabb appeared in which film?
12 Who played Thing in *The Addams Family*?
13 Who voiced Jasmine in the film *Aladdin*?
14 In which year was *Destry Rides Again* released?
15 Who was quoted as saying, 'Great talent is an accident of birth'?
16 Which movie is shown in the film *I Love You to Death*?
17 Who played Tony Moretti in the film *Action Jackson*?
18 Within ten minutes how long does *Sophie's Choice* last?
19 Who was Jim Carrey's make-up man for *The Mask*?
20 Who won the Best Actress Oscar for *Seventh Heaven*?
21 A character named Luis Molina appears in which film?
22 Which soap did Hollywood star Christian Slater star in?
23 Which Bill featured in *American Gigolo*?
24 Who was first choice for Sigourney Weaver's *Gorillas in the Mist* role?
25 Who won the Best Director Oscar for *From Here to Eternity*?

Answers Oscars – Who's Who? (see Quiz 7)
1 Poldek Pfefferberg (who told his story to Thomas Keneally). **2** Ralph Bellamy.
3 Elmer Bernstein. **4** Gary Busey. **5** Donfeld. **6** Alec Guinness. **7** Steven
Spielberg. **8** George Sanders (*All About Eve*). **9** Cuba Gooding Jr (*Jerry Maguire*).
10 John Corigliano. **11** *Bugsy*. **12** Yves Montand (Simone Signoret). **13** The
Shadows (John Farrar). **14** Mammy in *Gone with the Wind* (Hattie McDaniel).
15 Judy Holliday. **16** Margaret Herrick. **17** Johnny Carson. **18** Sophia Loren.
19 Ruth Gordon. **20** Edmund Goulding. **21** Alice Brady's. **22** Holly Hunter.
23 *The Pride of the Yankees*. **24** Ivan Jandl. **25** Richard Williams.

QUIZ 6 1930s

Answers – see page 224

1   Which movie was advertised as 'Garbo laughs'?
2   What was Johnny Weissmuller's first Tarzan movie called?
3   Which Russian-born choreographer worked on *The Goldwyn Follies*?
4   Who famously had a grapefruit squashed in her face by Cagney in *Public Enemy*?
5   In which movie did Marlene Dietrich sing 'See What the Boys in the Back Room Will Have'?
6   Who played Catherine the Great in *The Scarlet Empress*?
7   In which movie did Claudette Colbert say, 'The moment I saw you, I had an idea you had an idea'?
8   In which movie did Errol Flynn make his screen debut?
9   *The Country Doctor* was a movie about whose birth?
10 Which actress who appeared in *Anna Christie* wrote an autobiography called *The Life Story of an Ugly Duckling*?
11 Who played Sherlock Holmes in *The Sleeping Cardinal*?
12 Who was Janet Gaynor's most frequent partner of the 20s and 30s?
13 What was advertised as 'Garbo talks'?
14 If Leslie Howard is Professor Higgins, who is Eliza Doolittle?
15 In which of his own movies did King Vidor appear in 1934?
16 Which husband and wife were Oscar-nominated together in 1931?
17 Which movie had the ad line, 'He treated her rough and she loved it'?
18 Who played David Garrick to Anna Neagle's Peg Woffington in *Peg of Old Drury Lane* in 1935?
19 What was the first of Spencer Tracy's three Oscar nominations between 1936 and 1938?
20 Who played the title role in *Rembrandt* in 1936?
21 Which brother of Harold Lloyd was injured making *Scarface* in 1932?
22 Who played Captain Ahab in *Moby Dick*?
23 What were Mae West's two hits of 1933?
24 What did Miscah Auer impersonate in *My Man Godfrey*?
25 By what name did John Carradine star in movies between 1930 and 1935?

Answers Pot Luck 3 (see Quiz 8)
1 Book editor. **2** Barry McGuigan. **3** John Ford. **4** Jessica Lange. **5** Crewson.
6 *Godzilla*. **7** 83 mins. **8** Dabney Coleman. **9** Shelley Duvall (in *Popeye*).
10 Eddie Murphy. **11** Seven. **12** 'The Power of Love'. **13** New Jersey. **14**
Baseball. **15** Hedaya. **16** Howard Zieff. **17** 138. **18** Ralph Fiennes. **19** Frank
Coraci. **20** Patsy Kensit. **21** Johnny Rico. **22** Sound effects on *Robocop*. **23** 101
minutes. **24** Ron Howard. **25** Callow.

Answers – see page 221

1	Spielberg said he accepted for *Schindler's List* on whose behalf?
2	Which honorary winner's autobiography was called *When the Smoke Hits the Fan*?
3	Which composer was nominated for *The Man with the Golden Arm*?
4	Which nominee has been a member of Carp and a drummer with the Rubber Band?
5	Who was a nominee for costume for *Days of Wine and Roses*?
6	Who won an honorary award in 1979 for 'advancing the art of screen acting'?
7	Who did Amy Irving marry shortly after being nominated for *Yentl*?
8	Who won Best Supporting Actor the year Josephine Hull won Best Supporting Actress for *Harvey*?
9	Who did James Woods lose out to as Best Supporting Actor for *Ghosts from the Past*?
10	Who was nominated for music for *The Red Violin*?
11	What was Ben Kingsley's next nomination after his first win?
12	Who was the husband of the 1959 Best Supporting Actress?
13	The composer of the only nominated song from *Grease* was a member of which pop band?
14	The first black actress to win was honoured for which role?
15	Who won when Gloria Swanson was nominated for *Sunset Boulevard*?
16	Who supposedly named the Oscar, saying it looked like her uncle?
17	Who is the second most frequent host of the Oscars ceremony?
18	Who was the first performer to win an Oscar for a performance entirely in a foreign language?
19	Who was the Oscar winner in *Rosemary's Baby*?
20	Who in 1932 was the first director to see his film win Best Picture but not have a nomination himself?
21	In 1938, whose Oscar for *In Old Chicago* was received by an impostor and stolen?
22	Who was nominated for Best Actress and Best Supporting Actress in 1993?
23	What was the second of Gary Cooper's three nominations between 1941 and 1943?
24	Who won a Special Award for *The Search* aged nine?
25	Who won a Special Achievement Award for *Who Framed Roger Rabbit*??

Answers Pot Luck 2 (see Quiz 5)
1 Michael Caine (14.3.33). 2 *As Good As It Gets*. 3 Balsam. 4 85 minutes.
5 Rupert Everett. 6 Tim Burton. 7 Ronald Reagan. 8 LeMat. 9 Kauai. 10 Adolph
Hitler. 11 *Little Big Man*. 12 Christopher Hart. 13 Linda Larkin. 14 1939.
15 Woody Allen. 16 *Bridge on the River Kwai*. 17 Robert Davi. 18 157 minutes.
19 Jim Cannon. 20 Janet Gaynor. 21 *Kiss of the Spider Woman*. 22 *Ryan's Hope*.
23 Duke. 24 Jessica Lange. 25 Fred Zinnemann.

Answers – see page 222

1. What is the job of the Jack Nicholson character in *Wolf*?
2. Who coached Daniel Day-Lewis for his role in *The Boxer*?
3. Who won the Best Director Oscar for *The Informer*?
4. Who won the Best Actress Oscar for *Blue Sky*?
5. Which Wendy featured in *Air Force One*?
6. In which film did a character named Dr Niko Tatopoulos appear?
7. To the nearest five minutes, how long does *Snow White and the Seven Dwarfs* last?
8. Which actor played the womanizing boss in *9 to 5*?
9. Who played Robin Williams's wife in his first movie?
10. Which actor said, 'I've got a filthy mouth but it's my only sin'?
11. In how many films did Roger Moore play 007 altogether?
12. What was the theme tune to *Back to the Future*?
13. In which state was John Travolta born?
14. At what sport did William Baldwin excel?
15. Which Dan featured in *Alien: Resurrection*?
16. From whom did Penny Marshall take over the direction of *Jumpin' Jack Flash*?
17. Within 20, how many actors are named on the credits for the film *Gandhi*?
18. Which actor links *Wuthering Heights* and *Quiz Show*?
19. Who directed *The Wedding Singer*?
20. Which pop wife appeared in *The Great Gatsby* aged four?
21. What was the name of Casper Van Dien's character in *Starship Troopers*?
22. For what did Stephen Flick win a Special Award in 1987?
23. Within five minutes, how long does *The Wizard of Oz* last?
24. Who directed *Backdraft*?
25. Which Simon featured in *Ace Ventura: When Nature Calls*?

Answers – see page 227

1	Who composed the score for the 1995 movie *August*?
2	Who wrote the title song for *When the Wind Blows*?
3	Who sang the theme song for *North to Alaska*?
4	Who was Oscar-nominated for music for *The Cider House Rules*?
5	The Oscar-nominated 'Save Me' came from which movie?
6	Which three people successively sang the title song in *Someone to Watch Over Me*?
7	In which movie did jazz saxophonist Charlie Barnet play his hit recording of 'Cherokee'?
8	For which movie did Bernard Herrmann receive his first Oscar?
9	Who wrote the music for *Lawrence of Arabia*?
10	Which Shostakovich piece was used in *Eyes Wide Shut*?
11	Whose recording of 'Why Do Fools Fall in Love' featured on the soundtrack of *American Graffiti*?
12	Who wrote the score for *The Asphalt Jungle*?
13	Who provided the score for *Never on Sunday*?
14	Which music plays in the background in *10*?
15	Whose songs were on the soundtrack of *Philadelphia*?
16	Who wrote the songs for *Lady and the Tramp*?
17	Who was Oscar-nominated for the original score for *The Talented Mr Ripley*?
18	Who contributed a song for his 1957 film *Fire Down Below*?
19	'It Might Be You' comes from which movie?
20	Who wrote the songs for *Shanghai Surprise*?
21	Which famous son appeared as Michael Jackson's friend in *Moonwalker*?
22	*Don't Look Back* is an account of whose tour of Britain?
23	Whose zither music is haunting part of *The Third Man*?
24	Who wrote the score for *Double Indemnity*?
25	Which piece of music accompanies the prehistoric section of *Fantasia*?

.

Answers Pot Luck 4 (see Quiz 11)

1 Blue. **2** Ian McDiarmid. **3** Gene Wilder. **4** Paul Simon. **5** Penelope Spheeris.
6 158 minutes. **7** Warner Baxter. **8** *Night Shift*. **9** Harrison Ford. **10** Computer
salesman. **11** *US Marshals*. **12** *Licence to Kill*. **13** James L. Brooks. **14** England.
15 Mandy Patinkin. **16** Harris. **17** *Just a Gigolo*. **18** Charles Shaughnessy.
19 Ben Kingsley. **20** Morgan Freeman. **21** Golic. **22** 140 minutes. **23** Brolin.
24 Mary Pickford. **25** Jack Colton.

Answers – see page 228

1	Star of *Born on the Fourth of July*, when is his birthday?
2	What does he have in common with Robert De Niro and Charlie Chaplin?
3	What is his full real name?
4	What is the name of his character in *Days of Thunder*?
5	Who sang the title song of his first movie?
6	How old was he when he had his first movie role?
7	On which novel was *Taps* based?
8	Which 1999 movie was the last for its director?
9	Who directed him in the 1983 'brat pack' movie with Matt Dillon, Rob Lowe and others?
10	For which movie immediately after *Mission: Impossible* was he Oscar-nominated?
11	Who or what won an Oscar for *Top Gun*?
12	He received his first Oscar nomination for playing which role?
13	With which star of *Risky Business* did he have an off-screen romance?
14	Which 1986 movie won an Oscar for his co-star?
15	What is his job in the film which won his co-star Dustin Hoffman an Oscar?
16	Who was his wife prior to Nicole Kidman?
17	In which part of which state was he born?
18	Where did he spend a year before deciding to become an actor?
19	Which writer whose book a film was based on said, 'He's no more my Vampire Lestat than Edward G. Robinson is Rhett Butler'?
20	What 'award' did he win at high school?
21	What was his second film?
22	For which TV show did he make his directorial debut?
23	What was his next film after *Rain Man*?
24	What was the first movie he produced and starred in?
25	What was the first film he starred in with Nicole Kidman after their marriage?

Answers Disaster Movies (see Quiz 12)
1 264. **2** Hart Bochner. **3** Alfred Newman. **4** Ronald Neame. **5** Roger Simmons.
6 Alfred E. Green. **7** Jerry Bruckheimer. **8** On the beach. **9** Salvage hunter.
10 Industrial Light and Magic. **11** Ron Howard. **12** Elizabeth Hoffman. **13** 158
mins. **14** Jonathon Hensleigh. **15** Philip Lathrop. **16** Arthur Herzog. **17** Corey
Allen. **18** New York to New Jersey tunnel. **19** Laurence Rosenthal. **20** McCallum.
21 Spencer Tracy. **22** Max Catto. **23** Special effects. **24** Michael M. Mooney's.
25 Fox & MGM (*Towering Inferno*).

Answers – see page 225

1   The ghostly sisters seen by Danny wear what colour dresses in *The Shining*?
2   Who played the villain in *Return of the Jedi*?
3   Which movie star released a single called 'Pure Imagination' in 1970?
4   Which singer featured in *Annie Hall*?
5   Who directed *Wayne's World*?
6   Within five minutes, how long does *Where Eagles Dare* last?
7   Who won the Best Actor Oscar for *In Old Arizona*?
8   What was Michael Keaton's first film, in 1982?
9   Which actor links *Regarding Henry* and *Heroes*?
10 What does Helen think husband Harry does for a living in *True Lies*?
11 A character named Mark Sheridan appeared in which film?
12 What was Timothy Dalton's last film as James Bond?
13 Who won the Best Director Oscar for *Terms of Endearment*?
14 In which country was the whole of *Full Metal Jacket* filmed?
15 Who played Sam Francisco in the film *Alien Nation*?
16 Which Ed featured in *Apollo 13*?
17 What was Marlene Dietrich's last movie?
18 What was the name of Robert Mitchum's character in *Ryan's Daughter*?
19 Who said, 'I love British cinema like a doctor loves his dying patient'?
20 Which actor links *Street Smart* and *Glory*?
21 Which character did Paul McGann play in the film *Alien³*?
22 Within fifteen minutes, how long does *Apollo 13* last?
23 Which James starred in *The Amityville Horror*?
24 Who won the Best Actress Oscar for *Coquette*?
25 What was the name of Michael Douglas's character in *Romancing the Stone*?

Answers Music On Film (see Quiz 9)
1 Anthony Hopkins. 2 David Bowie. 3 Johnny Horton. 4 Rachel Portman.
5 *Magnolia*. 6 Sting, Gene Ammons & Roberta Flack. 7 *Jam Session*. 8 *All That Money Can Buy*. 9 Maurice Jarre. 10 Jazz Suite No. 2. 11 Frankie Lymon's.
12 Miklos Rozsa. 13 Monos Hadjidakis. 14 Ravel's *Bolero*. 15 Bruce Springsteen & Neil Young's. 16 Peggy Lee & Sonny Burke. 17 Gabriel Yared. 18 Jack Lemmon.
19 *Tootsie*. 20 George Harrison. 21 Sean Lennon. 22 Bob Dylan's. 23 Anton Karas's. 24 Miklos Rozsa. 25 Stravinsky's *Rite of Spring*.

Answers – see page 226

1   What is the body count of *Die Hard 2* said to be?
2   Who played Ellis in *Die Hard*?
3   Who wrote the score for *Airport*?
4   Who directed *The Poseidon Adventure*?
5   Which character is the technical expert responsible for the *Towering Inferno*?
6   Who directed the 50s movie *Invasion USA*?
7   Who produced *Armageddon*?
8   Where does the character Jenny die in *Deep Impact*?
9   What is the occupation of the character played by Bill Paxton in *Titanic*?
10   Which company provided the computer-generated images for *Twister*?
11   Who directed *Apollo 13*?
12   Who plays the grandmother of the Mayor's children in *Dante's Peak*?
13   Within ten minutes, how long does *Towering Inferno* run?
14   Who wrote *Die Hard with a Vengeance*?
15   Who was Oscar-nominated for *Earthquake*?
16   *The Swarm* is based on a novel written by whom?
17   Who directed *Avalanche*?
18   Where is *Daylight* set?
19   Who wrote the score for *Meteor*?
20   Which David featured in *A Night to Remember*?
21   Which actor received an Oscar nomination for *San Francisco*?
22   Who wrote the novel that *The Devil at Four O'Clock* is based on?
23   For what did *Krakatoa, East of Java* receive an Oscar nomination?
24   Upon whose novel is *The Hindenburg* based?
25   Which two studios made the movie based on *The Tower* and *The Glass Inferno*?

Answers Tom Cruise (see Quiz 10)
1 3rd July. **2** Left-handed. **3** Thomas Cruise Mapother IV. **4** Cole. **5** Lionel Richie ('Endless Love'). **6** 18. **7** *Father Sky*. **8** *Eyes Wide Shut* (Stanley Kubrick).
9 Francis Ford Coppola. **10** *Jerry Maguire*. **11** Song ('Take My Breath Away').
12 Ron Kovic (*Born on the Fourth of July*). **13** Rebecca De Mornay. **14** *The Color of Money*. **15** Salesman. **16** Mimi Rogers. **17** Syracuse, New York. **18** Franciscan monastery. **19** Anne Rice (*Interview with the Vampire*). **20** Least Likely to Succeed.
21 *Taps*. **22** *Fallen Angels*. **23** *Cocktail*. **24** *Mission: Impossible*. **25** *Far and Away*.

Answers – see page 231

1	What was his middle name?
2	Under which star sign was he born?
3	Which studio did he sign with when he first went to Hollywood?
4	What was the first movie where he was cast opposite Marlene Dietrich?
5	For which film was he nominated for his second Oscar?
6	With whose troupe did he go to America in 1920?
7	Which short saw his screen debut?
8	What did the studio want to change his name to when he first arrived at Paramount?
9	Which 1948 movies both featured the then Mrs Cary Grant?
10	Which of his co-stars mimicked him in the subsequent film he made?
11	Which of his movies was a remake of *The More the Merrier*?
12	He was a director of which cosmetics company after his retirement from the big screen?
13	After 1958 what percentage of the takings did he receive in lieu of salary in his films?
14	His second wife was heiress to which empire?
15	For which movie did he donate his salary to war relief?
16	Who was the only winner of an Oscar for *Suspicion*, in which he starred?
17	In which film did he say, 'Insanity runs in my family. It practically gallops'?
18	Mae West's invitation to Cary Grant to 'come up some time and see me' came from a movie based on which play?
19	Who played his wife in the first movie for which he was Oscar-nominated?
20	Who won Best Actor for the year Grant was given a special Oscar?
21	In 1937–38 he was under joint contract to which studios?
22	Who was the mother of his only child?
23	Who did he play in *Night and Day*?
24	What was his first film for Hitchcock?
25	Which wife survived him?

Answers Walt Disney (see Quiz 15)
1 Alfred Hitchcock. **2** *Flowers and Trees*. **3** Kansas City. **4** *Saludos Amigos; The Three Caballeros*. **5** *The Skeleton Dance*. **6** Alfred & Elma Milotte. **7** Made training films. **8** Laugh O Grams. **9** Julie Andrews (*Mary Poppins*). **10** Sagittarius. **11** One large Oscar and seven small ones. **12** *Jungle Book*. **13** Leopold Stokowski. **14** *Treasure Island*. **15** *Plane Crazy; Gallopin' Gaucho*. **16** Dippy Dawg. **17** *Victory Through Air Power*. **18** *Alice in Cartoonland*. **19** *Jungle Cat*. **20** 29. **21** Son-in-law. **22** *Oswald the Lucky Rabbit*. **23** Hayley Mills. **24** *The Happiest Millionaire*. **25** His daughter Diane.

Answers – see page 232

1. How many dollars did Eve Marie Saint tip the waiter to seat Cary Grant near her in *North by Northwest*?
2. Within fifteen minutes, how long does *Bambi* last?
3. Which Steve featured in *Armageddon*?
4. A character named Robert Kincaid appeared in which film?
5. Who directed *Awakenings*?
6. Within five minutes, how long does *When Harry Met Sally* last?
7. Who would not be billed below Paul Newman, so refused the part of Sundance?
8. For what did W. Howard Greene and Harold Rosson win a Special Award in 1936?
9. Which actor was born Ivo Livi in 1921?
10. Which singer appeared in *Eat the Rich*?
11. Jimi Hendrix's 'Foxy Lady' featured in which 90s movie?
12. Which actor links *Impromptu* and *Bitter Moon*?
13. Which character was played by Josh Charles in the film *Dead Poets Society*?
14. Which Laurie featured in *Assault on Precinct 13*?
15. In the 1990s who won the Best Actress Oscar the year before Helen Hunt?
16. In which year did Alfred Hitchcock die?
17. Who directed *The Usual Suspects*?
18. In the 1980s who said, 'The baby's...only problem is he looks like Edward G Robinson'?
19. Richard Williams won a Special Award in 1988 for animation direction on what?
20. Who played Paris Carver in *Tomorrow Never Dies*?
21. Which British actor said, 'Teeth are a vitally important part of an actor's equipment'?
22. A character named Dr Zira appeared in which film?
23. Within ten minutes how long does *Amadeus* last?
24. Who played the professional exterminator in *Arachnophobia*?
25. Which British actor married a former Miss Guyana in 1973?

Answers Partnerships (see Quiz 16)
1 Prince. **2** *Anchors Aweigh*. **3** Deanna Durbin. **4** Nicholas Roeg. **5** Three months. **6** Bruce Willis & Demi Moore. **7** *The Man Who Would Be King*. **8** Uma Thurman. **9** Sean Penn. **10** *Desk Set*. **11** Nancy Allen. **12** *Notorious*. **13** *The Naples Connection*. **14** *This Gun for Hire*. **15** Six. **16** Gary Oldman & Chloe Webb. **17** Dolly Parton. **18** James Caan. **19** *Losing Isaiah*. **20** William Powell. **21** Joanne Woodward, Nell Potts. **22** Simian Films. **23** Nanette Fabray. **24** Harry James. **25** *Adam's Rib*.

Answers – see page 229

1   Who said, 'Disney has the best casting. If he doesn't like an actor he just tears him up'?

2   In which 1932 film did he experiment with colour?

3   Where did he first meet Ub Iwerks?

4   Which movies were made as a result of a government goodwill tour of South America?

5   What was the first of the *Silly Symphonies* called?

6   A meeting with which photographers brought about the *True Life* nature films?

7   What was Disney's job during World War II?

8   What did Disney and Iwerks call their first cartoons?

9   Which actress won an Oscar for the last major film he made before his death?

10   What was his star sign?

11   Which special Oscar award did he receive for *Snow White and the Seven Dwarfs*?

12   Which animated film was he working on at the time of his death?

13   Who, with Disney, received a special Oscar for *Fantasia*?

14   What was the first of his all-live-action movies?

15   What were the first two silent Mickey Mouse cartoons called?

16   What was Goofy originally called?

17   Which morale-boosting movie did Disney make in 1943?

18   In 1923 what was the name of the animated live-action cartoons he produced with his brother Roy and Ub Iwerks?

19   What was the last film in the series which began with *Seal Island*?

20   How many Oscars did Disney win in his lifetime?

21   Which relative of Walt became chief executive of Disney in 1983?

22   Which series did Walt launch with Roy in 1927?

23   Which British child star did he bring to Hollywood in the late 50s?

24   Which musical was he working on at the time of his death?

25   Who wrote a biography of Disney, published in 1958?

Answers Cary Grant (see Quiz 13)
1 Alexander. 2 Capricorn. 3 Paramount. 4 *Blonde Venus*. 5 *None But the Lonely Heart*. 6 Bob Pender's. 7 *Singapore Sue*. 8 Cary Lockwood. 9 *Mr Blandings Build His Dream House; Every Girl Should Be Married*. 10 Tony Curtis (*Some Like It Hot*). 11 *Walk Don't Run*. 12 Fabergé. 13 75%. 14 Woolworths. 15 *The Philadelphia Story*. 16 Joan Fontaine. 17 *Arsenic and Old Lace*. 18 *Diamond Lil*. 19 Irene Dunne. 20 John Wayne. 21 RKO & Columbia. 22 Dyan Cannon. 23 Cole Porter 24 *Suspicion*. 25 Barbara Harris.

Answers – see page 230

1	Who was Kristin Scott Thomas's first co-star in 1986?
2	What was the first movie which teamed Gene Kelly with Frank Sinatra?
3	Who shared a 1938 Special Oscar with Mickey Rooney?
4	Which director did Theresa Russell marry?
5	For how long was James Caan married to Sheila Ryan?
6	Which married couple acted together in *Mortal Thoughts*?
7	In which movie did Mrs Michael Caine appear with him?
8	Which Mrs Ethan Hawke appeared in *Gattaca*?
9	Which husband of Robin Wright directed her in *The Crossing Guard*?
10	What was Spencer Tracy and Katharine Hepburn's penultimate film together?
11	How was Mrs Brian De Palma, star of *Dressed to Kill*, better known?
12	What was Cary Grant's second film with Hitchcock as director?
13	In which 80s movie did Mr and Mrs Harvey Keitel star?
14	What was Alan Ladd's first western opposite Veronica Lake?
15	How many real wives did the most famous Tarzan have?
16	Who played the title roles in *Sid and Nancy*?
17	Which singer/actress was Mrs Carl Dean?
18	Who co-starred with Bette Midler in *For the Boys*?
19	What was the first movie Samuel L. Jackson starred in with his wife?
20	Who played opposite Myrna Loy 13 times?
21	Which mother and daughter were in the title roles in *Rachel Rachel*?
22	Which production company was set up by Hugh Grant and Liz Hurley?
23	Who was the female triplet in the famous baby dance routine in *The Band Wagon*?
24	Which bandleader did Betty Grable marry in 1943?
25	What was the sixth Spencer Tracy/Katharine Hepburn movie?

Answers Pot Luck 5 (see Quiz 14)

1 Five. **2** 69 minutes. **3** Buscemi. **4** *The Bridges of Madison County*. **5** Penny Marshall. **6** 95 minutes. **7** Steve McQueen. **8** Colour cinematography. **9** Yves Montand. **10** Paul McCartney. **11** *Wayne's World*. **12** Hugh Grant. **13** Knox Overstreet. **14** Zimmer. **15** Frances McDormand. **16** 1980. **17** Bryan Singer. **18** Woody Allen. **19** *Who Framed Roger Rabbit?* **20** Teri Hatcher. **21** Peter Cushing. **22** *Planet of the Apes*. **23** 158 minutes. **24** John Goodman. **25** Michael Caine.

Answers – see page 235

1   Who said in 1985, 'When I grow up I still want to be a director'?
2   What was the name of Bruce Willis's character in *Twelve Monkeys*?
3   Within five minutes, how long does *Sleeping Beauty* last?
4   Which Cary featured in *Close Encounters of the Third Kind*?
5   What is the first name of Oliver Reed, who used his middle name in the movies?
6   Which Brian featured in *Cocoon*?
7   Who won the Best Actress Oscar for *The Divorcee*?
8   Which movie starts, 'I owe everything to George Bailey'?
9   Which actor was originally set to play Robert Redford's role in *Indecent Proposal*?
10 Who won the Best Director Oscar for *Marty*?
11 The song 'All The Way' came from which movie?
12 Which 1980 movie visited Sherwood Forest and the Titanic?
13 Which 1966 film did rock star Roy Orbison star in?
14 Which actor links *The Big Easy* and *Punchline*?
15 In which year did Orson Welles die?
16 Which writer directed *Tough Guys Don't Dance* in 1987?
17 In which film did a character named Roberta Glass appear?
18 'It Goes Like It Goes' won an Oscar when it was used in which movie in 1979?
19 Which Jon featured in *The Color of Money*?
20 Steve Martin was born in which American state?
21 In which movie did Clark Gable play Vic Norton?
22 What part does director Steve Miner play in *Friday the Thirteenth, Part 3*?
23 Who directed *Twister*?
24 In which film does a character named Freeman Lowell appear?
25 Which had the longest running time – *Dirty Dancing*, *Men in Black* or *The Color Purple*?

Answers Goldie Hawn (see Quiz 19)
1 Scorpio. **2** Peter Sellers. **3** *Good Morning World*. **4** Washington DC. **5** *The Sugarland Express*. **6** *Deceived*. **7** Juliet. **8** Left-handed. **9** Ingrid Bergman. **10** Fred Astaire. **11** Isabella Rossellini. **12** *The One and Only Genuine Original Family Band*. **13** *The Duchess and the Dirtwater Fox*. **14** Mel Gibson. **15** Steven Spielberg. **16** Librarian. **17** *In the Wild*. **18** Goldy Jeanne Hawn. **19** Meryl Streep. **20** Wyatt. **21** *Cactus Flower*. **22** *Sophie's Choice*. **23** Her film characters. **24** Gus Trikonis. **25** *Cactus Flower*.

Answers – see page 236

1   What was the first mainstream film to use the word 'virgin'?
2   What was the first Royal Command Performance film?
3   Which airline showed the first in-flight movie?
4   How old was Mae West when she made her movie debut?
5   What was Fritz Lang's first Hollywood film?
6   What did Kevin Kline play on the piano in his first movie, *Sophie's Choice*?
7   What was John Boorman's US directing debut?
8   Who was the first actor to receive $1 million for a single picture?
9   VistaVision was first used in which classic movie?
10   What was the first movie shown in Aromarama?
11   What was Milos Forman's first US movie?
12   What was the first movie to feature Dracula?
13   Which movie was the first to have Sensurround?
14   In which movie did Chow Yun-Fat make his US debut?
15   What was the first western to win an Oscar for best film?
16   What was the first film that teamed Mickey Rooney and Judy Garland?
17   What was Selznick's first movie from his own independent company?
18   Who was the first American to join the Young Vic company on an American tour?
19   What was the first production from the west allowed in Beijing's Forbidden City?
20   What was Shirley MacLaine's first movie?
21   What was Hitchcock's first film for an independent producer?
22   Who was the first US singer/actor to entertain the troops in Korea?
23   What was the first in-flight movie?
24   In which movie did Harrison Ford make his screen debut as a messenger boy?
25   What were the names of the first two film magazines in the US?

Answers Pot Luck 7 (see Quiz 20)
1 Mel Gibson. 2 Raquel Welch. 3 'I Got You Babe' by Sonny and Cher. 4 *Nil By Mouth*. 5 Greene. 6 *Dante's Peak*. 7 *The Young and the Restless*. 8 Scott Carey. 9 88 minutes. 10 Dog. 11 Mel Brooks. 12 *The Swan*. 13 Reese's Pieces. 14 True. 15 Jodi Benson. 16 Jeff Goldblum. 17 Cab driver. 18 William Friedkin. 19 Dustin Hoffman. 20 *Total Recall*. 21 Veronica Quaife. 22 Foley. 23 George Arliss. 24 Michael Schultz. 25 1 hour (1 hour 11 mins).

Answers – see page 233

1	Under what star sign was she born?
2	Which Goon was her co-star in her movie produced by John Boulting?
3	What was her first TV series?
4	Where was she born?
5	Which film was advertised as 'The true story of a girl who took on all of Texas and almost won'?
6	In which 1991 movie did she play an uncharacteristically serious role?
7	She made her professional debut in which role?
8	What does she have in common with Judy Garland and Marilyn Monroe?
9	Who was the female star of her first Oscar-nominated film?
10	Who did she say was the only person who had ever made her speechless?
11	Which daughter of Ingrid Bergman was a fellow co-star along with Meryl Streep?
12	What was her very first movie – for Disney?
13	Which movie had the advertising line, 'If the rustlers didn't get you...the hustlers did!'?
14	Who was her co-star in 1990 in a cast with David Carradine?
15	Who directed her in *The Sugarland Express*?
16	What was her occupation in *Foul Play*?
17	Which TV documentary did she make about elephants?
18	How was she billed in her very first film?
19	Who was she originally tipped to play opposite in *Thelma and Louise*?
20	What is the name of her son by the actor she met on the set of *The One and Only Genuine Original Family Band*?
21	For which movie did she receive her first Oscar nomination?
22	For which movie was she turned down in preference to Meryl Streep, who won an Oscar for the role?
23	Who or what are all her pets named after?
24	Who did she divorce to marry husband No. 2?
25	Which movie saw her debut as producer?

Answers Pot Luck 6 (see Quiz 17)
1 Steven Spielberg. **2** James Cole. **3** 75 minutes. **4** Guffrey. **5** Robert.
6 Dennehy. **7** Norma Shearer. **8** *It's a Wonderful Life.* **9** Warren Beatty.
10 Delbert Mann. **11** *The Joker Is Wild.* **12** *Time Bandits.* **13** *The Fastest Guitar Alive.* **14** John Goodman. **15** 1985. **16** Norman Mailer. **17** *Desperately Seeking Susan.* **18** Norma Rae. **19** Turturro. **20** Texas. **21** *The Hucksters.* **22** A newscaster. **23** Jan De Bont. **24** *Silent Running.* **25** *The Color Purple.*

Answers – see page 234

1   Which actor links *Tim* and *The Rest of Daniel*?
2   Which actress released the 1987 single 'This Girl's Back in Town'?
3   What song is playing every time Bill Murray wakes up on *Groundhog Day*?
4   Which film was Gary Oldman's directorial debut?
5   Which Graham featured in *Dances with Wolves*?
6   A character named Harry Dalton appeared in which film?
7   Which soap did Tom Selleck star in?
8   Who did Grant Williams play in *The Incredible Shrinking Man*?
9   Within five minutes, how long does *Sleeper* last?
10   Which animal mask does George Peppard steal in *Breakfast at Tiffany's*?
11   Who was quoted in *Newsweek* as saying, 'I only direct in self-defence'?
12   What was the last film Grace Kelly made before becoming a princess?
13   What type of sweets are used in the trail that E.T. follows in *E.T.*?
14   Which Rachel featured in *The Craft*?
15   Who voiced Ariel in *The Little Mermaid*?
16   Which actor links *California Split* and *Vibes*?
17   What is John Travolta's occupation in *Look Who's Talking*?
18   Who won the Best Director Oscar for *The French Connection*?
19   Who was offered the role of Rambo in *First Blood*, but turned it down?
20   In 1990 Eric Brevig won a Special Award for visual effects on which film?
21   What was the name of Geena Davis's character in *The Fly*?
22   Which Jeremy featured in *Dante's Peak*?
23   Who won the Best Actor Oscar for *Disraeli*?
24   Who directed *Car Wash*?
25   To the nearest hour, how long does the 30s movie *Frankenstein* last?

Answers Famous Firsts (see Quiz 18)
1 Otto Preminger's *The Moon Is Blue*. 2 *A Matter of Life and Death*. 3 Imperial
Airways. 4 40. 5 *Fury*. 6 Schumann's 'Scenes From Childhood'. 7 *Point Blank*.
8 Marlon Brando. 9 *White Christmas*. 10 *Behind the Great Wall*. 11 *Taking Off*.
12 *Nosferatu*. 13 *Earthquake*. 14 *The Replacement Killers*. 15 *Cimarron*. 16 *Love
Finds Andy Hardy*. 17 *Little Lord Fauntleroy*. 18 Richard Gere. 19 *The Last
Emperor*. 20 *Trouble with Harry*. 21 *Rope*. 22 Al Jolson. 23 *The Lost World*.
24 *Dead Heat on a Merry Go Round*. 25 *Photoplay; Motion Picture Story Magazine*.

Answers – see page 239

1   *Sommersby* was a remake of which Depardieu classic?
2   What was the only movie Hitchcock remade?
3   Who was the male star of the fourth version of *Daddy Long Legs*?
4   Who starred in a 1981 remake of a 1946 film noir with Lana Turner?
5   Who won an Oscar for the 1950 George Cukor movie remade in 1993 with Melanie Griffith?
6   Which 1997 film was a remake of Les Compères?
7   Whose final movie was a remake with sound of *The Unholy Three*?
8   *Move Over Darling* reworked which 40s classic with Cary Grant?
9   Which Warren Beatty movie was a remake of *Here Comes Mr Jordan*?
10   A 30s classic with Clark Gable and Claudette Colbert was remade as *You Can't Run Away from It* starring whom?
11   *Singapore Woman* was a remake of which Bette Davis Oscar-winner?
12   In which movie did Bette Midler recreate a Barbara Stanwyck role?
13   Who directed *Love Affair* and its remake *An Affair to Remember*?
14   Who played the wedding organizer in the 1991 remake of a 50s Spencer Tracy classic?
15   *The Badlanders* was a western remake of which Sterling Hayden movie which had a young Monroe in the cast?
16   *Silk Stockings* was the musical remake of which classic?
17   Which Humphrey Bogart movie was a remake of *Bordertown*?
18   What was the Julia Roberts remake of *Dr Jekyll and Mr Hyde* called?
19   Where was the 70s remake of *Invasion of the Body Snatchers* set?
20   Who played the Hayley Mills role in the 90s version of a 1961 movie about twins?
21   Which 60s movie was a remake of Bob Hope's *The Paleface*?
22   *One Sunday Afternoon* was remade twice, once with the same title and once as what?
23   Velvet Brown as a child was played by Elizabeth Taylor, but who was the adult 30 years later?
24   What was the remake of *Kid Galahad* which did not star Elvis?
25   How was *Sentimental Journey* remade with Lauren Bacall?

Answers Pot Luck 8 (see Quiz 23)
1 Yul Brynner. **2** Red. **3** Marie Dressler. **4** Peanut stall. **5** Frank Borzage.
6 Cromwell. **7** *The Jazz Singer.* **8** David Levinson. **9** *Give My Regards to Broad Street.* **10** *Silent Running.* **11** *The Living Daylights.* **12** Robinson. **13** 'Under the Sea'. **14** Terry Hayes. **15** Dirk Bogarde. **16** 1980. **17** John Cleese. **18** 1930s. **19** 105 minutes. **20** Dysart. **21** F. Murray Abraham. **22** A mood ring. **23** Bree Daniels. **24** Terry Gilliam. **25** Oates.

Answers – see page 240

1   Which actress links *Cookie* and *Angela's Ashes*?

2   Who played Sal in *The Beach*?

3   What was *Now and Then* star Thora Birch's first movie?

4   Who played the role of the lyricist in *Topsy Turvy*?

5   Who links *Independence Day* and *The Iron Giant*?

6   Who played Bonnie in *The Craft*?

7   Which actress links *Circle of Friends* and *GoldenEye*?

8   Who stars as Valerie Edmonds's 'old flame' in *One More Kiss*?

9   Who tries to eat Stuart Little?

10   Who played Wendy in *The Ice Storm*?

11   Who played Yul Brynner's role in the remake of *The King and I*?

12   Who links *Boogie Nights* and *The Myth of Fingerprints*?

13   What character did the actress who appeared in *The Mask* play in *My Best Friend's Wedding*?

14   Which actress played Glenn Close's role in the remake of *Dangerous Liaisons*?

15   Who played Glenn Gulia in *The Wedding Singer*?

16   Who links *The World is Not Enough* and *Wild Things*?

17   Which actress links *Mrs Doubtfire* and *Miracle on 34th Street*?

18   Who starred as Ray Liotta's daughter in *Corrina, Corrina*?

19   What role does ex-rapper Marky Mark play in *Three Kings*?

20   Who plays Sidney's boyfriend in *Scream 2*?

21   Who took Sir John Mills's role of Pip in the 90s adaptation of *Great Expectations*?

22   Who plays Maude in *The Big Lebowski*?

23   Which actress won a Golden Globe for *Boys Don't Cry*?

24   Where was Charlize Theron born?

25   Which actor starred in *Varsity Blues*?

Answers 1950s Stars (see Quiz 24)
1 Ace in the Hole. **2** Eight. **3** Bette Davis. **4** Mae Clarke. **5** Nat King Cole. **6** 19.
7 Ira Grossel. **8** Mrs Nancy Reagan. **9** *Picnic*. **10** Rhonda Fleming. **11** Stanley
Kowalski (*A Streetcar Named Desire*). **12** Cyd Charisse. **13** Maria Vargas. **14** Tab
Hunter. **15** *Separate Tables*. **16** Agnes Moorehead. **17** Preacher Harry Powell.
18 The chimp. **19** MacDonald Carey. **20** *Darby O'Gill and the Little People*.
21 Ava Gardner. **22** Vincent Winters. **23** Rosemary Clooney. **24** Ben Johnson.
25 Peter Lorre.

Answers – see page 237

1	Which great actor died on the same day as fellow star Orson Welles?
2	What colour is Deborah Kerr's suit in the final scene of *An Affair to Remember*?
3	Who won the Best Actress Oscar for *Min and Bill*?
4	What sort of stall does Chico have in *Duck Soup*?
5	Who won the Best Director Oscar for *Seventh Heaven*?
6	Which James starred in *Babe*?
7	What movie is shown within the film *Goodfellas*?
8	Who did Jeff Goldblum play in *Independence Day*?
9	What was the name of the last film that Ralph Richardson ever made?
10	*Armageddon, Scream 2, Silent Running* – which has the shortest running time?
11	In which film did Caroline Bliss replace Lois Maxwell as Miss Moneypenny?
12	Which Amy featured in *Mean Streets*?
13	Which song won Best Song Oscar for *The Little Mermaid*?
14	Who wrote the screenplay for *Mad Max Beyond Thunderdome*?
15	Which actor's memoirs include the volume *Snakes and Ladders*?
16	In which year did Peter Sellers die?
17	Who voiced Cat R. Ward in *An American Tail: Fievel Goes West*?
18	In which decade was *Morocco* released?
19	Within five minutes, how long does *Shine* last?
20	Which Richard featured in *The Hospital*?
21	Who won the Best Actor Oscar for *Amadeus*?
22	What kind of ring does Vada have in *My Girl*?
23	What was the name of Jane Fonda's character in *Klute*?
24	Who directed *Twelve Monkeys*?
25	Which Warren featured in *Badlands*?

Answers Remakes (see Quiz 21)
1 *The Return of Martin Guerre.* **2** *The Man Who Knew Too Much.* **3** Fred Astaire.
4 Jessica Lange & Jack Nicholson (*The Postman Always Rings Twice*). **5** Judy Holliday
(*Born Yesterday*). **6** *Father's Day.* **7** Lon Chaney. **8** *My Favorite Wife.* **9** *Heaven Can Wait.* **10** June Allyson & Jack Lemmon. **11** *Dangerous.* **12** *Stella.* **13** Leo McCarey. **14** Martin Short (*Father of the Bride*). **15** *The Asphalt Jungle.*
16 *Ninotchka.* **17** *They Drive by Night.* **18** *Mary Reilly.* **19** *San Francisco.*
20 Lindsay Lohan. **21** *The Shakiest Gun in the West.* **22** *The Strawberry Blonde.*
23 Nanette Newman. **24** *The Wagons Roll at Night.* **25** *The Gift of Love.*

Answers – see page 238

1   In which movie did Kirk Douglas say, 'I'm a thousand-a-day man, Mr Boot. You can have me for nothing'?

2   What number juror was Henry Fonda in *Twelve Angry Men*?

3   Who played Catherine the Great in *John Paul Jones*?

4   Which actress was the inspiration for Monroe's Lorelei Lee in *Gentlemen Prefer Blondes*?

5   Which singer appeared in *St Louis Blues* as W.C. Handy?

6   Ava Gardner married three times, but how many wives did her husbands have between them?

7   What was Jeff Chandler's real name?

8   What was the most famous married name of the actress who was born Anne Frances Robbins?

9   In which movie did William Holden say, 'I gotta get somewhere. I just gotta'?

10   Who played Cleopatra in *Serpent of the Nile*?

11   Which Broadway role did Brando recreate on screen in 1951?

12   How was Tula Ellice Finklea better known?

13   Which role did Ava Gardner play in *The Barefoot Contessa*?

14   Which 50s teenage idol's real name was Andrew Arthur Kelm?

15   What was the third of Deborah Kerr's three nominations between 1956 and 1958?

16   Who played Elizabeth I in *The Story of Mankind*?

17   Who did Robert Mitchum play in *The Night of the Hunter*?

18   Which Ronald Reagan co-star in *Bedtime for Bonzo* died before the movie premiere?

19   Who played Jesse James in *The Great Missouri Raid*?

20   In which 50s film did Sean Connery sing?

21   Who played Julie in *Showboat*, though her singing voice was dubbed?

22   Who won a Special Oscar for *The Little Kidnappers* aged six?

23   Who was the only star of *White Christmas* to live until the end of the 20th century?

24   Who won a World Champion Cowboy title in 1953?

25   Who was Nero in *The Story of Mankind*?

Answers Stars of the 21st Century (see Quiz 22)
1 Emily Lloyd. **2** Tilda Swinton. **3** *Purple People Eater*. **4** Jim Broadbent. **5** Harry Connick Jr. **6** Neve Campbell. **7** Minnie Driver. **8** Gerry Butler **9** Snowball the Cat. **10** Christina Ricci. **11** Chow Yun-Fat. **12** Julianne Moore. **13** Kimmy (Cameron Diaz). **14** Sarah Michelle Geller. **15** Matthew Glave. **16** Denise Richards. **17** Mara Wilson. **18** Tina Majorino. **19** Troy Barlow. **20** Jerry O'Connell. **21** Ethan Hawke. **22** Julianne Moore. **23** Hilary Swank. **24** South Africa. **25** James van der Beer.

Answers – see page 243

1   From which play was *Casablanca* adapted?
2   Who plays Charlotte Vale's mother in *Now, Voyager*?
3   Where do Jenny and Oliver first meet in *Love Story*?
4   Who plays the subway ghost in *Ghost*?
5   Within fifteen minutes, how long does *Brief Encounter* last?
6   On whose novel is *The English Patient* based?
7   To which country does Kathleen Turner travel to save her sister in *Romancing the Stone*?
8   In what year is *Ryan's Daughter* set?
9   How much money does Holly Golightly receive for going to the 'powder room' in *Breakfast at Tiffany's*?
10   Which film is *An Affair to Remember* a remake of?
11   Which character does Humphrey Bogart play in the 1954 film *Sabrina*?
12   What is Jennie's last name in the film *Portrait of Jennie*?
13   Where is Beau's ranch in the film *Bus Stop*?
14   Who is Doctor Zhivago's childhood sweetheart?
15   Where is *Romeo and Juliet* set in the 1996 film?
16   Who owns the hotel that Jennifer Grey visits in *Dirty Dancing*?
17   What is Sandra Bullock's job in *While You Were Sleeping*?
18   Which fictional character was 'incapable of love, or tenderness or decency'?
19   On whose novel is *The Bridges of Madison County* based?
20   By what age would Julianne and Michael marry each other if they were not already married in the film *My Best Friend's Wedding*?
21   Who plays Fiona's brother in *Four Weddings and a Funeral*?
22   What's the name of the character that Monroe rents an apartment from in *The Seven Year Itch*?
23   What is the name of the youngest Dashwood sister in *Sense and Sensibility*?
24   Who was lined up for Bogart's role in *Casablanca*?
25   In which country did Amy Jolly seek romance?

Answers Behind the Camera (see Quiz 27)
1 Orson Welles. **2** Marlon Brando. **3** *Things to Do in Denver when You're Dead.*
4 *The Other Half of the Sky.* **5** Robert Evans. **6** Jack Warner. **7** Nagisa Oshima.
8 *Shakespeare in Love.* **9** Howard Hawks (*The Big Sleep*). **10** Mike Leigh.
11 George Cukor. **12** Brian De Palma. **13** James Cameron. **14** James Whale.
15 Darryl F. Zanuck. **16** The street where he grew up – Mundy Lane. **17** *Ace: Iron Eagle III.* **18** Cher. **19** Marlon Brando. **20** Mel Brooks. **21** *The Hand.* **22** Jack Fisk. **23** Martin Scorsese. **24** Louis Malle. **25** *Everything You Always Wanted to Know About Sex... But Were Afraid to Ask.*

Answers – see page 244

1   What colour was the dress that Scarlett O'Hara made from her curtains?
2   What was Marlon Brando's first film, in 1950?
3   Within five minutes, how long does *Se7en* last?
4   Who directed the film *Body of Evidence*?
5   Which Jon featured in *Miller's Crossing*?
6   Who won the Best Actor Oscar for *The Champ*?
7   Who directed *Total Recall*?
8   In which film did a character named Leeloo appear?
9   What is Ted's middle name in *Bill & Ted's Excellent Adventure*?
10 Who did Joan Collins describe as, 'Short, myopic, not good looking'?
11 Which Pam starred in *Jackie Brown*?
12 Who was set to play Sofia Coppola's role in *The Godfather, Part III*, but pulled out on doctor's advice?
13 In which film did a pilot named Klaatu appear?
14 Who wrote the screenplay for the film *Billy Bathgate*?
15 Within fifteen minutes, how long does *Planet of the Apes* last?
16 Who directed *An Affair to Remember*?
17 Which Fiona featured in *The Avengers*?
18 In which film did Marisa Tomei make her debut?
19 Who wrote the screenplay for *The Bodyguard*?
20 For what did Ben Burtt win a Special Award in 1981?
21 What was the name of Spencer Tracy's character in *Father of the Bride*?
22 The song 'Secret Love' came from which movie?
23 Which Joan featured in *The Ice Storm*?
24 What movie is playing on a car radio in *The Flight of the Navigator*?
25 Who won the Best Director Oscar for *Cavalcade*?

Answers Superstars (see Quiz 28)
1 154. **2** 12 years. **3** Julie Andrews. **4** Robert Redford. **5** Shepherd. **6** Anthony Hopkins. **7** Charles Bronson. **8** Tony Curtis. **9** Lauren Bacall. **10** Holly Hunter. **11** Sylvester Stallone. **12** Alec Baldwin. **13** Philadelphia. **14** Meryl Streep. **15** Kim Basinger. **16** Harrison Ford. **17** Alec Guinness. **18** Syracuse Symphony Orchestra. **19** Lindsay Wagner. **20** *The Ugly American*. **21** Dan Aykroyd. **22** Julia Roberts. **23** Kim Basinger. **24** Michael Keaton. **25** Grimaldi.

Answers – see page 241

1   Which director wrote the novel *Mr Arkadin*?
2   About which of his performers did Bernardo Bertolucci say, 'an angel of a man, a monster of an actor'?
3   What was Gary Fleder's directorial debut?
4   Which Oscar-nominated documentary did Shirley MacLaine co-direct in 1975?
5   Whose autobiography was called *The Kid Stays in the Picture*?
6   Which mogul said of Clark Gable, 'What the hell am I going to do with a guy with ears like that?'?
7   Who directed *Merry Christmas Mr Lawrence*?
8   What was John Madden's follow up to *Mrs Brown*?
9   Who directed the second Bogart and Bacall movie?
10   Who said, 'Given the choice of Hollywood or poking steel pins in my eyes, I'd prefer steel pins'?
11   Who was the last man to direct Garbo?
12   Which director did Nancy Allen marry?
13   Who was the director of the second *Alien* movie?
14   Who first directed Boris Karloff as Frankenstein?
15   Which production executive is in the American Croquet Hall of Fame?
16   What did Denzel Washington name his film company after?
17   What was John Glen's first feature after directing five Bond movies?
18   About whom did Peter Bogdanovich say, 'Working with her is like being in a blender with an alligator'?
19   Who took over directing *One Eyed Jacks* when Stanley Kubrick was sacked?
20   Which actor's company funded *The Elephant Man*?
21   Which low-budget horror movie did Oliver Stone direct in 1981?
22   Which production designer did Sissy Spacek meet on the set of *Badlands* and then marry?
23   Who directed the sequel to *The Hustler*?
24   Which French director said, 'It takes a long time to learn simplicity'?
25   What was Woody Allen's third movie as actor/director?

Answers Romance (see Quiz 25)
1 *Everybody Comes to Rick's*. **2** Gladys Cooper. **3** In the library. **4** Vincent Schiavelli. **5** 86 minutes. **6** Michael Ondaatje. **7** Colombia. **8** 1916. **9** $50. **10** *Love Affair*. **11** Linus Larrabee. **12** Appleton. **13** Montana. **14** Tonya. **15** Venice Beach. **16** Max Kellerman. **17** Subway-ticket seller. **18** Rebecca de Winter (*Rebecca*). **19** Robert James Waller. **20** 28. **21** Simon Callow. **22** Richard Sherman. **23** Margaret. **24** Ronald Reagan. **25** Morocco (Dietrich character).

Answers – see page 242

1	Within five points either way, what is Sharon Stone's IQ?
2	How much older than Harrison Ford was Sean Connery when he played his father?
3	About whom did Moss Hart say, 'She has that wonderful British strength. It makes you wonder why they lost India'?
4	Who founded the Institute of Resource Management to increase co-operation between developers and environmentalists?
5	What does Marlon Brando have on his passport as his profession?
6	Who dubbed Olivier's voice for extra scenes added to the 1990 release of *Spartacus*?
7	Who is known in Italy as 'Il Brutto'?
8	After netting a weekend with which actor did the winner say she'd have preferred the second prize of a fridge?
9	Who played Barbra Streisand's mother in *The Mirror Has Two Faces*?
10	Joel and Ethan Coen wrote *Raising Arizona* with whom in mind?
11	Who said, 'I built my body to carry my brain around in'?
12	Who gave up the chance to star in the sequel to *Patriot Games* so he could play Stanley Kowalski on Broadway?
13	Sidney Poitier plays a cop from which state in *In the Heat of the Night*?
14	Who did Cher describe as 'an acting machine in the same sense that a shark is a killing machine'?
15	Who recorded a pop album called *The Color of Sex*?
16	Who was voted Film Star of the Century in the 100th issue of *Empire* magazine?
17	Whose autobiography was called *Blessings in Disguise*?
18	With which orchestra did Richard Gere play trumpet when he was 16?
19	Which actress was born on exactly the same day as Meryl Streep?
20	In which movie did Brando's sister Jocelyn appear with him?
21	Who made his directorial debut with *Nothing But Trouble*?
22	Who said, 'I'm too tall to be a girl. I'm between a chick and a broad'?
23	Which actress once pursued a singing career and was known as Chelsea?
24	Who played Dogberry in Kenneth Branagh's production of Much *Ado About Nothing*?
25	What was Grace Kelly's married name?

Answers Pot Luck 9 (see Quiz 26)
1 Green. **2** *The Men* **3** 107 minutes. **4** Uli Edel. **5** Polito. **6** William Beery.
7 Paul Verhoeven. **8** *The Fifth Element*. **9** Theodore. **10** James Dean. **11** Grier.
12 Winona Ryder. **13** *The Day the Earth Stood Still*. **14** Tom Stoppard. **15** 119
minutes. **16** Leo McCarey. **17** Shaw. **18** *The Flamingo Kid*. **19** Lawrence Kasdan.
20 Sound effects editing on *Raiders of the Lost Ark*. **21** Stanley T. Banks.
22 *Calamity Jane*. **23** Allen. **24** *Grease*. **25** Frank Lloyd.

Answers – see page 247

1   Which Anita featured in *Barbarella*?
2   Who won the Best Actress Oscar for *Norma Rae*?
3   What is the name of the third eldest child in *The Sound of Music*?
4   Who did Michael Douglas play in *The Wonder Boys*?
5   *Flipper* and *Almost an Angel* starred which actor?
6   Within five minutes, how long does *Schindler's List* last?
7   Which Peter featured in *Fargo*?
8   Who directed *Tomorrow Never Dies*?
9   Which author appeared in *All at Sea*?
10 In which film did a character named Herbert Bock appear?
11 Which Roy said, 'There's not much to acting as far as I'm concerned'?
12 'Call Me Irresponsible' won an Oscar when it was used in which movie in 1963?
13 Who was Gort the robot in *The Day the Earth Stood Still*?
14 Which Jennifer featured in *The Fabulous Baker Boys*?
15 Richard Edlund won a Special Award for what in *Return of the Jedi*?
16 Burt Reynolds was born in which American state?
17 Who was the first woman to win consecutive best actress Oscars?
18 What novel does Paul Sheldon write whilst under the 'care' of Annie Wilkes?
19 Which Melanie featured in *Missing*?
20 How long does the 60s movie *101 Dalmatians* last?
21 In which year was *Shadow of Doubt* released?
22 Who won the Best Actor Oscar for *Free Soul*?
23 In which film did a character named Gabe Walker appear?
24 Who won the Best Director Oscar for *Going My Way*?
25 Which Richard featured in *Misery*?

Answers 1940s (see Quiz 31)
1 *Adam's Rib*. 2 *All That Money Can Buy*. 3 *Foreign Correspondent*. 4 *The Palm Beach Story*. 5 *Two Faced Woman*. 6 Victor Mature & Hedy Lamarr. 7 *The Great Lie*. 8 *Lady in the Dark*. 9 *All That Money Can Buy*. 10 *The Pride of the Yankees*. 11 William Bendix. 12 *Pot O' Gold*. 13 Glenn Ford. 14 Paganini. 15 *The Tempest*. 16 Charlotte Bronte. 17 *Kiss of Death*. 18 *Champion*. 19 'World'. 20 Claude Jarman Jr. 21 *Highway 66*. 22 *The Bishop's Wife*. 23 Olivia de Havilland. 24 Waiting outside a phone box. 25 *Follow the Boys*.

Answers – see page 248

1   Whose marriage to Rudolph Valentino lasted just one day?
2   Who made his debut in *For France*?
3   Who were the stars of D.W. Griffith's *Broken Blossoms*?
4   Who was the star of the first feature to be made in 3D?
5   Who gave Clara Bow the title of the 'It Girl'?
6   Who was the star of D.W. Griffith's *The White Rose*?
7   In which movie did Rin Tin Tin make his debut?
8   What was the first sound movie made by Pickford and Fairbanks?
9   What was Mary Pickford's real name?
10   Fatty Arbuckle was arrested on charges of rape and manslaughter in 1920 after whose death?
11   Whose autobiography was called *An American Comedy*?
12   Who told Mary Pickford, 'You're too little and too fat but I may give you a job'?
13   What was Douglas Fairbanks's real name?
14   Who starred in 300 westerns as Bronco Billy but could hardly ride a horse?
15   Who was known as 'The Biograph Girl with the Curls'?
16   Who did Chaplin go to work for in 1915 – at $1,000 a week?
17   What was Mabel Normand's real surname?
18   Peter Noble's biography *Hollywood Scapegoat* was about whom?
19   Which silent-movie star did Betty Grable marry in 1937?
20   Which single movie did Lillian Gish direct?
21   Whose affair with an entire football team was revealed in a court case where she sued her secretary in 1931?
22   Which famous screamer's first movie was *Street of Sin* in 1928?
23   What was Mary Pickford's autobiography called?
24   Who did George Cukor describe as 'a beautiful nothing'?
25   Who played 'the man with a thousand faces' in a fifties biopic?

Answers Pot Luck 11 (see Quiz 32)
1 Prosky. **2** *Somerset*. **3** Bruce Willis. **4** Helen Hayes. **5** *Nell*. **6** Magee.
7 Richard White. **8** Anthony Hopkins. **9** Harrison Ford. **10** Shepard. **11** George Stevens. **12** Montana. **13** Sissy Spacek. **14** Nina. **15** *The River*. **16** Pee-Wee Herman. **17** Aiello. **18** Eric Stoltz. **19** Ron Howard. **20** Sound in *Fantasia*.
21 120 minutes. **22** *Mean Streets*. **23** Fierstein. **24** Singapore. **25** Peter Markle.

Answers – see page 245

1   Which movie had the ad line, 'The dangerous age for women is from three to seventy'?
2   In which movie did Walter Huston play the devil?
3   Which movie did Hitchcock make to encourage the US to enter World War II?
4   Which movie opens with the line, 'And so they lived happily ever after. Or did they?'?
5   Which movie did Garbo make immediately before retiring?
6   Who played the title roles in Cecil B de Mille's *Samson and Delilah*?
7   In which movie did Mary Astor say, 'If I didn't think you meant so well, I'd feel like slapping your face'?
8   In which film did Mischa Auer say, 'This is the end, the absolute end'?
9   Which William Dieterle movie was based on the Faust story?
10 What was the second of Gary Cooper's three Oscar nominations between 1941 and 1943?
11 Who played Babe Ruth in *The Babe Ruth Story*?
12 What did James Stewart say was the worst of all his movies?
13 Who had two teeth knocked out by Rita Hayworth during the making of *Gilda*?
14 Who did Stewart Granger play in *The Magic Bow*?
15 *Yellow Sky* was based on which Shakespeare play?
16 Which writer did Olivia de Havilland play in *Devotion*?
17 For which movie was Richard Widmark Oscar-nominated on his film debut?
18 In which 1949 movie did Kirk Douglas play a boxer?
19 What is the last word of *White Heat*?
20 Who won a Special Oscar for *The Yearling*, aged 12?
21 What was the working title of *The Grapes of Wrath*?
22 In which movie did Cary Grant play an angel?
23 Who played two parts in *The Dark Mirror* in 1946?
24 What is Hitchcock's cameo appearance in *Rebecca*?
25 In which 1944 movie did Orson Welles play himself?

Answers Pot Luck 10 (see Quiz 29)
1 Pallenberg. 2 Sally Field. 3 Louisa. 4 Grady Tripp. 5 Paul Hogan. 6 185 minutes. 7 Stormare. 8 Roger Spottiswoode. 9 Jackie Collins. 10 *The Hospital*. 11 Roy Rogers. 12 *Papa's Delicate Condition*. 13 Lock Martin. 14 Tilly. 15 Visual effects. 16 Georgia. 17 Luise Rainer. 18 *Misery's Child*. 19 Mayron. 20 79 minutes. 21 1943. 22 Lionel Barrymore. 23 *Cliffhanger*. 24 Leo McCarey. 25 Farnsworth.

Answers – see page 246

1   Which Robert featured in *Dead Man Walking*?
2   Which soap did Hollywood star Ted Danson star in?
3   Which movie star released an album called *Heart of Soul* in 1990?
4   Who won the Best Actress Oscar for *Sin of Madelon Claudet*?
5   A character named Jerome Lovell appeared in which film?
6   Which Patrick featured in *Barry Lyndon*?
7   Who voiced Gaston in the film *Beauty and the Beast*?
8   *Bookworm* and *Surviving Picasso* both starred which actor?
9   Who said, 'I ask for the money I want, they pay it. It's that simple'?
10   Which Sam featured in *Days of Heaven*?
11   Who won the Best Director Oscar for *A Place in the Sun*?
12   *The Horse Whisperer* is set in which US state?
13   Who plays the brain in the film *The Man with Two Brains*?
14   What was the name of Juliet Stevenson's character in *Truly, Madly, Deeply*?
15   In 1984 Kay Rose won a Special Award for sound effects editing on which movie?
16   Who plays Penguin's father in the film *Batman Returns*?
17   Which Danny featured in *Moonstruck*?
18   Who plays Rocky Dennis in *Mask*?
19   Who directed *Ransom*?
20   For what did Walt Disney win a Special Award in 1941?
21   Within five minutes, how long does *Platoon* last?
22   A character named Johnny Boy appeared in which film?
23   Which Harvey featured in *Mrs Doubtfire*?
24   What was the destination in the first *Road* film?
25   Who directed the film *Bat 21*?

Answers Stars of the Silent Years (see Quiz 30)
1 Jane Acker. **2** Erich von Stroheim. **3** Richard Barthelmess & Lillian Gish. **4** Noah Beery. **5** Elinor Glyn. **6** Ivor Novello. **7** *The Man from Hell's River*. **8** *The Taming of the Shrew*. **9** Gladys Smith. **10** Virginia Rappe. **11** Harold Lloyd's. **12** D.W. Griffith. **13** Douglas Ullman. **14** Gilbert M. Anderson. **15** Mary Pickford. **16** Essanay. **17** Fortescue. **18** Erich von Stroheim. **19** Jackie Coogan. **20** *Remodelling Her Husband*. **21** Clara Bow. **22** Fay Wray. **23** *Sunshine and Shadow*. **24** Louise Brooks. **25** James Cagney.

QUIZ 33 BLOCKBUSTERS ·· LEVEL THREE

Answers – see page 251

1   Which movie is *Twelve Monkeys* based on?
2   Who raised Hawkeye in *The Last of the Mohicans*?
3   Within fifteen minutes, how long does *The Godfather, Part II* last?
4   Who wrote the screenplay for *Unforgiven*?
5   What is the Penguin's real name in *Batman Returns*?
6   Which movie begins with 'No man's life can be encompassed in one telling'?
7   What film does Kevin Costner take Whitney Houston to see in The *Bodyguard*?
8   Which John co-directed *Aladdin*?
9   Who wrote the screenplay for *Basic Instinct*?
10   What colour are Woody's eyes in *Toy Story*?
11   What relation is Maid Marian to the King in *Robin Hood: Prince of Thieves*?
12   What is Peter Pan's job after he grows up in *Hook*?
13   Which character is played by Al Pacino in *Dick Tracy*?
14   Which president does Anthony Hopkins played in *Amistad*?
15   What colour ribbon holds together Jenny's chocolates in *Forrest Gump*, when Tom Hanks is sitting at the bus stop?
16   What is the name of Sam's scheming co-worker in *Ghost*?
17   What movie is playing within *When Harry Met Sally*?
18   Who plays Edward Scissorhands' father?
19   Which 80s hit was a remake of *Trois Hommes et un Couffin*?
20   The first script of which movie was called *The Man who Came to Play*?
21   Which palace was used for Kenneth Branagh's *Hamlet*?
22   Which daughter of a *Sound of Music* star appeared in *Pulp Fiction*?
23   In which publication did the Addams Family first appear?
24   Who plays Kevin Costner's father in *Robin Hood: Prince of Thieves*?
25   In what year is *The Last of the Mohicans* set?

Answers Pot Luck 12 (see Quiz 35)
1 Steven Spielberg. **2** Garry Marshall. **3** Colin Firth. **4** Ice Hockey. **5** Robert Duvall. **6** Helen Tasker. **7** 94 minutes. **8** *Captain Carey*. **9** Charles. **10** Madison. **11** *Wild at Heart*. **12** Elia Kazan. **13** Bob Hoskins. **14** Arndt. **15** Winchester '73. **16** Wayne Szalinski. **17** Marie. **18** *Slamdance*. **19** *Ghostbusters*. **20** Delpy. **21** Lisa Bonet. **22** Architecture. **23** 87 minutes. **24** Richard Blaney. **25** Spencer.

Answers – see page 252

1	Who was the oldest Marx Brother?
2	What was the name of their 1925 Broadway hit?
3	Which movie did they make immediately after *Monkey Business*?
4	Which brother's real name was Adolph but was also known as Arthur?
5	What was their last film for Paramount?
6	Who was Harpo cast as in *The Story of Mankind*?
7	Whose autobiography was called *Memoirs of a Mangy Lover*?
8	In which movie did they reunite after World War II?
9	Who directed their first movie for MGM?
10	Who replaced Harpo in *Androcles and the Lion* in 1952?
11	Which Brother made the shortest appearance in *Love Happy*?
12	What was the last movie they made before the death of producer Irving Thalberg?
13	What were the real names of the two brothers who left the team early on?
14	What was Harpo's most celebrated prop?
15	Which brother played romantic relief in their first five films?
16	What was the name of Groucho's son who published biographies of his father?
17	What was the name of their mother, daughter of vaudeville artists?
18	In which silent movie did Harpo make his debut?
19	To whom did Groucho say, 'Excuse me, I thought you were a fella I once knew in Pittsburgh'?
20	*Duck Soup* features the Presidency of which state?
21	Which Marx brother lived longest?
22	What was their name when they consisted of Groucho, Chico, Harpo, Gummo, their mother and her sister?
23	In which movie did they make their final appearance as a team?
24	What were Harpo's memoirs called?
25	Who received the only Oscar nomination for *A Day at the Races*?

Answers Famous Names (see Quiz 36)
1 Burt Reynolds. **2** Keith Carradine. **3** *Butch Cassidy and the Sundance Kid.*
4 Karuna. **5** David Hemmings. **6** *The Crow.* **7** Ellen McRae. **8** Brigitta. **9** Robert
Shaw. **10** Billy Crystal. **11** University of Wisconsin. **12** Hugh Grant. **13** Friday.
14 Argentina. **15** Tiffany. **16** *Together for Days.* **17** Winona Ryder. **18** Jane
Wyman (once Mrs Ronald Reagan). **19** Peter O'Toole. **20** Patrick Godfrey.
21 Andrew Blyth Barrymore. **22** Sally Field. **23** Bruce Willis. **24** Poppy (*Prime
Cut*). **25** Esterhuysen.

Answers – see page 249

1   Who said, 'The most expensive habit in the world is celluloid'?
2   Who directed *Pretty Woman*?
3   Who played Tommy Judd in the film *Another Country*?
4   At what sport did Keanu Reeves excel?
5   Who won the Best Actor Oscar for *Tender Mercies*?
6   What was the name of Jamie Lee Curtis's character in *True Lies*?
7   Within ten minutes, how long does *Porky's* last?
8   'Mona Lisa' won an Oscar when it was used in which movie in 1950?
9   Which Josh featured in *Dead Poets Society*?
10   What is the name of the mermaid in *Splash*?
11   In which film does a character named Sailor Ripley appear?
12   Who won the Best Director Oscar for *Gentleman's Agreement*?
13   *The Long Good Friday* and *Zulu Dawn* both starred which actor?
14   Which Denis featured in *Basic Instinct*?
15   Lin McAdam, played by James Stewart, searched for which stolen gun of his fathers?
16   What was the name of Rick Moranis's character in *Honey, I Shrunk the Kids*?
17   What is the first name of Debra Winger, who uses her middle name in the movies?
18   Which 1988 film did rock star Adam Ant star in?
19   In which movie does Bill Murray say, 'OK, so she's a dog'?
20   Which Julie starred in *Before Sunrise*?
21   Who played Epiphany Proudfoot in the film *Angel Heart*?
22   Which subject did James Mason study at Cambridge?
23   Within five minutes, how long does *Pinocchio* last?
24   What was the name of Jon Finch's character in *Frenzy*?
25   Which John featured in *Presumed Innocent*?

Answers – see page 250

1   Who said, 'My movies were the kind they showed in planes or prisons because nobody can leave'?

2   Which actor is the father of actress Martha Plimpton?

3   In which movie did Paul Newman say, 'Who are these guys?'?

4   What is Uma Thurman's middle name?

5   Which star actor was born on exactly the same day as Juliet Mills?

6   Brandon Lee, son of Bruce, died during the making of which movie?

7   How was Ellen Burstyn billed in the 1960s?

8   Which member of the Von Trapp family did Hugh Grant play while still at school?

9   Which film star wrote the novel *The Sun Doctor*?

10   Whose movie career began as a pregnant man in *Rabbit Test*?

11   Where did Willem Dafoe study before beginning his acting career?

12   Who did Robert Downey Jr describe as a 'self important, boring, flash-in-the-pan Brit.'?

13   On which day of the week was Tuesday Weld born?

14   Where was Olivia Hussey born?

15   What is Richard Gere's middle name?

16   What was Samuel L. Jackson's very first movie?

17   Which actress has siblings called Sunyata, Jubal and Yuri?

18   Who said, 'I recommend marriage highly to everyone but me'?

19   Whose autobiography was called *Loitering with Intent*?

20   Who played Leonardo da Vinci in *Ever After*?

21   What is Drew Barrymore's full name?

22   Who was originally earmarked for the Cher role in *Moonstruck*?

23   Which actor sang in a band called Loose Goose?

24   Sissy Spacek made her movie debut playing which character opposite Gene Hackman and Lee Marvin?

25   What does the E stand for in Richard E. Grant's name?

Answers The Marx Brothers (see Quiz 34)
1 Chico. 2 *The Cocoanuts*. 3 *Horse Feathers*. 4 Harpo. 5 *Duck Soup*. 6 Isaac Newton. 7 Groucho's. 8 *A Night in Casablanca*. 9 Sam Wood. 10 Alan Young. 11 Groucho. 12 *A Day at the Races*. 13 Milton (Gummo) & Herbert (Zeppo). 14 Taxi horn. 15 Zeppo. 16 Arthur. 17 Minnie Schoenberg. 18 *Too Many Kisses*. 19 Greta Garbo. 20 Fredonia. 21 Groucho. 22 The Six Musical Mascots. 23 *Love Happy*. 24 *Harpo Speaks!* 25 Dave Gould (choreography).

Answers – see page 255

1	What planet does Leslie Nielsen land on in *Forbidden Planet*?
2	Which actor said about which part, 'Take my name... I haven't a clue what it's meant to mean'?
3	Who provided the voice of Hal 9000?
4	What is the name of the monster in *Twenty Million Miles to Earth*?
5	Who played Lois Lane in the first Superman movie of the 1970s?
6	What is the name of Princess Leia's father?
7	Upon which planet does Barbarella live?
8	Who composed the music for *Planet of the Apes*?
9	Which studio released *The Day the Earth Stood Still*?
10	Who played the monster in *The War of the Worlds*?
11	Who plays Elliott's older brother in *E.T.*?
12	In what year was *Blade Runner: The Director's Cut* released?
13	What colour are Chewbacca's eyes in *Star Wars*?
14	What are the names of Dr John Hammond's grandchildren in *Jurassic Park*?
15	Upon what day does the film *Independence Day* begin?
16	How many years into the future is *Starship Troopers* set?
17	Which *Star Wars* role did Al Pacino reject?
18	What was Dr Niko Tatopoulos researching prior to Godzilla's appearance?
19	Within fifteen minutes, how long does *The Empire Strikes Back* last?
20	Who directed the third *Star Wars* movie?
21	What caused 'The Incredible Shrinking Man' to shrink?
22	What is the name of Major Don West's ship in *Lost in Space*?
23	*Invasion of the Body Snatchers* starts at a hospital in which city?
24	What is the name of the professor in *Twenty Thousand Leagues under the Sea*?
25	Which planet are the Robinson family sent to colonize in *Lost in Space*?

Answers 1950s (see Quiz 39)
1 John Longden. **2** *Marguerite of the Night*. **3** F. Scott Fitzgerald. **4** Julie Harris.
5 Double Bass. **6** *Fort Algiers*. **7** Donald O'Connor. **8** 8,552. **9** Dan O'Herlihy.
10 *The Love Lottery*. **11** Anthony Quinn. **12** *Somebody Up There Likes Me*.
13 Audrey Hepburn. **14** Karl Malden. **15** *Forever Darling*. **16** *Paris Holiday*.
17 Charles Laughton & Elsa Lanchester. **18** Dirk Bogarde. **19** Paul Gauguin.
20 Marilyn Monroe & Jean Hagen. **21** *Witness for the Prosecution*. **22** William
Holden. **23** Eli Wallach. **24** The atom bomb. **25** *The Tempest*.

Answers – see page 256

1   At which number do the Banks live in *Mary Poppins*?
2   Which Jim starred in *The Beverly Hillbillies*?
3   In which film does a character named William Somerset appear?
4   Who directed the 90s movie *The Nutty Professor*?
5   What movie is shown within the film *Field of Dreams*?
6   Within five minutes, how long does *Philadelphia* last?
7   *Casino Royale* and *The Assam Garden* starred which actress?
8   Who wrote, 'If you can drive a car, you can direct a movie'?
9   Who won the Best Director Oscar for *Letter to Three Wives*?
10   Which Mike featured in *Mad Max II*?
11   Who links the soundtracks of *Psycho* and *Taxi Driver*?
12   What advice did Mel Brooks give Burt Reynolds on directing?
13   The Nazi in *Marathon Man* had been hiding in which country?
14   Who directed *Clear and Present Danger*?
15   What was director Tony Richardson's final film?
16   What was the name of the American in *An American in Paris*?
17   In which year was *DOA* released?
18   Who won the Best Actress Oscar for *Network*?
19   Which song from *Papa's Delicate Condition* won an Oscar?
20   What was the name of Elizabeth Taylor's character in *Who's Afraid of Virginia Woolf*?
21   Within ten minutes, how long does *Pocahontas* last?
22   Who directed *City of Angels*?
23   Which song from *Song of the South* won an Oscar?
24   A character named Leonard Lowe appeared in which film?
25   Which John featured in *Beverly Hills Cop*?

Answers Oscars – Best Films & Directors (see Quiz 40)
1 *In Old Arizona.* **2** Seven. **3** Sam Mendes. **4** William Wyler. **5** Woody Allen.
6 Lewis Gilbert. **7** John Huston. **8** Bob Fosse, *Cabaret.* **9** Jonathan Demme.
10 Image Movers. **11** *The Apartment.* **12** *Johnny Belinda.* **13** Four. **14** *Jerry Maguire.* **15** Irving Pichel. **16** *Slow Dancing in the Big City.* **17** *Rebecca.* **18** *They Shoot Horses Don't They?* **19** Gardener. **20** *A Nervous Romance.* **21** American Zoetrope. **22** Barry Levinson's. **23** William Friedkin's. **24** Bob Fosse. **25** Oliver Stone.

Answers – see page 253

1   Who played Sherlock Holmes in *The Man with the Twisted Lip*?
2   In which movie did Yves Montand play the devil?
3   Which writer did Gregory Peck play in *Beloved Infidel*?
4   Who played Sally Bowles in *I Am a Camera*?
5   In *Strangers on a Train* what is Hitchcock seen carrying on to the train?
6   In which movie does Yvonne De Carlo sing 'I'll Follow You'?
7   Who played Keaton in *The Buster Keaton Story*?
8   To the nearest 100, how many animals were there in *Around the World in Eighty Days*?
9   Who played Crusoe in *The Adventures of Robinson Crusoe*?
10   In which 1954 movie did Humphrey Bogart play himself?
11   Who played the title role in *The Hunchback of Notre Dame*?
12   In which 1956 movie did Paul Newman play a boxer?
13   Who severely hurt her back making *The Unforgiven*?
14   Who dislocated Marlon Brando's shoulder making *A Streetcar Named Desire*?
15   In which movie did James Mason play an angel?
16   In which of his own movies did Preston Sturgess appear in 1958?
17   Which husband and wife were Oscar-nominated together in 1957?
18   Who played two parts in *Libel* in 1959?
19   Who did Anthony Quinn play on screen in *Lust for Life*?
20   Who played the gangsters' molls in *The Asphalt Jungle*?
21   In which movie did Tyrone Power have his final completed role?
22   Who played the innocent to Gloria Swanson's Norma Desmond in *Sunset Boulevard*?
23   Whose withdrawal from *From Here to Eternity* meant Frank Sinatra got the part?
24   *The Thing* was based on a fear of what?
25   *Forbidden Planet* was based on which Shakespeare play?

Answers Sci Fi (see Quiz 37)
1 Altair 4. **2** Alec Guinness, Ben Obi Wan Kenobi. **3** Douglas Rain. **4** Ymir.
5 Margot Kidder. **6** Bail Organa. **7** Sorgo. **8** Jerry Goldsmith. **9** 20th Century
Fox. **10** Charles Gemora. **11** Robert MacNaughton. **12** 1992. **13** Blue. **14** Lex
and Timmy. **15** July 2nd. **16** 400. **17** Hans Solo. **18** Chernobyl earthworms.
19 124 mins. **20** Richard Marquand. **21** A cloud of mist. **22** Jupiter 2. **23** San
Francisco. **24** Pierre Aronnax. **25** Alpha Prime.

Answers – see page 254

1   What was the first western to be nominated for Best Film?
2   How many nominations did *The Insider* have?
3   Which director holds the record for most nominations by a first-time non-American director?
4   Who won his third Best Director for his third Best Picture in 1959?
5   Who directed the first two films for which Dianne Wiest won an award?
6   Who did Carol Reed replace on *Oliver!*?
7   Which winner was an amateur lightweight boxing champion in the early 20s?
8   Who was the only 70s director to win but not see his movie win Best Film?
9   Which 90s winning director is a former producer for New World Productions?
10 Which company did Robert Zemeckis found in 1997?
11 What was the last black-and-white picture to win Best Film before *Schindler's List*?
12 Which multi-nomination movie had the ad line, 'There was temptation in her helpless silence – then torment'?
13 Out of 12 nominations, how many awards did *The Song of Bernadette* win?
14 What was James L. Brooks's first nomination of the 90s?
15 Who was the unseen narrator of *How Green Was My Valley*?
16 What was John G. Avildsen's next movie after his first award?
17 In which movie did Judith Anderson say, 'You're overwrought, madam. I've opened a window for you....'?
18 Which Jane Fonda movie gave Sydney Polack his first nomination?
19 What was The Last Emperor's job in Mao's Republic?
20 What was the subtitle of *Annie Hall*?
21 Which studio did Coppola set up after the success of *The Godfather*?
22 Whose first wife was screenwriter Valerie Curtin?
23 Whose biography was called *Hurricane Billy*?
24 Who was nominated for a 70s movie based on his own life?
25 Who, on receiving his award said, 'I think you are really acknowledging the Vietnam veteran...'?

Answers Pot Luck 13 (see Quiz 38)
1 17. 2 Varney. 3 *Se7en*. 4 Tom Shadyac. 5 *Harvey*. 6 119 minutes.
7 Deborah Kerr. 8 John Landis. 9 Joseph L. Mankiewicz. 10 Preston. 11 Bernard Herrmann. 12 Fire someone on the first day. 13 Uruguay. 14 Phillip Noyce.
15 *Blue Sky*. 16 Jerry Mulligan. 17 1950. 18 Faye Dunaway. 19 'Call Me Irresponsible'. 20 Martha. 21 81 mins. 22 Brad Silberling. 23 'Zip-A-Dee-Doo-Dah'. 24 *Awakenings*. 25 Ashton.

Answers – see page 259

1   Which film star was born on the same day as Gymnast Olga Korbut?
2   Who designed The Riddler's costume in *Batman Forever*?
3   Who won the Best Director Oscar for *Rocky*?
4   Which movie featured 5,000 unpaid New Yorkers as extras?
5   What was Doris Day's first film, in 1948?
6   In which film does a character named Louis Dega appear?
7   Which Ralph featured in *The Bodyguard*?
8   Who played the villain in *Moonraker*?
9   Within five minutes, how long does *The Piano* last?
10 Who won the Best Actor Oscar for *The Informer*?
11 *King Kong* and *All That Jazz* starred which actress?
12 Who links *Forbidden Planet* made in 1956 and *Spy Hard* in 1996?
13 Who directed *My Best Friend's Wedding*?
14 What does Julie Andrews hold in her left hand on *The Sound of Music* movie poster?
15 What was the name of Alan Rickman's character in *Truly, Madly, Deeply*?
16 Where in America was Raquel Welch born?
17 Which film includes clips from *Dracula* and *Strangers on a Train*?
18 Who was the butler in *Princess Caraboo*?
19 Which Ron featured in *Reversal of Fortune*?
20 In which film does a character named Jim Stark appear?
21 Which writer directed *Dream Wife* in 1953?
22 How old was Sam Raimi when he directed *The Evil Dead*?
23 Who has a production company called Edited?
24 Which John featured in *The Pelican Brief*?
25 In which film does a character named Jane Spencer appear?

Answers James Bond   (see Quiz 43)
1 Ian Fleming. 2 *Goldfinger*. 3 *Casino Royale*. 4 Two. 5 Hamburg.
6 *GoldenEye*. 7 *Licence to Kill*. 8 *Dr No*. 9 *Never Say Never Again*. 10 Barbara
Bach. 11 George Lazenby. 12 *Live and Let Die*. 13 117 minutes. 14 Stoke Poges.
15 *Thunderball*. 16 *You Only Live Twice*. 17 *A View to a Kill*. 18 Spectre.
19 Auric. 20 *You Only Live Twice*. 21 *Dr No*. 22 Carver. 23 Ian Fleming's home
in Jamaica. 24 'No news is bad news'. 25 *A View to a Kill*.

Answers – see page 260

1   For which movie did Shirley MacLaine win Best Actress at Berlin in 1971?
2   What won the International Jury Prize at the first Cannes festival?
3   Who took the Palme D'Or at Cannes in 1985 for *When Father Was Away on Business*?
4   What is the full name of the Best Film award at Venice?
5   Who shared Golden Lions in 1980 for *Gloria* and *Atlantic City*?
6   What was the nationality of the 1996 winner in Berlin?
7   In what year was the Palme D'Or inaugurated at Cannes?
8   How many prizes were given at Cannes in 1947 for all film genres?
9   Between which years was the Venice Film Festival suspended?
10   For which movie did Edward G. Robinson win at Cannes at the last festival of the 40s?
11   Which 1990s movie won a Golden Lion for Neil Jordan?
12   For which movie did Elodie Bouchez and Natacha Regnier share Best Actress at Cannes in 1998?
13   For which movie did Cher win Best Actress at Cannes in 1985?
14   Who won at Cannes the year before starring in *Evita*?
15   In what year after its inauguration was no Golden Bear given?
16   Which actress won in Venice in 1993 for *Three Colours: Blue*?
17   Who won Best Actress at Cannes for *Cal* and *The Madness of King George*?
18   Which two Brits won Best Actor and Actress at Cannes in 1965?
19   Who won the Best Actress award at Cannes in 1997?
20   How was Ingmar Bergman's Golden Bear winner *Smultonstallet* also known?
21   Which very English collection of stories was a winner in Berlin for Pasolini in 1972?
22   Who won Best Actress at Cannes for *La Reine Margot*?
23   Who won the inaugural Golden Bear award?
24   What were the short-lived European Film Awards called?
25   Who received the Golden Lion for *Rosencrantz and Guildenstern Are Dead*?

Answers Pot Luck 15 (see Quiz 44)
1 *As the World Turns.* **2** Daryl Hannah. **3** James Frawley. **4** Taylor. **5** 101 minutes. **6** *Don't Look Now.* **7** 1940s. **8** Patricia Neal. **9** Miller. **10** Burt Reynolds. **11** 141 minutes. **12** Adrian Cronauer. **13** *Aladdin.* **14** Ford. **15** *Cabaret.* **16** Alan J. Pakula. **17** *Drugstore Cowboy.* **18** Skerritt. **19** Leo McCarey. **20** Tom Topor. **21** Goldie Hawn. **22** Daniella Bianchi. **23** Tasmania (Australia). **24** *Planet of the Apes.* **25** Daniels.

Answers – see page 257

1   Who described James Bond as 'a blunt instrument wielded by a government department'?
2   Which 007 movie did Sean Connery make prior to *Marnie*?
3   Which Bond film did Deborah Kerr appear in?
4   How many Bond films were released during Ian Fleming's lifetime?
5   Where is the first hour of *Tomorrow Never Dies* set?
6   Which movie's villain was Xenia Onatopp?
7   Which movie first had the toothpaste with plastic explosive?
8   What is the only Bond movie not to have an action sequence before the credits?
9   In which movie did Rowan Atkinson (a.k.a. Mr Bean) make his big-screen debut?
10   Which Bond girl married a Beatle?
11   Which 007 backed the restaurant chain the Spy House?
12   Which movie had the electromagnetic watch with the spinning blade?
13   Within fifteen minutes, how long does *You Only Live Twice* last?
14   Which golf course featured in *Goldfinger*?
15   What was the most successful Bond film of the 70s and 80s in terms of cinema admissions?
16   What was the final Bond movie, as far as Ian Fleming was concerned?
17   May Day was the Bond girl in which film?
18   In the films, what replaced the Soviet organization Smersh which existed in the books?
19   What was Goldfinger's first name?
20   In which movie did Blofeld kidnap US and USSR spaceships to try and gain planetary control?
21   Which Bond movie opened during the Cuban missile crisis?
22   What is the name of the villain in the movie that preceded *The World Is Not Enough*?
23   What was *GoldenEye* named after?
24   What is the motto of the villain in *Tomorrow Never Dies*?
25   What was the last film where Lois Maxwell played Miss Moneypenny?

Answers Pot Luck 14 (see Quiz 41)
1 Debra Winger (16.5.55). 2 Jim Carrey. 3 John G. Avildsen. 4 *King Kong* remake. 5 *Romance on the High Seas*. 6 *Papillon*. 7 Waite. 8 Michael Lonsdale. 9 120 minutes. 10 Victor McLaglen. 11 Jessica Lange. 12 Leslie Nielsen. 13 P.J. Hogan. 14 Guitar case. 15 Jamie. 16 Chicago. 17 *Innocent Blood*. 18 Kevin Kline. 19 Silver. 20 *Rebel Without a Cause*. 21 Sidney Sheldon. 22 19. 23 Jack Lemmon. 24 Heard. 25 *Naked Gun: From the Files of Police Squad*.

Answers – see page 258

1   Which soap did Meg Ryan star in?
2   Which actress links *Blade Runner* and *Legal Eagles*?
3   Who directed *The Muppet Movie*?
4   Which Christine featured in *The Wedding Singer*?
5   Within ten minutes, how long does *The Mask* last?
6   A character named John Baxter appeared in which film?
7   The action of *The Godfather* starts in which decade?
8   Who won the Best Actress Oscar for *Hud*?
9   Which Larry featured in the 90s movie *The Nutty Professor*?
10   Which movie star released a single called 'I Like Having You Around' in 1974?
11   Within five minutes, how long does *The Pelican Brief* last?
12   Who did Robin Williams play in *Good Morning, Vietnam*?
13   Which 1990s movie concerned the city of Agrabah?
14   Which Steven featured in *When Harry Met Sally*?
15   Philosophy student Brian Roberts turns up in which movie?
16   Who directed *Klute* and *The Pelican Brief*?
17   Which film is based upon an unpublished novel by James Fogle, written whilst he was in prison?
18   Which Tom featured in *A River Runs Through It*?
19   Who won the Best Director Oscar for *The Awful Truth*?
20   Who wrote the screenplay for *The Accused*?
21   Which actress links *Dollars* and *Butterflies Are Free*?
22   Who played the Bond girl in *From Russia with Love*?
23   In which country was Errol Flynn born?
24   John Chambers won an Honorary Oscar Award in 1968 for make-up in which film?
25   Which William featured in *The Parallax View*?

Answers Film Festivals (see Quiz 42)
1 *Desperate Characters*. **2** *The Battle of the Rails*. **3** Emir Kusturica. **4** Golden Lion of St Mark. **5** John Cassavetes & Louis Malle. **6** Taiwanese (Ang Lee). **7** 1955. **8** Six. **9** 1942 & 1946. **10** *House of Strangers*. **11** *Michael Collins*. **12** *Dream Life of Angels*. **13** *Mask*. **14** Jonathan Pryce. **15** 1970. **16** Juliette Binoche. **17** Helen Mirren. **18** Terence Stamp & Samantha Eggar. **19** Kathy Burke. **20** *Wild Strawberries*. **21** *The Canterbury Tales*. **22** Virna Lisi. **23** Gene Kelly. **24** Felixes. **25** Tom Stoppard.

Answers – see page 263

1 What was William Wyler's third movie with Audrey Hepburn?
2 Which role did John Wayne play in *North to Alaska*?
3 What was Marilyn Monroe's penultimate completed movie?
4 For which movie did Burt Lancaster win an Oscar for his second nomination?
5 Who did Robert Mitchum play in *The Sundowners*?
6 In which movie did Zero Mostel say, 'He who hesitates is poor'?
7 What was the first of Richard Burton's three Oscar nominations between 1964 and 1966?
8 Who inspired the David Hemmings role in Antonioni's *Blow Up*?
9 What was the sequel to *One Million Years BC*?
10 Who wrote the novel *A Christmas Story* the same year as starring in *Night of the Iguana*?
11 In which film of her father's did Anjelica Huston make her screen debut?
12 Sean Connery's first father-in-law was a world authority on what subject?
13 In *The Birds*, Hitchcock walks past Tippi Hedren with what?
14 Which then husband and wife starred in *The Illustrated Man*?
15 Who played Elizabeth I in *Seven Seas to Calais*?
16 Which actor 'killed' Ronald Reagan in his final film *The Killers*?
17 Which singer was Oscar-nominated for his role as a shell-shocked GI in *Captain Newman MD*?
18 Who did Alec Guinness play in *Lawrence of Arabia*?
19 Who played Bob & Ted, in *Bob and Carol and Ted and Alice*?
20 Julie Christie won an Oscar for *Darling* after which US actress turned the part down?
21 Who links *The Dirty Dozen* and *Rosemary's Baby*?
22 Who directed and starred in *Charlie Bubbles* in 1968?
23 Who is the only US actor in *King Rat*?
24 Who played the title role in *Dr No*?
25 Which Redgrave appeared in *A Man for All Seasons*?

Answers Pot Luck 16 (see Quiz 47)
1 Chocolate. **2** Barry Sonnenfeld. **3** Wood. **4** Mark Rutland. **5** Tatum O'Neal. **6** 110 minutes. **7** Barbara Hershey. **8** Morse. **9** 'Baby It's Cold Outside'. **10** John Book. **11** Walter & John Huston. **12** Brestoff. **13** Katherine Hepburn. **14** Richard Marquand. **15** *Jackie Brown*. **16** Art Carney. **17** *The Accidental Tourist*. **18** Joel Schumacher. **19** 1993. **20** 'Last Dance'. **21** Russo. **22** Richard Attenborough. **23** Moor Azeem. **24** 117 minutes. **25** Norman.

Answers – see page 264

1   Who founded Lightstorm Entertainment with James Cameron?
2   Who has a company called Flower Productions?
3   Who became an independent producer after appearing as Jethro in *The Beverley Hillbillies*?
4   Who bought Vitagraph in 1925?
5   Who founded New World Pictures in 1970?
6   Who set up M & M Productions?
7   Which studio made the 1954 *Godzilla* movie?
8   Who founded the Oz Film Manufacturing Company in 1914?
9   Who was the only female founder member of First Artists?
10 What was Warner Brothers' follow-up talkie to *The Jazz Singer*?
11 Who announced a $65 million loss after the failure of *Meet Joe Black*?
12 In which film did Paramount introduce Vistavision?
13 Which record company bought Universal in 1952?
14 What were Pinewood Studios first used for at the start of World War II?
15 What was the most successful company that made B movies?
16 Who replaced Louis B. Mayer at MGM in 1951?
17 Which Moscow-born composer was head of RKO's music department from 1941 to 1952?
18 Which company asked Oliver Stone to make *Salvador*?
19 Menaham Golan and Yoram Globus took over which company in 1979?
20 What was First Artists' first movie after Steve McQueen joined the company?
21 What is Denzel Washington's film company called?
22 Which millionaire bought 20th Century Fox in 1981?
23 What was Fox's wide screen system pioneered in 1929 called?
24 Who set up the computer-effects company Digital Domain?
25 Who acquired Paramount in 1966?

Answers John Ford (see Quiz 48)
1 Sean Aloysius O'Feeney. 2 Aquarius. 3 12. 4 Member of the Ku Klux Klan.
5 *The Iron Horse; Four Sons*. 6 Monument Valley. 7 *The Battle of Midway; December 7th*. 8 Four. 9 Orson Welles. 10 1973. 11 *The Tornado*. 12 *Three Bad Men*. 13 *How Green Was My Valley*. 14 Argosy Productions. 15 *She Wore a Yellow Ribbon*. 16 Mervyn LeRoy. 17 *Seven Women*. 18 *Mogambo*. 19 Peter Bogdanovich. 20 *The Quiet Man*. 21 *Drums Along the Mohawk*. 22 George O'Brien. 23 *The Quiet Man*. 24 Universal. 25 *Straight Shooting*.

Answers – see page 261

1	What type of sauce was used in the shower scene in *Psycho*?
2	Who directed *Men in Black*?
3	Which John featured in *War Games*?
4	What was the name of Sean Connery's character in *Marnie*?
5	Who was the youngest performer in the 20th century to win an Oscar open to adults?
6	Within ten minutes, how long does *Mission: Impossible* last?
7	Which actress links *Splitting Heirs* and *The Portrait of a Lady*?
8	Which David featured in *The Rock*?
9	Which song from *Neptune's Daughter* won an Oscar?
10	Who does Harrison Ford play in *Witness*?
11	Which father and son, actor and director, won Oscars for *The Treasure of the Sierra Madre*?
12	Which Richard featured in *Car Wash*?
13	Who played Tracy Lord in *The Philadelphia Story*?
14	Who directed *Return of the Jedi*?
15	What was Quentin Tarantino's third film as a director?
16	Who won the Best Actor Oscar for *Harry and Tonto*?
17	A character named Muriel Pritchett appears in which film?
18	Who directed *Batman Forever*?
19	In which year did Audrey Hepburn die?
20	Which song won Best Song Oscar for *Thank God It's Friday*?
21	Which James featured in *My Own Private Idaho*?
22	Who was Jane Seymour's first father-in-law?
23	What was the name of Morgan Freeman's character in *Robin Hood: Prince of Thieves*?
24	Within five minutes, how long does *Patriot Games* last?
25	Which Zack featured in *Romancing the Stone*?

Answers 1960s Stars (see Quiz 45)

1 *How to Steal a Million*. 2 *Big Sam*. 3 *Let's Make Love*. 4 *Elmer Gantry*. 5 Paddy Carmody. 6 *The Producers*. 7 *Becket*. 8 David Bailey. 9 *When Dinosaurs Ruled the Earth*. 10 Richard Burton. 11 *A Walk with Love and Death*. 12 Tropical medicine (Diane Cilento's father). 13 Two dogs. 14 Rod Steiger & Claire Bloom. 15 Irene Worth. 16 Lee Marvin. 17 Bobby Darin. 18 Prince Feisal. 19 Elliott Gould & Robert Culp. 20 Shirley MacLaine. 21 John Cassavetes. 22 Albert Finney. 23 George Segal. 24 Joseph Wiseman. 25 Corin.

Answers – see page 262

1   What was John Ford's real name?
2   Under what star sign was he born?
3   How many older siblings did he have?
4   He appeared in *Birth of a Nation* as an extra, playing what?
5   Which two silent movies did he direct in 1924 and 1928?
6   Where, on the Arizona–Utah line, did he make nine movies?
7   Which two of his World War II documentaries won Oscars?
8   How many times did he win the New York Film Critics Award?
9   Who, when asked which US directors appealed to him most, said, 'The Old Masters. John Ford, John Ford and John Ford'?
10 In what year did Ford die?
11 What was his first two-reeler called?
12 Which 20s movie was about the Oklahoma land rush?
13 What did he win an Oscar for the year after *The Grapes of Wrath*?
14 Which company did he form with Merian C. Cooper?
15 What was the middle film of his so-called Cavalry Trilogy?
16 Who replaced him on the set of *Mister Roberts* after he reputedly argued with Henry Fonda?
17 What was his final feature film?
18 Which of his films was a remake of *Red Dust*?
19 Who made the documentary *Directed By John Ford*?
20 Which film starred John Wayne and was set in the Emerald Isle?
21 In which 1939 film did he direct Henry Fonda and co-star Claudette Colbert?
22 Which star of *The Iron Horse* did he direct again in *Salute*?
23 For which movie did he win an unprecedented fourth Oscar?
24 What was the first Hollywood studio he worked for?
25 What was his first feature film?

Answers Film Companies & Studios (see Quiz 46)
1 Lawrence Kasanoff. 2 Drew Barrymore. 3 Max Baer Jr. 4 Warner Brothers.
5 Roger Corman. 6 Michael Caine. 7 Toho Studios. 8 Frank L. Baum. 9 Barbra
Streisand. 10 *The Singing Fool*. 11 Universal. 12 *White Christmas*. 13 Decca.
14 Food storage. 15 Republic Studios. 16 Dore Schary. 17 Constantin
Bakaleinikoff. 18 Hemdale. 19 Cannon Films. 20 *Pocket Money*. 21 Mundy Lane.
22 Marvin Davis. 23 Fox Grandeur. 24 James Cameron. 25 Gulf Western.

Answers – see page 267

1 Who sets out to trap Pierce Brosnan in *The Thomas Crown Affair*?
2 What is Jim Carrey's middle name?
3 Which English actress said, 'When you're called a character actress it's because you're too ugly to be called a leading lady'?
4 Where was Samuel L. Jackson born?
5 Who does Nicolas Cage play in *Face/Off*?
6 Who played Leonardo DiCaprio's mother in *This Boy's Life*?
7 Which 90s Oscar nominee made his debut aged five in *Pound*?
8 Which star of TV's *Taxi* starred in *Independence Day*?
9 Who replaced Mia Farrow in *Manhattan Murder Mystery*?
10 Which star of *Heavenly Creatures* was Oscar-nominated a year later?
11 Who directed and starred in *Hoffa* in 1992?
12 Which actress, also an accomplished artist, exhibited with Christian Fenouillat in 1994?
13 In which movie did Kate Winslet have her first nude scene?
14 What is Ralph Fiennes's middle name?
15 Who played John Lennon in *Backbeat*?
16 Which painter did Joss Ackland play in *Surviving Picasso*?
17 Which star of *Mouse Hunt* runs Little Mo Productions?
18 Which perfume house did Rupert Everett model for in adverts?
19 Who was Woody Allen's ex wife in *Deconstructing Harry*?
20 John Candy died during the making of which movie?
21 What was Whitney Houston's follow-up to *The Bodyguard*?
22 Which 90s Oscar nominee is a founder of the Atlanta-based Just Us Theatre Company?
23 Which aunt of Macaulay Culkin appeared in *Shadow of a Doubt*?
24 What was Hugh Grant's first movie to be made in Hollywood?
25 Who played Lyon Gaultier in the 90s movie *AWOL*?

Answers Warren Beatty (see Quiz 51)
1 Henry Warren Beaty. 2 Aries. 3 Buck Henry. 4 Natalie Wood. 5 *Shampoo*.
6 Director (*Reds*). 7 'Sooner or Later'. 8 Vivien Leigh. 9 Tess Trueheart. 10 Gene Hackman. 11 Diane Keaton. 12 *The Many Loves of Doby Gillis*. 13 *Shampoo*.
14 *The Pick Up Artist*. 15 *Butch Cassidy and the Sundance Kid*. 16 Paula Prentiss.
17 *Here Comes Mr Jordan*. 18 *Reds*. 19 Frank Sinatra. 20 Madonna. 21 Charles Boyer & Irene Dunne. 22 Elaine May. 23 Bugsy Siegel. 24 Kansas. 25 Woody Allen.

Answers – see page 268

1   *Jackie Brown* is based on whose bestseller, *Rum Punch*?
2   Which Diane featured in *The Wicker Man*?
3   Who directed *Lost in Space*?
4   Who starred with Terence Stamp in 60s movie *The Collector*?
5   Which actress links *Raising Arizona* and *Once Around*?
6   Within five minutes, how long does *Pale Rider* last?
7   Who was Daniel Day-Lewis's actress mother?
8   Who played Charlie's handsome colleague in *Roxanne*?
9   What was the name of Edward Woodward's character in *The Wicker Man*?
10 Who played Addy in the film *City Heat*?
11 Who won the Best Director Oscar for *The Divine Lady*?
12 In which land is *The Neverending Story* set?
13 Within ten minutes, how long does *Invasion of the Body Snatchers* last?
14 Which Paul featured in *Romeo + Juliet*?
15 What was the name of Anthony Hopkins's character in *The Elephant Man*?
16 Who directed *Butterfield 8*?
17 Who won the Best Director Oscar for *The Last Emperor*?
18 Who played Peter Falk's grandson in *The Princess Bride*?
19 Who played Bonnie Rayburn in the film *City Slickers*?
20 In which film did a character named Griffin Mill appear?
21 The song 'Swinging on a Star' came from which movie?
22 Who played opposite Elliott Gould in the 70s remake of *The Lady Vanishes*?
23 Which Carrie featured in *Pale Rider*?
24 Who won the Best Actress Oscar for *Two Women*?
25 Who directed *The Cable Guy*?

Answers – see page 265

1   What is his full real name?
2   Under what star sign was he born?
3   Who was his co-director in *Heaven Can Wait*?
4   Who was his co-star in his feature film debut?
5   Which of his movies was set on the eve of the 1968 election?
6   In what capacity did he win an Oscar for the movie based on *Ten Days that Shook the World*?
7   What song won Best Song Oscar in his movie with Madonna?
8   Who was his co-star in *The Roman Spring of Mrs Stone*?
9   Which character was his true love in *Dick Tracy*?
10   Who played his brother in his first Oscar-nominated movie?
11   Who was his female co-star in the movie where he played John Reed?
12   In which US TV series did he appear in the 50s?
13   Which movie gave him his second Oscar nomination?
14   He was executive producer on which movie in the same year that *Ishtar* flopped?
15   Which movie did he turn down to do *The Only Game in Town*?
16   Who was his co-star in *The Parallax View*?
17   His third movie with Julie Christie was a remake of which movie?
18   Which movie was advertised as 'Never since *Gone with the Wind* has there been a great romantic epic like it'?
19   Who did he replace on *The Only Game in Town*?
20   In whose documentary *Truth or Dare* did he feature in 1991?
21   Who were the original stars of *Love Affair*, which he remade in 1994?
22   Who directed the 80s comedy flop where he starred with Dustin Hoffman?
23   Who was the subject of the biopic where he met his wife?
24   Where was his first feature-length movie set?
25   Who said if he came back in another life he wanted to be Warren Beatty's fingertips?

Answers – see page 266

1.   What was Gary Cooper's job before he became an actor?
2.   Which movie was John Wayne working on when he won his Oscar for *True Grit*?
3.   Which silent-movie star turned director using the pseudonym William Goodrich?
4.   Who appeared in a 30s classic and was Oscar-nominated for her final film in 1984?
5.   Which superstar did Lew Ayres marry after Lola Lane?
6.   In which movie did Clark Gable play Blackie Norton?
7.   How was William Mitchell better known?
8.   Cartoonist Al Capp based Li'l Abner on which late actor?
9.   Who said of Clark Gable, 'His ears made him look like a taxicab with both doors open'?
10.   When a journalist wired Cary Grant's agent saying, 'How old Cary Grant?' what did Cary Grant himself reply?
11.   What was Vivien Leigh's first movie after *Gone with the Wind*?
12.   Which pioneer's catchphrase was 'Leave 'em wanting'?
13.   What was the name of Ava Gardner's dog, to which she left a maid and a limo in her will?
14.   Which actor was US diving champion in 1932?
15.   In what year did Charlie Chaplin eventually receive a knighthood?
16.   Which comedy actor was a former vice president of the London Judo Society?
17.   How did Vivien Leigh die?
18.   Whose marriage to Katharine Hepburn lasted just three weeks?
19.   What was Natalie Wood's last movie?
20.   Which Italian actress was the twin of Marisa Pavan?
21.   Which movie did Sinatra make shortly after paying a ransom on his son's kidnap?
22.   Marilyn Monroe died during the making of which movie which was never finished?
23.   How was Anne Leppert better known?
24.   Where is there a museum celebrating Audrey Hepburn's work as a UN Ambassador?
25.   Which queen did Charles Laughton's real-life wife play in *The Private Life of Henry VIII*?

Answers Pot Luck 17 (see Quiz 50)

1 Elmore Leonard. **2** Cilento. **3** Stephen Hopkins. **4** Samantha Eggar. **5** Holly Hunter. **6** 115 minutes. **7** Jill Balcon. **8** Rick Rossovich. **9** Sergeant Neil Howie. **10** Jane Alexander. **11** Frank Lloyd. **12** Fantasia. **13** 80 minutes. **14** Sorvino. **15** Dr Frederick Treves. **16** Daniel Mann. **17** Bernardo Bertolucci. **18** Fred Savage. **19** Helen Slater. **20** *The Player*. **21** *Going My Way*. **22** Cybill Shepherd. **23** Snodgrass. **24** Sophia Loren. **25** Ben Stiller.

Answers – see page 271

1   How many rooms does the Bates Motel have?
2   What was the name of Jessica Tandy's character in *Fried Green Tomatoes at the Whistle Stop Café*?
3   Who won the Best Actor Oscar for *Story of Louis Pasteur*?
4   Who directed *A League of Their Own*?
5   Which Samantha featured in *Little Women*?
6   Does *Groundhog Day* last around 85, 100 or 120 minutes?
7   In which film did the character Major General Roy Urquhart appear?
8   A Charles Portis novel became which late 60s classic movie?
9   Which Richard featured in *Logan's Run*?
10 In which film did a sailor named Ned Land appear?
11 *No Minor Chords: My Days in Hollywood* was whose autobiography?
12 Which actress links *Mr North* and *The Witches*?
13 A character named Charles Horman appeared in which film?
14 Which film actor's voice was that on Michael Jackson's video *Thriller*?
15 What is the first name of Bruce Willis, who uses his middle name in the movies?
16 Within five minutes, how long does *9 to 5* last?
17 Which Martin featured *in Little Big Man*?
18 Whose memoirs of Limerick were made into a film with Emily Watson?
19 In which film does the character named Sean Thornton appear?
20 In 1984 which movie star released the pop single 'The Christmas Song'?
21 How is actor/director Nobby Clarke better known?
22 What movie is shown within the film *The Fabulous Baker Boys*?
23 A character named Doris Murphy appeared in which film?
24 Which Chris featured in *The Fifth Element*?
25 What's the name and number of the computer in *2001*?

Answers Alfred Hitchcock (see Quiz 55)
1 Leytonstone. **2** Leo. **3** Title card illustrator. **4** *Elstree Calling*. **5** *The Lady Vanishes*. **6** Daphne Du Maurier (*Rebecca*). **7** St Ignatius College, London. **8** *The Lodger*. **9** James Allardice. **10** Alma Reville. **11** David O. Selznick. **12** Carole Lombard. **13** *The Case of Jonathan Drew*. **14** He won with his first! **15** Blondes. **16** Julie Andrews. **17** Bernard Herrmann. **18** *Frenzy*. **19** *Elstree Calling*. **20** *Suspicion* (Cary Grant). **21** Mount Rushmore. **22** Pierre Boileau & Thomas Narcejac. **23** *Rope*. **24** *Shadow of a Doubt*. **25** Madeleine Carroll.

Answers – see page 272

1	Which movie had the ad line, 'Don't give away the ending; it's the only one we have'?
2	Who injured his leg making *Cat Ballou*, eventually requiring an amputation?
3	*A Fistful of Dollars* was based on which samurai classic?
4	Which composer did Dirk Bogarde play in *Song Without End*?
5	Who played Catherine the Great in *Great Catherine*?
6	Who turned down the Clark Gable role in *The Misfits* as he said he didn't understand it?
7	In which movie did Lon Chaney play the devil?
8	Who played Wyatt Earp in *Hour of the Gun*?
9	Which role did Ava Gardner play in *The Night of the Iguana*?
10	Who played Elizabeth I in *The Fighting Prince of Donegal*?
11	For which movie was Terence Stamp Oscar-nominated on his film debut?
12	Who played Jean Harlow in *Harlow*?
13	In *The Birds*, Hitchcock walks past Tippi Hedren with what?
14	Who played Sherlock Holmes in *A Study in Terror*?
15	In which movie did John Philip Law play an angel?
16	Who played two parts in *Fahrenheit 451* in 1966?
17	Which husband and wife were Oscar-nominated together in 1963?
18	*The Jackals* was based on which Shakespeare play?
19	In which of his own movies did John Huston appear in 1966?
20	In which 1962 movie did Anthony Quinn play a boxer?
21	'Shut up and deal' is the last line of which movie?
22	What is the nickname of 'The Man With No Name'?
23	Who turned down the role of Lara in *Dr Zhivago*?
24	What was the name of Jackie Gleason's character in *The Hustler*?
25	What was the third of Richard Burton's three Oscar nominations between 1964 and 1966?

Answers Pot Luck 19 (see Quiz 56)
1 *Cleopatra*. 2 Elizabeth Taylor. 3 Benjamin. 4 1987. 5 Hera. 6 *Abbott and Costello Meet Frankenstein*. 7 *War Hunt*. 8 120 minutes. 9 Goodall. 10 *A Star Is Born*. 11 Lewis Milestone. 12 Faye Dunaway. 13 *Legends of the Fall*. 14 Garfield. 15 Rebecca De Mornay. 16 *Airplane!* 17 1980. 18 Judy Holliday. 19 Danny Cannon. 20 Robert Thorn. 21 96 minutes. 22 *How I Won the War*. 23 Sam Bowden. 24 *Basic Instinct*. 25 128 minutes.

Answers – see page 269

1	In which part of London was Hitchcock born?
2	What is his star sign?
3	What was his first job in the movie industry?
4	In which movie did he have his only pie-throwing scene?
5	What was the last hit movie he made in the UK before leaving for Hollywood?
6	Who wrote the novel on which his first Hollywood movie was based?
7	At which school was he enrolled at an early age?
8	What was the British title of the film he made that saw his first cameo appearance?
9	Who wrote the commentary for his *Alfred Hitchcock Presents* TV anthology series?
10	Who did he marry in 1926?
11	Which producer first signed him to work in the USA?
12	Who was the star of his 1941 romantic comedy?
13	How was *The Lodger* titled in the USA?
14	How many Hollywood films did he make before winning his first Oscar for Best Film?
15	Who did Hitchcock say made the best victims?
16	Who played the double agent's girlfriend in *Torn Curtain*?
17	Who wrote the score for the shower scene in *Psycho*?
18	Which hit film did he make in Britain after a 30-year gap in Hollywood?
19	Which of his early movies was based on *The Taming of the Shrew*?
20	What was his first movie to star the actor born Archibald Leach?
21	On which mountain was much of *North by Northwest* shot?
22	Whose novel was *Vertigo* based on?
23	What was his first movie in colour?
24	What was reputedly his own favourite among his films?
25	Who played the starring female role Hitchcock created for *The Thirty-Nine Steps*?

Answers Pot Luck 18 (see Quiz 53)
1 12. **2** Ninny Threadgoode. **3** Paul Muni. **4** Penny Marshall. **5** Mathis. **6** 100.
7 *A Bridge Too Far.* **8** *True Grit.* **9** Jordan. **10** *20,000 Leagues Under the Sea.*
11 André Previn. **12** Anjelica Huston. **13** *Missing.* **14** Vincent Price. **15** Walter.
16 110 minutes. **17** Balsam. **18** Frank McCourt's. **19** *The Quiet Man.* **20** Billy
Crystal. **21** Bryan Forbes. **22** *It's a Wonderful Life.* **23** *A League of Their Own.*
24 Tucker. **25** HAL 9000.

Answers – see page 270

1	Producer Buddy Adler died during the making of which blockbuster movie?
2	Which movie star released a single called 'Wings in the Sky' in 1976?
3	Which Richard featured in *Catch 22*?
4	In which year did Fred Astaire die?
5	Who did Honor Blackman play in *Jason and the Argonauts*?
6	Which movie is shown in the film *Into the Night*?
7	What was Robert Redford's first film, in 1961?
8	Within fifteen minutes, how long does the 1990s *Emma* last?
9	Which Caroline featured in *Schindler's List*?
10	A character named Esther Blodgett appeared in which film?
11	Who won the Best Director Oscar for *Two Arabian Knights*?
12	Which actress links *Barfly* and *American Dreamers*?
13	*Legends of the Fall, Liar Liar, The Lion King* – which runs the longest?
14	Which Allen featured in *The Candidate*?
15	When Roger Vadim remade *And God Created Woman*, who played the role originally played by his first wife?
16	In which film did a character named Ted Striker appear?
17	In which year was *Time Bandits* released?
18	Who won the Best Actress Oscar for *Born Yesterday*?
19	Who directed *Judge Dredd*?
20	What was the name of Gregory Peck's character in *The Omen*?
21	Within five minutes, how long does *Night of the Living Dead* last?
22	Which 1967 film did rock star John Lennon star in?
23	Who did Nick Nolte play in *Cape Fear*?
24	In which film did a character named Beth Curran appear?
25	Within fifteen minutes, how long does *Ghost* last?

Answers 1960s (see Quiz 54)

1 *Psycho.* 2 Jay C. Flippen. 3 *Yojimbo.* 4 Franz Liszt. 5 Jeanne Moreau.
6 Robert Mitchum. 7 *The Devil's Messenger.* 8 James Garner. 9 Maxine Falk.
10 Catherine Lacey. 11 *Billy Budd.* 12 Carroll Baker. 13 Two dogs. 14 John
Neville. 15 *Barbarella.* 16 Julie Christie. 17 Rex Harrison & Rachel Roberts.
18 *The Tempest.* 19 *The Bible.* 20 *Requiem for a Heavyweight.* 21 *The Apartment.*
22 Blondie. 23 Jane Fonda. 24 Minnesota Fats. 25 *Who's Afraid of Virginia Woolf?*.

Answers – see page 275

1   Who did John Belushi play in his first movie?
2   Who was the only woman to have major billing for *A Bridge Too Far*?
3   Which 70s Best Actress Oscar nominee became co-artistic director of the Actors Studio after the death of Lee Strasberg?
4   Who became his country's top star of the 70s and was dubbed the Dutch Paul Newman?
5   Who directed and starred in *The Last Movie* in 1971?
6   Which Hitchcock film trailer saw the director floating in the Thames?
7   Which 70s star was the granddaughter of fashion designer Elsa Schiaparelli?
8   Who was Best Actress at Cannes for *An Unmarried Woman*?
9   Which movie featured Michael York, Jacqueline Bisset and Lauren Bacall?
10   Which future Oscar-winner made his debut as a car vandal in *Sunday Bloody Sunday*?
11   In which movie did Julie Christie first star opposite Warren Beatty?
12   In which movie did Robert De Niro play a dying baseball player?
13   What was Tom Selleck's first film, in 1970?
14   Who starred as the editor of the newspaper in question in *All the President's Men*?
15   Who made his directorial debut with *Hide in Plain Sight* in 1980?
16   What was Peter Ustinov's first film as Agatha Christie's Belgian detective?
17   Which ex circus performer was Oscar-nominated for his role in *The Heartbreak Kid*?
18   Who did Dudley Moore replace in *10*?
19   What was Sting's first movie?
20   In 1970 who won the LA Silver Annual Handball Tournament?
21   Who was the first director to cast Goldie Hawn in a straight film?
22   In which movie did Jane Fonda play Lilian Hellman?
23   Which star of *Bugsy Malone* was once Pamela Anderson's fiancé?
24   In which movie did Richard Dreyfuss have his first romantic lead?
25   Stacy Keach replaced whom in *Fat City*?

Answers Pot Luck 20 (see Quiz 59)
1 Gymnastics. **2** John McTiernan. **3** 14. **4** Morton. **5** *48 Hours*. **6** Ian Ogilvy.
7 Adam Ant. **8** 150. **9** *Guiding Light*. **10** Criena Rohan's. **11** Donat. **12** Julie
Edwards (Julie Andrews). **13** Mia Farrow. **14** Red (National colour of Wales –
Richard Burton). **15** 'I'm Easy'. **16** John Belushi. **17** Irving Berlin. **18** 105 minutes.
19 Natalie Wood. **20** Sidney Poitier. **21** 93 minutes. **22** Muldoon. **23** *Scent of a Woman*. **24** Jane Powell. **25** Sheila McCarthy.

Answers – see page 276

1   What was his real first name?
2   Under what star sign was he born?
3   In which 1925 Von Stroheim movie did he appear?
4   Which of his wives was 14 years his senior?
5   Which movie studio turned him down in 1930?
6   In which movie, where he had second billing to Leslie Howard, did he make his name?
7   Which medals did he receive in World War II?
8   What was his first movie after the death of his third wife?
9   Who did he marry while making the movie where he played Rhett Butler?
10 Who directed him in his final movie?
11 In which movie did he star opposite the actress who 'wanted to be alone'?
12 Which studio 'borrowed' Gable for *It Happened One Night*?
13 Which production executive once screen tested him and said he looked like an ape?
14 Who was the mother of his only child, though he died before the child was born?
15 In which movie did he sing 'Puttin' on the Ritz'?
16 Who did he famously punch on the chin in *Night Nurse*?
17 In which two 1934 movies did he star with Myrna Loy?
18 Which movie had to be altered several times after his co-star died during filming?
19 On the set of which movie did he meet Carole Lombard?
20 Who was his first wife after he was widowed?
21 Which 1948 movie was a big-screen version of his Broadway play?
22 Who wrote the screenplay of his final movie?
23 His fourth wife was the widow of which actor?
24 In which movie did he play Peter Warne?
25 What was the name of his character in *Red Dust*?

Answers Headline Makers (see Quiz 60)
1 *Calponia harrisonford.* **2** Mia Farrow. **3** Hugh Grant & Liz Hurley. **4** *The Island of Doctor Moreau.* **5** Mae West. **6** Bridget Fonda (as Mandy Rice-Davies). **7** Zsa Zsa Gabor. **8** Philip Glass. **9** Melanie Griffith. **10** Marvin Hamlisch. **11** Howard Hughes. **12** Jill Ireland. **13** John Garfield. **14** Andy Garcia. **15** *Doombeach.* **16** Hedy Lamarr. **17** 4454813. **18** *Ulee's Gold* (1997). **19** Irene Dunne. **20** Somalia. **21** Greta Scacchi. **22** Felipe De Alba. **23** Audie Murphy. **24** Celeste Holm. **25** Bob Hope.

Answers – see page 273

1	At what sport did Richard Gere excel?
2	Who directed *The Hunt for Red October*?
3	How many people are killed in the gangster movie *Dick Tracy*?
4	Which Joe featured in *Speed*?
5	In which film does a character named Jack Cates appear?
6	Who played Chagall in the film *Death Becomes Her*?
7	Which singer appeared in *Slam Dance*?
8	Within ten minutes, how long does *The Firm* last?
9	Which soap did Kevin Bacon star in?
10	Whose novel is the film *The Delinquents* based on?
11	Which Peter featured in *The China Syndrome*?
12	Under what name has the Oscar nominee for *Victor/Victoria* written books for children?
13	Which actress links *A Wedding* and *Blind Terror*?
14	Elizabeth Taylor's fifth husband was buried wearing which colour?
15	Which song won Best Song Oscar for *Nashville*?
16	The movie Wired was based on whose life story?
17	About whom did Jerome Kern say, he 'has no place in American music. He is American music'?
18	Within five minutes, how long does *My Best Friend's Wedding* last?
19	*Brainstorm* and *Meteor* both feature which actress?
20	Who won the Best Actor Oscar for *Lilies of the Field*?
21	Within fifteen minutes, how long does *Look Who's Talking* last?
22	Which Patrick featured in *Starship Troopers*?
23	A character named Charlie Simms appeared in which film?
24	Who played opposite Howard Keel in *Seven Brides for Seven Brothers*?
25	Who played Samantha Copeland in the film *Die Hard 2*?

Answers – see page 274

1   What name was given to the species of spider named after the star of the Indiana Jones movies?
2   Whose 1997 autobiography was called *What Falls Away*?
3   In 1996 whose mattress from their holiday home fetched £550 at auction?
4   What was Brando's last movie of the 20th century?
5   Who said, 'Don't forget dear, I invented censorship'?
6   Who said the infamous, 'Well he would, wouldn't he' line in *Scandal*?
7   Whose husbands include George Sanders and Conrad Hilton?
8   Which composer, along with Richard Gere, founded the Tibet House in Greenwich Village in 1988?
9   Who fell in love with at 14, and later married, her mother's co-star of *The Harrad Experiment*?
10   Who was the first person to win three Oscars in one night?
11   Which director designed the plane called the Spruce Goose?
12   Which star of *Breakheart Pass* and *Death Wish II* was a spokeswoman for the American Cancer Society in the 80s?
13   How was Julius Garfinkle better known when he was blacklisted during the McCarthy era?
14   Which star of *The Untouchables* had fled the Castro regime aged five?
15   What was Glenda Jackson's final movie before she embarked on a political career?
16   Which actress invented an anti-jamming device for the Allies which laid the foundations for secure military communications?
17   What suspect number did Hugh Grant have when he was arrested with Divine Brown on Sunset Strip?
18   For which movie did Peter Fonda receive his first Oscar nomination after finding fame in *Easy Rider*?
19   Which Hollywood star was appointed by President Eisenhower as an alternate delegate to the UN's 12th General Assembly?
20   Audrey Hepburn made a highly publicized visit to which country for UNICEF just before her final illness took hold?
21   Who needed hospital treatment making *Turtle Beach* when a coconut fell on her head?
22   Whose marriage to Zsa Zsa Gabor lasted just eight days?
23   Which actor was the US's most decorated soldier ever?
24   Which star of *Oklahoma!* was knighted by King Olaf of Norway, the country of her birth, in 1979?
25   Which comedy star gave his name to a golfing Desert Classic?

Answers Clark Gable (see Quiz 58)

1 William. **2** Aquarius. **3** *The Merry Widow*. **4** Josephine Dillon. **5** MGM. **6** A *Free Soul*. **7** Distinguished Flying Cross & Air Medal. **8** *Adventure*. **9** Carole Lombard. **10** John Huston. **11** *Susan Lenox: Her Fall and Rise*. **12** Columbia. **13** Darryl F. Zanuck. **14** Kay Spreckels. **15** *Idiot's Delight*. **16** Barbara Stanwyck. **17** *Men in White; Manhattan Melodrama*. **18** *Saratoga* (with Jean Harlow). **19** *No Man of Her Own*. **20** Lady Sylvia Ashley. **21** *Command Decision*. **22** Arthur Miller. **23** Douglas Fairbanks. **24** *It Happened One Night*. **25** Dennis Carson.

Answers – see page 279

1	What was Frank Capra's third Oscar in five years, in 1938?
2	Which movie had seven nominations but lost out to *Forrest Gump*?
3	Which movie broke all records by winning in all categories for which it was nominated in 1988?
4	Which 1964 Cary Grant movie won Oscars for writers Peter Stone and Frank Tarloff?
5	Who was Oscar-nominated for music for *American Beauty*?
6	Whose original screenplay was nominated for *The Sixth Sense*?
7	Which future Mrs Janusz Kaminski won an Oscar the same night he did in 1993?
8	What was the second of Brando's four consecutive nominations between 1951 and 1954?
9	Who was the first British actor to win Best Actor?
10	Who was the first Best Actress, British born of British parents?
11	Ingrid Bergman won for which film, marking her return from Hollywood exile?
12	Which 60s Oscar-winner was narrated by Michael MacLiammoir?
13	Who was the first actress of British parents who won an Oscar twice?
14	Who is the third most frequent host of the Oscars ceremony?
15	Which 1962 winner studied medicine at the University of California?
16	In which three categories did *E.T.* win?
17	Which Sammy Cahn Oscar-winning song had the longest title?
18	John Mollo won an Oscar in *Star Wars* in which category?
19	Who in 1989 was the first director since 1932 to see his film win Best Picture but not to have an Oscar nomination himself?
20	Who won a Special Award for *The Little Kidnappers* aged 10?
21	What was the first film to be nominated for Best Special Effects?
22	Who was nominated for *Pasha* in the 60s movie with Julie Christie and Omar Sharif?
23	What was the second of Gregory Peck's three nominations between 1945 and 1947?
24	For which character was Dustin Hoffman nominated in 1969?
25	Who was the only winner of an Oscar and a BAFTA for *Platoon*?

Answers Box Office Successes (see Quiz 63)
1 Dodi Fayed. **2** *The Full Monty*. **3** Shelley Michelle. **4** Running for a bus.
5 Estelle Reiner. **6** Match. **7** Anthony Shaffer. **8** *Jaws: The Revenge*. **9** Charles
Fleischer. **10** Miami. **11** 1938. **12** Kelly Macdonald. **13** Carl Denham (*King Kong*). **14** Henry Hill. **15** 39. **16** Kieran Culkin. **17** The Funky Chicken.
18 Martin Brest. **19** Matthew Modine. **20** P.J. Hogan. **21** Amon Goeth. **22** 112
minutes. **23** Wai Lin. **24** Steve Martin. **25** Teacher.

Answers – see page 280

1   Who directed *Groundhog Day*?
2   In which film does a character named Bud Fox appear?
3   In the 50s epic, what colour horses pull Ben Hur's chariot during the race?
4   Which Josh featured in *Teenage Mutant Ninja Turtles*?
5   Within five minutes, how long does *Mrs Doubtfire* last?
6   Who did Ray Milland play in *National Velvet*?
7   How many crew members were there in the Nostromo in *Alien*?
8   What movie is being watched in *Home Alone 2: Lost in New York*?
9   Which British actor won an Oscar for *Separate Tables*?
10   Within fifteen minutes, how long does *Lost in Space* last?
11   Which Nicholas featured in *Chariots of Fire*?
12   Who was the first non-professional actor to win an acting Oscar?
13   Which actress links *Drop Dead Fred* and *Soapdish*?
14   Which actor was originally set to play Tom Cruise's role in *Born on the Fourth of July*?
15   Which writer directed *Night Breed* in 1990?
16   Which 1988 film had the highest fee ever for a commissioned script?
17   Who played Brandi in the film *Boyz N the Hood*?
18   Which 1990 film had the highest ratio ever of stunt men to actors?
19   Who appears as a gravedigger in the film *LA Story*?
20   The song 'Buttons and Bows' came from which movie?
21   Which Ron featured in *Swingers*?
22   Who won the Best Actress Oscar for *The Rose Tattoo*?
23   A character named Joe Turner appeared in which film?
24   Who directed *Gremlins*?
25   Who played Lucy Westenra in the film *Bram Stoker's Dracula*?

Answers The Silent Years (see Quiz 64)
1 *America*. **2** Pittsburgh. **3** *The Adventures of Kathlyn*. **4** Winsor McCay. **5** Bill Bitzer. **6** Archibald & Edgar Selwyn. **7** *Dream Street*. **8** *The Toll of the Sea*. **9** Columbia Pictures. **10** *The Power of Love*. **11** Santa Monica. **12** Thomas Ince. **13** *The Glorious Adventure*. **14** *Greed*. **15** Roxy Theater, New York. **16** Gilbert M. Anderson & George K. Spoor. **17** *A Study in Scarlet*. **18** Pathé Weekly. **19** *My Four Years in Germany*. **20** Electric Theatres. **21** *Tillie's Punctured Romance*. **22** *The Cure, Easy Street*. **23** Willis O'Brien. **24** *Birth of a Nation*. **25** Jack the Ripper.

Answers – see page 277

1   Which producer who tragically died in 1997 co-produced *Chariots of Fire*?
2   Which movie did *Titanic* overtake as a record UK earner?
3   Who was Julia Roberts's body double in the opening scene of *Pretty Woman*?
4   What is Hitchcock's cameo appearance in *North by Northwest*?
5   Who utters the famous line, 'I'll have what she's having' in *When Harry Met Sally*?
6   Who does Billy Zane play in *Back to the Future*?
7   Who adapted *Evil Under the Sun* for the big screen?
8   Which movie was Michael Caine filming so that he could not pick up his Oscar for *Hannah and Her Sisters*?
9   Who played Roger in *Who Framed Roger Rabbit*?
10   Where is *Scarface* set?
11   In which year did Indiana Jones ride the Hindenburg in *Indiana Jones and the Last Crusade*?
12   Who plays Diane in *Trainspotting*?
13   Which character said, in which movie, 'It wasn't the airplanes. It was beauty killed the beast'?
14   Upon whose life is *Goodfellas* based?
15   How many different hats does Madonna wear in *Evita*?
16   Who plays Fuller in *Home Alone*?
17   What type of dance does Paul Barber say he can do in *The Full Monty*?
18   Who directed *Scent of a Woman*?
19   Who was Oscar-nominated for *Married to the Mob*?
20   Who directed *My Best Friend's Wedding*?
21   What character did Ralph Fiennes play in *Schindler's List*?
22   Within fifteen minutes, how long does *Goldfinger* last?
23   Which character does Michelle Yeoh play in *Tomorrow Never Dies*?
24   Who adapted the play *Cyrano de Bergerac* into the movie *Roxanne*?
25   What was Captain John Miller's job before he entered the army in *Saving Private Ryan*?

Answers Oscar Trivia (see Quiz 61)
1 *You Can't Take it with You.* **2** *The Shawshank Redemption.* **3** *The Last Emperor.*
4 *Father Goose.* **5** Thomas Newman. **6** M. Night Shyamalan's. **7** Holly Hunter.
8 *Viva Zapata.* **9** George Arliss. **10** Julie Andrews. **11** *Anastasia.* **12** *Tom Jones.*
13 Olivia de Havilland. **14** Billy Crystal. **15** Gregory Peck. **16** Music; Sound;
Visual Effects. **17** *Three Coins in the Fountain.* **18** Costume. **19** Bruce Beresford.
20 Jon Whitley. **21** *Only Angels Have Wings.* **22** Tom Courtenay. **23** *The Yearling.* **24** Ratso Rizzo (*Midnight Cowboy*). **25** Oliver Stone.

Answers – see page 278

1	Which D.W. Griffith movie had the American Revolution as its subject?
2	Where did the first nickelodeon in the USA open?
3	What was the name of the first serial – in 13 parts – to be shown in cinemas?
4	Who created the cartoon *Gertie the Dinosaur* in 1914?
5	Who photographed *Birth of a Nation*?
6	Who founded Goldwyn Pictures with Samuel Goldfish?
7	Which movie did D.W. Griffith make in 1921 using synchronized sound on disc?
8	What was the first movie made in two-colour Technicolor?
9	What did the CBC Film Sales Corporation become in 1924?
10	What was the first feature to be made in 3D?
11	Where did Vitagraph open a studio in 1913?
12	Who set up Triangle Films with D.W. Griffith and Mack Sennett?
13	What was the first movie to be made in colour in England?
14	What was the epic *McTeague* called when it was finally released in 1923?
15	What was dubbed The Cathedral of the Motion Picture?
16	Who formed the Essanay company in Chicago?
17	What was the first Sherlock Holmes feature film, made in 1914, called?
18	What was the name of the first newsreel in the US?
19	What was Warner Brothers' first major feature?
20	What was the name of the first British cinema chain?
21	What was the name of Mack Sennett's first comedy feature?
22	What were Chaplin's first two two-reel comedies?
23	Who created the special effects for *The Lost World* which showed a dinosaur rampaging through London?
24	What was the first movie screened at the White House?
25	Who was Hitchcock's movie *The Lodger* about?

Answers Pot Luck 21 (see Quiz 62)
1 Harold Ramis. **2** *Wall Street*. **3** White. **4** Pais. **5** 125 minutes. **6** Don Birman.
7 Five. **8** *It's a Wonderful Life* (in Spanish). **9** David Niven. **10** 109 minutes.
11 Farrell. **12** Harold Russell (*Best Years of Our Lives*). **13** Carrie Fisher. **14** Al
Pacino. **15** Clive Barker. **16** *Rain Man*. **17** Nia Long. **18** *The Rookie*. **19** Rick
Moranis. **20** *The Paleface*. **21** Livingston. **22** Anna Magnani. **23** *Three Days of the Condor*. **24** Joe Dante. **25** Sadie Frost.

QUIZ 65 POT LUCK 22 ·· LEVEL THREE

Answers – see page 283

1 What was the first movie to have a budget of $100 million?
2 Who directed *GoldenEye*?
3 Who won the Best Actor Oscar for *Watch on the Rhine*?
4 What colour hat is Andie MacDowell wearing in her first scene in *Four Weddings and a Funeral*?
5 Which Kevin featured in *Sleeping with the Enemy*?
6 In the film *Baby Boom* who played Dr Jeff Cooper?
7 Who played Biff Tannen in the film *Back to the Future*?
8 Who won the Best Director Oscar for *All Quiet on the Western Front*?
9 Within ten minutes, how long does *Mad Max* last?
10 Which movie star released the 1960s album *Everything I've Got*?
11 Which John featured in *1941*?
12 Which actress links *Candleshoe* and *The Little Girl Who Lives Down the Lane*?
13 A character named Robert Gold appeared in which film?
14 The father of which director was first flute of the NBC Symphony Orchestra under Toscanini?
15 Who directed *Escape from New York*?
16 The title of which 70s film was the date of the death of James Dean?
17 What is the name of 'The Horse Whisperer'?
18 Which song won Best Song Oscar for *Here Comes the Groom*?
19 How many days did it take John Hughes to write *The Breakfast Club*?
20 What unbilled role does Jack Nicholson play in *Broadcast News*?
21 Within five minutes, how long does *Monty Python's Life of Brian* last?
22 Which Henry featured in *Clear and Present Danger*?
23 A character named Loretta Castorini appeared in which film?
24 In which year was *San Francisco* released?
25 Who directed *Grease*?

Answers Bette Davis (see Quiz 67)
1 Carl Laemmle, President of Universal. 2 *Cabin in Cotton*. 3 *Broken Dishes*. 4 *My Mother's Keeper*. 5 Empress Carlota Von Hapsburg. 6 *The Letter*. 7 George Cukor. 8 Peter Ustinov. 9 Bill Sampson. 10 Apple Annie (*Pocketful of Miracles*). 11 *Now Voyager*. 12 *The Petrified Forest*. 13 Goldwyn. 14 *The Private Lives of Elizabeth and Essex*. 15 *Whatever Happened to Baby Jane*? 16 Arthur Farnsworth. 17 American Film Institute's Lifetime Achievement Award. 18 George Arliss. 19 San Sebastian. 20 Catherine the Great. 21 *Old Acquaintance*. 22 Mildred the waitress. 23 *Hush Hush Sweet Charlotte*. 24 *The Lonely Life*. 25 ' She did it the hard way'.

Answers – see page 284

1   Who cast Cher in the play, then movie of *Come Back to the Five and Dime, Jimmy Dean, Jimmy Dean*?

2   How old was Richard Gere when he played a young recruit in *An Officer and a Gentleman*?

3   Which actress's husband designed the Olympic Gateway for the 1984 Los Angeles Olympics?

4   Who directed and starred in *The Four Seasons* in 1981?

5   For which 1985 film did Gerard Depardieu win Best Actor at Venice?

6   Which actor's voice was dubbed by Rich Little in *Curse of the Pink Panther* because he was so ill?

7   For which role was Willem Dafoe an Oscar-winner for *Platoon*?

8   Who did Faye Dunaway play in *Network*?

9   In the movie based on *Les Liaisons Dangereuses* who was Glenn Close?

10   As which character in *Frances* did Kevin Costner have one speaking line?

11   In which 80s movie did Sammy Davis Jr make a comeback?

12   Who played Mrs La Motta in *Raging Bull*?

13   Who did Schwarzenegger's co-star in *Twins* marry after the movie was finished?

14   Which Oscar-winner for *Cocoon* shared the Best Actor prize at Venice for *Things Change*?

15   Who came to international attention after appearing in Almodovar's *Women on the Verge of a Nervous Breakdown*?

16   Who played Bogey in *The Man with Bogart's Face*?

17   As which character did Kirstie Alley make her movie debut?

18   What was the name of Alan Rickman's character in *Die Hard*?

19   Who was the only female lead actress in Barry Levinson's directorial debut?

20   Who graduated from child to adult acting roles as Shirley Muldowney in *Heart Like a Wheel*?

21   Who plays the author of the book in *The Man Who Would Be King*?

22   In *Plenty* which British actress/comedienne was Meryl Streep's eccentric friend?

23   For which movie did Nicolas Cage have two teeth pulled out?

24   In *A Royal Love Story*, who played Princess Diana?

25   Who sang with Joan Jett on *Light of Day* in 1986?

Answers Pot Luck 23 (see Quiz 68)
1 River Phoenix (31.10.93). **2** Penny Marshall. **3** *How the West Was Won*.
4 Claude. **5** 100 minutes. **6** I Got Worms. **7** John Huston. **8** Bud Fox . **9** Edson.
10 Nicholas Kazan. **11** Steve Guttenberg. **12** *Along Came a Spider*. **13** *The Wind and the Lion*. **14** Whitfield. **15** Two hours. **16** Leo. **17** Alan Metter. **18** Dickey.
19 'It Might As Well Be Spring'. **20** Mrs Canby. **21** Shirley Booth. **22** Roland Emmerich. **23** Anderson. **24** *Aria*. **25** *My Own Private Idaho*.

Answers – see page 281

1   Who said she had as much sex appeal as Slim Summerville?
2   In which movie did she say, 'I'd like to kiss ya but I just washed my hair!'?
3   In which show did she make her Broadway debut?
4   What was the name of the autobiography written by her daughter?
5   What role did she play in *Juarez*?
6   What was her third Oscar nomination in the run of five starting with *Jezebel*?
7   Which director fired her on her first professional engagement?
8   Who played the sleuth in the Agatha Christie movie she made?
9   Which role did her husband play in *All About Eve*?
10   Who did she play in her 1961 movie directed by Frank Capra?
11   In which movie did she say, 'Jerry, don't let's ask for the moon; we have the stars'?
12   Which movie did she make after receiving her first Oscar?
13   With which studio did she fail a screen test before signing for Universal?
14   What was the first movie in which she played a Tudor queen?
15   For which movie did she receive her tenth and final Oscar nomination?
16   By which husband was she widowed?
17   In 1977 she became the first woman to be honoured with which award?
18   Whose leading lady was she in *The Man Who Played God*?
19   Which film festival was she returning from when her terminal cancer claimed her life?
20   In *John Paul Jones* she played a cameo role as whom?
21   In which movie did she say, 'There comes a time in every woman's life where the only thing that helps is a glass of champagne'?
22   What was her name and her profession in *Of Human Bondage*?
23   Which was her next hit movie after her tenth Oscar nomination?
24   What was the name of her first autobiography?
25   What did she say would be put on her tombstone?

Answers Pot Luck 22 (see Quiz 65)

1 *True Lies*. **2** Martin Campbell. **3** Paul Lukas. **4** Navy Blue. **5** Anderson. **6** Sam Shepard. **7** Thomas F. Wilson. **8** Lewis Milestone. **9** 90 minutes. **10** Honor Blackman. **11** Belushi. **12** Jodie Foster. **13** *Darling*. **14** Francis Ford Coppola. **15** John Carpenter. **16** *September 30th 1955*. **17** Tom Booker. **18** 'In the Cool, Cool, Cool of the Evening'. **19** Three. **20** An anchorman. **21** 93 minutes. **22** Czerny. **23** *Moonstruck*. **24** 1936. **25** Randal Kleiser.

Answers – see page 282

1   Which actor died on the same day as film director Federico Fellini?
2   Who directed *Big*?
3   A character named Linus Rawlings appeared in which film?
4   What did the C stand for in W.C. Fields's name?
5   Within five minutes, how long does *Love Story* last?
6   What is the name of the shop that the two characters from *Dumb and Dumber* want to open?
7   Who said, 'I never killed an actor. Nearly lost a few'?
8   What was the name of Charlie Sheen's character in *Wall Street*?
9   Which Richard featured in *Do the Right Thing*?
10   Who wrote the screenplay for the film *At Close Range*?
11   *High Spirits* and *Diner* starred which actor?
12   What was the original title for the film *Arachnophobia*?
13   In which film did the splendidly named Mulay Ahmed Mohammed el Raisuli the Magnificent appear?
14   Which Mitchell featured in *My Cousin Vinny*?
15   To the nearest hour, how long does *LA Confidential* last?
16   What was the first name of Albert Finney's character in *Miller's Crossing*?
17   Who directed the film *Back to School*?
18   Which James featured in *Deliverance*?
19   Which song from *State Fair* won an Oscar?
20   Who did Kathy Bates play in the film *Arthur 2: On the Rocks*?
21   Who won the Best Actress Oscar for *Come Back, Little Sheba*?
22   Who directed *Godzilla*?
23   Which Jeff starred in *Clerks*?
24   Which film was Bridget Fonda's debut film?
25   In which film does a character named Mike Waters appear?

Answers 1980s Stars (see Quiz 66)
1 Robert Altman. **2** 30. **3** Anjelica Huston. **4** Alan Alda. **5** *Police*. **6** David Niven. **7** Sergeant Elias. **8** Diana Christensen. **9** Marquise de Merteuil. **10** Luther Adler. **11** *Tap*. **12** Cathy Moriarty. **13** John Travolta. **14** Don Ameche. **15** Antonio Banderas. **16** Robert Sacchi. **17** Lt Saavik (*Star Trek II*). **18** Hans Gruber. **19** Ellen Barkin (*Diner*). **20** Bonnie Bedelia. **21** Christopher Plummer. **22** Tracey Ullman. **23** *Birdy*. **24** Catherine Oxenberg. **25** Michael J. Fox.

Answers – see page 287

1   What was the name of the novel on which *Goodfellas* was based?
2   Which conflict is depicted in *Land and Freedom*?
3   Who does John Wayne play in *Sands of Iwo Jima*?
4   In which movie based on his own book did Audie Murphy play himself?
5   Who was the target in the 90s remake of *The Day of the Jackal*?
6   Which Hitchcock remake had 'Que Sera Sera' as its theme song?
7   Who drove the booby-trapped bus in *Speed*?
8   *You Only Live Once* was partly based on the life of which duo?
9   How many *Die Hard* movies were made before Samuel L. Jackson joined as Bruce Willis's sidekick?
10   Which women have an action-packed fight in *Destry Rides Again*?
11   Which Shakespeare play was turned into a gangland movie in *Men of Respect*?
12   In terms of admissions, what was the least successful Bond movie?
13   To the nearest hour, how long does *Dirty Harry* last?
14   Which '*Die Hard* on a plane' type movie was criticized as being as 'fresh as an in-flight meal'?
15   Who took next billing after Goldie Hawn in *Sugarland Express*?
16   Who plays the arch enemy in *French Connection II*?
17   Shaun Ryder's movie debut was in which movie?
18   Which race was the setting for *Cannonball*?
19   What were the two remakes of *The Asphalt Jungle* called?
20   Which movie opens with the line 'I believe in America'?
21   Who replaced Steve McQueen and Ali McGraw in a 90s remake of an action thriller?
22   Which two actors rejected *Bridge on the River Kwai* before Alec Guinness got the lead role?
23   Where did the boat chase take place in *Puppet on a Chain*?
24   Which character did Sylvester Stallone play in *Cop Land*?
25   Who directed the chariot race in *Ben Hur*?

Answers Pot Luck 24 (see Quiz 71)
1 *Rebecca*. **2** Meg Tilly. **3** Terry Gilliam. **4** Fats Domino. **5** 110. **6** Marley.
7 *Sunset Boulevard*. **8** George Stevens. **9** *Taps*. **10** Hulce. **11** 93 minutes.
12 Prahka Lasa. **13** Lerner. **14** Paul Hogan. **15** Kissy Suzuki. **16** Joel Coen.
17 *Hud*. **18** Nancy Travis. **19** Gene Hackman. **20** 1937. **21** David Warner.
22 Francis. **23** 129 minutes. **24** Tess Harper. **25** Adrian Lyne.

Answers – see page 288

1	What was John Barrymore's pet vulture called?
2	Who found fame in *Beau Brummel* opposite John Barrymore, who became her lover?
3	Who played Dr Kildare in a series of 30s films?
4	Who was Oscar-nominated for *Jezebel* and *White Banners*?
5	Who said, 'They used to photograph Shirley Temple through gauze. They should photograph me through linoleum'?
6	Who played the title role in *The Mighty Barnum*?
7	Jean Harlow died during the making of which movie?
8	Which former child star was one of the Three Smart Girls?
9	Who was fired as Norman Maine in the 1934 version of *A Star Is Born*?
10	Who was Hitler's favourite actress?
11	Which other Bennett sisters acted along with Constance?
12	Which comedienne's husbands included the promoter of the Todd AO wide screen system?
13	How was Etienne Pelissier de Bujac better known?
14	*The Prisoner of Zenda* was made from whose book?
15	How did *Gone with the Wind* star Butterfly McQueen meet her death?
16	Who played Bottom in *A Midsummer Night's Dream*?
17	Who said, 'I was shot to death in six films between 1931 and 1937'?
18	In which book did Sir Cecil Beaton describe his deep romance with Greta Garbo?
19	What was Carole Lombard's real name?
20	Which film star wrote the novel *Today Is Tonight*?
21	What did Irene Dunne receive her second Oscar nomination for?
22	Which actor directed the two movies which ended the career of John Gilbert?
23	In which movie did Jeanette MacDonald and Nelson Eddy first appear together?
24	What was the second of Spencer Tracy's three Oscar nominations between 1936 and 1938?
25	Who won the 400 yards freestyle gold at the 1932 Olympics?

Answers Unforgettables (see Quiz 72)
1 Jean Harlow's. 2 *Father Goose*. 3 Dorothy Stratten. 4 Rudy Vallee. 5 Peggy Middleton. 6 Susan Blanchard. 7 Harrison Ford. 8 Kathryn Grayson. 9 *The Cat and the Canary*. 10 Ray Milland. 11 Tom Mix. 12 *Green Grow the Rushes*. 13 Gloria Swanson. 14 Dirk Bogarde. 15 Charles Farrell. 16 *Where's the Rest of Me?* 17 Calcutta (he was born in Omaha). 18 Drowned. 19 South Africa. 20 Orson Welles. 21 His pet Airedale dog. 22 *The Big Broadcast*. 23 James Stewart. 24 Sir Noel Coward. 25 Bing Crosby.

Answers – see page 285

1	What movie is showing within the film *Desperately Seeking Susan*?
2	Which actress was to play the role of Constanze in the film *Amadeus* before Elizabeth Berridge took over?
3	Who directed *The Fisher King*?
4	Which singer appeared in *Every Which Way You Can*?
5	Did *A Fish Called Wanda* last around 90, 110 or 130 minutes?
6	Which John featured in *Love Story*?
7	In which 1950 movie did Cecil B. de Mille appear on screen?
8	Which George won the Best Director Oscar for *Giant*?
9	What was Sean Penn's first film, in 1981?
10	Which Tom featured in *Mary Shelley's Frankenstein*?
11	Within ten minutes how long does *Honey, I Shrunk the Kids* last?
12	Which character in the film *All of Me* was played by Richard Libertini?
13	Which Michael featured in *Godzilla*?
14	Who wrote the screenplay for the film *Almost an Angel*?
15	What was the name of the Bond girl in *You Only Live Twice*?
16	Who directed *The Big Lebowski*?
17	In which film does a character named Lon Bannon appear?
18	Who was the main adult female actress in *Three Men and a Baby*?
19	*Bonnie and Clyde* and *Young Frankenstein* both featured which actor?
20	In which year was *Lost Horizon* with Ronald Colman released?
21	Who played the villain in the 80s movie *Time Bandits*?
22	What is the first name of 'Baby' Houseman in *Dirty Dancing*?
23	Within five minutes, how long does *The Lost World: Jurassic Park* last?
24	Who plays Rosa Lee in *Tender Mercies*?
25	Who directed *Flashdance*?

Answers Action (see Quiz 69)
1 *Wiseguy*. **2** Spanish Civil War. **3** Sergeant Stryker. **4** *To Hell and Back*. **5** The First Lady. **6** *The Man Who Knew Too Much*. **7** Sandra Bullock. **8** Bonnie & Clyde. **9** Two. **10** Marlene Dietrich & Una Merkel. **11** *Macbeth*. **12** *The Man with the Golden Gun*. **13** 2 hours (102 mins). **14** *Passenger 57*. **15** Ben Johnson. **16** Fernando Rey. **17** *The Avengers*. **18** Trans American Grand Prix. **19** *The Badlanders; Cairo*. **20** *The Godfather*. **21** Alec Baldwin & Kim Basinger. **22** Noel Coward & Charles Laughton. **23** Amsterdam. **24** Freddy Heflin. **25** Andrew Marton.

Answers – see page 286

1   According to Jack Warner, Rin Tin Tin died with his head on whose lap?
2   What was Cary Grant's penultimate movie?
3   *The Killing of the Unicorn* was Peter Bogdanovich's book about the murder of which of his lovers?
4   Alice Faye was a singer in whose band?
5   What was Yvonne De Carlo's real name?
6   Which wife of Henry Fonda was a stepdaughter of Oscar Hammerstein II?
7   Which namesake of an 80s/90s star appeared in *The Mysterious Mrs M* in 1917?
8   How was Zelma Hedrick better known?
9   In which movie did Bob Hope say, 'I get goose pimples. Even my goose pimples get goose pimples'?
10 Which Welsh-born actor's autobiography was called *Wide Eyed in Babylon*?
11 Who was described as being as elegant on a horse as Fred Astaire on a dance floor?
12 What was Richard Burton's last UK film before turning to Hollywood?
13 Whose marriage to Wallace Beery lasted just three weeks?
14 Which film star wrote the novel *West of Sunset*?
15 Who played opposite Janet Gaynor 12 times?
16 What was Ronald Reagan's autobiography called?
17 Where did Marlon Brando's first press release say he had spent the first six months of his life?
18 How did Natalie Wood die?
19 Where was Basil Rathbone born?
20 Whose was the voice narrating Agatha Christie's *And Then There Were None*?
21 Who did John Wayne get his nickname 'Duke' from?
22 In which movie did Bob Hope find his theme tune?
23 Who collected Gary Cooper's final Oscar?
24 Which British writer, actor and director had two bit parts in D.W. Griffith's *Hearts of the World* in 1918?
25 Who died in 1977 stipulating that his sons could not touch a trust fund of money until they were 65?

Answers – see page 291

1 Which movie had the ad line, 'You don't assign him to cases – you just turn him loose'?
2 Which former teen star made his debut in *Over the Edge*?
3 Who ate dog droppings in *Pink Flamingos*?
4 What was Mark Hamill's follow-up to *Star Wars*?
5 Which role did Al Pacino play in the 1975 Sidney Lumet movie?
6 *The Taking of Pelham One Two Three* is about the hijack of what?
7 Who played Valentino in *The World's Greatest Lover*?
8 In which state does the action start in *The Sting*?
9 Which movie had the ad line, 'The damnedest thing you ever saw'?
10 What's the name of the prostitute played by Jane Fonda in *Klute*?
11 Who played Sherlock Holmes in *The Seven Per Cent Solution*?
12 To the nearest hour, how long does *The Andromeda Strain* last?
13 What was the first film to use Dolby sound?
14 Who played Moses in *Moses*?
15 Who did Robert Mitchum play in *Ryan's Daughter*?
16 Who made the film of the biggest hippy festival ever?
17 Which flop prompted its producer to declare, 'It would have been cheaper to lower the Atlantic'?
18 In which movie did Burgess Meredith play the devil?
19 Who was Jugs in *Mother, Jugs and Speed*?
20 What was the first of Jack Nicholson's three nominations between 1973 and 1975?
21 Who was originally cast to play Evelyn Mulwray in *Chinatown* before she divorced the movie's producer?
22 In which 1972 movie did Stacey Keach play a boxer?
23 *Bound for Glory* was about which star?
24 Where and when was *The Man Who Would Be King* set?
25 Who played Carole Lombard in *Gable and Lombard*?

Answers Pot Luck 25 (see Quiz 75)
1 Murphy. 2 Arizona. 3 *The Inn of the Sixth Happiness*. 4 Luc Besson. 5 *Search for Tomorrow*. 6 118 minutes. 7 Richard Adams. 8 Sylvester Stallone. 9 James Foley. 10 Cliff Robertson. 11 Nurse Costello. 12 *The Big Lebowski*. 13 Larry Hagman. 14 *Madam Sousatzka*. 15 Hall. 16 126 minutes. 17 Oliver Stone. 18 Elliott. 19 1954. 20 Sally Field. 21 *The Right Stuff*. 22 Jane Wyman. 23 Tom. 24 Sydney Pollack. 25 Emmerich.

Answers – see page 292

1. What is his full real name?
2. Which character did he win his first Oscar for?
3. What was the name of the second Oscar-nominated film he made for Billy Wilder?
4. Who directed him in *Days of Wine and Roses*?
5. Under what star sign was he born?
6. Which director described him as somewhere between Chaplin and Cary Grant?
7. For which 1959 film was he Oscar-nominated and a BAFTA winner?
8. Which movie also featured Shirley MacLaine as Miss Kubelik?
9. Who did he play in *The Odd Couple*?
10. Who starred in and produced *The China Syndrome*?
11. What was billed as 'the greatest comedy ever made'?
12. Who won the Oscar for musical director in his film *Irma La Douce*?
13. What was the name of his character in *Avanti!*?
14. Who was the spouse in the movie whose title suggested how she could be dispensed with?
15. He was the son of a president of a company that made what?
16. What film was his directorial debut?
17. To which 1957 movie did he contribute a song?
18. For which two movies was he named Best Actor at Cannes?
19. Whose estranged father did he play in *Short Cuts*?
20. Where is his son missing, in *Missing*?
21. In which 1980 movie did he recreate his Broadway role as a dying playwright?
22. In which 1986 movie did he co-star with his wife and son?
23. Which movie was a remake of the French *L'Emmerdeur*?
24. In which movie did he play opposite Walter Matthau, who played Walter Burns?
25. At which film festival did he receive the Best Actor award for *Glengarry Glen Ross*?

Answers Biopics (see Quiz 76)
1 Roshan Seth (Nehru). 2 J. Edgar Hoover (Bob Hoskins). 3 Walter Brennan.
4 Vincent van Gogh. 5 Missionary Gladys Aylward. 6 Iain Softley. 7 Beethoven.
8 Lionel Barrymore. 9 Billie Burke. 10 Calamity Jane. 11 Ruth Ellis (last woman to be hanged in Britain). 12 Lilian Roth. 13 Frank Loesser. 14 David Bowie.
15 Ambrose Bierce. 16 C.S. Lewis & Joy Gresham. 17 Anthony Hopkins (Nixon).
18 James Brolin. 19 *Bonnie and Clyde*. 20 Gary Busey. 21 The Dalai Lama.
22 Stephen Fry (Oscar Wilde). 23 Kafka. 24 Beethoven. 25 Phineas T. Barnum.

Answers – see page 289

1   Which Michael featured in *Manhattan*?
2   To which American state is Janet Leigh's car registered in *Psycho*?
3   What was Robert Donat's final film?
4   Who directed *The Fifth Element*?
5   Which soap did Kevin Kline star in?
6   Within five minutes, how long does *Logan's Run* last?
7   Who did Michael Douglas play in *The China Syndrome*?
8   Who is Q. Moonblood better known as on the credits of *First Blood*?
9   Who directed the film *After Dark, My Sweet*?
10 Who won the Best Actor Oscar for *Charly*?
11 What was the name of Julie Kavner's character in *Awakenings*?
12 In which movie does Jeff Bridges play The Dude?
13 *Superman* and *Nixon* both featured which actor?
14 For which movie did Shirley MacLaine win Best Actress at the Venice Film Festival in 1988?
15 Which Albert featured in *Malcolm X*?
16 Within ten minutes, how long does *Good Will Hunting* last?
17 Whose directing did Tom Cruise say was 'like seeing Bruce Springsteen live for the first time'?
18 Which Sam featured in *Tombstone*?
19 In which year was *Sabrina* first released?
20 Which movie star released an album called *The Star of the Flying Nun* in 1967?
21 In which film does a character named Chuck Yeager appear?
22 Who won the Best Actress Oscar for *Johnny Belinda*?
23 What was the name of Gabriel Byrne's character in *Miller's Crossing*?
24 Who directed *The Firm*?
25 Which Noah featured in *The Truman Show*?

Answers 1970s (see Quiz 73)
1 *Dirty Harry*. 2 Matt Dillon. 3 Divine. 4 *Corvette Summer*. 5 Sonny Wortzik (*Dog Day Afternoon*). 6 Subway train. 7 Gene Wilder. 8 Illinois. 9 *Nashville*. 10 Bree Daniels. 11 Nicol Williamson. 12 Two hours (131 mins). 13 *A Clockwork Orange*. 14 Burt Lancaster. 15 Charles Shaughnessy. 16 Michael Wadleigh (*Woodstock*). 17 *Raise the Titanic*. 18 *The Sentinel*. 19 Raquel Welch. 20 *The Last Detail*. 21 Ali McGraw. 22 *Fat City*. 23 Woody Guthrie. 24 Afghanistan in the 1880s. 25 Jill Clayburgh.

Answers – see page 290

1   Who played the future Indira Gandhi's father in *Gandhi*?
2   Which role did the star of *Mona Lisa* and *Who Framed Roger Rabbit?* play in *Nixon*?
3   Who played Judge Roy Bean in *The Westerner*?
4   Who was the subject of *Lust for Life*?
5   Whose story was told in *Inn of the Sixth Happiness* with Ingrid Bergman?
6   Who directed the 1995 biopic about the Beatles' early days in Hamburg?
7   Who was the subject of *New Wine*, with Albert Basserman?
8   Who did Errol Flynn play in *Too Much Too Soon*?
9   What was the name of Mrs Florenz Ziegfeld, as played by Myrna Loy in the biopic?
10   Who did Ellen Barkin play in *Wild Bill*?
11   *Dance with a Stranger* was about whom?
12   Which singer did Susan Hayward play in *I'll Cry Tomorrow*?
13   Who wrote the songs in the Danny Kaye movie about Hans Christian Andersen?
14   Who played Andy Warhol in *Basquiat*?
15   Which writer did Gregory Peck play in *Old Gringo*?
16   Who are the two main characters in *Shadowlands*?
17   Who played the first US president to resign while in office?
18   Who played Clark Gable in *Gable and Lombard*?
19   Which movie opens with the line, 'Hey boy, what you doin' with my momma's car'?
20   Who played the title role of the rock singer who sang 'Peggy Sue'?
21   *Kundun* is Martin Scorsese's biography of whom?
22   Who played the title role in the 90s movie about the author of *The Importance of Being Earnest*?
23   Who was the subject of the movie in which Jeremy Irons starred after he won his first Oscar?
24   Which composer did Gary Oldman play in *Immortal Beloved*?
25   Who did Wallace Beery play in *A Lady's Morals* in 1930?

Answers – see page 295

1   Which studio did he make his first professional movies with?
2   What was Amblin's logo?
3   Who gave Spielberg his first professional contract?
4   With whom did he found Dreamworks?
5   What was his 1989 movie a remake of?
6   What was the name of the police chief in his first blockbuster?
7   Who was his wife when he made *Always*?
8   Under what star sign was he born?
9   Who does he say he is always thinking of when he is directing?
10   In which 1980 movie did he have a cameo role?
11   On whose eyes were *E.T.*'s eyes based?
12   Who wrote the book on which his first Oscar-winner as director was based?
13   Which movie did he reissue as *The Special Edition* because he was initially dissatisfied with it?
14   Which Indiana Jones movie did Mrs Spielberg star in?
15   With which movie did he win an amateur contest aged 13?
16   On whose novel was his 1987 movie based?
17   What was his first film after *Close Encounters of the Third Kind*?
18   Which company did he form in 1984?
19   What was his 70s debut as a feature-film director?
20   Which animated features did he make prior to *Who Framed Roger Rabbit*?
21   What was the second film which earned him a Best Director Oscar nomination?
22   Who wrote the book on which his first adult movie was based?
23   Which award did he win at the 1987 Oscar ceremony?
24   At which film festival was his first professional movie shown?
25   His sister won her first Oscar in what capacity for which movie?

Answers Hollywood Heyday (see Quiz 79)
1 Doris Day. **2** *The Ghost Breakers*. **3** Joan Crawford. **4** David Niven. **5** *Major Barbara*. **6** Bing Crosby. **7** Ginger Rogers. **8** Spottiswoode Aitken. **9** *Private Worlds*. **10** Katharine Hepburn. **11** Jean Arthur. **12** Joseph Cotten. **13** Betty Grable. **14** Joan Crawford. **15** George Cukor. **16** *Monkey Business*. **17** Swedish. **18** Brigadier General. **19** Sri Lanka (Ceylon). **20** Charlotte Bronte. **21** Tallulah Bankhead. **22** Colin Clive. **23** Bing Crosby. **24** Peter Lorre. **25** June Allyson.

Answers – see page 296

1   What colour T-shirt is James Dean wearing in *Rebel Without a Cause* during the car race?

2   What is Private Benjamin's first name?

3   Who formed his own company, Bryna Productions, in 1955?

4   Which movie star released a single called 'Do It to Me' in 1979?

5   Who won the Best Actor Oscar for *A Double Life*?

6   Which Shelley featured in *Labyrinth*?

7   Who won the Best Director Oscar for *The Quiet Man*?

8   Which actress links *Cherry 2000* and *Close to Eden*?

9   The final car chase in *What's Up Doc* takes place in which city?

10   The songs 'On the Atchison', 'Topeka', and 'The Santa Fe' came from which movie?

11   Who played Sera in *Leaving Las Vegas*?

12   From 1936 to 1950 Judy Garland was with which studio?

13   Who wrote the screenplay for *Casualties of War*?

14   Onna White won a Special Award in 1968 for doing what in *Oliver!*?

15   Which Noah featured in *Shine*?

16   Who played Ronald Miller in the film *Can't Buy Me Love*?

17   To the nearest hour, how long does *The Graduate* last?

18   Which song won Best Song Oscar for *A Hole in the Head*?

19   What sort of car did Woody Allen have in *Sleeper*?

20   What is the first name of Robert Redford, who uses his middle name in the movies?

21   Who won the Best Actress Oscar for *The Heiress*?

22   *Star Wars* and *Kafka* both starred which actor?

23   Within five minutes, how long does *Jurassic Park* last?

24   Who directed *Face/Off*?

25   Which Kirsten featured in *Doctor Dolittle*?

Answers Woody Allen (see Quiz 80)

1 Stewart. **2** Marshall Brickman. **3** *Zelig.* **4** *Getting Even; Without Feathers; Side Effects.* **5** *Don't Drink the Water.* **6** Orion. **7** Ralph Rosenblum. **8** Alvy Singer. **9** Meryl Streep (*Manhattan*). **10** *The New Yorker.* **11** Yale; Michael Murphy. **12** Bette Midler. **13** Mira Sorvino (*Mighty Aphrodite*). **14** *The Purple Rose of Cairo.* **15** *A Midsummer Night's Sex Comedy.* **16** Maureen O'Sullivan & Mia Farrow (*Hannah and Her Sisters*). **17** Louise Lasser. **18** *Husbands and Wives.* **19** Michael's Pub, New York. **20** *Interiors.* **21** Sagittarius. **22** *Stardust Memories.* **23** Jimmy Bond. **24** Satchel Paige. **25** Tony Lacey.

Answers – see page 293

1	Who was the only actress to be billed above James Cagney in 30 years of film-making?
2	In which movie did Bob Hope say, 'The girls call me pilgrim because every time I dance with one I make a little progress'?
3	Who was known during part of her career as Billie Cassin?
4	Which film star wrote the novel *Once Over Lightly*?
5	What was Deborah Kerr's first film?
6	Who said his epitaph should be, 'He was an average guy who could carry a tune'?
7	Whose first movie was *Campus Sweethearts* with Rudy Vallee?
8	Who played Dr Cameron in D.W. Griffith's *Birth of a Nation*?
9	What was Claudette Colbert's next Oscar nomination after her win with *It Happened One Night*?
10	Who won a bronze medal for skating aged 14 at Madison Square Garden?
11	Which actress, born Gladys Georgianna Greene, made her screen debut in John Ford's *Cameo Kirby*?
12	Who debuted in *Too Much Johnson* after starring on Broadway opposite Katharine Hepburn in *The Philadelphia Story*?
13	Sam Goldwyn changed which star's name to Frances Dean?
14	Which Hollywood star married the head of Pepsi Cola in 1956?
15	Which director was fired from the set of *Gone with the Wind* only ten days into production?
16	In which movie did the Marx Brothers hide in barrels of kippered herring?
17	What nationality is Warner Oland, a screen Charlie Chan?
18	Which rank did James Stewart reach in the US Air Force?
19	Where was Merle Oberon born?
20	Who did Olivia de Havilland play in *Devotion*?
21	Which star of Hitchcock's *Lifeboat* was a daughter of a Speaker of the US House of Representatives?
22	Who played Frankenstein in the 30s classic?
23	Whose autobiography was called *Call Me Lucky*?
24	Which movie star is named in Al Stewart's song 'The Year of the Cat'?
25	Who played a role in *Best Foot Forward* on Broadway in 1943 which she recreated in the movie two years later?

Answers Steven Spielberg (see Quiz 77)

1 Universal. **2** Bicycle from *E.T.* **3** Sidney Sheinberg. **4** David Geffen & Jeffrey Katzenberg. **5** *A Guy Named Joe* (remade as *Always*). **6** Martin Brody. **7** Kate Capshaw. **8** Sagittarius. **9** The audience. **10** *The Blues Brothers*. **11** Einstein's. **12** Thomas Keneally. **13** *Close Encounters of the Third Kind*. **14** *Indiana Jones and the Temple of Doom*. **15** *Escape to Nowhere*. **16** J.G. Ballard (*Empire of the Sun*). **17** *1941*. **18** Amblin. **19** *The Sugarland Express*. **20** *An American Tail; The Land Before Time*. **21** *Raiders of the Lost Ark*. **22** Alice Walker (*The Color Purple*). **23** Irving G. Thalberg Award. **24** Atlanta. **25** Screenwriter, *Big*.

Answers – see page 294

1	What is his middle name?
2	With whom did he share his Oscar for the screenplay of *Annie Hall*?
3	In which movie did he play a human chameleon in 1983?
4	Which three books did he write in the 60s?
5	In the 60s what did he write for Broadway along with *Play it Again Sam*?
6	Which film studio did he join after leaving United Artists?
7	Who was the editor on his first film as director?
8	What was Allen's character called in his 1977 movie with Diane Keaton?
9	In his last film of the 70s, who played his ex-wife who had left him for another woman?
10	For which newspaper did he write comic essays in the 60s?
11	In *Manhattan*, what is the name of his best friend, and who plays him?
12	Who was his co-star in *Scenes from a Mall*?
13	Who won the Oscar for the 1995 movie for which he was nominated as writer?
14	For which 80s movie did he win the International Critics Prize at Cannes?
15	What was the name of his first film with Mia Farrow?
16	Which famous mother and daughter starred in his film for which Michael Caine won an Oscar?
17	Who was his wife when he made *What's Up, Tiger Lily*??
18	Which film was released soon after his affair with his partner's adopted daughter was exposed?
19	Where did he perform for several decades as a jazz clarinetist?
20	What was his first straight drama called?
21	What is his star sign?
22	What was his last film for United Artists?
23	Which character did he play in a James Bond movie?
24	After whom did he name his natural son with Mia Farrow?
25	In *Annie Hall* what is the name of the pop singer played by Paul Simon?

Answers Pot Luck 26 (see Quiz 78)
1 White. **2** Judy. **3** Kirk Douglas. **4** Britt Ekland. **5** Ronald Colman.
6 Thompson. **7** John Ford. **8** Melanie Griffith. **9** San Francisco. **10** *The Harvey Girls*. **11** Elisabeth Shue. **12** MGM. **13** David Rabe. **14** Choreography.
15 Taylor. **16** Patrick Dempsey. **17** Two hours. **18** 'High Hopes'. **19** Volkswagen Beetle. **20** Charles. **21** Olivia de Havilland. **22** Sir Alec Guinness. **23** 127 minutes. **24** John Woo. **25** Wilson.

Answers – see page 299

1   At what sport did Chevy Chase excel?
2   In which film did the character named Kimberly Wells appear?
3   Who directed *The Empire Strikes Back*?
4   Which Matt featured in *The Driver*?
5   Which entertainer died on the same day as muppet maestro Jim Henson?
6   What was the name of Michael O'Keefe's character in *Caddyshack*?
7   Within five minutes, how long does *Jungle Book* last?
8   *Flash II* and *Village of the Damned* both starred which actor?
9   Which Jeremy features in *Saving Private Ryan*?
10   Who plays Miss Millie in the film *The Color Purple*?
11   Who changed Bernie for Tony in his first film, *Criss Cross*?
12   Which actor played Elliott in *E.T.*?
13   Who said, 'The characters I play have a need to be cuddled'?
14   Which British actor said, 'Eight times my heart stopped'?
15   Who wrote the screenplay for *Clean and Sober*?
16   Who played Gregory Peck's feeble neighbour in *To Kill a Mockingbird*?
17   Which Donald featured in *Escape from New York*?
18   Who won the Best Actress Oscar for *The Farmer's Daughter*?
19   A character named Laura Burney appeared in which film?
20   In which year was *Duel in the Sun* released?
21   Olympia Dukakis was a champion in what sport while at university?
22   Who did Kevin Dillon play in *The Doors*?
23   What is the name of Raquel Welch's actress daughter?
24   Within fifteen minutes, how long does *The Godfather* last?
25   Which star of *Pretty Woman* was born Jay Greenspan?

Answers Oscars – Best Actors & Actresses (see Quiz 83)
1 Edmund Gwenn. **2** Barry Fitzgerald. **3** Robert Donat. **4** Five. **5** *Bonnie and Clyde*. **6** Sacheen Littlefeather. **7** *The Robe*. **8** Red Buttons. **9** *Rambling Rose*. **10** Patty Duke. **11** Daniel Day-Lewis. **12** *Broadcast News* (Holly Hunter). **13** *Dr Jekyll and Mr Hyde*. **14** Angelo Maggio (*From Here to Eternity*). **15** *The Search*. **16** Elisabeth Shue. **17** Humphrey Bogart. **18** *Thunderbolt and Lightfoot*. **19** *Heaven Knows Mr Allison*. **20** Judy Holliday. **21** *Double Indemnity*. **22** *The Spy Who Came in from the Cold*. **23** Ada McGrath. **24** James Dean. **25** *The Story of Adele H.*

Answers – see page 300

1	Which future TV comedian was the child clinging to Marie Dressler's skirts in *Tillie's Punctured Romance* in 1914?
2	How is former child star Suzanne Caputo better known?
3	Who starred in *Reunion* when they were two?
4	Which teen star was Stewart Granger's brother in *North to Alaska*?
5	About which seven-year-old did Paderewski say, 'Some day that boy might take my place'?
6	Roddy McDowall found fame as a child and adult actor, and in which other branch of the arts?
7	Which former child star appeared in *Carmen Jones* and *Porgy and Bess*?
8	In which movie did Liza Minnelli appear as a baby with her mother?
9	How was Anne Shirley known in her early days as a child star?
10	Which actor was torn between Meryl Streep and Dustin Hoffman in a 70s classic?
11	Who played Michael, the little boy that Mary Poppins was nanny to?
12	In which movie did the unknown Alan Barnes steal the show from a more famous Hayley Mills?
13	Whose debut was in *Uncle Buck*?
14	Who played the youngest Frank McCourt in *Angela's Ashes*?
15	Which star of Little Miss Thoroughbred received a 1945 Oscar for being 'outstanding as a child actress'?
16	Who played the brother in *The Railway Children*?
17	Who played the title role in David Lean's classic *Oliver Twist* and went on to be a TV producer?
18	Who played young Charlie in Richard Attenborough's *Chaplin*?
19	Whose marriage to Drew Barrymore lasted just six weeks?
20	Who played Gregory Peck's daughter in *To Kill a Mockingbird*?
21	Who won a Special Oscar for *The Window* aged 12?
22	Which star of *Captains Courageous* and *Kidnapped* went into advertising when his adult film career foundered?
23	What was Matthew Beard's nickname?
24	Who played Gene Tierney's daughter in the 1947 movie which also starred Rex Harrison and George Sanders?
25	Which former member of the *Our Gang* movies appeared in *That's Entertainment III* in her seventies?

Answers Pot Luck 28 (see Quiz 84)
1 Nora Ephron. **2** Bernard Herrman. **3** Meryl Streep. **4** Douglas McGrath. **5** *The Guns of Navarone*. **6** Nelson. **7** Woody Harrelson. **8** 135 minutes. **9** Marshall Will Kane. **10** Fiorentino. **11** *Giant*. **12** Bette Midler. **13** Roger Moore. **14** Rebecca Miller. **15** Marion. **16** Colicos. **17** Sally Field. **18** Wind In His Hair. **19** Nouri. **20** 1940s. **21** 2 hours. **22** 'Lullaby of Broadway'. **23** Archer. **24** *Reversal of Fortune*. **25** *Big Broadcast of 1938*.

Answers – see page 297

1   Who was 72 when he won for *Miracle on 34th Street*?
2   Who was the first person to be nominated as Best Actor and Best Supporting Actor for the same role?
3   The only major award *Gone with the Wind* did not win went to whom?
4   How many Oscar nominations did Shirley MacLaine have before the one with which she won for *Terms of Endearment*?
5   For which movie was Estelle Parsons nominated on her film debut?
6   Who accepted Brando's Oscar for him for *The Godfather*?
7   For which movie did Richard Burton get his second nomination?
8   Which actor, real name Aaron Chwatt, won for *Sayonara*?
9   What was Laura Dern's first nomination for?
10   Which teenager was a winner for *The Miracle Worker*?
11   Which winner became Arthur Miller's son-in-law?
12   For which movie did the winner from *The Piano* win her first nomination?
13   For which movie did Frederic March win the first of his two Oscars?
14   For which character did Frank Sinatra first win Best Supporting Actor?
15   For which movie was Montgomery Clift nominated on his film debut?
16   Which actress was nominated in the movie which won Nicolas Cage an award in 1995?
17   Who was a winner and deprived Brando for *A Streetcar Named Desire*?
18   For which movie did Jeff Bridges win his second supporting actor nomination?
19   What was the second of Deborah Kerr's three nominations between 1956 and 1958?
20   Who won when Bette Davis was nominated for *All About Eve*?
21   For which movie did Barbara Stanwyck lose out on a 1944 Oscar to Ingrid Bergman?
22   What was the second of Richard Burton's three nominations between 1964 and 1966?
23   For which character did Holly Hunter win Best Actress in 1993?
24   Who was the first actor to be nominated for two posthumous Oscars?
25   For which movie did Isabelle Adjani receive her first nomination?

Answers Pot Luck 27 (see Quiz 81)
1 Tennis. 2 *The China Syndrome*. 3 Irvin Kershner. 4 Clark. 5 Sammy Davis Jnr (16.5.90). 6 Danny. 7 78 minutes. 8 Mark Hamill. 9 Davies. 10 Dana Ivey. 11 Tony Curtis. 12 Henry Thomas. 13 Dudley Moore. 14 Peter Sellers. 15 Tod Carroll. 16 Robert Duvall. 17 Pleasence. 18 Loretta Young. 19 *Sleeping with the Enemy*. 20 1946. 21 Fencing. 22 John Densemore. 23 Tahnee Welch. 24 175 minutes. 25 Jason Alexander.

Answers – see page 298

1   Who won an Oscar for her first screenplay, *Silkwood*?
2   Martin Scorsese dedicated *Taxi Driver* to the memory of which composer who finished the score just before he died?
3   Which movie star released a single called 'Amazing Grace' in 1984?
4   Who directed 90s movie *Emma*?
5   A character named Keith Mallory appeared in which film?
6   Which Barry featured in *The Shining*?
7   *Wildcats* and *Wag the Dog* both starred which actor?
8   Within five minutes, how long does *Jerry Maguire* last?
9   What was the name of Gary Cooper's character in *High Noon*?
10 Which Linda featured in *Men in Black*?
11 A character named Jett Rink appeared in which 50s film?
12 Which actress once 'packed pineapples at a local cannery in Honolulu'?
13 Which uncredited actor appears as Clouseau at the end of *The Curse of the Pink Panther*?
14 Who played Kay Otis in the film *Consenting Adults*?
15 Who did Karen Allen play in *Raiders of the Lost Ark*?
16 Which John featured in *The Postman Always Rings Twice*?
17 Who founded the company Fogwood Films?
18 Who was played by Rodney A. Grant in *Dances with Wolves*?
19 Which Michael starred in *Flashdance*?
20 In which decade was *Crossfire* released?
21 To the nearest hour, how long does *Blade Runner* last?
22 Which song from *Gold Diggers of 1935* won an Oscar?
23 Which Anne featured in *Fatal Attraction*?
24 In which film did a character named Claus von Bulow appear?
25 The song 'Thanks for the Memory' came from which movie?

Answers Child Stars (see Quiz 82)
1 Milton Berle. 2 Morgan Brittany. 3 The Dionne Quins. 4 Fabian. 5 Liberace.
6 Photography. 7 Dorothy Dandridge. 8 *In the Good Old Summertime*. 9 Dawn O' Day. 10 Justin Henry (*Kramer versus Kramer*). 11 Matthew Garber. 12 *Whistle Down the Wind*. 13 Macaulay Culkin. 14 Joe Breen. 15 Peggy Ann Garner.
16 Gary Warren. 17 John Howard Davies. 18 Hugh Downer. 19 Jeremy Thomas.
20 Mary Badham. 21 Bobby Driscoll. 22 Freddie Bartholomew. 23 Stymie.
24 Natalie Wood (*The Ghost and Mrs Muir*). 25 Nanette Fabray.

QUIZ 85 1980s ··· LEVEL THREE

Answers – see page 303

1   Who are the two main characters who write to each other in *84 Charing Cross Road*?
2   What were the furry creatures called in *Gremlins*?
3   Which 1982 movie did Hugh Grant make while still at Oxford?
4   In which movie did Robert De Niro play the devil?
5   Within fifteen minutes, how long does *Arthur* last?
6   What was the name of the giant grizzly which starred in *Clan of the Cave Bear*?
7   Who did Faye Dunaway play in *Chinatown*?
8   What was Emilio Estevez's first movie as writer/director?
9   Who played Robinson Crusoe in *Crusoe*?
10   What was the occupation of Madame Sousatzka?
11   In which movie was Isabelle Adjani Oscar-nominated for playing Rodin's mistress?
12   What was the real name of the actress who played the title role in *Octopussy*?
13   Which movie is famous for the fact that all Kevin Costner's scenes were cut out of it?
14   Who played Frances Farmer in *Frances*?
15   In which 1984 movie did Liza Minnelli play herself?
16   Who played Mozart's rival in *Amadeus*?
17   What was the name of the brain in the jar in *The Man with Two Brains*?
18   Which film is being screened on TV during *Gremlins*?
19   Who played Richie Valens in *La Bamba*?
20   In which movie did Harry Dean Stanton play an angel?
21   What was the name of Kristin Scott's character in *A Handful of Dust*?
22   Which movie had the ad line, 'In Vietnam the wind doesn't blow – it sucks'?
23   Who was decapitated during the making of *Twilight Zone: The Movie*?
24   Which star of *Seinfeld* made an appearance in *Pretty Woman*?
25   In whose stately home was *Greystoke* filmed?

Answers Pot Luck 29 (see Quiz 87)
1 Billy. **2** *The Outsiders*. **3** Tobolowsky. **4** *Freejack*. **5** *Stir Crazy*. **6** Betty Thomas. **7** Sean Young. **8** Ramis. **9** Angela Lansbury. **10** 125 minutes. **11** Norman Taurog. **12** Preston Sturges. **13** Five. **14** Nelligan. **15** *A Fire over England*. **16** Judy Davis. **17** James Clavell. **18** *Always*. **19** *Blue Sky*. **20** Joe Eszterhas. **21** Charlton Heston. **22** Spike Lee. **23** *Awakenings*. **24** Olivia de Havilland. **25** Webb.

Answers – see page 304

1   Which musical has the song, 'Why Can't a Woman Be More Like a Man'?
2   Who were the singing voices of Tony and Maria in *West Side Story*?
3   Who does Debbie Reynolds play in *Singin' in the Rain*?
4   Who wrote the score of the musical remake of *Ninotchka*?
5   June Allyson sang 'Thou Swell' in which movie?
6   In which 70s movie did 'Starsky' of *Starsky and Hutch* fame star?
7   Which character sings 'Sit Down You're Rockin' the Boat' in the Frank Loesser musical?
8   Who played the third sailor 'On the Town' with Frank Sinatra and Gene Kelly?
9   Which character did Stubby Kaye play in *Li'l Abner*?
10   Whose voice was dubbed by Marilyn Horne in *Carmen Jones*?
11   In *An American in Paris* the ex GI is in Paris to learn how to do what?
12   Which musical was the first to be shown in Todd AO?
13   In *Guys and Dolls* where does the double wedding take place?
14   In which 60s musical movie did Richard Attenborough sing?
15   Who played Peron's teenage mistress in *Evita*?
16   Who was the black female star of *Stormy Weather*?
17   Which character discovers the Von Trapps hiding in the abbey in *The Sound of Music*?
18   In what type of building does the opening scene of *Evita* take place?
19   Who choreographed the dance routines in *Half a Sixpence*?
20   Who played Barbra Streisand's husband in the follow-up to *Funny Girl*?
21   *Follow the Fleet* was based on which two Broadway plays?
22   In which Liza Minnelli musical is TV's Jane Krakowski from *Ally McBeal* one of the dancers?
23   Who wrote the score for the 1953 movie with Fred Astaire & Cyd Charisse?
24   Within fifteen minutes, how long does *Gigi* last?
25   What colour is Mary Poppins's sash when she's dancing with the penguins?

Answers Animation (see Quiz 88)
1 Joan Cusack. **2** Art Babbitt. **3** Maurice Chevalier. **4** James Earl Jones. **5** *Plane Crazy*. **6** *Porky's Hare Hunt*. **7** *The Chain Gang*. **8** Joanna Lumley & Miriam Margolyes. **9** 1932. **10** Bach's Toccata & Fugue in D Minor. **11** John Lasseter. **12** Richard Williams. **13** 76 minutes. **14** MGM. **15** Universal. **16** Bob Hoskins. **17** Ralph Bakshi. **18** Don Bluth. **19** Michael J. Fox. **20** *Tin Toy*. **21** Columbia. **22** *Lady and the Tramp*. **23** *Fast and Furry Outs*. **24** Monstro. **25** Hans Zimmer.

Answers – see page 301

1	What was the name of the Kramers' son?
2	What was Rob Lowe's first film, in 1983?
3	Which Stephen featured in *Groundhog Day*?
4	Which 1992 film did rock star Mick Jagger star in?
5	Skip Donahue and Harry Monroe were characters in which film?
6	Who directed the 90s movie *Doctor Dolittle*?
7	Which actress was originally set to play the role of Vicki Vale before Kim Basinger took over in *Batman*?
8	Which Harold featured in *Ghostbusters*?
9	*National Velvet* and *Company of Wolves* starred which actress?
10	Within five minutes, how long does *Jaws* last?
11	Who won the Best Director Oscar for *Skippy* in 1931?
12	Which writer/director was the inventor of kissproof lipstick?
13	How many times was John Huston married?
14	Which Kate featured in *US Marshals*?
15	The relationship between Laurence Olivier and Vivien Leigh began on the set of which movie?
16	Who played Audrey Taylor in the film *Barton Fink*?
17	Which writer directed *To Sir, With Love* in 1967?
18	What was the last film Audrey Hepburn appeared in?
19	What was the last movie made by director Tony Richardson?
20	Who wrote the screenplay for the film *Basic Instinct*?
21	*Wayne's World 2* and *Hamlet* link which actor?
22	Who directed *Do the Right Thing*?
23	The character Dr Malcolm Sayer appeared in which film?
24	Who won the Best Actress Oscar for *To Each His Own*?
25	Which Chloe featured in *Twins*?

Answers 1980s (see Quiz 85)

1 Helene Hanff & Frank Doel. **2** Mogwais. **3** *Privileged*. **4** *Angel Heart*. **5** 97 minutes. **6** Bart. **7** Evelyn Mulwray. **8** *Men at Work*. **9** Aidan Quinn. **10** Piano teacher. **11** *Camille Claudel*. **12** Maude Wikstrum (Maud Adams). **13** *The Big Chill*. **14** Jessica Lange. **15** *The Muppets Take Manhattan*. **16** F. Murray Abraham. **17** Anne Uumellmahaye. **18** *It's a Wonderful Life*. **19** Lou Diamond Phillips. **20** *One Magic Christmas*. **21** Brenda Last. **22** *Full Metal Jacket*. **23** Vic Morrow. **24** Jason Alexander. **25** Duke of Roxburghe.

Answers – see page 302

1 Who is the voice of Jessie in *Toy Story 2*?
2 Who drew the wicked queen in *Snow White*?
3 Who sang the title song in *The Aristocats*?
4 Who was the voice of Mufasa in *The Lion King*?
5 The Mickey Mouse character first appeared in which cartoon, when he was briefly known as Mortimer?
6 In which movie did Bugs Bunny first appear?
7 Pluto made his big-screen debut in which movie?
8 Who voiced Spiker and Sponge in *James and the Giant Peach*?
9 In what year did Goofy appear in *Mickey's Review*?
10 With which piece of music does *Fantasia* open?
11 Who directed the first feature-length computer-generated film?
12 Who won an Oscar for animation for *Who Framed Roger Rabbit*?
13 Within fifteen minutes, how long does *Peter Pan* last?
14 Fred Quimby headed whose cartoon studio?
15 Which studio released *Oswald the Rabbit*?
16 Who was the voice of the Russian goose in *Balto*?
17 Who made the more adult animation, *Fritz the Cat*?
18 Whose production company released *An American Tail* in the 80s?
19 Who provided the voice of Chance in *Homeward Bound: The Incredible Journey*?
20 Which short movie did John Lasseter receive an Oscar for before he made *Toy Story*?
21 Which studio created *Color Rhapsodies*?
22 What was the only feature film in the 1950s devised by Disney from an original story?
23 In which movie did Road Runner have his first screen outing?
24 What is the name of the whale in *Pinocchio*?
25 Who wrote the score for *The Lion King*?

Answers Musicals (see Quiz 86)
1 *My Fair Lady*. 2 Jimmy Bryant & Marni Nixon. 3 Kathy Seldon. 4 Cole Porter.
5 *Words and Music*. 6 *Fiddler on the Roof*. 7 Nicely Nicely Johnson. 8 Jules Munshin. 9 Marryin' Sam. 10 Dorothy Dandridge. 11 Paint. 12 *Oklahoma!*.
13 Times Square. 14 *Dr Dolittle*. 15 Andrea Corr. 16 Lena Horne. 17 Rolf.
18 Cinema. 19 Gillian Lynne. 20 James Caan. 21 *Shore Leave* & *Hit the Deck*.
22 *Stepping Out*. 23 Arthur Schwarz & Howard Dietz (*The Band Wagon*). 24 116 minutes. 25 Red.

Answers – see page 307

1	Which movie did Kim Basinger back out of and lose a multi-million pound lawsuit as a result?
2	Who was the first actor ever to refuse an Oscar?
3	Which actor, who worked with the Resistance in Rome in World War II, made his first Hollywood appearance in *Little Women*?
4	Who walked out on her contract with 20th Century Fox after the failure of *Fallen Angel*?
5	Which Bond villain was identified by a Holocaust survivor as having saved her family from the Nazis?
6	Which actor, born Orson Whipple Hungerford III, was expelled from Spain in 1974?
7	Who was arrested in a Florida cinema in 1991 during a showing of *Naughty Nurses*?
8	Who was awarded a medal in 1938 by Goebbels and was appointed head of his film company Tobis?
9	Why did MGM sack Sinatra in 1949?
10	Which actor was the first glider pilot to land Allied troops behind Japanese lines in Burma?
11	Who received the Jean Hersholt Humanitarian Award during the 1977 Oscar ceremony?
12	Where was Leslie Howard returning from when he was shot down in World War II?
13	Who made his debut as a mugger in Woody Allen's *Bananas*?
14	Which cause does Paul Newman give the profits of his salad dressing business to?
15	Who set up the American Foundation for AIDS Research?
16	Which actress's daughter stabbed her boyfriend to death but was acquitted on grounds of protecting her mother?
17	What could 007 hero turned villain Sean Connery change in *The Avengers*?
18	Who did Gregory Peck play in *The Boys from Brazil*?
19	Who plays the villain alongside Quentin Tarantino in *From Dusk Till Dawn*?
20	Which actor famous for wholesome roles played the villain in *Double Indemnity*?
21	Which villain did Richard Widmark play in *Kiss of Death* in 1947?
22	Who played the first cinema vampire in *Nosferatu*?
23	Whose make-up turned Boris Karloff into one of the great screen performers of all time?
24	Where was Stacy Keach arrested in April 1984?
25	Who wrote *Mommie Dearest*?

Answers Comedy (see Quiz 91)

1 $3,000. **2** *A Shot in the Dark*. **3** Nixon & Kennedy. **4** 98 minutes. **5** Sherman Klump. **6** Gonzo. **7** Car Salesman. **8** Leaf Phoenix. **9** A gopher. **10** Vincent Cadby. **11** Punxsutawney. **12** Alabama. **13** A bouncer. **14** Wyld Stallyns. **15** Elizabeth Taylor. **16** *Blazing Saddles*. **17** *The Bride and the Wolf*. **18** 1962. **19** Waco. **20** *A Day at the Races*. **21** Franck Eggelhoffer. **22** Fozziwig the rubber chicken factory owner. **23** *Kindergarten Cop*. **24** *Bedtime Story*. **25** Thora Birch.

Answers – see page 308

1   Which high flyer appeared in *The Boy in the Plastic Bubble*?
2   What is the last word of *Sleepy Hollow*?
3   Within five minutes, how long does *JFK* last?
4   Which Tony featured in *Ghost*?
5   Who directed *Deep Impact*?
6   What was the name of Audrey Hepburn's character in *The Nun's Story*?
7   In which film did a character named Stephen McCaffrey appear?
8   Edith Head contributed to some 1,000 movies, doing what?
9   *Four Rooms* and *A League of Their Own* starred which performer?
10   Who won the Best Actor Oscar for *All the King's Men* in 1949?
11   Which Paul featured in *Raiders of the Lost Ark*?
12   Who directed *Diamonds Are Forever*?
13   Who directed *Agnes Browne*?
14   Who played Pa Kent in the 1978 *Superman* movie?
15   Which soap did Hollywood star Tommy Lee Jones star in?
16   *The Year of Living Dangerously* was concerned with which year?
17   Which British actor won an Oscar for *A Double Life*?
18   In which year did David Niven die?
19   Which Paul featured in *The Full Monty*?
20   Who directed the film *Alive*?
21   Within fifteen minutes, how long does *Casablanca* last?
22   In which film did a character named C.R. MacNamara appear?
23   Which Barry featured in *Saturday Night Fever*?
24   Who won the Best Actress Oscar for *The Trip to Bountiful*?
25   Which 1943 film is Spielberg's 80s movie *Always* a remake of?

Answers Oscars – Best of the Rest (see Quiz 92)
1 *The Turning Point.* **2** Luise Rainer. **3** Writer. **4** Peter Shaffer. **5** Costume design.
6 Francis Ford Coppola. **7** *The Bells of Saint Mary's; Say One For Me.*
8 *Ordinary People.* **9** *The English Patient; Shakespeare in Love.* **10** Carmine.
11 *Tom Jones.* **12** Three (Brando, Hoffman, Hanks). **13** Murdered on his way home
from a rehearsal. **14** University of Hull. **15** Cinematography. **16** Douglas
Fairbanks. **17** Sound effects. **18** *The Circus.* **19** Make-up. **20** *On the Waterfront;
The Godfather; The Godfather Part II.* **21** 1937. **22** *The Last Command; The Way of
All Flesh.* **23** Lewis Milestone. **24** Darryl Zanuck. **25** Three.

Answers – see page 305

1   What was *Pretty Woman* originally to have been called?
2   In which film did Peter Sellers first star as Clouseau?
3   Which presidents does Tom Hanks meet in *Forrest Gump*?
4   Within fifteen minutes, how long does *The Muppet Movie* last?
5   Who does Eddie Murphy play in the 90s remake of the Jerry Lewis comedy?
6   Who was the author in *The Muppet Christmas Carol*?
7   What is Ted Danson's job in *Made in America*?
8   Who plays Gary in the film *Parenthood*?
9   What type of animal drives Bill Murray mad in *Caddyshack*?
10   Who does Simon Callow play in *Ace Ventura: When Nature Calls*?
11   In which town is *Groundhog Day* set?
12   In which state is Vinny's cousin accused of murder in *My Cousin Vinny*?
13   What part does Meat Loaf play in *Wayne's World*?
14   What is the name of Bill & Ted's rock group in *Bill and Ted's Bogus Journey*?
15   Who played John Goodman's mother in law in *The Flintstones*?
16   In which film does railwayman Cleavon Little become sheriff?
17   What was *Moonstruck* originally to have been called?
18   In what year is *National Lampoon's Animal House* set?
19   Where was Steve Martin born?
20   'Marry me, Emily, and I'll never look at another horse' is the last line of which movie?
21   Which character does Martin Short play in the 90s film *Father of the Bride*?
22   Who did Fozzie Bear play in *The Muppet Christmas Carol*, and what was his job?
23   What was Arnold Schwarzenegger's first comedy movie of the 90s?
24   Which film was remade as *Dirty Rotten Scoundrels*?
25   Which actress links *Hocus Pocus* and *Now and Then*?

Answers Heroes & Villains (see Quiz 89)
1 *Boxing Helena*. 2 George C. Scott. 3 Rossano Brazzi. 4 Alice Faye. 5 Gert Frobe (*Goldfinger*). 6 Ty Hardin. 7 Pee Wee Herman. 8 Emil Jannings. 9 He insulted boss Louis B. Mayer. 10 Jackie Coogan. 11 Charlton Heston. 12 Lisbon. 13 Sylvester Stallone. 14 Holiday camps for children with life-threatening diseases. 15 Elizabeth Taylor. 16 Lana Turner's daughter Cheryl. 17 The weather. 18 Joseph Mengele. 19 George Clooney. 20 Fred MacMurray. 21 Tommy Udo. 22 Max Schreck. 23 Jack Pierce. 24 Heathrow Airport. 25 Christina Crawford (daughter of Joan).

Answers – see page 306

1   Which 70s film had 11 nominations but won nothing?
2   Who was the first actress to win in consecutive years?
3   Out of 11 nominations *Becket* had one winner; in which category?
4   On whose play was F. Murray Abraham's Oscar-winning performance based?
5   In what capacity was Anna Biedrzycka Sheppard nominated for *Schindler's List*?
6   Who said, 'I probably have genius but no talent'?
7   Which two subsequent movies featured the lead character of *Going My Way*?
8   Which movie had the ad line, 'Everything is in its proper place except the past'?
9   In which two 90s Best Films did Colin Firth appear?
10 Which Coppola won an Oscar for *The Godfather Part II*?
11 What was the first movie to have three nominations for Best Supporting Actress?
12 Of all the actors with two wins, how many were still alive at the end of the 20th century?
13 How did the nominee director for *Rebel Without a Cause* meet his death?
14 Where did Anthony Minghella teach before being an Oscar winner?
15 In which category did Russell Carpenter win for *Titanic*?
16 Who was the first president of the Academy which presents the Oscars?
17 For what did Peter Berkos win a Special Award with *The Hindenburg*?
18 For which movie did Chaplin win his first Special Award?
19 In which category did William Turtle win a Special Award?
20 Which three films have received three nominations for *Best Supporting Actor*?
21 In what year was the Irving Thalberg award introduced?
22 For which two films was the first Best Actor given his award?
23 Who was the first person to win two awards for direction?
24 Who won the first Irving Thalberg award?
25 How many Oscars did Tim Rice win in the 1990s?

Answers Pot Luck 30 (see Quiz 90)
1 Buzz Aldrin. 2 Way ('And home is this way'). 3 189 minutes. 4 Goldwyn.
5 Mimi Leder. 6 Gabrielle Van Der Mal. 7 *Backdraft*. 8 Costume design.
9 Madonna. 10 Broderick Crawford. 11 Freeman. 12 Guy Hamilton. 13 Anjelica
Huston. 14 Glenn Ford. 15 *One Life to Live*. 16 1965. 17 Ronald Colman.
18 1983. 19 Barber. 20 Frank Marshall. 21 102 minutes. 22 *One, Two, Three*.
23 Miller. 24 Geraldine Page. 25 *A Guy Named Joe*.

Answers – see page 311

1   Under what name does Janet Leigh sign in to the Bates Motel?
2   In which film does a character named Louise Bryant appear?
3   Which movie star was born on the same day as fellow star Marlon Brando?
4   To the nearest hour, did *Alfie* run 1, 2 or 3 hours?
5   Which Roger directed *Dante's Peak*?
6   Who won the Best Actress Oscar for *The Great Ziegfeld*?
7   What colour is Melanie's dress in *The Birds*?
8   Within fifteen minutes, how long does *Citizen Kane* last?
9   Which Chris featured in *The Princess Bride*?
10   A character named Prissy Bronte appeared in which film?
11   The song 'The Way You Look Tonight' came from which movie?
12   Who won the Best Director Oscar for *Bad Girl*?
13   Meryl Streep said you can't get spoiled if you do your own what?
14   Which John featured in the 80s version of *The Fly*?
15   Which movie star released a single called 'Lonely for a Girl' in 1965?
16   Who did Ralph Richardson play in *Time Bandits*?
17   What was the name of Deborah Kerr's character in *An Affair To Remember*?
18   Who directed the film *Air America*?
19   Which Robert featured in *Private Benjamin*?
20   For what did Les Bowie win a Special Award in 1978?
21   What movie is shown in the film *Hot Shots!*?
22   Within five minutes, how long does *Jackie Brown* last?
23   Who directed *The Craft*?
24   What was the name of Spencer Tracy's character in *Inherit the Wind*?
25   Which Matt featured in *Honey, I Shrunk the Kids*?

Answers Writers (see Quiz 95)
1 William Nicholson. **2** Bob Hope & Danny Kaye. **3** *Delusions of Grandma*.
4 Dulwich College. **5** Alfred Uhry's. **6** Hans Christian Andersen. **7** Carl
Woodward. **8** Billy Hayes's. **9** Spielberg. **10** Michael Crichton. **11** *The Lost
World*. **12** Roger Avary. **13** Preston Sturges. **14** Henry Graham. **15** *Red Dragon*
by Thomas Harris **16** Norman Mailer. **17** Neil Simon. **18** Harrison Ford (Melissa
Mathison). **19** *Blue Collar*. **20** Winona Ryder. **21** Richard Stark. **22** Robin Ruzan.
23 Dan O'Bannon. **24** Nora Ephron & Carl Bernstein. **25** *The Age of Innocence*.

Answers – see page 312

1   Who did Julia Roberts want for the part of Shakespeare in *Shakespeare in Love*, so turned down the movie herself?
2   Who played Margaret Schlegel's younger sister in *Howard's End*?
3   What did Jim Carrey have removed shortly after making *The Mask*?
4   *Backbeat* was about which pop star?
5   Which two Johns are Gwyneth Paltrow's prospective lovers in *Sliding Doors*?
6   Who played the unwitting drugs carriers in *Brokedown Palace*?
7   Where was Ms Heslop's home in *Muriel's Wedding*?
8   Who plays the prospective bride in *My Best Friend's Wedding*?
9   Who or what was *Andre* in the film of the same name?
10   What is the epidemic that breaks out in Spielberg's animated *Balto*?
11   What was Woody Allen's follow-up to *Everyone Says I Love You*?
12   Within fifteen minutes, how long does *Nell* last?
13   Who played Babe Ruth in *Babe*?
14   Which writer did Johnny Depp play in *Fear and Loathing in Las Vegas*?
15   What was the name of the gangster played by Ray Liotta in *Goodfellas*?
16   In *Quiz Show*, what is the quiz show called?
17   For which movie did Jamie Lee Curtis win her second Golden Globe Award?
18   *Devil's Candy* was written about the making of which movie?
19   *A Thousand Acres* was loosely based on which Shakespeare play?
20   Which father and son starred in *A Boy Called Hate*?
21   Who played Vincent van Gogh in *Vincent and Theo*?
22   River Phoenix died during the making of which movie?
23   Who did Al Pacino play in the 1990 movie with Warren Beatty and Madonna?
24   Who played two parts in *A Kiss Before Dying* in 1991?
25   Which movie had the ad line, 'The coast is toast'?

Answers Pot Luck 32 (see Quiz 96)
1 Eldred. 2 Cellist. 3 German. 4 *Apocalypse Now*. 5 Mie Hama. 6 'You'll Never Know'. 7 Gary. 8 *Presumed Innocent*. 9 Michael Bay. 10 *Lady Jane*. 11 Jose Ferrer. 12 Judy Bernly. 13 100 minutes. 14 'All the Way'. 15 Schneider. 16 *Out of the Past*. 17 Meg Tilly. 18 Hutton. 19 111 minutes. 20 Simon West. 21 Kitchen. 22 1940s. 23 Michelle Pfeiffer. 24 Ronald Regan. 25 *The Unforgiven*.

Answers – see page 309

1   On whose play was *Shadowlands* based?
2   Who did Billy Wilder originally write *Some Like It Hot* for?
3   What was the name of the Carrie Fisher novel on which *Postcards from the Edge* was based?
4   Which school links P.G. Wodehouse, Raymond Chandler and A.E.W. Mason who all wrote for the movies?
5   On whose one-act play was *Driving Miss Daisy* based?
6   Whose work was the inspiration for *The Red Shoes*?
7   Who wrote *Wired* about John Belushi, which was later filmed?
8   Whose memoirs did Oliver Stone use to script *Midnight Express*?
9   Who did the director of *Home Alone* first work for when he began as a screenwriter?
10 Who was paid $10 million for the screen rights to his novel *Airframe*?
11 What is Arthur Conan Doyle's contribution to tales for the cinema other than Sherlock Holmes?
12 Who co-wrote *Pulp Fiction* with Quentin Tarantino?
13 Which writer turned director in *The Great McGinty*?
14 How is Graham Greene billed in his cameo role in *Day for Night*?
15 On which book by which author was *Manhunter* based?
16 Who wrote the novel on which Warner Brothers' *American Dream* was based?
17 Which playwright was Woody Harrelson's father-in-law until 1986?
18 Who is the husband of the writer of the screenplay for *E.T.*?
19 What was the directorial debut of Paul Schrader, who scripted *Taxi Driver*?
20 About whom did Arthur Miller say, 'She's as good as it gets'?
21 On whose novel was *Point Blank* based?
22 Which writer married Mike Myers?
23 Who scripted Ridley Scott's 1979 sci-fi movie with Sigourney Weaver?
24 Whose marriage is the subject of *Heartburn*?
25 Which Pulitzer Prize-winning novel by Edith Wharton was brought to the big screen by Martin Scorsese in 1993?

Answers Pot Luck 31 (see Quiz 93)
1 Marie Samuels. 2 *Reds*. 3 Doris Day (3.4.24). 4 2 hours. 5 Roger Donaldson.
6 Luise Rainer. 7 Green. 8 120 minutes. 9 Sarandon. 10 *Green Card*.
11 *Swingtime*. 12 Frank Borzage. 13 Ironing. 14 Boushel. 15 Oliver Reed.
16 The Supreme Being. 17 Terri McKay. 18 Roger Spottiswoode. 19 Webber.
20 Visual effects on *Superman*. 21 *Flight of the Intruder*. 22 154 minutes.
23 Andrew Fleming. 24 Henry Drummond. 25 Frewer.

Answers – see page 310

1   What is the first name of Gregory Peck, who uses his middle name in the movies?
2   What is Sigourney Weaver's job in *Ghostbusters*?
3   What is the first language to be spoken in *The Lady Vanishes*?
4   A character named Lieutenant Willard appears in which film?
5   Who played the Bond girl in *You Only Live Twice*?
6   Which song from *Hello, Frisco, Hello* won an Oscar?
7   Which Lorraine featured in *Jaws*?
8   In which film does a character named Rusty Sabich appear?
9   Who directed *Armageddon*?
10   What was Helena Bonham Carter's first film, in 1984?
11   Who won the Best Actor Oscar for *Cyrano de Bergerac*?
12   What was the name of Jane Fonda's character in *9 to 5*?
13   To the nearest 10 minutes, how long does *The Italian Job* last?
14   Which song won Best Song Oscar for *The Joker Is Wild*?
15   Which Rob featured in *Judge Dredd*?
16   Which 1947 film is the 80s movie *Against All Odds* based upon?
17   Who played Agnes in the film *Agnes of God*?
18   *Ordinary People* featured which Timothy?
19   Within fifteen minutes, how long does *Dr No* last?
20   Who directed *Con Air*?
21   Which Michael featured in *Out of Africa*?
22   In which decade was *Mom and Dad* released?
23   *A Midsummer Night's Dream* and *Sweet Liberty* both star which actress?
24   Who links *Cowboys from Brooklyn*, *Tugboat Annie Sails Again* and *An Angel from Texas*?
25   A character named Rachel Zachery appears in which film?

Answers 1990s (see Quiz 94)
1 Daniel Day-Lewis. **2** Helena Bonham Carter. **3** His gall bladder. **4** John Lennon. **5** Lynch & Hannah. **6** Kate Beckinsale & Claire Danes. **7** Porpoise Spit. **8** Cameron Diaz. **9** Seal. **10** Diphtheria. **11** *Deconstructing Harry*. **12** 113 minutes. **13** John Goodman. **14** Hunter S. Thompson. **15** Henry Hill. **16** *Twenty One*. **17** *True Lies*. **18** *The Bonfire of the Vanities*. **19** *King Lear*. **20** Scott & James Caan. **21** Tim Roth. **22** *Dark Blood*. **23** Big Boy Caprice. **24** Sean Young. **25** *Volcano*.

Answers – see page 315

1   What is his star sign?
2   Whose voice was he in a 1995 Disney hit?
3   Where are the friends from in *Gallipoli*?
4   Which pop star wife starred in *Lethal Weapon 2*?
5   How was the sequel to *Mad Max* titled in the US?
6   Who played his mother in his first Shakespearean venture?
7   In which movie did he play Sissy Spacek's husband?
8   In which 1993 movie did he direct himself?
9   Where was *Air America* filmed?
10   Where did he study in Australia?
11   Which 1979 movie earned him the Australian equivalent of an Oscar?
12   What was his second movie directed by Peter Weir?
13   In which 1984 movie did he play a role previously played by Clark Gable and Marlon Brando?
14   Who was the subject of *Immortal Beloved*?
15   Which film was advertised as: 'From a place you may never have heard of, a story you'll never forget'?
16   Where was *Attack Force Z* set?
17   Who directed his first movie of a Shakespeare play?
18   What was the name of his character in *Lethal Weapon*?
19   What was the name of the 1993 biography by Roland Perry?
20   What is his production company called?
21   Where are the villains from in *Lethal Weapon 2*?
22   In which city was *Mrs Soffel* set?
23   In which city in which state was he born?
24   On which river was *The River* set?
25   Who played Gibson's murdered wife in *Braveheart*?

Answers Pot Luck 33 (see Quiz 99)
1 Demi Moore. **2** Evil Genius. **3** *Fried Green Tomatoes at the Whistle Stop Café.*
4 Susan. **5** Orange. **6** Molen. **7** Robert Wise. **8** Emily Lloyd. **9** 145 minutes.
10 'Sweet Leilan'. **11** *Splash*. **12** *The Empire Strikes Back*. **13** Perez. **14** Frank
Capra. **15** Nicholas Evans. **16** *Another World*. **17** Sound effects – *Star Wars*.
18 Romeo. **19** Sinise. **20** 188 minutes. **21** Joanna Lumley. **22** *The Conversation*.
23 Natasha Richardson. **24** Luise Rainer. **25** William Peter Blatty.

Answers – see page 316

1   What was the second of Ingrid Bergman's three Oscar nominations between 1943 and 1945?

2   What was the nickname of the house David Niven shared with Errol Flynn?

3   Which star of *Rebecca* was the first woman lawyer in Texas?

4   Whose autobiography was called *Intermission*?

5   In *Mildred Pierce* which actor famously said, 'Oh boy! I'm so smart it's a disease!'?

6   Who played Catherine the Great in *A Royal Scandal*?

7   How did the star of *Forever Amber* meet her death?

8   Rita Hayworth and Hedy Lamarr advertised which cosmetics house in the 40s?

9   Who was married to Dick Powell between 1945 and 1963?

10 Who played Cleopatra in Pascal's *Caesar and Cleopatra*?

11 How old was Sydney Greenstreet when he made his very first movie?

12 Who had a biography called *Divine Bitch*?

13 What was the first of Gregory Peck's three Oscar nominations between 1945 and 1947?

14 Who said, 'All they did at MGM was change my leading men and the water in my swimming pool'?

15 In which movie did Errol Flynn say, 'Now for Australia and a crack at those Japs'?

16 Which part did Henry Fonda play in *The Ox-Bow Incident*?

17 What was Glenn Ford's real first name?

18 Who played Judy McPherson in *Only Angels Have Wings*?

19 Stan Laurel married eight times, but to how many different women?

20 How did Veronica Lake die?

21 In which 1943 movie did Johnny Weissmuller play himself?

22 Bill Mead died during the making of which movie?

23 In which 1949 movie did Robert Ryan play a boxer?

24 What was the first of Ingrid Bergman's three nominations between 1943 and 1945?

25 Who won a Special Oscar for *Meet Me in St Louis* aged eight?

Answers Classics (see Quiz 100)
1 Book shop. **2** Beethoven's Pastoral Symphony. **3** Swats a little boy with a newspaper. **4** *The Apartment.* **5** 1 hour (80 mins). **6** *The Third Man.* **7** *Holiday Inn* ('White Christmas'). **8** *Suspicion.* **9** South America. **10** Fred MacMurray & Jack Oakie. **11** Elwood P. Dowd. **12** *The Lodger.* **13** Walter Pidgeon. **14** *It Happened One Night.* **15** Rhett. **16** Dying sea captain. **17** *Road to Hong Kong.* **18** 1946. **19** Ub Iwerks. **20** Osgood Fielding III. **21** *Brief Encounter.* **22** *Grand Hotel.* **23** Cary Grant; William Holden. **24** *Going My Way.* **25** Art Babbitt.

Answers – see page 313

1 Which actress has children called Scout and Rumer?
2 What was the name of the villain in *Time Bandits*?
3 A character named Evelyn Couch appeared in which film?
4 What was the name of Jill Eikenberry's character in *Arthur*?
5 What colour dress is Jane Banks wearing when we first meet her in *Mary Poppins*?
6 Which Jerry featured in *Rain Man*?
7 Who directed *The Andromeda Strain*?
8 *Cookie* and *Scorchers* both starred which actress?
9 To the nearest 10 minutes, how long does *Independence Day* last?
10 Which song from *Waikiki Wedding* won an Oscar?
11 What was the first film put out by the Disney subsidiary, Touchstone?
12 Brian Johnson won a Special Award in 1980 for visual effects on which movie?
13 Which Rosie featured in *Night on Earth*?
14 Who won the Best Director Oscar for *You Can't Take it with You*?
15 Who wrote the novel *The Horse Whisperer*?
16 Which soap did Hollywood star Morgan Freeman star in?
17 For what did Benjamin Burtt Jr win an Oscar Special Award in 1977?
18 What was the name of Joan Wilder's cat in *Romancing the Stone*?
19 Which Gary featured in *Ransom*?
20 Within fifteen minutes, how long does *Gandhi* last?
21 *Shirley Valentine* and *Curse of the Pink Panther* link which actress?
22 In which film does a character named Harry Caul appear?
23 Which daughter of Vanessa Redgrave featured in *Nell*?
24 Who won the Best Actress Oscar for *The Good Earth*?
25 Which writer directed *The Exorcist III* in 1990?

Answers Mel Gibson (see Quiz 97)
1 Capricorn. **2** Captain John Smith (*Pocahonatas*). **3** Perth, Australia. **4** Patsy Kensit. **5** *The Road Warrior*. **6** Glenn Close. **7** *The River*. **8** *The Man Without a Face*. **9** Thailand. **10** National Institute of Dramatic Arts. **11** *Tim*. **12** *The Year of Living Dangerously*. **13** *The Bounty* (Fletcher Christian). **14** Beethoven. **15** *Gallipoli*. **16** Japan. **17** Franco Zeffirelli. **18** Martin Riggs. **19** *Lethal Hero*. **20** Icon Productions. **21** South Africa. **22** Pittsburgh. **23** Peekskill, New York. **24** Holston River, Tennessee. **25** Catherine McCormack.

Answers – see page 314

1 In *Funny Face*, where is Audrey Hepburn working prior to becoming a model?
2 In *Fantasia* which piece of music accompanies the scenes set on Mount Olympus?
3 What is Hitchcock's cameo appearance in *Blackmail*?
4 Which movie opens with the line 'On November 1 1959, the population of New York City was 8,042,783'?
5 To the nearest hour, how long does *Rope* last?
6 In which movie did Trevor Howard play Major Calloway?
7 Which movie had the best-selling single ever until Elton John's 'Candle in the Wind' replaced it?
8 Francis Iles's *Before the Fact* was the basis for which Hitchcock film?
9 About which continent is Audrey Hepburn reading in the library in *Breakfast at Tiffany's*?
10 Who were the original male choices for the series which starred Hope, Crosby and Lamour?
11 What was the name of the 'owner' of the six-foot-tall rabbit Harvey?
12 What was the first Hitchcock movie with one of his cameo roles?
13 Who played Mr Miniver in the Greer Garson classic?
14 Which 30s classic was originally to have been called *Night Bus*?
15 Who wore most costumes in *Gone with the Wind* – Rhett, Melanie or Ashley?
16 What part did Walter Huston play in son John's first movie as director?
17 What was the seventh *Road* film?
18 In what year did Universal stop making Sherlock Holmes films with Basil Rathbone?
19 Who did most of the trick work for *The Birds*?
20 Which character amorously pursues Daphne in *Some Like It Hot*?
21 Which movie inspired Billy Wilder to make *The Apartment*?
22 *Hotel Berlin* was the sequel to what classic?
23 Who was first tipped for the role of Shears in *The Bridge on the River Kwai*, and who actually got it?
24 In which movie did Bing Crosby first play Father O'Malley?
25 Who drew the dance of the mushrooms in *Fantasia*?

Answers 1940s Stars (see Quiz 98)
1 *Gaslight*. 2 Cirrhosis by the Sea. 3 Florence Bates (Mrs Van Hopper). 4 Anne Baxter.
5 Jack Carson. 6 Tallulah Bankhead. 7 Fire (Linda Darnell). 8 Max Factor.
9 June Allyson. 10 Vivien Leigh. 11 61. 12 Susan Hayward. 13 *The Keys of the Kingdom*. 14 Esther Williams. 15 *Desperate Journey*. 16 Gil Carter. 17 Gwyllyn.
18 Rita Hayworth. 19 Four. 20 Hepatitis. 21 *Stage Door Canteen*. 22 *They Died With Their Boots On*. 23 *The Set Up*. 24 *For Whom the Bell Tolls*. 25 Margaret O'Brien.

Answers – see page 319

1	Who directed *Fratelli e Sorelle*?
2	Who died the day after completing *Il Postino*?
3	Which 1996 Patrice Leconte movie won a BAFTA and four Cesars?
4	Which 1960 Palme D'Or winner so exhausted its director that he did not make another movie for three years?
5	In which movie did Garbo make her Swedish debut as an extra?
6	What was the first Indian talkie called?
7	Who directed Sophia Loren for the first time in *The Gold of Naples*?
8	Who starred in Akira Kurosawa's *Seven Samurai*?
9	*Accatone* was which director's first movie?
10	Which Swedish actor went to Hollywood to appear in *The Greatest Story Ever Told*?
11	Who played Falstaff in *Chimes at Midnight*, which was made in Spain?
12	Who directed the classic Indian film *Pather Panchali*?
13	Who made *I Am Curious (Yellow)*?
14	Which is the only country in the world never to have imposed censorship for adult films?
15	Where was Simone Signoret born?
16	Which director wrote the novel *Les Enfants Terribles*?
17	Who played the philosophy teacher in Andre Techine's *Les Voleurs*?
18	Who collaborated with Bunuel to make *L'Age d'Or* in 1930?
19	Who directed *Les Enfants du Paradis*?
20	What was Louis Malle's first film after he returned to France from America, in 1992?
21	Which 1985 film was based on the John Osborne play *A Patriot for Me*?
22	Who was the Cambodian director of *Les Gens de la Rizière*?
23	Who was the only human in the Belgian movie *Romeo–Juliet*?
24	What is the name of the cat in *Chacun Cherche Son Chat*?
25	*None But the Brave* was a collaboration between the US and which other country?

Answers Westerns (see Quiz 103)
1 Joe. **2** *Shenandoah*. **3** Johnny Mack Brown. **4** Joel McCrea. **5** *High Noon*.
6 William Boyd. **7** John Ford. **8** *How the West Was Won*. **9** Where the hero kisses his horse at the end but now worries about it. **10** *The Kentuckian*. **11** *The Wild Bunch*. **12** $1,000. **13** Robert Duvall. **14** *Tombstone*. **15** Cleavon Little.
16 Jerome Moross (*The Big Country*). **17** Kurt Russell. **18** The marshall throws his badge in the dust at the end. **19** Kevin Costner. **20** None. **21** *Bad Girls*.
22 *Butch Cassidy and the Sundance Kid*. **23** Matthew Garth. **24** Warner Baxter.
25 Monument Valley.

Answers – see page 320

1 What colour are the elevator doors in *The Shining*?
2 At what sport did Tommy Lee Jones excel?
3 Who won the Best Actor Oscar for *Marty*?
4 Who directed *Zulu*?
5 Which Jack featured in *Play Misty for Me*?
6 Which movie star released a single called 'Raisin' Heaven and Hell Tonight' in 1989?
7 A character named Reggie Hammond appeared in which film?
8 Within fifteen minutes, how long does *Jailhouse Rock* last?
9 Which actor died on the same day as fellow actor Raymond Massey?
10 Which Adam starred in *Full Metal Jacket*?
11 How many catsuits did Michelle Pfeiffer wear in *Batman Returns*?
12 Which song won Best Song Oscar for *The Poseidon Adventure*?
13 Who wrote the novel on which *Dances with Wolves* was based?
14 *Tim* and *Return to Oz* both starred which actress?
15 Who won the David Di Donatello award in Italy for *Amadeus*?
16 What movie is shown in the film *Hannah and her Sisters*?
17 Who played Alias in *Pat Garret and Billy the Kid*?
18 *Dark Journey* and *A Yank at Oxford* both starred which actress?
19 Who directed *Arthur*?
20 Who won the Best Actress Oscar for *Places in the Heart*?
21 In which film does a character named Gloria Wandrous appear?
22 Within five minutes, how long does *Gone with the Wind* last?
23 Which Fred featured in *The Player*?
24 In which decade was *Maytime* released?
25 What was the name of Robert Patrick's character in *Terminator 2: Judgment Day*?

Answers The 21st Century (see Quiz 104)
1 *The Green Mile*. 2 *Shopping*. 3 New York. 4 Allan Corduner. 5 Blythe Danner.
6 My So-Called Life. 7 Gary Oldman. 8 *21 Jump Street*. 9 Wilhelm. 10 The Kids.
11 Tawny Madison. 12 Anna Friel. 13 *The Wonder Boys*. 14 Mike Figgis.
15 Om Puri. 16 Ndingombaba. 17 John Hannah. 18 1985. 19 Michael Mann.
20 Johnny Lee Miller. 21 Melissa Joan Hart. 22 John Irving. 23 *Princess Ida*.
24 Winona Ryder. 25 Katie Holmes.

QUIZ 103 WESTERNS ··· LEVEL THREE

Answers – see page 317

1   What is the name of 'The Man With No Name'?
2   Which James Stewart western had such a moving soliloquy it was released on record?
3   Who played Billy the Kid in the 1930 film of the same name?
4   Which star of westerns was married for 57 years to actress Frances Dee?
5   Which movie was based on *The Tin Star* by John W. Cunningham?
6   Who was Hopalong Cassidy's most famous alter ego?
7   Which director made *Cheyenne Autumn*?
8   What was the first western in Cinerama?
9   How did comic Milton Berle describe an adult western?
10   Which Burt Lancaster-directed movie was based on *The Gabriel Horn* by Felix Holt?
11   Who were 'nine men who came too late and stayed too long'?
12   What was the reward in *Unforgiven*?
13   Who played Jesse James in *The Great Northfield Minnesota Raid*?
14   Which 90s western was a remake of *Gunfight at the OK Corral*?
15   What is the name of the first black sheriff in town in the western spoof *Blazing Saddles*?
16   Who wrote the theme tune for the 1958 western for which Burl Ives won an Oscar?
17   Who played Wyatt Earp in *Tombstone*?
18   Why did John Wayne say *High Noon* was un-American?
19   Which actor/director was described by a critic as having 'feathers in his hair and feathers in his head'?
20   How many Oscar-nominated westerns won between 1930 and 1990?
21   Who are Andie McDowell, Drew Barrymore, Madeleine Stow and Mary Stuart Masterson in the 1994 movie?
22   Which movie opens with the line 'Most of what follows is true'?
23   What was the name of John Wayne's ward in *Red River*?
24   Who first played the Cisco Kid in *Old Arizona*?
25   Which valley saw the climax of *Stagecoach*?

Answers World Cinema (see Quiz 101)
1 Pupi Avati. **2** Massimo Troisi. **3** *Ridicule*. **4** *La Dolce Vita* (Fellini). **5** *A Fortune Hunter*. **6** *Alam Ara*. **7** Vittorio de Sica. **8** Toshiro Mifune. **9** Pasolini. **10** Max von Sydow. **11** Orson Welles. **12** Satyajit Ray. **13** Vilgot Sjöman. **14** Belgium. **15** Germany. **16** Jean Cocteau. **17** Catherine Deneuve. **18** Salvador Dali. **19** Marcel Carné. **20** *Damage*. **21** *Colonel Redl*. **22** Rithy Panh. **23** John Hurt (the rest were cats). **24** Gris Gris. **25** Japan.

Answers – see page 318

1   Which Frank Darabont movie received an Oscar nomination at the beginning of the millennium?

2   What was Jude Law's first film?

3   From which American city did Annie MacLean work in *The Horse Whisperer*?

4   Who played the writer of the music in *Topsy Turvy*?

5   Who is Gwyneth Paltrow's mother?

6   What was the name of Claire Danes's TV series?

7   To whom was Uma Thurman married before Ethan Hawke?

8   In which TV series did Johnny Depp play a character named Tom Hanson?

9   What is Leonardo DiCaprio's middle name?

10   In which band did Johnny Depp play lead guitar?

11   Which character does Gwen DeMarco play in *Galaxy Quest*?

12   Which UK actress turned down a starring role in *Boys and Girls*?

13   Which movie is about professor Grady Tripp?

14   Who directed *Time Code 2000*?

15   Who plays the lead role in *East Is East*?

16   What is Eddie's last name in *Guest House Paradiso*?

17   Which actor links *Sliding Doors* and *Pandaemonium*?

18   In which year did Ethan Hawke make his screen debut?

19   Who directed *The Insider*?

20   Which actor is set to star in the film *Wasp Factory*?

21   Who stars in the teen movie *Drive Me Crazy*?

22   Who adapted *The Cider House Rules* for the big screen?

23   *Topsy Turvy* begins after the flop of which G & S opera?

24   Which actress stars in *Autumn in New York*?

25   Which actress links *Go* and TV series *Dawson's Creek*?